COMPLETE GUIDE TO
GUNS & SHOOTING

by
John Malloy

DBI BOOKS, INC.

STAFF

Senior Staff Editors
Harold A. Murtz
Ray Ordorica

Production Manager
John L. Duoba

Editorial/Production Associate
Jamie L. Puffpaff

Editorial/Production Assistant
Holly J. Porter

Electronic Publishing Manager
Nancy J. Mellem

Electronic Publishing Associate
Robert M. Fuentes

Managing Editor
Pamela J. Johnson

Publisher
Sheldon Factor

About Our Covers

The exciting world of guns and shooting is filled with a variety of firearms for different purposes and games. Our covers show just a few of the types of guns you'll likely encounter as you journey into this wonderful field.

At the top is Ruger's Red Label 12-gauge over/under chambered for 2³⁄₄-inch shells. It sports a rare blued receiver and fixed Modified and Improved Cylinder chokes. This shotgun is a very popular choice for hunters and competitive shooters alike.

The revolver is Colt's premier model, the Python. Chambered for 357 Magnum, this wheelgun has been a favorite of sport shooters, law enforcement personnel and hunters for many years, and is well known for its silky-smooth action. Shown here is the 6-inch barrel model with target stocks.

At left center is the famous Browning Hi-Power autoloading pistol in 9mm Parabellum. With the grip, feel and reliability by which others are judged, the Hi-Power is one of the most popular pistols in the world. This example is shown with target sights.

At bottom is the Ruger M77R Mark II bolt-action rifle in caliber 30-06. Since its introduction in the late 1960s, the M77 rifle has appeared in many forms, in myriad chamberings, and is the rifle of choice for many hunters because it represents excellent value. It's shown here with a Redfield 2¹⁄₂-7x Tracker scope in Ruger mounts.

Photo by John Hanusin.

ISBN 0-87349-166-1

Library of Congress Catalog Card 95-67032

CONTENTS

INTRODUCTION

NO GENERAL-TOPIC book on guns and shooting is ever really complete. Whole shelves of books have been written on the topics covered in each chapter of this book. Still, I hope you find it complete in one sense—all the major aspects of guns and shooting are covered. Covered well enough, I hope, so that newcomers, casual shooters and dedicated experts will all find something of interest on these pages.

Over the years, there have been many general books on guns and shooting. Over the years, I have read quite a number of them. I enjoyed them and learned a lot from them.

Although each book had its strong points, there was seldom any common method of presentation between one book and the next. It seemed that all the books had the "Ten Commandments of Safety," but they were not always the same ten commandments. Adding up all of them could produce fifteen to twenty of the "ten commandments." All good, but far too many for a new shooter to remember.

Since I ran my first Boy Scout shooting program way back in 1956, I have been asked to recommend books for further reading. The ideal book would have some familiar ground for the reader interested in firearms and the shooting sports.

The years went by. "Familiar ground" for many people came to be the basic shooting courses of the National Rifle Association and the handbooks used with those courses. The Boy Scout merit badge requirements and other shooting programs are based on the NRA courses and their handbooks.

This book is a very different sort of thing, but I want the readers to be on familiar ground. I have used a sequence of presentation similar to that of the NRA handbooks when it seems appropriate.

There are, of course, ten basic rules of safety, and they are essentially the same ones used in NRA courses, with the same stress on the first three. How many different types of shotguns are there? Depends on how you want to classify them. The NRA shotgun handbook divides them into four types, and I have used this breakdown. In similar fashion, the fundamentals of shooting are presented in a sequence similar to that of the NRA courses.

I hope this approach makes it easier for a newcomer to the shooting sports to use this book. Its expanded information may also be useful to both students and instructors, as a supplement to other material.

As you read these pages, it will become obvious that no one person can be expert in all aspects of guns and shooting. Much of the information here comes from my personal experience. However, many more things are from reading what knowledgeable people have written, listening to what knowledgeable people say, and watching knowledgeable people do things.

As a boy, I gained information from reading the works of great hunters who had bagged the greatest trophies of several continents; I enjoyed hunting, too, but a good hunt could be a couple of rabbits or a limit of ducks. I learned from great competitive rifle, pistol and shotgun shooters, some so good they shot in the Olympics; I won some local matches here and there. I learned from great shooting coaches of worldwide reputation; I instructed Boy Scouts and other young shooters. I learned from gun collectors of vast knowledge who had put together superb gun collections; I accumulated some nondescript but interesting guns.

A pattern formed. As the years went by, I did almost everything that the "greats" of guns and shooting did, but I did all this in the very ordinary ways that the average person would.

I had a lot of fun doing all this—and still do—and I hope this wide range of interests gives me a perspective that will be of interest to the reader.

As you read, I hope you will become aware of three things.

First, notice the evolution of guns and shooting. Not only the guns have changed, but the shooting sports themselves have changed with time. With increasing experience, the techniques of shooting have also changed.

This is not to say that new guns have replaced old guns, or that new sports or new techniques have made all the others obsolete. A shooting club can sponsor an event that dates back to the 1800s one week and a relatively new event the next. The guns and techniques used may be the latest or may date far back, varying with the age or preference of the shooter. The only thing that seems certain is that tomorrow's guns and tomorrow's sports and tomorrow's accessories will evolve into things different from those we enjoy now.

Second, notice the great diversity of guns and types of shooting sports. There are guns and shooting activities to suit just about any interest. Yet, while the activities of the casual plinker, Action Pistol shooter, Olympic air rifle shooter, muzzle-loading deer hunter and Skeet shooter might seem to have little in common, there is a common bond among the participants in the shooting sports. Each has a stake in the future of shooting. Each can learn something from the others.

Third, I hope that these pages show you some of the fun of being involved with guns and shooting. Some sports are fun only if you win. In shooting, you are always competing against yourself. You can "win" by improving your skills and doing better each time you try. Also, shooting is an equal-opportunity sport, open to men and women, young and old. People from all walks of life can enjoy a lifelong interest in guns and shooting.

Some of the best times I have ever had, and some of the most wonderful people I have ever met, have come through guns and the shooting sports.

I hope reading these pages will increase your store of knowledge about guns and shooting. If you become more knowledgeable, build your shooting skills and enjoy your activities more, this book will have served its purpose.

John Malloy

BASIC TYPES OF FIREARMS

GUNS ARE FASCINATING things. Hardly anything else made by man has the romance and aura of history that guns do. Certainly few things as useful as guns conjure up that feeling. In genius of design and sheer numbers of mechanical variations, guns are perhaps rivaled only by automobiles. However, while automobiles last a relatively few years and are then discarded, guns are often handed down for generations.

Variations seem almost limitless. Guns of various types have been in common use for hundreds of years. They may be long or short, light or heavy, simple or complex, slow-firing or quick-firing, shoot a single projectile or many projectiles, and can be breathtakingly beautiful to plain or even downright... well...unbecoming.

In order to discuss them, we must make patterns out of all these variations. Traditionally, we consider three main categories: rifles, handguns and shotguns. Not all the guns we'll encounter in this book fall neatly into these categories, and some of the nonconformists are fascinating, indeed. However, the traditional use of the terms *rifle, handgun* and *shotgun* gives us a framework on which to build.

To make certain that we are thinking about the same things, let's agree on a few definitions. *Guns* are devices that propel projectiles of some sort through tubular barrels. Two common examples are airguns and firearms.

Airguns use the expansion of a compressed gas, such as air or carbon dioxide (CO_2), to provide the power that propels the projectile. We'll discuss airguns separately in Chapter 18 so most of our present discussion will involve firearms.

Firearms use the pressure of rapidly expanding gases generated by burning granular chemical compounds called powders. The powder may be blackpowder (the original "gunpowder" that played such a big part in the history of the world), or it may be that more modern class of propellant powders called smokeless powder. Blackpowder today is used primarily in muzzle-loading firearms, a subject we'll cover separately in Chapter 17.

Most of our present discussion will concern modern firearms. Modern? Of course, everything is relative. Let us say that "modern" firearms are those made from about a century ago to now.

At this point, we must continue with our definitions at a very basic level. For you experts, please continue to pay attention. You may have to explain all this to a beginner some day, and this may prove to be a good way to do it.

Rifles and *shotguns* are considered long guns. They are generally a yard or more in length and designed to be fired from the

A rifle can fire a single bullet with precision. Here, the writer sights-in a Marlin lever-action 30-30 rifle in preparation for deer season.

Muzzle-loading rifles are still used, not only for hunting and target shooting, but in Civil War reenactments, such as this reenactment of the Battle of Galveston.

shoulder, using both hands and both arms. Rifles and shotguns are generally identified by action type. The "action" of a rifle or shotgun is the mechanism used to lock the cartridge into the chamber—the rear portion of the bore—for firing. In the case of firearms that hold more than one shot, the action also includes the mechanism that feeds cartridges into the chamber. *Handguns* are short, generally less than a foot in length, and are designed to be fired with one hand at the end of an extended arm. As we shall see, though, two hands are often used.

Rifles

Rifles are designed to shoot a single projectile, usually called a *bullet*. Bullets are generally long in relation to their diameter, so they need something to provide stability on their way to the target. Rifles accomplish this by spinning the bullet.

Think about it: A spinning football will travel straight when thrown; a football lobbed down the field will flip end-over-end. In the same manner, a spinning bullet will travel straight.

This rotation is imparted to the bullet by *rifling*—shallow grooves cut into the inner surface of the barrel. These grooves form a spiral, and as the bullet contacts these grooves, the bullet rotates as it passes through the barrel. After exiting the muzzle, it continues to rotate as well. Thus, the rifle shoots a single, well-stabilized projectile.

A rifle is a relatively large firearm, and the support provided by a shoulder and two hands and arms makes it relatively steady to hold. Thus, the rifle's primary use has always been for making precise, accurate hits on specific targets, usually relatively stationary targets. Rifles are commonly used for many types of small and big game hunting, and for target shooting.

At this Cub Scout Day Camp, the airgun range was the most popular spot. The writer is working with a group of Webelos Scouts using Daisy Model 845 airguns.

Common rifle types are bolt action, lever action, slide action, semi-automatic, hinge-type (single- and double-barrel) and falling block. We'll go into these in detail in Chapter 5.

Shotguns

A shotgun is of the same basic shape as a rifle. It is fired from one shoulder, using two hands and two arms to steady its hold. The primary differences: The bore inside the barrel is generally larger in diameter than that of a rifle, and, most importantly, it is smooth and unrifled.

The reason for the smooth bore is that the shotgun does not use a single projectile, rather it fires many small spherical projectiles at one time. These small projectiles are called *shot*. (See why the gun is a shotgun?) The amount fired at one time—it may be several hundred pellets of shot—is called a shot charge.

At the instant this shot charge leaves the muzzle, it is the same diameter as the bore. However, as it gets farther from the gun, the shot charge enlarges at a fairly regular rate, covering a much greater area. This enlarging pattern of shot is not as precise as a rifle's single bullet, but allows hits on moving targets. The small pellets of shot slow down rapidly after leaving the barrel, so the shotgun is limited to relatively short ranges. Because of this limitation, shotguns may be fired safely in situations in which rifles are not allowed. Shotguns are commonly used for many types of hunting, most often small game and bird hunting, and sports involving moving clay targets.

Common shotgun types are slide action (more commonly known as pump), hinge action (single- and double-barrel), semi-automatic and bolt action. We'll cover these in some detail in Chapter 15.

A shotgun is suited for close shots at moving targets. The writer shoots clay pigeons with an early Marlin pump shotgun.

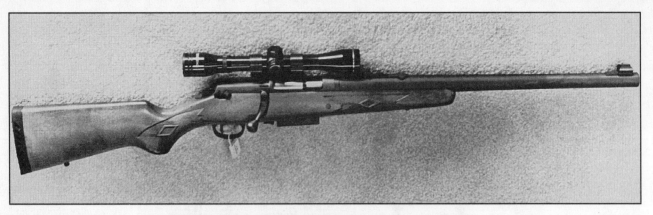

This Marlin Model 512 Slugmaster shotgun is designed for use with slugs and has a rifled bore, rather than a smooth one. This noncon-formist does not fit neatly into our rifle-shotgun-handgun categories.

A quick review:

A rifle is a long gun that fires a single rotating bullet with pre-cision. It allows accurate shots into small areas at short, inter-mediate or long ranges.

A shotgun is a long gun that fires a charge of shot that allows fast shots at moving targets at short range.

A rifle is designated by the spiral grooves—the rifling—in its bore. A shotgun is designated by the projectiles—shot—it is designed to shoot.

Handguns

Now for the third category: A *handgun* is designated by the manner in which is was designed to be shot, that is, from one hand.

Handguns are more closely related to rifles than to shotguns. They have rifled bores, with a spiral pattern of lands and grooves, as do rifles. Therefore, handguns are designed to fire single bullets as well.

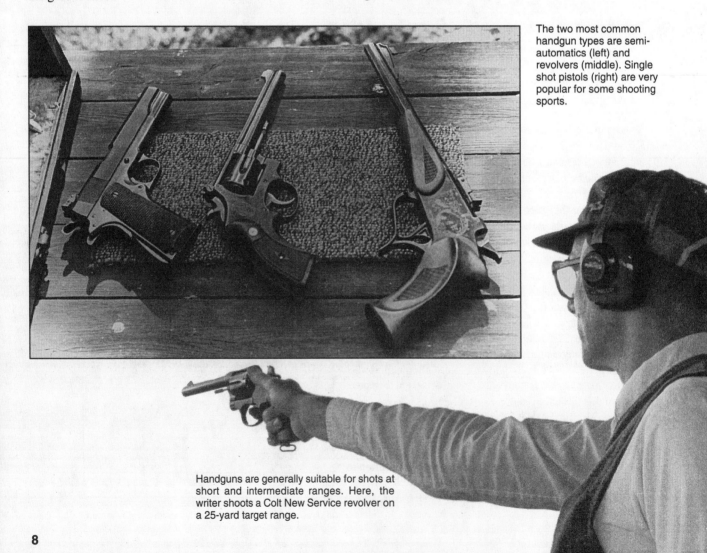

The two most common handgun types are semi-automatics (left) and revolvers (middle). Single shot pistols (right) are very popular for some shooting sports.

Handguns are generally suitable for shots at short and intermediate ranges. Here, the writer shoots a Colt New Service revolver on a 25-yard target range.

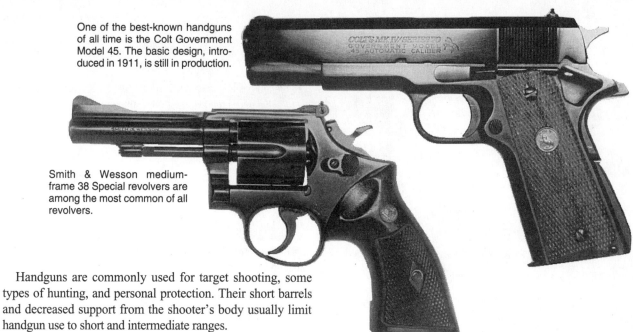

One of the best-known handguns of all time is the Colt Government Model 45. The basic design, introduced in 1911, is still in production.

Smith & Wesson medium-frame 38 Special revolvers are among the most common of all revolvers.

Handguns are commonly used for target shooting, some types of hunting, and personal protection. Their short barrels and decreased support from the shooter's body usually limit handgun use to short and intermediate ranges.

The two most common types of handguns in use today are revolvers and semi-automatics. Single shot handguns are not as common, but are popular for certain types of hunting and target shooting. We'll cover all the various handgun types in more detail in Chapter 8.

For now, let's just touch on one aspect of handgun terminology. What is a pistol? Generally, the terms **handgun** and **pistol** can be used interchangeably. Frequently, in technical writing or discussion, **pistol** is used to describe handguns which have a single fixed chamber (such as semi-automatics and single shots) and **revolver** is used for handguns with several chambers in a revolving cylinder.

Machineguns

Let's devote just a little space to machineguns and submachine guns. They are basically military firearms. Because of the legal restrictions and expense involved, civilian target shooting with machineguns and submachine guns is not very common.

However, should you have a chance to attend one of the rare machinegun shoots, you will be treated to a spectacular *sporting* event. Military and police use of these firearms for target shooting has a far more serious side, but the skills are the same.

Basically, a machinegun is a rifled firearm designed to shoot full-power rifle ammunition. Machineguns are often described as full automatic, meaning they use the power generated by firing one cartridge to load and fire the next cartridge. The mechanism and ammunition feed systems are such that when the trigger is pressed, the gun will continue to fire until the trigger is released or the ammunition supply runs out. Perhaps the best-known examples are the Browning machineguns of 30- and 50-caliber that have served our country so well for the better part of a century.

A submachine gun is also a full-automatic firearm. It differs from a machinegun in that it is smaller, lighter and, most impor-

These WWII motorcycle couriers look fierce and well-armed with their 45-caliber pistols and Thompson submachine guns. (Photo courtesy of Harley-Davidson)

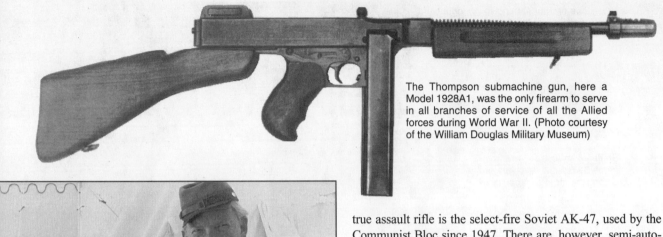

The Thompson submachine gun, here a Model 1928A1, was the only firearm to serve in all branches of service of all the Allied forces during World War II. (Photo courtesy of the William Douglas Military Museum)

By the end of the Civil War, a successful mechanical machinegun—the Gatling—was in use. This Civil War reenactor proudly shows off his small-scale working model.

tantly, chambered for handgun cartridges. In Europe, submachine guns are generally called machine pistols. The use of pistol cartridges obviously restricts these weapons to limited ranges for military use. Also, submachine guns may be of the select-fire type, which means that a selector switch allows either continuous full-automatic fire or semi-automatic (one shot for each press of the trigger) fire. Perhaps the most easily recognized submachine gun ever made is the Thompson—the only firearm used by every branch of service of every Allied country during World War II.

Machineguns are older than you might think. Mechanical machineguns such as the Gatling date back to the Civil War, and fully automatic ones were common by the end of the 1800s. Submachine guns made their appearance at the end of World War I.

Then, by the end of World War II, a new type—the *Sturmgewehr* or assault rifle—had been introduced by the Germans. Designed to help massed infantry "storm" or "assault" fixed positions, it favored rapid-fire over power. The new rifles used ammunition intermediate in power between pistol ammunition and that of full-power rifles. After the war, the Communist countries adopted the idea. Perhaps the most easily recognized

true assault rifle is the select-fire Soviet AK-47, used by the Communist Bloc since 1947. There are, however, semi-automatic versions of similar appearance made for civilian hunting and target shooting.

That's plenty about machineguns. We've devoted some space to them here because we won't discuss them again in this book. Most people will do all their shooting with traditional rifles, shotguns or handguns.

Other Firearm Types

While reading about rifles, shotguns and handguns, I'm sure you were already thinking of some guns that did not fit neatly into our definitions. There are indeed a number of nonconformists in the world of guns.

Combination guns have two or more barrels, at least one of which is a rifle and one, a shotgun. European guns have been made with two, three and four barrels for different combinations of rifle and shotgun use. Perhaps the most familiar to Americans is the Savage Model 24, made in various forms since 1938, with a rifle barrel atop a shotgun barrel. How do we file such things? As rifles or shotguns? Even catalogs of firearms have trouble figuring where to list them.

Another type hard to pigeonhole is what we'll call, for want of a really descriptive name, the *utility gun.* With this type, the same frame will accept interchangeable shotgun and rifle barrels. Thus, such a gun could be either a shotgun or a rifle, depending on the barrel in place at a certain time. Examples being made today are the New England Firearms Handi-Rifle and the Thompson/Center Contender Carbine.

British Paradox guns of the 1800s were smoothbored for most of their barrel length, but rifled near the front end or muzzle. This configuration was supposed to allow use of either shot loads or single bullets.

Some decades ago, Mossberg made 22-caliber Targo guns, smoothbored for the little 22 Long Rifle shot cartridge. To increase the usefulness, the company offered a 4-inch screw-on rifle adapter. With this installed, the little smoothbore gun could be used as a rifle. The bullet would zip straight through the smooth bore, then suddenly slam into the rifling. Accuracy was not great, but was good enough for small game at close range.

The restrictions against high-power rifle use in some locales have given rise to a new type of shotgun that will accurately shoot single slugs instead of a charge of shot. Remember how

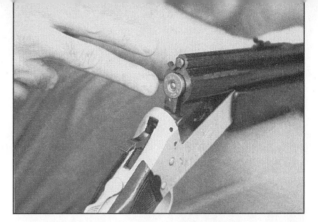

(Left and right) Rifle or shotgun? This combination gun, a Savage Model 24, has a rifle barrel on top of a shotgun barrel.

(Below) This New England Firearms kit has both a shotgun barrel and a rifle barrel that will fit the same frame. It can be either a rifle or a shotgun.

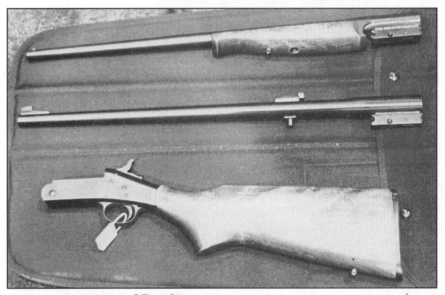

This Mossberg Targo gun, Model 42T, has a short rifled barrel that screws to the front of its smoothbore barrel.

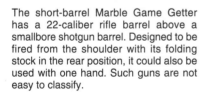

The short-barrel Marble Game Getter has a 22-caliber rifle barrel above a smallbore shotgun barrel. Designed to be fired from the shoulder with its folding stock in the rear position, it could also be used with one hand. Such guns are not easy to classify.

our definition of a shotgun was based on the fact that it had a smooth bore and was designed to shoot shot? This new breed of shotgun is rifled and designed for slug use only.

In decades past, the firms of Harrington & Richardson and Ithaca made shotguns with very short barrels and one-hand grips. Later restricted by federal regulations, these guns are rare today, even in collections. Are they shotguns or handguns?

Perhaps the most difficult firearm to categorize is the Marble Game Getter, made after the turn of the century. A short two-

barrel gun, it had a 22-caliber rifle barrel above a small-bore shotgun barrel. A folding metal stock was pivoted from a pistol grip that allowed one-handed shooting. Was it a rifle, shotgun or handgun?

Obviously, it is difficult to put some of these oddities into our neat rifle-shotgun-handgun pigeonholes. Certainly, they are all interesting, and we may touch on some of them later. For the most part, however, we'll stick with the more conventional types.

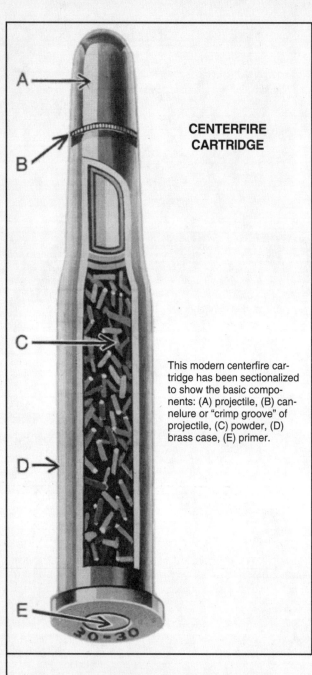

CENTERFIRE CARTRIDGE

This modern centerfire cartridge has been sectionalized to show the basic components: (A) projectile, (B) cannelure or "crimp groove" of projectile, (C) powder, (D) brass case, (E) primer.

Ammunition

Now, let's take a look at the ammunition these guns use, which is an interesting subject in itself. Many people collect ammunition, either in connection with their shooting or gun-collecting activities, or because of historical significance.

In days gone by, all ammunition was "loose." That is, the projectiles, the powder, the priming agent (the method of igniting the powder) and any other components were all purchased or acquired separately. Even if you have never shot a muzzle-loader, you are probably aware that they were loaded with loose components.

By the mid-1800s, the separate components of ammunition had been combined into nice little packages called *cartridges,* which made the components waterproof. Cartridges were easy to load into a gun, and they allowed the invention of repeating firearms.

Two cartridges, both 22-caliber—the 22 Long Rifle on the left is a rimfire, the 223 Remington is a centerfire. The rimfire case is less expensive, but higher pressures and thus more power can be obtained with the centerfire system.

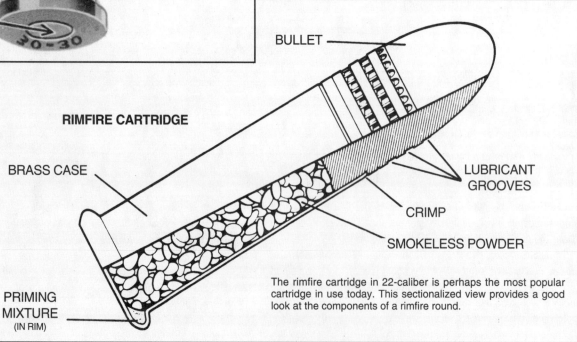

RIMFIRE CARTRIDGE

BULLET

LUBRICANT GROOVES

CRIMP

SMOKELESS POWDER

BRASS CASE

PRIMING MIXTURE (IN RIM)

The rimfire cartridge in 22-caliber is perhaps the most popular cartridge in use today. This sectionalized view provides a good look at the components of a rimfire round.

Of course, loose ammunition did not just disappear. Because so many muzzle-loading guns had been made, loose components stayed in common use for many decades after the introduction of cartridges. Even today, the sport of muzzleloader shooting continues.

Rifle and handgun cartridges consist of four components: bullet; powder; primer; cartridge case.

The *bullet* is the projectile, the object that will be shot from the gun. It is generally made of lead or lead alloy. Often, the lead is plated with a copper-alloy coating, or "jacketed" with a covering of a copper-alloy material. Some bullets are made of solid bronze or copper.

The *powder* is the chemical propellant that pushes the bullet. Modern propellant powders burn when ignited, forming a tremendous volume of gas. This expanding gas is what actually pushes the bullet through the bore of the firearm and on its way.

The *primer* ignites the powder. It contains a chemical that is sensitive to impact. When struck by a firearm's firing pin, the primer emits a flash of flame that ignites the powder.

The *cartridge case* is what makes up the package we call a cartridge. Generally made of brass, the case is the container into which the primer, powder and bullet are inserted. It holds everything together allowing us to keep all the components ready to use.

Types of Cartridges

Rifle and handgun ammunition may be grouped by the type of priming method used. The two modern types are *rimfire* and *centerfire*.

The simpler type, called rimfire, dates back to before the Civil War. The first firearm using a rimfire cartridge was a Smith & Wesson revolver, introduced in 1857. The cartridge for which it was chambered was the 22 Short, and that cartridge is still in production today. The famous Civil War rifles, the Henry and the Spencer rifle and carbine, used rimfire cartridges. Calibers were 44 for the Henry, and 56 for the Spencer.

In the rimfire cartridge, the fold of the cartridge case that forms the rim is hollow. Into this hollow space is inserted the priming compound. When the firing pin strikes the rim, the rim is crushed, detonating the priming compound. The resulting flash from the ignited compound in turn ignites the powder.

This rimfire system is simple and inexpensive, but can be used only with relatively low-powered cartridges. Think about it: If the brass of the case is thin enough to be crushed by the firing pin, it will not be strong enough to withstand much pressure from the burning powder. Although large-caliber rimfires have been made, they were all low-pressure rounds.

In the centerfire system, the cartridge case can be thick and

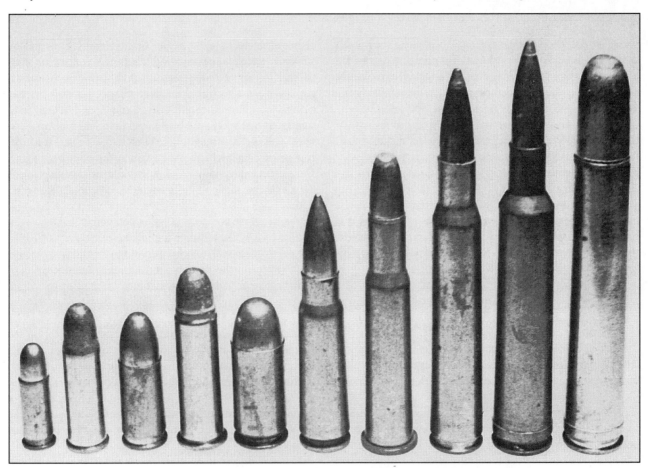

The centerfire system can handle a wide range of pressures: 25 Automatic, 32 Smith & Wesson Long, 9mm Luger, 38 Special, 45 Automatic (five handgun cartridges), and 7.62x39mm, 30-30, 30-06, 7mm Remington Magnum and 458 Winchester Magnum (five rifle cartridges).

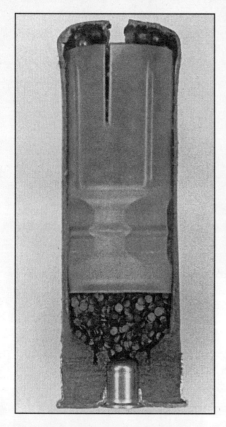

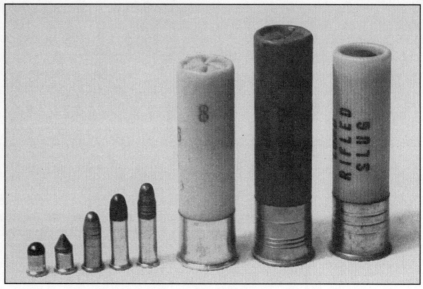

A 22-caliber/20-gauge combination gun can use all these different types of cartridges: 22 BB Cap, 22 CB Cap, 22 Short, 22 Long, 22 Long Rifle, 20-gauge field load, 3-inch Magnum load and rifled slug load.

A sectioned shotgun shell shows (from bottom) the primer, powder, and plastic wad holding the shot, just visible through the wad and at the top of the shell.

strong. A completely separate primer, containing the priming compound, is made of thinner brass. This primer is inserted into a hollow primer pocket in the center of the cartridge case's base. This way, the firing pin can easily indent the relatively thin primer, while the thick case can withstand great pressure.

Rifle and pistol cartridges are often referred to as metallic cartridges because the cartridge case is made of metal, generally brass.

On the other hand, the cartridges used in shotguns have cases generally made nowadays of plastic, although for many decades they were made of rolled paper. Paper or plastic is much less expensive than brass, but is not as strong. That is all right, though, because shotgun pressures (from gas generated as the burning powder pushes the shot) are generally much, much lower than those of rifles and handguns.

All-brass shotgun cartridge cases, as well as those of other metals, have been made and may still be available. They are much costlier, though, and offer little advantage for regular shotgun use.

Now, be aware that it is entirely proper to call shotgun cartridges "cartridges" and to call shotgun cartridge cases "cartridge cases." However, few people do. Most shotgun shooters call the loaded cartridges "shotgun shells" or just "shells." Most shotgun shooters also call the empty cartridge cases, "shotgun shells" or just "shells." This would seem to be a bit confusing, and sometimes it is. Just one of the things we have to live with.

The parts of a shotgun cartridge (or shell, if you've already begun using that term) are essentially the same as for metallic cartridges, with a couple of differences.

As with rifle and handgun cartridges, the powder is the chemical that burns to form gases to act as the propellant. The primer detonates to ignite the powder. The cartridge case is the container that holds everything together in a nice, compact package. As we've already mentioned, the case of modern shotgun shells is ordinarily of plastic, sometimes paper, but it may have a base of brass or some other metal. Note that high-pressure loads often have the brass base extended higher on the sides. This is often thought to be necessary to contain the higher pressures, and perhaps at some time in the past this was true. The system today, however, is strictly one of identification, as the plastic case alone is plenty strong enough for shotgun pressures.

The first three components—powder, primer and case—are thus essentially the same as for rifle and handgun cartridges. The major difference in shotgun cartridges lies in the projectile. The fourth component is the shot, which is a charge of spherical pellets, generally lead, but sometimes of steel for waterfowl hunting. This charge of shot forms the composite projectile that will be sent toward the target.

Obviously, if the shot were just dumped in on top of the powder, the two components could get mixed together. So, the fifth component of shotgun ammunition—the wad—separates shot from powder. Wads are made almost exclusively of plastic now, but it wasn't all that long ago that fiber or cardboard was used. The wad forms a cushion and a seal, allowing the powder gases to push the shot uniformly through the bore.

At this point, you know some things about types of guns and ammunition that many people who have used them for years do not know. But no one can be considered really knowledgeable about the field of firearms until he or she has a good understanding of gun safety, which is our next topic.

CHAPTER TWO

FIREARM SAFETY

"SAFETY IS THE most important thing," remarked a friend of mine. At the time, he was talking about operating machine tools, but as a shooter, he applies that concept to firearms, too.

Such consciousness has made the shooting sports among the safest of all sports. This is a surprise to many people. Perhaps, because accidents involving firearms are so rare, they receive dramatic treatment as news stories and, therefore, appear to be much more commonplace than they really are. The truth is that insurance rates on shooting ranges are relatively inexpensive, compared to other sports facilities. Few accidents ever happen, so insurance companies offer favorable treatment. Hunting accidents still occur, but have been decreasing steadily for many years. Studies show that only one in 1000 hunters is likely to be involved in a hunting accident. You are much more likely to have a traffic accident going to or from a hunting location than to have an accident while hunting. Hunter education programs deserve large credit for this happy state of affairs.

Here in my home state of Florida, I assisted with the recent State Games. For four days, over 11,000 people participated in thirty-five categories of sporting events. At the conclusion of the Games, Shooting Sports was the *only* category that had no accidents and no injuries. The Shooting Sports coordinator said he was worried that some shooters might have had problems with sunburn or ant bites and thus spoil the record, but even those problems did not occur.

This rather good record of firearms safety did not just happen. Being in control of a firearm means that you are responsible for handling and shooting it safely. Most shooters accept this responsibility. Understanding and accepting this responsibility means that you must:

1. Have *knowledge* of firearms safety.
2. Develop the proper *skills* for safe gun handling.
3. Have a safe *attitude.*

Note that attitude is an extremely important—perhaps the most important—factor. Your attitude must be one that will allow you to use your knowledge and skills every time you pick up a gun.

Let's start with the knowledge every shooter needs. I'm sure you've all probably read the Ten Commandments of Safety as they apply to firearms. Different publications sometimes word them differently. So, if you have done a lot of reading on the subject before opening this book, you may have already come up with well over ten. Even so, they are all good safety rules.

However, it is difficult to keep fifteen or twenty safety rules in your head all at one time, every time you pick up a gun. To make the situation a bit simpler, let's break the rules into two different categories: rules for handling a gun; and rules for shooting and storing one. The first three rules pertain to the former, while the last seven apply to the latter.

The Ten Commandments of Firearm Safety

Rule 1. Always keep the gun pointed in a safe direction. This is the most important and most basic rule of firearms safety. Many instruction courses call this the "Golden Rule" of gun safety. Think about it: No matter what else goes wrong, if the muzzle is pointed in a safe direction, an injury—to the shooter or another person—cannot occur.

How well a person incorporates this basic rule into his attitude can mark him to other shooters. I remember going into a gun collectors' meeting in a new town years back. There were several dozen people in that room and probably hundreds of guns. Everyone was handling guns, showing them to others and comparing features. It looked as if guns were swinging around and pointing in all directions.

But they weren't.

During that evening, though guns were handled constantly, never once did I see a gun pointed toward another person. In that group, I felt comfortable. Those people thoroughly understood the golden rule of firearms safety. Following that rule was not a chore; it did not take away any of the fun. Rather, it made the evening more enjoyable.

This is what safety is all about. If you enjoy activities such as hunting and shooting, you do not want anything to spoil that enjoyment. Not for you or anyone else. That is why we know the rules of safety, know how to apply them, and always maintain a safe attitude.

You can see where all of this is leading. If Rule 1 can prevent an accident even if something goes wrong, then Rules 2 and 3 will make things even safer by keeping things from going wrong in the first place.

Rule 2. Always keep your finger off the trigger until ready to shoot. I know; believe me, I know—everyone's natural tendency is to put the index finger on the trigger as soon as you pick up a gun. Every once in a while I come across an old picture of me holding a gun with my finger on the trigger. It seemed natural at the time; now, it absolutely makes me cringe. Fight this tendency! It is difficult, but it can (and must) be done.

More than one shot has been fired unintentionally just

Hunting is one of the safest outdoor sports, because hunters generally know and obey the rules of safe gun handling. Here, the writer's hunting companion keeps his shotgun pointed in a safe direction, even as he scans the skies for the presence of game.

(Above) Keeping the finger off the trigger until ready to shoot becomes a natural habit. Here, the writer uses cartridges in half-moon clips to load a Mark IV Webley revolver that has been converted to 45 ACP.

(Left) The writer was obviously much younger in this old duck-hunting photo. Gun is pointed in a safe direction, but, alas, my index finger rests on the trigger of this Winchester 97.

because someone was resting his finger on the trigger. Think positively about this: Won't you feel more comfortable when all the friends with whom you hunt and shoot keep their fingers off the trigger until ready to shoot? Won't they feel comfortable when you do?

Get in the habit of keeping that trigger finger around the grip, on the side of the gun, or across the trigger guard until you are ready to begin shooting. Others may not mention it, but they will have you spotted as someone who knows his stuff.

Rule 3. Always keep the gun open and unloaded until ready to shoot. On a shooting range, you will see that experienced shooters arrive with their guns open and unloaded, leave with them open and unloaded, and keep them open and unloaded until the command to commence fire is given. Those nearby will notice they are in the presence of safe shooters.

While hunting, no commands are given, of course. A hunter never knows when he will have a shot—he must be ready at all times while hunting. Common sense rules here. You are not hunting if you are in your camp, in your vehicle, or climbing into your treestand. Your gun should be open and unloaded. If, at any time, you should happen to pick up a closed gun, open it immediately.

What follows are seven rules which pertain to safety while shooting or storing a gun. Be aware, however, that special situations will often require special rules.

Rule 4. Be sure the gun is safe to operate. Before you actually begin shooting, check your gun. The bore should be free of obstructions. I'm sure you've heard some variation of the story about a gun "blowing up" because there was a wasp's nest, dead mouse or some other such obstruction in the bore. It is easy to see that a projectile accelerating rapidly through the bore does not want to encounter any kind of obstruction. If it does, something has to give, and nothing good can happen. Results can range from an almost imperceptible bulge to a burst barrel and an injured shooter.

Guns need regular maintenance. Make sure everything is operating properly and smoothly. If there is any question about a gun's capacity to function properly, do not shoot it! Have it checked out by a knowledgeable shooter or a competent gunsmith to make sure it is safe before using it.

Rule 5. Know how to safely use the gun. The more experience you gain with firearms, the more likely you are to be the knowledgeable shooter we just mentioned. Before using a gun, learn—and understand—how it operates. Learn the basic parts and function. Learn how to work the action, how to load it, how to unload it.

This Sporting Clays shooter is carrying his shotgun open and unloaded. Because of shooters such as this, the shooting sports are among the safest outdoor activities.

(Above) Make sure your gun is safe to shoot. Before shooting this Mossberg bolt-action 20-gauge shotgun, the writer checks to make sure the bore is free of obstructions.

Know how to safely use a gun. Before shooting, the writer and his brother, Robert Malloy, check out the unusual operating features of a rare French MAB Modele R 9mm pistol.

This couple positions a target frame so that the bullets will safely strike the backstop. Always know your target and what is beyond it.

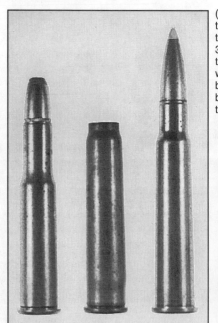

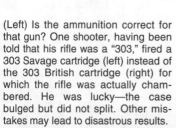

(Left) Is the ammunition correct for that gun? One shooter, having been told that his rifle was a "303," fired a 303 Savage cartridge (left) instead of the 303 British cartridge (right) for which the rifle was actually chambered. He was lucky—the case bulged but did not split. Other mistakes may lead to disastrous results.

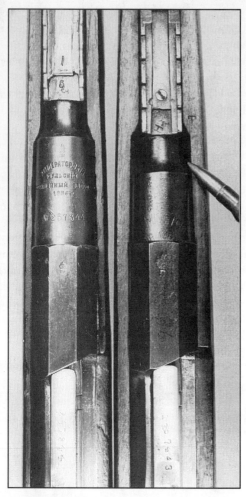

(Above) Look at the space indicated by the pointer. Compared to the unaltered rifle on the left, it indicates this Russian 1891 military rifle has had the barrel set back and rechambered. For what cartridge? Better make sure before you shoot.

(Right) This young lady has just completed an NRA Basic Pistol Shooting course. Let's check her out: safe direction, finger off trigger, eye protection, ear protection—not bad.

Know how the safety operates, but never trust it. Even the best safeties are only mechanical devices, and they can fail. Use the safety, but remember that it only supplements safe gun handling.

Rule 6. Use only the correct ammunition for your gun. Sounds pretty basic, doesn't it? However, people have used cartridges that were not the correct ones. Just because something goes into the chamber does not mean it is suitable for a particular firearm.

Most modern guns have the type of ammunition for which they were designed stamped on the barrel. Match this information with the information printed on the ammunition box or stamped on the cartridge. Be aware that many military arms do not have a cartridge designation stamped on them. If there is *any* question as to the right ammunition for a gun, do not shoot it until it has been checked out.

Rule 7. Know your target and what is beyond. When target shooting with a rifle or pistol, be sure that your target has an appropriate backstop behind it. Never shoot at the surface of water or any flat hard surface that could cause a ricochet. When shooting a shotgun at clay targets, make sure there is an adequate safety zone for the shot you are using. Be aware that big shot travels farther than small-diameter shot.

While hunting, be sure you have identified your game beyond any doubt. Then think beyond your target—could a shot endanger anyone? If there is any doubt about taking the shot, pass it up. Real hunters respect someone who passes on a questionable shot.

Rule 8. Wear ear and eye protection. Eyes and ears, unfortunately, are not renewable resources. Loud noises can damage your hearing, and almost any firearm makes enough noise to do this. Surprisingly, this was not common knowledge among shooters until well into the 1960s. Many older shooters who shot a lot prior to the '60s (your writer included) have experienced at least some degree of hearing loss. Be kind; speak up when talking to us. But don't let it happen to you!

Very effective plug and muff-type hearing protectors are available today. They can be used in combination, and while the protection does not double, it does increase. Wearing hearing protectors also reduces distraction while shooting—many airgun shooters wear them for that reason.

There is always the chance that a flaw in a cartridge case could leak some gas or debris toward your eye. The chance is actually very small, but why take it, when wearing eye protection could prevent eye injury? Special shooting glasses are available, but ordinary eyeglasses or sunglasses are generally adequate.

Rule 9. Never use alcohol or drugs before or during shooting. You certainly don't want anything to impair your judgment while you are in control of a firearm. Alcohol always has this effect. Illegal drugs have unpredictable effects and are dangerous in any circumstance.

Ordinary over-the-counter medications or prescription drugs may affect your ability to handle a gun safely. If there is any doubt, you should check this out before shooting. As a

---

TEN COMMANDMENTS OF FIREARM SAFETY

1. Always keep the gun pointed in a safe direction.
2. Always keep your finger off the trigger until ready to shoot.
3. Always keep the gun open and unloaded until ready to shoot.
4. Be sure the gun is safe to operate.
5. Know how to safely use the gun.
6. Use only the correct ammunition for your gun.
7. Know your target and what is beyond.
8. Wear ear and eye protection.
9. Never use alcohol or drugs before or during shooting.
10. Safely store guns.

---

general rule, if a medication warns of drowsiness, or cautions against driving or operating machinery, do not shoot when taking it.

Rule 10. Safely store guns. Safe storage means storing your guns so they are not accessible to unauthorized persons. Generally, this means storing them in such a way that children (or other untrained people) cannot get to them and possibly create a hazardous situation.

Hidden storage, locked cabinets, vaults and trigger locks are some of the options you might want to consider. Situations vary from person to person, household to household, and your decision on safe storage should be based on an evaluation of your situation.

Well, there are the Ten Commandments, so to speak, of Firearms Safety. Please be aware, though, that special shooting activities and certain types of guns require additional safety precautions. As we get into these special situations, we'll look at some specific safety tips.

Don't ever forget that *knowledge* is the foundation for safety. You must then develop *skills* based on that knowledge and constantly display an *attitude* of safety.

Safety on Shooting Ranges

More and more of our shooting is done on shooting ranges. Shooting ranges are safe places because, in general, shooters understand and follow the rules of safety. To be able to follow the rules, you must know what they are. The rules we've just discussed—the three basic rules of gun handling and the seven additional rules—are always in effect.

Ranges may be commercial, club-operated, private or public, and their specific rules and procedures may be posted or, perhaps, not posted. If you are not sure of the procedures, feel free to ask. By expressing your concern for safety, you show yourself to be a safe shooter and establish your welcome at the range.

There are two standard commands on shooting ranges:

"Commence Fire" means that you are allowed to begin shooting.

"Cease Fire" means to stop shooting.

The "Commence Fire" command is ordinarily given only by the Range Officer, the person chosen to be in charge of the range, either by formal appointment or informal agreement.

"Cease Fire," the command to stop, is also ordinarily voiced by the Range Officer. However, in the interest of safety, "Cease Fire" may be called by anyone. A child could inadvertently step forward of the firing line, but be out of sight of the Range Officer. In such a case, anyone who observed an unsafe situation could bring shooting to a halt by calling "Cease Fire." For this reason, cease fire means to stop shooting *immediately*. Even if you have begun to squeeze the trigger when you hear the command, immediately release pressure, then open and unload your gun and set it down.

During a cease-fire period, shooters may go downrange to retrieve or put up targets. All guns should be unloaded, open and set down. Also, during this time when shooters are forward of the firing line, no firearms should be handled by those remaining back at the line.

When everyone is back behind the firing line, a separate command to handle or load may be given. If not, guns may be handled and loaded after the command to commence fire.

Simple, isn't it? Only two basic commands to remember—"Commence Fire" and "Cease Fire."

I regret to tell you that although these are the standard commands for any range, they may not be the only ones you will hear. Some ranges use whistle or buzzer commands. No problem—just be sure you understand them.

Shooting ranges are among the safest places for outdoor recreation. Be aware of any special rules a range might have and obey them.

(Below) This trap range has specific rules for shooters to obey. Read, understand and abide by any special rules when shooting at a range.

During a smallbore rifle match, this Winchester 52B target rifle sits open and unloaded between stages of shooting.

Marion Hammer, originator of the NRA's "Eddie Eagle" safety program for kids, poses with a couple of the reasons why she did it. Caroline and Natalie Pararo enjoyed talking with Hammer at Florida's 1994 Sunshine State Games.

Some shooters are used to the "hot" and "cold" terminology of range operation. Because this is still common, you should be aware of it. When someone calls "the line is hot," it means that shooting is permitted, and it is safe to commence firing. When "the line is cold" is called, it means that shooting is no longer permitted, and the range has ceased firing. A new shooter here in Florida, coming on to a range when the temperature is hovering near 90 degrees, may agree that the range is indeed hot, but may be surprised to hear it declared cold.

When you have the opportunity to call commands on a range, please use the standard "Commence Fire" and "Cease Fire." Sometimes, usually on unsupervised ranges where the shooters don't know each other, the call "All Clear!" will go down the line. This makes my blood run cold. Does it mean to commence or cease fire? It could mean either, depending on when it is used. Or is it a report on the weather? To make things worse, some people use it for both commands. Please avoid using this term, at least as a range command. As a safe shooter, you are also justified in asking for a clarification if someone else uses it. To keep things friendly, if I hear "All Clear," I'll politely add, "All clear for a Commence Fire." Then I'll try to steer the commands to the basic "Commence Fire" and "Cease Fire."

You go to the range to have fun shooting. Range procedures and range commands exist to make sure nothing spoils that fun. Each time you go to a new range, take a few moments to familiarize yourself with the procedures and commands of that range. And, if a new shooter seems uncertain, be willing to help out by explaining what you know.

CHILDREN. . . IF YOU FIND A GUN

Stop
Don't Touch
Leave the Area
Tell an Adult

Kids and Guns

Perhaps one of the most-discussed aspects of safety is that of kids and guns. At what age should a child be instructed in the use of guns? Allowed to shoot? Under supervision? By himself? Be permitted to own a gun?

In some cases, the answers to these questions are dictated by law. Parents seeking answers should be aware of the laws in their area. In some cases, parents may make the decisions.

At what age can a youngster be trusted with a gun? A youngster who has demonstrated a sense of responsibility in other areas is probably ready to use a gun under adult supervision. Some might be ready at age ten; others not until in their teens.

As a guide, Cub Scouts in school grades four and five have shot airgun target-shooting programs. Boy Scouts of ages eleven through seventeen can enter shooting programs and work on Rifle Shooting and Shotgun Shooting merit badges.

Here is some advice from a pamphlet printed shortly after World War II, "What Every Parent Should Know When a Boy or Girl Wants a Gun." It suggests that parents ask themselves: *Would you trust him to carry the neighbor's baby across the street, or take a $20 bill to the grocery store, or carry a really important and confidential message, or look after the house while you are gone for a day?*

Well, times have changed. Today, we might fear more for the safety of the youngster, instead of evaluating his level of responsibility. Still, the concept is valid—if a youngster already shows a sense of responsibility, he may be ready to shoot. Safely handling a gun will increase that sense of responsibility. This is a good thing, for soon he will be old enough to legally control the most potentially dangerous object ever devised by man— the automobile!

An entirely different aspect of safety is involved with youngsters too young to have reached the age of responsibility. Parents are well advised to make these children aware of the Eddie Eagle program of the National Rifle Association, which teaches a four-step message to young children who might unexpectedly encounter a gun: Stop; don't touch; leave the area; tell an adult.

As we noted at the beginning of this chapter, safety really is the most important factor in the sport of shooting—no matter what your age. Do everything you can to increase your knowledge and skill, so you too can promote an attitude of safety.

CHAPTER THREE

UNDERSTANDING THE MODERN RIFLE

RIFLES HAVE A special place in American history. First used in Europe, probably before 1500, they were by 1700 fairly common in Germany and Switzerland, soon making their way to America with German gunsmiths settling in Pennsylvania. By 1735, rifles designed for American use—balanced for carrying, with small bores and long barrels—were becoming part of the American scene. With the expansion of the American frontier during Colonial days, the usefulness of the rifle became evident. A firearm that could deliver a small projectile with great accuracy was well suited for the wilderness. And, small bores required smaller amounts of lead and powder, hard items to acquire in the wilderness. This distinctly American style of rifle came to be called the "Kentucky" or "Pennsylvania" rifle.

Rifles played decisive roles in American history. They were instrumental during the American Revolution, accompanied Lewis and Clark on their expedition, and influenced both the War of 1812 and the Mexican War. The use of the rifle in the Civil War changed military tactics forever and helped expand the Western frontier. Rifles designed and used by Americans also influenced the outcomes of the two World Wars.

As special as rifles have been to our country on a historical level, they are special to many people on a personal level as well. For generations, a boy's first 22 was a rite of passage, a sign he was considered a responsible person by adults. That tradition has dwindled in our large metropolitan areas, but is still an American tradition nonetheless.

My first rifle was a Winchester Model 67, a manually cocked bolt-action single shot. I bought it with my lawn mowing money at age eleven, which was some time ago. To me, that little 22 seemed like an artillery piece. It seemed as if I were in control of more power than I had ever before imagined.

From that simple rifle, I learned a lot. Its few parts made me curious as to how a rifle worked, and knowing something about rifle parts is basic to understanding rifles. Since rifles are usually classified by action type, we must know something about the parts of a rifle in order to group them into categories of action types.

Rifles may also be classed according to the ammunition used—either rimfire or centerfire. Today's rimfires are all 22 caliber. The other classification, centerfire, consists of rifles that have greater power and range.

However, as we have already said, the usual way of classify-

ANATOMY OF A RIFLE

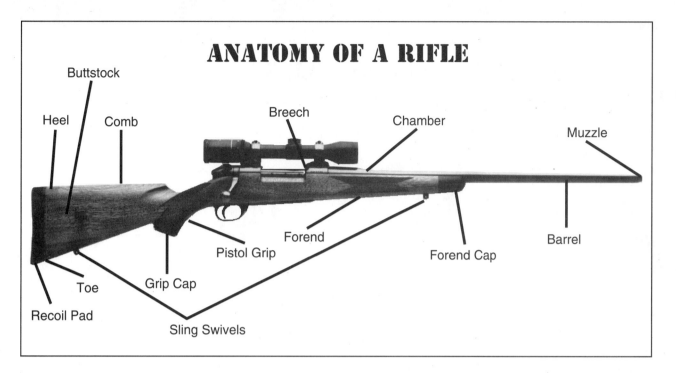

Buttstock
Heel Comb
Breech Chamber
Muzzle
Forend
Pistol Grip
Forend Cap
Barrel
Toe Grip Cap
Recoil Pad
Sling Swivels

ing rifles is by action type. Although they may differ in scale and details, rimfire and centerfire rifles use the same types of actions. Let us therefore define **action:** The breech mechanism that allows the shooter to load, shoot, and unload the rifle.

Parts of a Rifle

Since the parts of an action are critical to our classification, let's first go over all the parts of a rifle. The stock is the simplest part, so let's take that first.

The Stock

For this discussion, we will assume the stock is made of wood. More and more stocks are being made of synthetic materials now, but most of the terminology still applies.

Beginning at the rear, the **butt** is the portion, generally flat or slightly curved, that fits against the shoulder. The top of the butt is the **heel** and the bottom is the **toe**. Going forward, the shooter's cheek rests on the **comb** of the stock. Continuing forward, the stock becomes small. This is the **small** of the stock, or more commonly, the **grip**. If the top and bottom lines are straight, it is called a **straight grip**. If the bottom line curves like the grip of a pistol, it is called a **pistol grip**.

Continuing forward, we come to the **forend** or **forearm**. In some cases, it is a continuation of the same piece of wood. In others, it is a separate piece of wood.

Now we need to address a question that is not easy to answer. When is it correct to use "forend" and when is it correct to use "forearm?" The NRA basic handbooks use the term "forend"

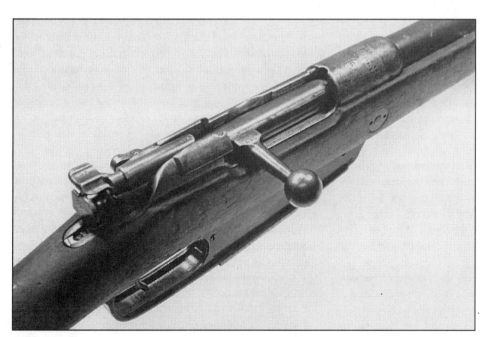

This close-up shows the bolt and receiver of a German 1888 Commission bolt-action rifle.

ANATOMY OF A SINGLE SHOT ACTION

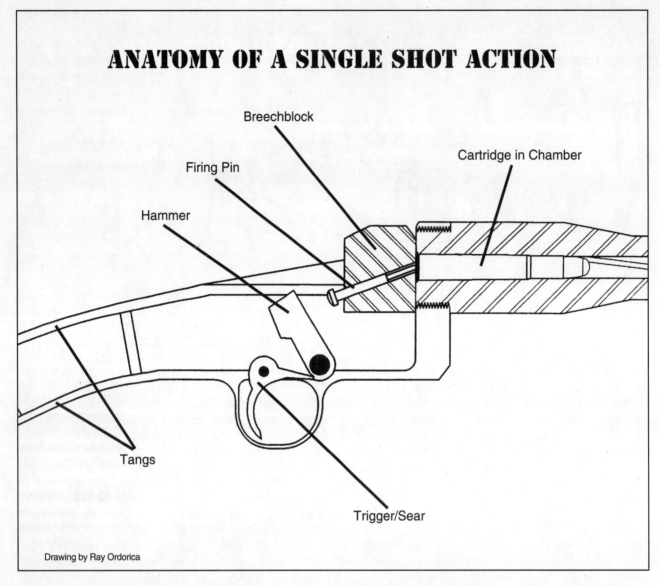

Breechblock

Firing Pin

Cartridge in Chamber

Hammer

Tangs

Trigger/Sear

Drawing by Ray Ordorica

when it is a continuous piece of wood; "forearm" is used to define the separate front piece of a two-piece stock. If you are taking an NRA course, by all means keep your instructor happy by using the terms in this fashion. Be aware, though, that some authorities use the two terms in exactly the opposite manner. Many use them interchangeably.

Until I began writing this, I really was not sure how I used these two terms. I found that, when speaking, I tended to use the terms interchangeably. When writing, I generally used "forearm" for all cases.

Some rifles based on modern military patterns may have features other than those we've discussed. They may have a completely separate pistol grip, or a buttstock that folds for compactness. Some hunters, including Florida Governor Lawton Chiles, use such rifles for hunting because of ease of transport. However, it is the traditional stock we will deal with in this book.

Attached to the stock may be a number of items. A *buttplate* generally covers the butt to protect the wood from cracking or splitting. Some centerfire rifles have substantial recoil and may have a rubber *recoil pad* attached. A *grip cap* may be at the end

of a gracefully curved pistol grip—perhaps for protection, perhaps for aesthetics. A *forend cap* may cover the front end of the stock. In most cases, I think a forend cap is primarily used for looks, but many feel that covering the grain of the wood here deters moisture from entering and thus prevents the wood from warping.

Sling swivels may be installed to allow the use of a sling or carrying strap. On target rifles, an *accessory rail* or *adapter* in the forend allows the use of a hand stop or palm rest.

The Barrel

The barrel is the hollow steel tube into which the cartridge is inserted and through which the bullet passes on its way to the outside world.

The hole through the center of the barrel is called the bore. Spiral grooves are cut into the bore to impart a rotation or "spin" to the bullet as it travels through the bore. The grooves are called, logically enough, *grooves*. The highs between the groove valleys are called *lands*. This combination of lands and grooves is called "rifling," which of course gives a rifle its name.

The rifling curves either to the left or right going through the

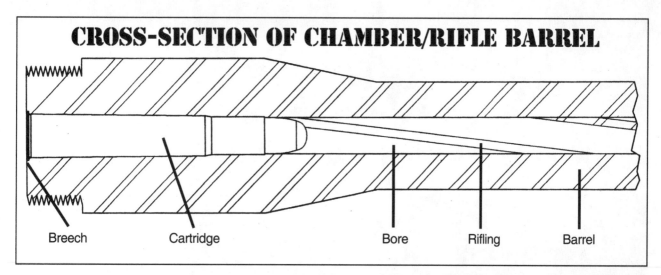

CROSS-SECTION OF CHAMBER/RIFLE BARREL

Breech   Cartridge   Bore   Rifling   Barrel

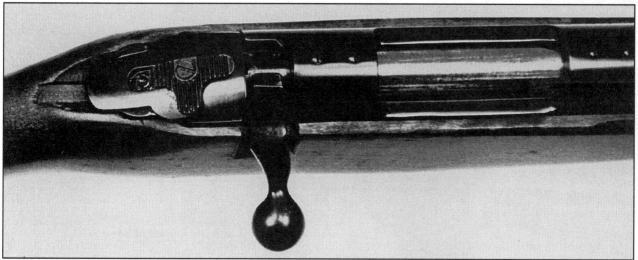

Become familiar with your rifle's safety and how it works. This bolt-action 308-caliber Mossberg rifle has a sliding safety on the rear of the bolt.

bore. In almost all cases, this curve is constant. At some pre-determined point in the bore, the rifling will make one full rotation. The distance at which this occurs is usually determined by the manufacturer, suited for the cartridge used, and is generally an even number of inches. Thus, we talk of the *twist* of the rifling. For example, a rifle may have a twist rate of one turn in 10 inches, or 1:10.

The rear of the barrel is the *breech*. At the breech, the rifle's bore is enlarged to form a *chamber* which allows insertion of the cartridge for which the rifle is designed or chambered.

If a rifle barrel has the same outside diameter for its entire length (some target rifles do), it is said to be a straight, unta-pered barrel. Most barrels are smaller at the muzzle end than at the breech. This reduction is accomplished usually by tapering the barrel, sometimes by stepping it, and sometimes by a com-bination of steps and taper.

The front of the barrel is the *muzzle*. The metal of the muzzle end of the barrel may be crowned, curved both toward the bore and the outside, or countersunk. This crowning protects the rifling and also has a positive effect on accuracy. Items such as sights or bands also may be installed on the barrel.

The Action

The action of a modern rifle is the combination of moving parts that allows a shooter to load, fire and unload the rifle. All rifles have a *receiver*, a metal frame onto which all the other parts are attached. All rifles have this in common: A way to open the action, place a cartridge into the chamber and close the bolt or breechblock. When the rifle is thus loaded, a trigger mechanism can release the hammer or strik-er mechanism, causing the firing pin to strike the primer of the cartridge.

In addition, most rifles have a *magazine*. This is a device that stores ammunition and allows individual cartridges to be fed automatically into the chamber. In addition, every rifle has some sort of mechanical safety device, which may be of a number of different types. If the design permits, the safety should be engaged whenever a rifle is loaded or unloaded.

Rifles are primarily classified by action type. The actions of modern rifles fall into six main categories: bolt action, slide (pump) action, lever action, semi-automatic, hinge (breakopen) action, falling block action.

Bolt-action rifles are still seen in High Power Rifle matches. Here, the writer squeezes off a shot from a 1903A3 Springfield during the standing stage.

Bolt Action

The bolt-action rifle is probably the most common type of rifle used in America. It is so named because the bolt resembles the common turning door bolt which was in use for some time before the concept was applied to firearms.

During the 1840s, bolt-action rifles were in common use in Europe in the form of the Prussian Needle Gun. This early form of bolt action used a paper cartridge and did not seal well at the breech. Thus, soldiers got a puff of powder gas coming back at them with each shot. Still, this inefficient breechloader was very successfully used against military muzzleloaders of the day.

The prize for the first bolt action to use metallic cartridges

Bolt-action tubular-magazine 22 rifles have fallen from popularity, but there are still a lot of them around. This is a Remington Model 34.

Bolt-action 22-caliber rifles with removable box magazines have been around for a long time. This Winchester Model 69 was the first rifle owned by Robert Malloy, the brother of the writer.

The bolt action is considered to be the most accurate type of action for target shooting. This is a heavy-barrel Winchester Model 52B target rifle.

The Mauser '98 was probably the most important bolt-action rifle design ever produced. Many other designs are modifications of the Mauser '98. The basic design has a non-detachable magazine and can be loaded with single cartridges or from a stripper clip.

BOLT-ACTION SINGLE SHOT

A bolt-action rifle, action open.

A bolt-action rifle, action closed.

Bolt-action single shot rifles include two types: the least expensive beginner's rifles, usually 22s, and the most expensive expert's target rifles. The least expensive, because machining is simpler without a magazine cut in the receiver; target rifles, because the receiver is stiffer and flexes less without a magazine cut.

To load:
1. Open the bolt.
2. Insert a cartridge into the chamber.
3. Close the bolt.

Some very inexpensive rifles require manually pulling back the cocking piece at the end of the bolt, an additional step before shooting. If the rifle has an automatic safety, the safety will be on when the bolt is closed and must be taken off to fire. Recall, however, that in Chapter 2 we agreed the safety is only a mechanical device that supplements safe gun handling.

To unload:
1. Open the bolt. The cartridge or empty case will be ejected.
2. Visually inspect the chamber to make sure it is empty.

BOLT-ACTION REPEATER WITH NON-REMOVABLE MAGAZINE

Examples of this type include most centerfire hunting and military surplus rifles.

To load:
1. Open the bolt.
2. Place a cartridge into the open action and press downward into the magazine. Repeat to load additional cartridges.
3. Close the bolt.

To unload:
1. Open the bolt. The cartridge or empty case in the chamber will be ejected.
2. If the floorplate can be removed, release it and empty the remaining cartridges from the magazine. If the floorplate cannot be removed, open and close the bolt repeatedly until the magazine is empty.
3. Visually check the chamber and magazine.

Most bolt-action centerfire rifles, here a 308-caliber Mossberg, load by pushing cartridges down into the magazine.

BOLT-ACTION REPEATER WITH REMOVEABLE MAGAZINE

Examples of this type are most box-magazine 22 rifles and some centerfire rifles such as the Savage 340 and Remington 788.

To load:
1. Open the bolt.
2. Remove the magazine.
3. Load the magazine.
4. Insert the loaded magazine back into the rifle.
5. Close the bolt.

Some bolt-action rifles, such as this 30-30 Stevens Model 325, have a removable box magazine.

To unload:
1. Open the bolt. The chambered cartridge or empty case will be ejected.
2. Remove the magazine.
3. Remove the cartridges from the magazine.
4. Visually check the chamber and magazine.

BOLT-ACTION REPEATER WITH TUBE MAGAZINE

These rifles are almost exclusively 22-caliber, and for many decades, they were very popular plinking and small game rifles. Recently, their popularity has waned compared to bolt-action box-magazine repeaters. Lots of them were made, however, and many models made by Winchester, Remington, Mossberg, Marlin, Savage and Stevens are still in use.

To load:
1. Open the bolt.
2. Release the inner magazine tube and pull it out until the cartridge loading port in the outer tube is open.
3. Load cartridges into the magazine through the opening.
4. Push the tube into its original position and secure it.
5. Close the bolt to position the first cartridge, then open and close it to chamber the first cartridge.

To unload:
1. Open and close the action until all cartridges have been ejected from the rifle.
2. With the action open, visually check the chamber and magazine.

With all tubular magazine 22-caliber rifles, it is possible to unload most of the cartridges by withdrawing the inner magazine tube completely and pouring out the cartridges. There is a reason this method is *not recommended*. It is possible for a cartridge to hang up in the magazine or feed mechanism when the plunger force is removed. Working the cartridges through the action reduces this possibility.

---

goes to a little-known American rifle, the Palmer carbine, patented in 1863. About a thousand of these 44 rimfire carbines were used by Union troops during the Civil War. By 1867, the Swiss were starting production of the Vetterli rifle, a somewhat more powerful 10.4mm (41-caliber) rimfire rifle. The Vetterli was the first bolt-action repeater.

In 1871, the single shot German Mauser, a powerful 11mm rifle using a centerfire blackpowder cartridge, became the first really successful bolt-action military rifle. In 1886, France adopted the Lebel, the first smokeless-powder bolt-action rifle.

The race was on. By 1891, every major world power had adopted a bolt-action repeating military rifle using smokeless powder cartridges except the United States. We corrected this

deficiency in 1892 with the adoption of the 30-40 Krag; then, a decade later, the 1903 Springfield.

Yet, the lever-action rifle was still the rifle of the American hunter. That situation did not change until after World War I. American "doughboys" had used bolt actions during that conflict and wanted similar rifles for hunting afterwards. Before too long, the bolt action became America's number one hunting rifle.

Bolt-action rifles are favored for their strength and their accuracy. All bolt-action rifles share the common "up-and-back, forward-and-down" operation of the bolt, but they come in many styles and types: bolt-action single shot; bolt-action repeater with removable or non-removable magazines; bolt-action with tube magazine.

Slide or Pump Action

The slide-action, or pump, rifle is operated by sliding (or pumping) the forearm of the stock back and forth. When doing so, rods connected to the forearm open and close the action. At the rear of the stroke, a cartridge case is ejected. At the forward stroke, a new round is chambered.

The slide-action rifle never attained the popularity of the bolt-action or lever-action types, but a lot of them have been made, most in 22-caliber. Because the hand that controls the trigger stays in place, leaving the other hand to operate the slide, the slide action is the fastest of all manually operated rifles. The forward movement of the forearm in closing the action also tends to help point the rifle toward the target. Thus, this type is favored by some for woods hunting, where a follow-up shot may be desired.

The slide action is moderately popular in America, but hardly anywhere else. Here, the Colt slide-action Lightning rifle was introduced about 1885. There were three frames: small, medium and Express. Calibers ranged from 22 to the big 50-95.

In 1890, Winchester brought out its handy little 22 pump rifle. The rifle went through several modifications, ending as the Model 62. In 1959, Winchester discontinued the rifle and subsequently sold the machinery to Rossi of Brazil; the basic design is still in production as the Rossi Gallery model. Other slide-action 22s have been made by Winchester, Remington, Marlin, Savage, Stevens, Noble, H&R, and High Standard. Centerfire pump hunting rifles have been made by Remington, Savage, Marlin and Action Arms.

As with bolt actions, it is important to understand how to load and unload slide-action rifles. There are three basic types: rimfire with tube magazine; centerfire with tube magazine; centerfire with removable box magazine.

RIMFIRE SLIDE-ACTION REPEATER WITH TUBE MAGAZINE

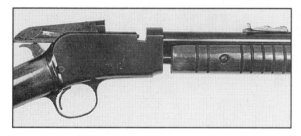

A slide-action rifle, action open.

A slide-action rifle, action closed.

Most 22-caliber slide-action rifles have tubular magazines under the barrel. These magazines have a removable inner tube that contains a spring and plunger.

To load:
1. Open by pressing the action release and pulling the forearm to the rear.
2. Release the magazine and pull the plunger past the cartridge opening in the outer magazine tube.
3. Place cartridges in magazine opening.
4. Push inner magazine tube to original position and latch, then push the forearm forward to close it. A cartridge is now in the carrier mechanism.
5. Open and close the action to feed a cartridge into the chamber.

To unload:
1. Press the action release.
2. Open and close the action until all cartridges have been ejected from the rifle. (Some old-timers slap the stock

The slide-action rifle is almost always a hunting rifle. Here the writer sights in a Savage Model 170.

to jar the rifle, then work the action again at this point, to make sure a cartridge has not hung up in the magazine.)
3. With the action open, visually check the chamber and magazine to be sure the rifle is completely unloaded.

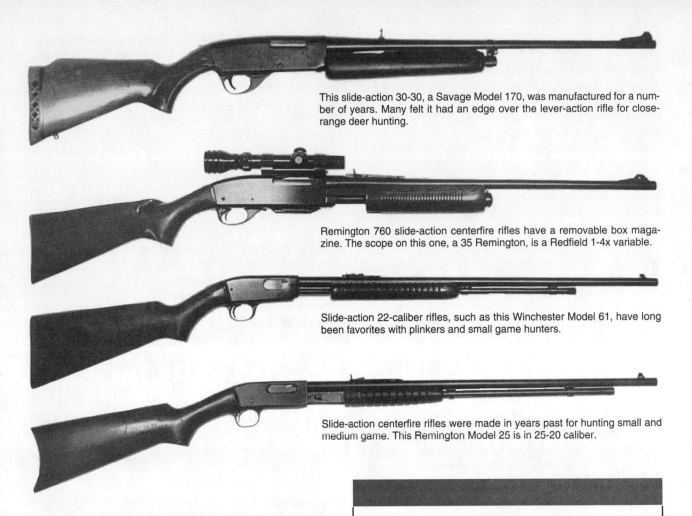

This slide-action 30-30, a Savage Model 170, was manufactured for a number of years. Many felt it had an edge over the lever-action rifle for close-range deer hunting.

Remington 760 slide-action centerfire rifles have a removable box magazine. The scope on this one, a 35 Remington, is a Redfield 1-4x variable.

Slide-action 22-caliber rifles, such as this Winchester Model 61, have long been favorites with plinkers and small game hunters.

Slide-action centerfire rifles were made in years past for hunting small and medium game. This Remington Model 25 is in 25-20 caliber.

CENTERFIRE SLIDE-ACTION REPEATER WITH REMOVABLE BOX MAGAZINE

The most common example in use today is the Remington Model 760.

To load:
1. Press the action release and open the action.
2. Remove the magazine and load cartridges into it.
3. Insert the magazine back into the rifle.
4. Move the forearm forward to close the action. This chambers the first cartridge.

To unload:
1. Press the action release and open the action.
2. Remove the magazine and take the cartridges out of it.
3. Visually inspect the chamber and magazine.

CENTERFIRE SLIDE-ACTION REPEATER WITH NON-REMOVABLE TUBE MAGAZINE

Examples still in fairly common use are the Savage 170 and the Remington 141.

To load:
1. Push cartridges into the magazine through the bottom of the receiver (M170) or the magazine tube opening forward of the receiver (M141).
2. Press the action release.
3. Open and close the action to feed a cartridge into the chamber. The magazine will now accept an extra cartridge.

To unload:
1. Press the action release.
2. Open and close the action until all cartridges have been ejected.
3. Visually check the chamber and magazine.

Lever Action

Although there are probably more bolt-action rifles in use in America than all other types combined, the lever action is still considered by many as the traditional American rifle.

The lever-action repeater was introduced to Americans during the Civil War in the form of the Henry and Spencer repeating rifles. After the Civil War, large numbers of these rifles went west and played a significant role in the westward expansion and settlement.

Oliver Winchester, a shirt manufacturer, headed up the company that manufactured the Henry. In 1866, he brought out an improved version under the name Winchester. When the Spencer company went bankrupt in 1868, Winchester bought the failed company in 1869 and discontinued the Spencer, leaving the Winchester without any serious competition for some years.

Before long, the Winchester design of an outside-hammer rifle with a tubular magazine under the barrel became the traditional lever-action rifle of America.

New Models 1873 and 1876 became popular, then were replaced by a later series of rifles designed by John M. Browning. These reached their peak of popularity in the Model 1894, which is still in production.

The Winchester lever action became the favored rifle of America not just because of availability, but because it worked well and suited the needs of the times. By the 1890s, other

One of the most famous lever-action rifles of all time is the Winchester '73. Here the writer shoots one in 32-20 caliber.

lever-action repeaters, such as the Marlin and the Savage, had entered the market.

Even so, military use of the lever-action rifle has been limited, though the Henry and Spencer rifles were decisive in the American Civil War. The history books show us that in every major engagement where Union troops were equipped with Spencer rifles, they were victorious. (Except, for some reason, in Florida.)

However, after the Civil War, the repeaters were sold as sur-

RIMFIRE LEVER-ACTION REPEATER WITH REMOVABLE TUBE MAGAZINE

Common examples are the Marlin Model 39A and the Winchester 9422. Most lever-action 22-caliber rifles are of this type.

To load:
1. Open the action by pivoting the lever forward.
2. Remove the inner magazine tube enough so that the plunger clears the cartridge cutout in the outer tube.
3. Load cartridges into the cutout, then return the tube to its original position.
4. Close the action. A cartridge is now ready to be chambered.
5. Open and close the action. A cartridge is now in the chamber, and the rifle is ready to fire.

To unload:
1. Open and close the action until all cartridges have been ejected.
2. Visually inspect the chamber and magazine.

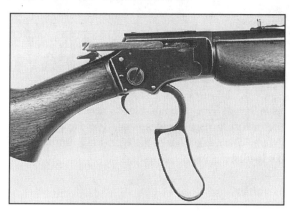

A lever-action rifle, action open.

A lever-action rifle, action closed.

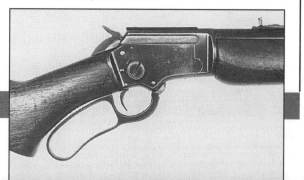

plus, and United States troops were armed with a single shot rifle, the "trapdoor" Springfield. European military minds were equally slow to see the advantages of the repeating rifle. By 1877, most European countries were armed with single shot bolt-action rifles.

Despite this fact, an energetic Winchester salesman had sold the Turkish government 30,000 Winchester Model 1866 rifles. At the 1877 battle of Plevna, Turkish defenders faced a massed Russian army that was twice as large. The Turks issued 100 rounds with each Winchester. Also, before the battle, an extra box of 500 rounds was placed beside each defender. When it was over, the hail of bullets from the Winchesters had cut the Russian army to pieces. Over 30,000

Russian soldiers were killed during two mass assaults, and the lesson was not lost. The battle marked the end of the single shot military rifle, but it was replaced by the bolt-action repeater, not the lever action.

In America, by the turn of the century, three basic centerfire lever-action types had appeared and were in common use—the Winchester 1894, Marlin 1893 and hammerless Savage 1899. Variants of these designs are still in production as the Winchester 94, Marlin 336 and Savage 99. For a time, Mossberg also made a lever-action centerfire rifle of traditional design.

The Savage 99 with its rotary magazine has an advantage over the Winchester and Marlin designs. Because the tubular

CENTERFIRE LEVER-ACTION REPEATER WITH TUBE MAGAZINE

Most lever-action rifles such as the Winchester 94 and the Marlin 336, the common "30-30 deer rifles," are of this type, although they may be of calibers other than 30-30.

To load:
1. Load cartridges through the loading port.
2. Open the action.
3. Close the action.

To unload:
1. Open and close the action until all cartridges are out.
2. Visually inspect chamber and magazine.

Most centerfire lever-action rifles load through a loading port in the right side of the receiver. This is a 30-30 Winchester Model 94.

LEVER-ACTION REPEATER WITH REMOVABLE BOX MAGAZINE

Centerfire rifles such as the Winchester 88, late-version Savage 99 with removable magazine, and Browning Lever Rifle generally represent this type. For a short time, Marlin also made rifles of this type, in 22 rimfire as well as 30 Carbine and 256 Winchester.

To load:
1. Open the action.
2. Remove the magazine and load cartridges into it.
3. Insert the magazine back into the rifle and close the action.

To unload:
1. Open the action.
2. Remove the magazine and unload the cartridges from it.

Only a few lever-action rifles load with a detachable box magazine. This is a 22-caliber Marlin Model 56.

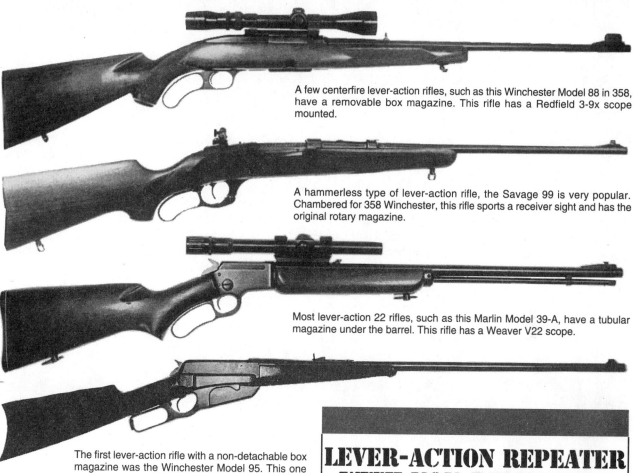

A few centerfire lever-action rifles, such as this Winchester Model 88 in 358, have a removable box magazine. This rifle has a Redfield 3-9x scope mounted.

A hammerless type of lever-action rifle, the Savage 99 is very popular. Chambered for 358 Winchester, this rifle sports a receiver sight and has the original rotary magazine.

Most lever-action 22 rifles, such as this Marlin Model 39-A, have a tubular magazine under the barrel. This rifle has a Weaver V22 scope.

The first lever-action rifle with a non-detachable box magazine was the Winchester Model 95. This one is chambered for 30-40 Krag.

magazine of the Winchester and Marlin put the nose of the cartridge's bullet against the primer of the one ahead, these designs are limited to the use of blunt-bullet ammunition. The Savage 99 can use pointed bullets, and its action is strong enough for high-pressure loads that the Winchester and Marlin can't handle.

The Winchester 88, introduced in 1955, was a hammerless box-magazine lever-action rifle capable of handling high-pressure cartridges and pointed bullets. It was dropped after twenty years, whereas the "traditional" Model 94 continued in production. In 1971, Browning tried a compromise—a modern lever-action box-magazine rifle with the traditional outside hammer. It found favor with many.

Because of their common use in Western movies, lever-action rifles are probably familiar even to those who have never shot one. They operate by forward and rearward rotation of an operating lever pivoted under the receiver. The operating lever under the grip is hinged in front of the trigger, and it forms the trigger guard of the rifle. When the lever is pivoted forward, the breech bolt is moved to the rear, opening the action. This opening action extracts the empty cartridge case from the chamber and positions the next cartridge. The rearward movement of the lever moves the bolt forward, chambers the cartridge, and closes and locks the action.

LEVER-ACTION REPEATER WITH NON-REMOVABLE BOX MAGAZINE

Rifles in this category are the Savage 99 with original rotary magazine and, to a lesser extent, the Winchester Model 95. Lots of 99s are still in the field, but most of the 95s rest in collections now. However, some of the Winchesters still see service, and Browning made a number in replica form not too long ago, so they are worth considering here also.

To load:
1. Open the action.
2. For the 99, lay a cartridge in the open action and push it into the magazine until it clicks into place. Continue until the magazine is loaded. For the 95, place the base of the cartridge under the lips at the rear of the magazine, then rock the cartridge forward into the magazine. Continue until the magazine is loaded.
3. Close the action.

To unload:
1. Open and close the action until all cartridges have been ejected.
2. Visually check the chamber and magazine.

Semi-Automatic Action

Semi-automatic rifles use the energy of one shot to operate the action, making the rifle ready for the next shot. Either through recoil or gas energy, the mechanism ejects the empty cartridge case, feeds the next one and closes the bolt. Because they eliminate the manual operations of the previous types, semi-automatics are often called self-loaders or autoloaders.

Semi-automatic rifles seem very modern, and many are. However, many designs are very old, and this method of operation is much older than many people believe.

In the early 1880s, an American, Hiram Maxim, developed the first practical self-loading mechanism for firearms. By the early 1890s, both Maxim and another American, John M. Browning, had patented designs for gas- and recoil-operation machineguns. Semi-automatic pistols were already in commercial production by 1892.

In 1903, Winchester introduced a 22-caliber semi-automatic rifle for small-game hunting. Then in 1905, they brought out a centerfire version that was suitable for deer at short ranges. The following year, 1906, Remington introduced a more powerful semi-automatic rifle, their Model 8. This spurred Winchester to bring out more powerful versions of its design in 1907 and 1910. These early designs found favor with police as well as with hunters and saw limited service in WWI.

The advantages of the semi-automatic system were obvious to many military planners, and developments continued. Mexico officially adopted a semi-auto rifle for their military in 1908, the Mondragon. They were also used by German aviators in WWI.

In 1936, the United States adopted a semi-automatic rifle, the M1 Rifle developed by John C. Garand. This was followed in 1941 by the M1 Carbine.

World War II and its aftermath saw tremendous development of semi-automatic military rifles. As had happened with the bolt

A semi-automatic rifle, action open.

A semi-automatic rifle, action closed.

The M1 Garand rifle, adopted by the United States in 1936, was the first general-issue military semi-automatic rifle. It proved its worth in WWII and Korea, and before long, most nations had adopted semi-automatics.

The first successful 22 semi-automatic rifle, the Winchester 03 (below) was later replaced by the Model 63 (above) which stayed in the Winchester line from 1933 to 1958. The tubular magazine is in the stock and loads through the port in the right side.

The most popular 22 semi-automatic rifle of all time, the Marlin Model 60, has a tubular magazine beneath the barrel.

RIMFIRE SEMI-AUTOMATIC WITH TUBE MAGAZINE

These rifles have a removable magazine tube with a spring and plunger. Location of the magazine may be under the barrel or inside the buttstock.

To load:
1. Open the action. In some early designs, the action will not stay open; such rifles must be loaded with the action closed, so extra care must be taken to make this operation safe.
2. Remove the magazine inner tube until the plunger has passed the cartridge cutout or loading port.
3. Load the cartridges through the loading port.
4. Push the inner tube of the magazine back into its original position and secure it.
5. Open the action and let it fly forward, feeding a cartridge into the chamber.

To unload:
1. Open and close the action until all cartridges have been ejected from the rifle.
2. Visually examine the chamber and magazine.

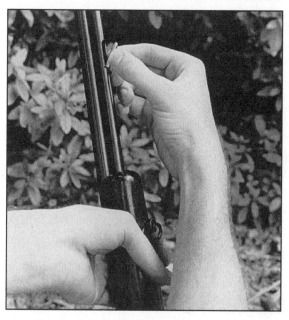

Many 22-caliber rifles with tubular magazines under the barrel have a loading port through which cartridges may be loaded.

SEMI-AUTOMATIC WITH REMOVABLE BOX MAGAZINE

Such rifles may be relatively simple 22-caliber arms, such as several Marlin models, Ruger's 10/22 or Survival Arms' AR-7. A number of centerfire arms have removable box magazines. Among those designed as sporting rifles, perhaps the most common now are the Browning BAR and Remington 7400. A number of rifles originally designed for military service are now used for hunting and target shooting, and are frequently encountered. Among them are the M1 Carbine, various semi-automatic offspring of the AK-47, Springfield M1A and Colt AR-15.

To load:
1. Open the action.
2. Remove the magazine and load it with cartridges.
3. Replace the magazine.
4. Close the action.

To unload:
1. Open the action.
2. Remove the magazine and unload the cartridges.
3. Visually inspect the chamber and magazine.

Early semi-automatic designs were very interesting and sometimes very strange. Military historian William Douglas explains the operation of a 30-06 Thompson Autorifle to the writer. This design was under development about the time of World War I.

action after World War I, American servicemen liked the semi-automatic rifles they had used and wanted similar rifles for hunting. New 22-caliber semi-automatic rifles were already on the market. Soon, Remington, Winchester, Ruger, Harrington & Richardson and Browning were supplying modern semi-automatic centerfire hunting rifles. Target shooters began to use rifles similar to military semi-automatics and, later, semi-automatic versions of selective-fire (semi- or full-automatic) military rifles.

The importation of large quantities of military surplus semi-automatic rifles during the 1980s and 1990s has spurred the interest in, and the use of, semi-automatic rifles.

There are a number of different types of semi-automatic rifles in common use: rimfire with tube magazine and centerfire with removable or non-removable magazine.

Clip vs. Detachable Magazine

Our remaining two types of rifles do not use magazines, so perhaps this is a good time to make a short side trip. Often times, removable or detachable box magazines are mistakenly called "clips." I have mentioned this not because I think it is a particularly good idea, but because it is common usage. Because the use of "clip" for "removable magazine" is so widespread, all shooters should be aware of it.

Actually, there are parts that can be correctly called clips, and I have mentioned them relative to the M1 and SKS rifles. Technically, clips are devices used to hold (or clip) cartridges together for inserting into a magazine, and there are two types.

Charger clip: The entire clip of cartridges goes into the magazine and actually becomes a part of the magazine as long as cartridges remain. The magazine will not function without the clip. Examples are the clips used to charge the magazine of the M1 Garand, a semi-automatic. Many early bolt-action military rifles—such as the German 1888 Commission rifle, Italian Carcano, Austrian 1895 straight-pull and French Berthier rifle—used charger clips. They are also called *en bloc* clips.

Stripper clip: These clips of cartridges are placed above the magazine into a slot which correctly positions them. Then the cartridges are pushed, or stripped, out of the clip into the magazine. Some examples are the 1903 Springfield rifle, German Mauser rifles, British SMLE and Russian SKS. The SMLE uses stripper clips to load a detachable magazine; however, most stripper clips are used to load a fixed magazine; the M14/M1A can be loaded from stripper clips directly into its (detachable) magazine.

Now you know the difference between clips and magazines, so let's continue with our discussion of action types.

SEMI-AUTOMATIC WITH NON-REMOVABLE MAGAZINE

Common rifles in this category are the M1 Garand and the SKS rifles made in Russia and China.

To load:
1. Open the action by drawing back the operating handle until the bolt locks open.
2. For the M1, place a loaded clip of cartridges on the follower; press down until it latches. Release thumb pressure. Bolt will run forward, chambering a cartridge. For the SKS, push cartridges, one at a time or from a clip, into the magazine. Slightly pull back on the operating handle and release; the bolt will run forward, chambering a cartridge.

To unload:
1. For the M1, open the bolt to eject the chambered cartridge and firmly hold it back. Press the clip latch on the left side of the receiver to eject the clip and remaining cartridges. For the SKS, open the magazine box latch and empty cartridges from the bottom. Open the bolt to eject the round from the chamber.
2. Visually inspect the chamber and magazine.

A number of semi-automatic rifles have non-removable magazines. This 7.62x39mm SKS rifle can be loaded with single rounds or, as shown, from a stripper clip.

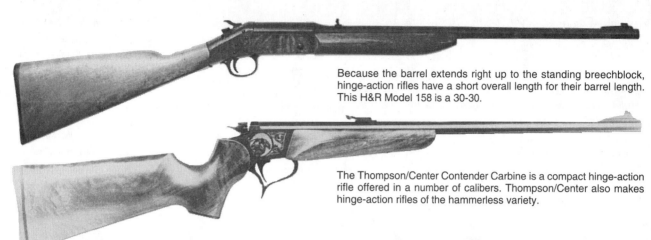

Because the barrel extends right up to the standing breechblock, hinge-action rifles have a short overall length for their barrel length. This H&R Model 158 is a 30-30.

The Thompson/Center Contender Carbine is a compact hinge-action rifle offered in a number of calibers. Thompson/Center also makes hinge-action rifles of the hammerless variety.

Hinge Action

Hinge-action rifles are commonly known as "breakopens." The opening movement is similar to that of a door hinge. When the action release is opened, the barrel (or barrels) pivot downward away from the frame. The part of the frame that is directly behind a cartridge in firing position is sometimes called the "standing breech." We know that the breech of a firearm is actually the rear end of the barrel, so a more proper term would be "standing breechblock."

Hinge-action rifles are most commonly seen in America with one barrel, but versions with two or three may be encountered. Double rifles may have the barrels in either a side-by-side or under/over configuration. Three-barrel guns most commonly have a combination of rifle and shotgun barrels and are often called by the German name, *drilling*.

Hinge-action rifles have been around since the middle 1800s. The big double elephant rifles used in Africa are of this type. In America, the more common hinge-action shotguns were sometimes fitted with an extra rifle barrel for greater usefulness.

Modern hinge-action single shot rifles are offered today in a number of calibers by New England Firearms and Thompson/Center Arms.

Falling Block Action

The falling block action uses a breechblock that falls or drops down away from the breech to allow the loading of a cartridge into the chamber. The action is operated by a lever beneath the action, which either forms the trigger guard or is located near it. Falling block rifles are all single shots.

The falling block system was very popular in America in the latter part of the 1800s. It could handle the large, powerful cartridges that the early repeating rifles could not. The Sharps buffalo rifles, Browning and Winchester single shots, and some designs by Remington, Stevens and others were of the falling block type. Many of the best of the old blackpowder target rifles were falling blocks.

As repeaters developed, they could handle more powerful cartridges. The widespread use of bolt-action rifles by the turn of the century indicated that this system was potentially stronger and more accurate than the falling block. The Winchester Single Shot stayed in production until 1920, and a few of the Stevens rifles stayed in production until World War II. The falling block single shot rifle was essentially dead at that point.

Then, a combination of sportsmanship and nostalgia brought it back. Many good riflemen felt that if one shot were well placed, fast follow-up shots would not be needed. They liked the challenge of making that one perfect shot with a single shot rifle, as the old-timers had.

In 1967, Ruger put its Number 1 rifle into production and found a market. It was a modernized falling block rifle chambered for modern cartridges. For some years, a Number 3 Carbine was also offered, with a nostalgic choice of

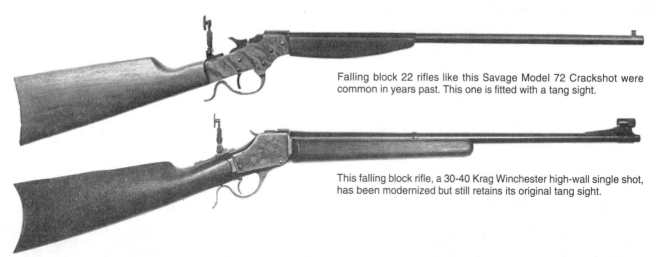

Falling block 22 rifles like this Savage Model 72 Crackshot were common in years past. This one is fitted with a tang sight.

This falling block rifle, a 30-40 Krag Winchester high-wall single shot, has been modernized but still retains its original tang sight.

cartridges that included 45-70 (1873) and 30-40 Krag (1892).

A small, light 22-caliber falling block, the Savage 72, a modernized replica of the old Stevens Crackshot, was introduced in 1972. Browning and a number of smaller companies have made modern versions of the old Winchester Single Shot.

Falling block rifles do not form a large part of the rifle world, but they appeal to careful marksmen with a sense of history.

Have we covered all possible types of rifles? I think you know by now that there will always be some nonconformists that refuse to fit into our neat categories.

Straight-pull rifles had some popularity in the decades just before and after the turn of the 20th century. These rifles use a back-and-forth movement of a bolt by the shooter, while mechanical camming locks and unlocks the action. Theoretically, it is faster to operate than a traditional bolt action, but in practice it had little real advantage. Still, Hungary and Austria used a Mannlicher design as their military rifle for some time. The Swiss used the beautifully made but somewhat clumsy Schmidt-Rubin, and the Canadians used the Ross straight-pull until it had problems in the trenches of World War I.

Even the United States Navy tried a straight-pull rifle. The 6mm Lee rifle was adopted as the standard Navy rifle in 1895.

HINGE-ACTION

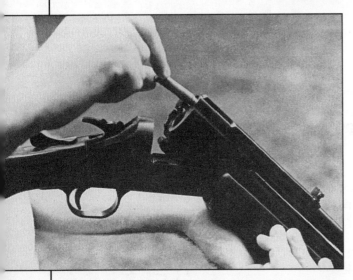

In terms of loading procedures, hinge-type rifles include combination guns, such as this Savage 24V, in 30-30/20-gauge. To load the rifle barrel, simply open the gun and insert a cartridge into the chamber.

A hinge-action rifle, action open.

To load:
1. Open the action by operating the release and pivoting the barrel(s) downward.
2. Place the cartridge(s) into the chamber(s).
3. Close the action.

To unload:
1. Open the action.
2. Remove the cartridge(s).

This young shooter finds a hinge-action H&R 30-30 rifle is just the right size for hunting a North Florida Wildlife Management Area.

A hinge-action rifle, action closed.

FALLING BLOCK

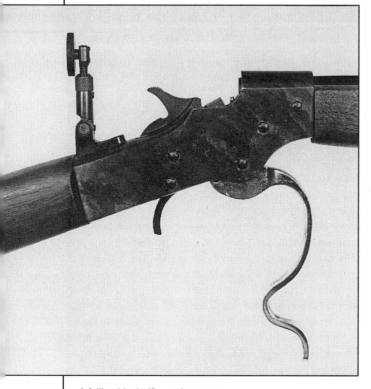

A falling block rifle, action open.

A falling block rifle, action closed.

To load:
1. Open the action by lowering the lever.
2. Load a cartridge into the chamber.
3. Close the action by pulling the lever back to its original position.

To unload:
1. Open the action.
2. Remove the cartridge.

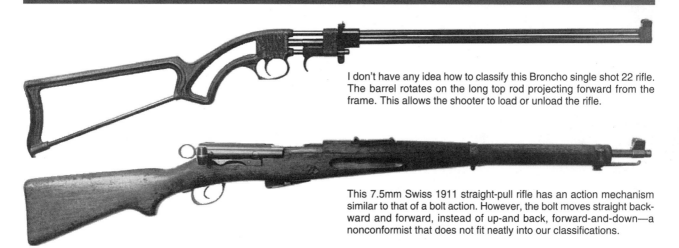

I don't have any idea how to classify this Broncho single shot 22 rifle. The barrel rotates on the long top rod projecting forward from the frame. This allows the shooter to load or unload the rifle.

This 7.5mm Swiss 1911 straight-pull rifle has an action mechanism similar to that of a bolt action. However, the bolt moves straight backward and forward, instead of up-and-back, forward-and-down—a nonconformist that does not fit neatly into our classifications.

In more recent years, Browning offered a straight-pull 22 rifle, the T-Bolt, in 1965. The straight-pull design, however, is something of a curiosity and is little used today.

Back in the late 1890s, the Burgess rifle was made in several calibers popular at the time. The Burgess action operated by means of the grip sliding backward and forward at the small of the stock. How would one classify this action? Fortunately, we don't need to. Burgess rifles are extremely rare, and we are unlikely to see one outside a museum.

For a number of years, a small rifle called the Broncho was sold. Designed for backpackers and others with a need for a light 22, it was a single shot that opened by rotating the barrel on a long rod that projected forward from the frame—another odd type that is difficult to classify.

There is not much point in spending a lot of time on these. However, our friends may mention them, and we want to maintain our reputations as people knowledgeable about various types of rifles.

CHAPTER FOUR

RIFLE AMMUNITION

RIFLES ARE precision instruments, but, of course, they must have ammunition in order to accomplish anything. As a quick review, recall that rifle cartridges have four components: cartridge case; primer; powder; bullet.

The *cartridge case* is the container into which the other components are assembled. The *primer* is the chemical compound that detonates on impact to ignite the powder. The *powder* burns to generate high-pressure gas. The *bullet* is the projectile which is expelled through the bore and heads toward the target. Recall, also, that cartridges may be classed as *rimfire* and *centerfire*.

Rimfire ammunition has the priming chemical inside the hollow rim at the base of the cartridge case. The rim is soft enough so that when the firing pin strikes, it dents the case and crushes the priming compound. The priming compound detonates and the flash ignites the powder charge.

The metal of the case rim must be thin and easily dented. This means the case itself is thin and suitable only for relatively low-pressure loads.

In centerfire ammunition, the primer is a separate component pressed into the center of the cartridge case base. Thus, the case can be quite strong. The metal of the primer, however, is softer and easily dented by the firing pin. The strike of the firing pin indents the primer, crushing the priming compound, which detonates to ignite the powder. High-power rifle cartridges are all centerfire.

Firing a rifle is not instantaneous. It involves a whole chain of actions and reactions, and this will be important to remember when we arrive at the shooting principles of Chapter 6. The shooter's finger presses the trigger. The trigger releases the firing mechanism which drives the firing pin forward to strike the primer. The firing pin indentation crushes the priming compound, causing it to detonate. The flash of detonation quickly ignites the powder charge. The powder charge begins to burn. As it burns, it generates gas in large volumes. The pressure of this expanding gas pushes in all directions at once. The cartridge case expands against the chamber walls and the bolt of the rifle.

The only way the tremendous increase in pressure can be relieved is to push the bullet out of the way. The pressure pushes the bullet out of the case and into the bore. The bullet forcibly contacts the rifling and begins to turn. It continues to turn as it is pushed through the bore. It finally exits out the muzzle and continues spinning toward the target.

Cartridges introduced in 1873 that use black-powder cartridge designations: (from left) 44-40 Winchester, 45-70-500 and 45-70-405. Rifles chambered for these cartridges are still in use.

The first smokeless-powder cartridge, the 8mm Lebel (left), was adopted by France in 1886. It was soon followed by the 8mm Mauser (Germany, 1888); 6.5mm Carcano (Italy, 1891); 7.62mm Russian (Russia, 1891); and 30-40 Krag (U.S., 1892.)

This all takes place in a tiny fraction of a second. But it does take *some* time, and that is important to remember.

How do we identify rifle ammunition? By caliber. The term "caliber" simply means the diameter of the bore of a rifle or pistol. Usually expressed in hundredths or thousands of an inch, the term is also used in metric designations.

Thus, a 50-caliber muzzleloader has a bore of $^{50}/_{100}$-inch or $^1/_2$-inch. A 30-caliber or 300-caliber rifle has a $^{30}/_{100}$-inch bore, or 0.3-inch, or 300 thousandths of an inch. The metric designation is 7.62mm. Caliber is often used to designate a particular cartridge.

Cartridge Names

When cartridges came into common use—during and after the Civil War—new designations were needed because several different cartridges could have the same bore diameter. Cartridges had to have more specific names.

Was some master plan of cartridge designation then carefully worked out to avoid all confusion? No, of course not. Cartridge names just grew. So there may be some confusion, but when we understand how this system grew, the confusion clears up.

Let's go back to the Civil War. The first rimfire cartridge used in the Spencer rifles was the 56-56 Spencer cartridge. It had a cartridge case diameter of 56-caliber (0.56-inch) and a bullet diameter exactly the same size. The caliber of later Spencers was reduced to 50-caliber, exactly $^1/_2$-inch. Cartridges to supply these smaller bore rifles were made by tapering the original 56-caliber cases to hold a 50-caliber bullet. The new round was called the 56-50 cartridge, indicating a case of 56-caliber and a bullet of 50-caliber. This kept people clear about the outside dimensions of the cartridge.

The Henry was a 44-caliber rifle. The cartridges were simply called 44 Henry or 44 Flat, the latter designation because the bullet had a flat nose to rest against the base of the next cartridge in the magazine.

By 1873, Winchester had introduced a new centerfire rifle and a new cartridge for it, the 1873 Winchester with its 44-40 cartridge. The Henry had used a 44-caliber bullet with 28 grains of blackpowder. The new centerfire cartridge was also a 44-caliber, but was much more powerful with its load of 40 grains of blackpowder. The new round was variously called the 44 Winchester or 44 WCF (for Winchester Center Fire), but the most common designation, indicating its 40-grain powder charge, was 44-40.

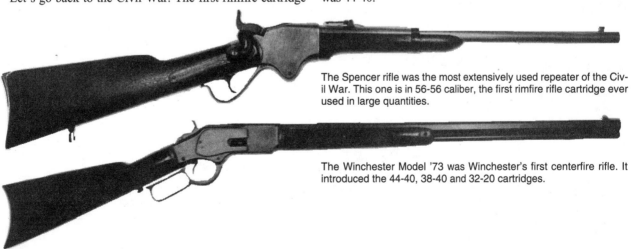

The Spencer rifle was the most extensively used repeater of the Civil War. This one is in 56-56 caliber, the first rimfire rifle cartridge ever used in large quantities.

The Winchester Model '73 was Winchester's first centerfire rifle. It introduced the 44-40, 38-40 and 32-20 cartridges.

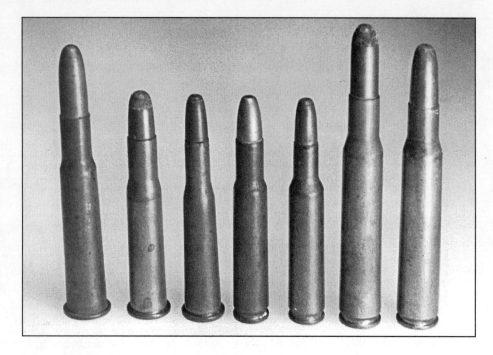

Early American smokeless-powder cartridges: (from left) 30-40 Krag (1892); 30-30 (1895); 25-35 (1895); 32 Remington (1906); 25 Remington (1906); 30-03 (1903); and 30-06 (1906).

That same year, the United States government adopted a long 45-caliber rifle cartridge, using 70 grains of blackpowder. It was known as the 45-70. Two loads were issued: a heavy-bullet load (500 grains) for rifles and a lighter-bullet load (405 grains) for carbines. The weight of the bullet was added to the cartridge designation, and the two loads became 45-70-500 and 45-70-405.

At any rate, most blackpowder cartridges introduced before the mid-1890s used either a two-number or three-number system of identification, with the first number always the caliber.

By then, smokeless powder was replacing black. The U.S. Army's 30-40 Krag cartridge (1892) and Winchester's new 30-30 cartridge (1895) were both 30-caliber. The second number, as with the old system, was the number of grains of powder, but in these cases, smokeless powder.

However, while the composition of blackpowder was consistent, the new smokeless powders were of a variety of chemical compositions. They could not really be compared by weight. The old two- and three-number cartridge names faded away. Remington's 1906 cartridges, brought out in competition with Winchester's 30-30 and 25-35, were simply called 30 Remington and 25 Remington.

In 1903, the U.S. Army adopted a new rifle and cartridge, developed at Springfield Armory. The cartridge was a 30-caliber. It was known as the "30 Government, 1903." Everyone soon called it the 30-'03. Three years later, the neck was shortened and the bullet lightened, and the cartridge became "30 Government, 1906." This famous cartridge is known now as the 30-06 Springfield.

Designating the caliber in hundredths of an inch was fine,

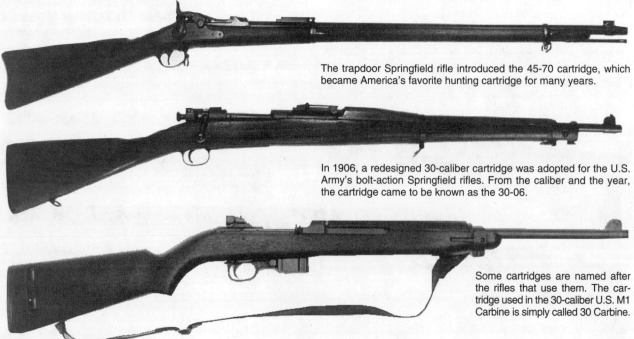

The trapdoor Springfield rifle introduced the 45-70 cartridge, which became America's favorite hunting cartridge for many years.

In 1906, a redesigned 30-caliber cartridge was adopted for the U.S. Army's bolt-action Springfield rifles. From the caliber and the year, the cartridge came to be known as the 30-06.

Some cartridges are named after the rifles that use them. The cartridge used in the 30-caliber U.S. M1 Carbine is simply called 30 Carbine.

A number of cartridges have been based on pre-existing cartridges: (left) 30-06 with its offspring 25-06, 270 Winchester, 280 Remington, and 35 Whelen. The 308 Winchester was the basis for the 243, 7mm-08 and 358 Winchester.

but eventually you can get a number of different cartridges of the same bullet diameter. What then to call them? In 1920, Savage solved the problem by calling its short new 30-caliber cartridge the 300 Savage. This substituted thousandths of an inch for hundredths of an inch to come up with the caliber designation.

Another early Savage offering, now called the 250 Savage, was originally introduced with a longer name. With an 87-grain bullet, the little 250 would attain the unheard-of (for the time) velocity of 3000 feet per second. It was accordingly introduced as the 250-3000, to increase publicity. Later, the 250 Savage case was necked down to 22-caliber. The resulting cartridge is known as the 22-250.

Another way of differentiating cartridges is to designate them by groove diameter instead of bore diameter. Thus we have the 257 Roberts, a 25-caliber round, and the popular 308 Winchester, a 30-caliber round.

Sometimes the manufacturers fudge things just a little. Not too long ago, Winchester introduced an effective new 30-caliber cartridge for its Model 94 lever-action rifle. The designation 308 Winchester had already been used, so the company simply called the new round the 307 Winchester. Close enough.

For a long time, new cartridges have been made by redesigning existing cartridge cases. The 257 Roberts cartridge was created by reducing the neck of the 7mm Mauser case (28-caliber) to 25-caliber.

The names of cartridges are important as well. They have had more influence on sales than you might expect. About a decade after World War II, Remington introduced new car-

The 30-30 Winchester, introduced in 1895 for the 1894 Winchester rifle, was America's first smokeless-powder sporting cartridge. Here, the writer shoots an early '94 Carbine in 30-30 caliber.

tridges, among them the 244 Remington and 280 Remington. The 244 was a 257 Roberts (itself a "neck-down") necked-down to 6mm. The 280 was the 30-06 case necked down to 7mm. Neither cartridge sold particularly well so the names were then changed to 6mm Remington and 7mm Express Remington. Sales of the "new" 6mm boomed; sales of the "new" 7mm stalled out, and later the name was changed back to 280 Remington.

Recently, we have really been reaching deep for cartridge names. A wildcat (non-standard) cartridge of the 1920s was standardized by Remington in 1969. Based on the 30-06 necked down to 25-caliber, it was introduced as the 25-06 Remington. Well, it is easy to remember, but it doesn't have anything to do with the year 1906. About 1980, the company brought out a new cartridge. They necked the 308 Winchester down to 7mm and introduced it as the 7mm-08 Remington! It seems to be a useful cartridge, and it is easy to remember, but what a ghastly name!

Now, I'm sure you've heard the term "magnum." As applied to firearms, it simply means more powerful than standard. Thus, a 7mm Mauser will shoot a 175-grain bullet at about 2400 feet per second. A 7mm Remington Magnum, a completely different cartridge of the same bore size, will shoot the same weight bullet at about 2800 feet per second. While magnum is a catchy name, some cartridge designers have used it in questionable circumstances.

Metric Cartridge Names

In Europe and other places, our metric brethren have not done a much better job of keeping things straight. The meter is the standard unit of the metric system. The meter was intended to be (and almost is) one ten-millionth of the distance from the equator to the pole of our earth. Considering that the measurements were made in 1791, I am too impressed to quibble that the standard meter is not quite right. At any rate, there is a standard meter, and one one-thousandth

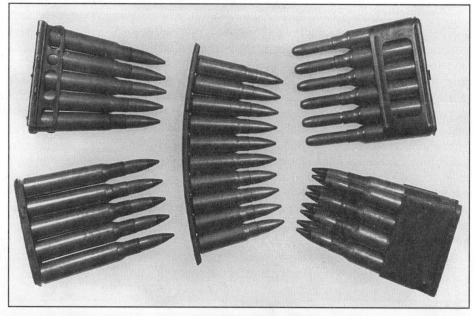

Some rifle magazines may be loaded from stripper slips and some must be loaded with charger clips. Three stripper clips: five-shot 303 British (top left); five-shot 30-06 for Springfield rifle (bottom left); and ten-shot 7.62x39mm for SKS (center). Two charger clips: 6.5 Italian Carcano (top right) and eight-shot M1 Garand (bottom right).

(Below) Some people just seem to like the challenge of shooting old obsolete rifles for which ammunition is not readily available. Here the writer lines up a shot with an 1891 Italian rifle chambered for the 6.5mm Carcano cartridge.

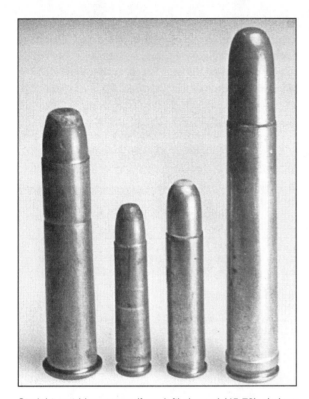

Straight cartridge cases: (from left) rimmed (45-70); rimless (30 Carbine); semi-rimmed (351 Winchester Self-Loading); and belted (458 Winchester Magnum.)

Bottleneck cartridge cases: (from left) rimmed (30-30 Winchester); rimless (30-06 Springfield); semi-rimmed (220 Swift); and belted (7mm Remington Magnum). The 284 Winchester on the right is rebated.

of a meter is a millimeter. European cartridges are designated in millimeters.

The first metric system rifle cartridges with which we should be familiar are military 11mm versions. In the late 1860s and early 1870s, a number of countries adopted rifles of about 11mm bore diameter. Among them were Denmark in 1867, Egypt in 1870, Germany and Spain in 1871, Austria in 1873, and France and Turkey in 1874. When France developed smokeless powder and adopted the 8mm Lebel rifle in 1886, most other countries soon dropped their 11s and adopted 8mm rifles, or even smaller bores.

Some sporting cartridges eventually filled the 8-11mm gap, but most military metric rifle cartridges have, since the 1890s, been 8mm or smaller. One exception is the 12.7x99, otherwise known as the 50 BMG. The 50 BMG is used by many NATO countries as their heavy machinegun cartridge.

The metric system has some disadvantages and some advantages. On the up side, metric designations are generally given as the bullet diameter followed by the case length. Thus, the 7mm Mauser in full metric designation would be 7x57. This defines a cartridge in which the bullet is of 7mm-caliber and has a case that is 57mm (about 2¼ inches) long.

Alas, the system is not as precise as one might expect. For example, the famous German 8mm Mauser cartridge (8x57) also carries the designations 7.9mm and 7.92mm. Rifle bores and bullets for this cartridge vary in diameter and are differentiated by letters only. Thus the 8x57J cartridge has a .318-inch bullet, while the 8x57JS has a .323-inch bullet. For an easy conversion between metric and inch systems, multiply the metric

designation by four. Thus a rifle of 7mm caliber may be seen to have a bore size of approximately .28-inch. This is not precise, because a millimeter is actually .03937-inch, but it's good enough to impress a few folks.

Cartridge Cases

Rifle cartridge cases are of several types. In general shape, they may be straight or bottlenecked. Straight cases have little or no change in dimension from base to mouth. Bottleneck cases are nearly straight for most of their length, then there is a shoulder, and a noticeable reduction in the diameter.

Some older designs such as the 32-40 Winchester defy our classification and just sort of taper from back to front. We should be aware that they exist, but for all practical purposes we can ignore them.

Straight or bottleneck cases may have one of four different base designs: rimmed; rimless; semi-rimmed; belted. These different base types have to do with the positioning of the cartridge in the chamber.

The *rimmed* case is the oldest type. The cartridge rim limits the distance the cartridge can go into the chamber. An extractor acting against the rim withdraws the case from the chamber. All the blackpowder cartridges were rimmed, and almost all smokeless ones used in America were also rimmed until about the beginning of the 20th century.

The *rimless* case came into common use in 1888, with the 8mm Mauser cartridge and German Commission rifle. The box magazine of the Commission rifle was designed to smoothly feed cartridges without rims. Positioning of the cartridge in the chamber was therefore by a precision fit between the shoulder of the case and the bolt behind it. Extraction is facilitated by the extractor groove near the rear of the case. The diameter of the case behind the extractor groove is essentially the same as that forward of it. Most modern military and sporting cartridges now are of the rimless type.

In the rare instances in which a rimless rifle case does not have a shoulder (such as the straight-case 30 Carbine), the forward positioning of the case is achieved by the case mouth contacting a step at the front of the chamber.

Semi-rimmed cases attempted to combine the smooth feeding of the rimless type with the positive positioning of a rim. The diameter of the case behind the extractor groove is slightly larger than the body of the case, forming a semi-rim. An example is the 6.5mm Japanese Arisaka cartridge of 1897. In sporting cartridges, perhaps the best known is the 220 Swift, introduced in 1935. The line of cartridges for the early Winchester semi-automatic rifles—32, 35, 351 and 401 Winchester Self Loading—were all semi-rimmed. Perhaps the first semi-rimmed cartridge was one of 50-caliber for the Bullard repeating rifle, made in about 1886.

The *belted* case is another attempt to provide smooth feeding with positive positioning. The belt acts as a small-diameter rim to position the cartridge in the chamber. Holland & Holland of England experimented with this design about 1905. The famous 375 Holland & Holland Magnum was introduced in 1912 and was very successful. Most of our modern belted magnum cartridges are based on the 375 case. Note that the belt does not add strength to the case, but is a positioning device.

Naturally, something always has to spoil our neat classifications. In this case, it is the case with the rebated rim. The diameter of the rim of a rebated case is actually smaller than

EXAMPLES OF CASE TYPES

Case	Type	Cartridge Examples
Straight	Rimmed	45-70, 444 Marlin
Straight	Rimless	30 Carbine
Straight	Semi-rimmed	351, 401 Win. Self-Loading
Straight	Belted	458 Winchester Magnum
Bottleneck	Rimmed	30-30, 30-40 Krag, 303 British
Bottleneck	Rimless	30-06, 308 Win., 6mm Rem.
Bottleneck	Semi-rimmed	220 Swift, 6.5mm Arisaka
Bottleneck	Belted	7mm Rem. Mag., 300 Win. Mag.

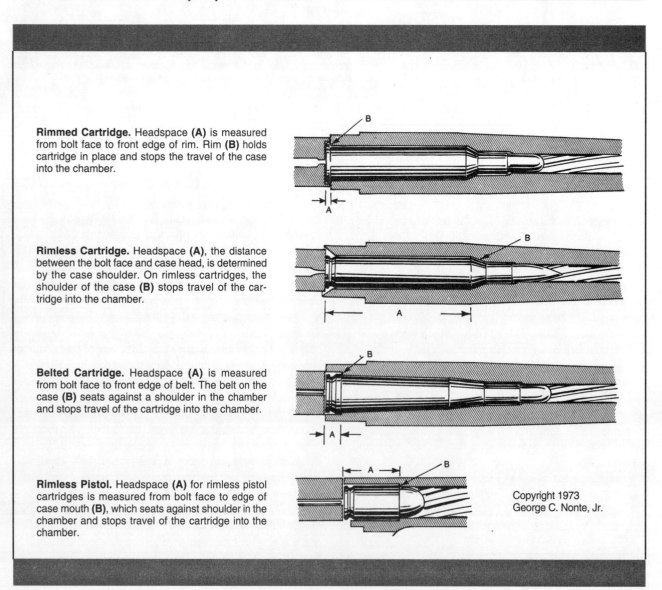

Rimmed Cartridge. Headspace **(A)** is measured from bolt face to front edge of rim. Rim **(B)** holds cartridge in place and stops the travel of the case into the chamber.

Rimless Cartridge. Headspace **(A)**, the distance between the bolt face and case head, is determined by the case shoulder. On rimless cartridges, the shoulder of the case **(B)** stops travel of the cartridge into the chamber.

Belted Cartridge. Headspace **(A)** is measured from bolt face to front edge of belt. The belt on the case **(B)** seats against a shoulder in the chamber and stops travel of the cartridge into the chamber.

Rimless Pistol. Headspace **(A)** for rimless pistol cartridges is measured from bolt face to edge of case mouth **(B)**, which seats against shoulder in the chamber and stops travel of the cartridge into the chamber.

Copyright 1973
George C. Nonte, Jr.

the diameter of the case body. The design allows a large cartridge to be used with the bolt face and extractor of a rifle designed for a smaller cartridge. In reality, it is just a modification of the rimless category, so we need not get too upset. A number of European cartridges have used this design, but in America only the 284 Winchester rifle cartridge is of this type.

Headspace

When we think about the positioning of cartridges in the chamber of a rifle, we must understand headspace. Headspace is usually defined as the distance from the bolt or breechblock to that part of the chamber that positions the cartridge and supports it against the strike of the firing pin.

Let's simplify that a bit. Let us think of headspace as the space between the head, or base, of the cartridge case and the rifle's bolt. This space should be minimal, just enough so that cartridges from all lots of all manufacturers will work smoothly in the rifle.

We can see that with cases of the rimmed, semi-rimmed or belted design, the headspace will be the same no matter what the length of the case. However, with cases of the rimless variety, the length of the case from base to shoulder controls the positioning of the cartridge, and therefore the headspace. A change in this length will change the headspace.

We've probably all heard of a rifle that had to go to the gunsmith for work because it "had headspace." Well, as we know now, all rifles have headspace. It is only when they have *excess* headspace that a problem exists. And, generally, the problem of excess headspace exists primarily in rifles chambered for rimless cartridges. If the chamber is too long or the cartridge is too short (the relationship is the same in either case), then the problem exists.

Here's why too much headspace is a problem: When the firing pin strikes, the case is pushed forward in the chamber. As the pressure of the burning powder gas increases, the brass case is expanded against the chamber walls. The rear of the case is too far forward, and the gas pressure pushes back on it. Howev-

HEADSPACE AND SAFETY

- Most problems of excess headspace occur in rifles chambered for rimless cartridges.
- Excess headspace problems can be caused either by a too-long chamber, a too-short cartridge or an improper bolt.
- Excess headspace can be caused by loading bottleneck ammunition that is too short. If the problem is under stood, it can be cured by loading ammunition of the proper length.
- No manufacturer of either sporting or military rifles produces rifles with excess headspace. It is created later by misuse, excessive wear or by swapping bolts from one rifle to another.
- If you buy a used rifle and do not know what has been done to it, it is not a bad idea to have a gunsmith check it out, including a check of headspace.

er, by then, the front of the case is already sealed against the chamber walls by pressure. The only way the rear of the case can go backwards is by stretching the sides of the brass case. This stretching thins and weakens the brass. In some cases, the brass can split, with the possibility of sending high-pressure gas back into the action and toward the shooter.

Bullets

The whole purpose of a rifle is to place a bullet where the shooter wants it, so let's give bullets some thought.

Bullet Shape

Bullets are basically cylindrical with variations in shape at the front (the point) and the back (the base.)

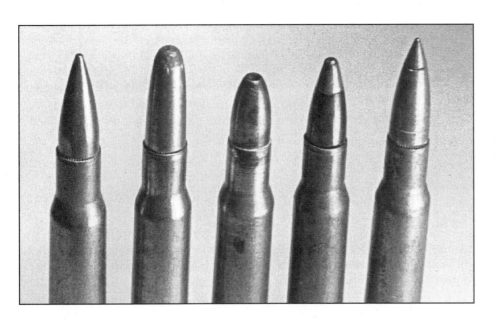

Different bullet types, all in 30-06 loads: full metal jacket, softpoint, hollowpoint, Silvertip (Winchester) and Bronze Point (Remington.)

Bullet Points

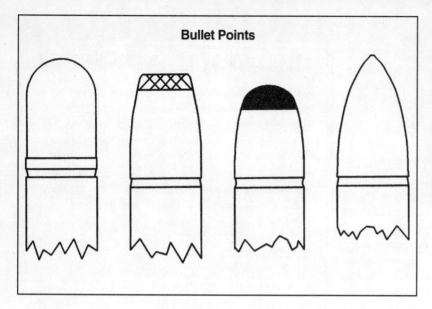

(Left) Four of the most common rifle nose shapes (left to right): round- or blunt-nosed solid, commonly used in the hunting of large dangerous game. Bullets of this type are made of homogeneous bronze or covered with a full jacket of steel. Next is a flat-nosed softpoint, a design used in tubular-magazine rifles, such as the Winchester lever actions. The flat point won't set off the primer of the round in front of it. Third is a round-nose softpoint, useful for brush hunting and low-velocity cartridges. Fourth is a spirepoint, shown full-metal-cased, and is most typical of military bullets. This bullet shape may also be of soft-nose design.

(Below) Rifle bullet bases are generally of two types, flat base and boattail. The flat base is easier and cheaper to manufacture, hance is most common. The boattail shape cuts air drag, which helps the bullet retain its velocity over long ranges.

Bullets can be classed by shape, and we'll do that quickly, for there are other characteristics to consider. The front of a bullet may be flat, rounded or pointed. The base of a bullet may be flat or may taper back into a boattail.

Flatpoint bullets are generally used in cartridges designed for lever-action rifles with tubular magazines, so the primer of the first cartridge does not have the sharp point of the next bullet pressing against it during recoil. Such a condition could cause the first bullet to detonate.

Rounded bullets are common for moderate-range loads. Pointed (or spitzer, after the original German term) bullets have less air resistance and are preferred for long-range shooting.

As for bullet bases, the flat-base bullet is the type most commonly used, because it is relatively inexpensive to manufacture.

Bullets with boattail bases are aerodynamically better and are used when maximum long-range performance is desired.

Bullet Material and Construction

Bullets may be roughly grouped into lead bullets and jacketed bullets. Rimfire cartridges predominantly use lead bullets; most centerfire rifle cartridges are factory-loaded with jacketed bullets. Let's use "jacketed" to mean that the lead core of the bullet has a cover or jacket of a copper-alloy material such as gilding metal.

Bullet jackets may be full, sometimes called full metal jacket (FMJ) or full patch. FMJ bullets are generally used for the largest of African big game, in which case they are often called solids. Military bullets are also FMJ, completely covered at the front. These bullets can sometimes be obtained more cheaply than hunting bullets and have found favor with civilian target shooters. Paper targets don't really care what type of bullet is fired at them.

While the construction of FMJ bullets completely covers the front, it generally leaves an opening at the rear. Hunting bullets are designed to expand, so they usually have the opening at the front and are closed at the rear.

Bullet Bases

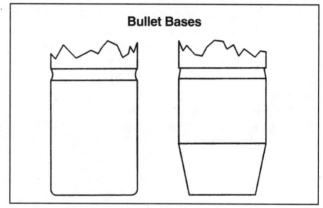

The front opening may be hollow, in which case it is termed a hollowpoint. Sometimes it may show exposed lead (softpoint). Also, several bullet designs have extra features to control expansion. Remington's Bronze Point has a separate metal point that moves rearward on impact to begin expansion. Winchester's Silvertip is a softpoint coated with a silvery aluminum cap to control expansion.

Recently, new designs of solid copper-alloy bullets have appeared on the market. Examples are Winchester's Fail-Safe bullet and Barnes' all-copper X-Bullet.

Cartridges for Specific Purposes

Certain calibers have proven themselves in hunting and target-shooting situations over the years. It is not completely valid to generalize the performance and usefulness of groups of rifle cartridges, but let's do it anyway.

22 Rimfire

The 22 rimfire, in its modern Long Rifle loadings, is the king of rifle cartridges. It is the least expensive and probably the most accurate of rifle cartridges, used for informal plinking, Olympic-level competitive target shooting and small game hunting. Numerous 22 rimfire variations are available, including the BB Cap and CB Cap for almost noiseless short-range shooting, as well as the Short, Long and Long Rifle, in a mix-

Some cartridges in the 22-caliber family: 22 Hornet, 222 Remington, 223 Remington, 22-250 Remington and 220 Swift.

Some useful cartridges in the 24- and 25-caliber family: 243 Winchester, 6mm Remington, 250 Savage, 257 Roberts and 25-06.

ture of solid and hollowpoint loads. Special loads using shot, blanks and extra-velocity loadings are offered. All will fit the same chamber. For those who would like more power for hunting, the 22 Winchester Magnum Rimfire (WMR) is available.

17 and 22 Calibers—Centerfire

Let's include the little 17 Remington and all the 22 centerfires here. They are widely used for informal and competitive target shooting, but are also certainly suitable for small game and varmint hunting. Common examples are the 22 Hornet, 222 and 223 Remington, and 22-250.

These are useful little cartridges, but some find it almost

embarrassing that the current standard U.S. military cartridge, the 5.56mm (223 Remington), is in this category. At any rate, there is a good supply of brass for handloading this caliber.

24 and 25 Calibers

These are crossover cartridges that are small enough for varmints, big enough for deer. In general, the lighter bullets offered are used for varmint hunting, while the heavier numbers are better suited for deer. Some of these cartridges have been widely used for benchrest rifle competition. Examples in this class are 243 Winchester, 6mm Remington, 250 Savage, 257 Roberts and 25-06.

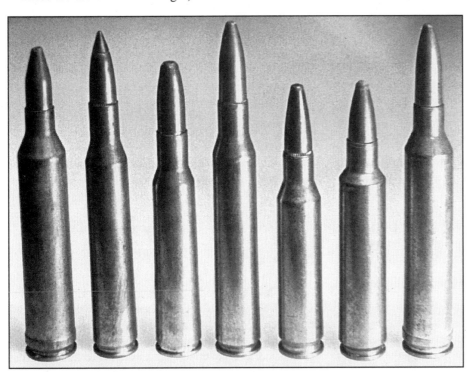

Some cartridges in the 26- to 28-caliber family: 264 Winchester Magnum, 270 Winchester, 7mm Mauser, 280 Remington, 7mm-08 Remington, 284 Winchester and 7mm Remington Magnum.

Some cartridges in the versatile 30-caliber family: 30 Carbine, 30-30 Winchester, 308 Winchester, 30-06 Springfield, 300 Holland & Holland Magnum and 300 Winchester Magnum.

The 31 and 32 calibers have never been particularly popular in this country and are now represented primarily by foreign military calibers: (from left) 7.62x39mm Russian, 7.62x54R (7.62 Russian), 303 British and 8mm Mauser.

26, 27 and 28 Calibers (6.5mm through 7mm)

These are primarily hunting calibers, although the early cartridges in these bore sizes began as military rounds. Some hunters consider rifles chambered for this class of cartridges to be generally capable of taking most North American big game. Other hunters consider them to be on the small size for the largest North American game. Some examples are the 264 Winchester Magnum, 270 Winchester, 7mm Mauser, 7mm-08, 280 Remington, 284 Winchester and 7mm Remington Magnum.

30 Calibers

The 30-caliber cartridges are considered by many to be the best all-around and most versatile of all the bore sizes. Widely used for competitive target shooting (and lots of informal target shooting as well), they offer a large range of power for hunting. The little 30 Carbine is suitable for small game; the 30-30 is good on deer; the larger 30s are capable of taking most North American game. In this latter class, the 308 Winchester (the 7.62x51mm NATO cartridge), the tried-and-true 30-06, the old 300 H&H Magnum and the 300 Winchester Magnum are popular choices. Not only is the range of cartridges versatile, but the versatility of a single cartridge is also great. The 30-06 is not a first choice for woodchucks, but varmint loads are available for it and it will do. On the other end of the scale, the 30-06 also might not be a first choice for the huge brown bears, but heavy loads are available for it and it will do.

31 and 32 (8mm) Calibers

These bore sizes live on mainly because of the large number of foreign military rifles being used in the United States. They are often starters for competitive High Power rifle

shooting, but can be effective hunting rifles, equivalent to much of the 30-caliber family and limited mainly by their military sights. In this category, the 303 British, 7.62x39mm Russian, 7.62x54R Russian and 8mm Mauser are well known.

33 to 35 Calibers

With the exception of the 35 Remington, a very effective close-range deer cartridge, rifles of these bore sizes were primarily designed for hunting the biggest species of big game found on the North American continent. In this category, you may see the 338 Winchester Magnum, the old 348 Winchester, 358 Winchester, 35 Whelen and 350 Remington Magnum.

375 to 458 Calibers

The biggest of these big boomers were designed primarily for African big game. The 375 Holland & Holland Magnum and 458 Winchester Magnum are among the most popular. They are sometimes used for hunting large American game.

Other cartridges in this caliber range are pretty widely used in America. The 44 Magnum, designed as a powerful revolver cartridge, is also a popular short-range rifle cartridge for deer. Stepping up a notch, the old 45-70 and 444 Marlin are good for most game on this continent at short to moderate ranges.

458 On Up

There are many rifles chambered in this range, mostly British, still being fired today. These include the British elephant cartridges, and Federal Cartridge Co. makes loaded ammo today for the 470. Cartridges in this class range up to the mighty 700 Nitro, chambered in a recent rifle made by Holland and Holland. Many of these rifles were designed for use against

The 35 Remington on the left is an excellent woods cartridge for deer, but most of the other members of the 33- to 35-caliber family were designed for larger game: 338 Winchester Magnum, 348 Winchester, 358 Winchester, 35 Whelen and 350 Remington Magnum.

(From left) The 375 Holland & Holland Magnum and 458 Winchester Magnum were designed for African game. Other big-bore rounds for American hunting are the 44 Remington Magnum, 444 Marlin and 45-70 Government.

dangerous game, but the blackpowder versions of these rifles were designed for use against ordinary big game. Examples include the 450, 500, and 577 Expresses, big in size but ordinary in performance. In the U.S., the big 50-caliber Sharps rifles are very popular, and we also need to mention the recent interest in bolt-action sniper and sporting rifles chambered for the 50 Browning cartridge. Many of these big rifles are being used today to hunt ordinary game, and they work very well for that purpose.

It might seem that all possible rifle cartridges for all possible uses have already been designed. However, it probably seemed that way a hundred years ago, too. New cartridges are introduced periodically. Sometimes they catch on; sometimes they fizzle out.

At any rate, we can expect to see some new cartridges from time to time, as well as new developments in bullet types and loads. Still, the old standard rifle cartridges and rifle bullets will be with us for the foreseeable future.

What should you use? If you are going into a new sport or a new hunting area, talk to as many shooters as possible. Find out what cartridges they use successfully. Loads? If you are not a handloader, you are at no disadvantage with factory loads. Factories load what sells, and what sells is what works well for shooters.

Rifle shooting is full of individual preferences. Some shooters like to be up-to-date; others enjoy being old-fashioned. Some want maximum power; others want mild loads. Most like ready availability; some like the challenge of shooting an unusual cartridge. For some, all bullets must go into half an inch at 100 yards; for others, staying in a target the size of a deer heart at half that range is all that is desired. Whatever you are looking for, there are plenty of choices to find the rifles and rifle ammunition that suit your needs.

Somewhat more powerful than the 458 are the 450 NE, 500/450, and the 470, shown here in original Kynoch version and latest nickel-cased load from Federal Cartridge Co.

CHAPTER FIVE

RIFLE
SIGHTS AND SIGHTING-IN

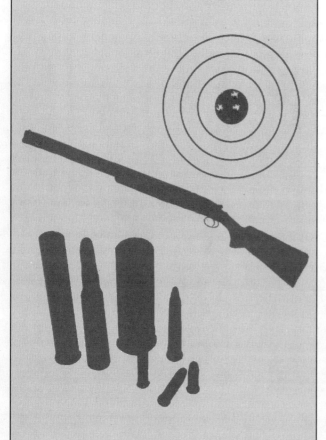

RIFLES ARE PRECISION instruments capable of accurate shooting with proper ammunition. By themselves, however, they have no idea where the target is. The shooter must orient the rifle in the proper direction, and sights give the shooter a way to consistently align the rifle with the target.

Sights were probably an afterthought in the development of firearms. Early firearms such as hand cannons—simple tubes with some sort of handle, scaled for one-man use—did not need sights. They were used at very short ranges and were just sort of pointed toward the target.

As musketry developed for military use, it was found that a front sight of some sort, often a bead, would allow the musket to be pointed more specifically. Eventually, people found that a front and rear sight gave even better results.

Front and rear sights had already been developed for crossbows. However, smoothbore muskets and pistols, until the time of the American Revolution, were made with two sights, one sight, or even no sights at all.

By the time rifles came on the scene, it was logical to have both sights to make use of the improved shooting accuracy. In America, they took the form of an upright front and a flat rear with some sort of notch. These were generally adjusted until they enabled the owner to put a bullet where he wanted it at a certain range.

This sighting arrangement remained in general use for centuries. It is still the type most used, because most rifles come from the factory with variations of such sights.

There are many different types of rifle sights. Generally, they can be put into three categories: open sights; aperture sights; optical sights.

Open Sights

Most shooters today recognize the disadvantages of open sights. However, there are also some advantages, or such sights would have been abandoned by now. True to historical form, open sights have an upright front and a flat, upright rear which has some sort of notch in it.

Here, front sights fall into two main groups—bead and post sights. The bead front sight is a relatively thin upright piece topped with a cylinder, seen by the shooter as a circle or bead. The post front sight is a blade of metal with a square top, appearing to the shooter as a flat-topped post. This post is generally thicker and wider than the bead sight.

The critical portion of the open rear sight is the notch through

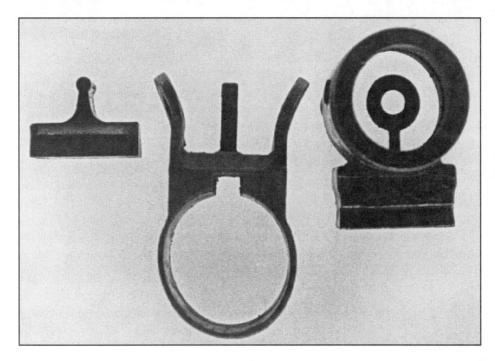

The three common types of rifle front sights are bead, post (here with protective "ears") and aperture.

which the front sight is seen. Notches are basically of four types: V-notch; U-notch; square-notch; shallow-V.

The V-notch type was primarily used on European military rifles of the late 1800s and early 1900s, and generally were teamed with an inverted-V front sight. A lot of these rifles are still in use. I have seen a few sporting rifles that had a V-notch rear sight, but not many.

The U-notch is generally teamed with a bead front sight. The size of the bead and notch are often designed so that shooters with normal eyes will see the bead more or less filling the notch.

The square-notch is most often used (and should be used) with a square-topped post. This system is called Patridge, named after the early pistol target shooter who developed it. Because is has no curved surfaces, it allows the most precise alignment of the sights possible with an open-sight system.

There is another type of rear sight—the shallow-V—that is seldom seen in this country. This wide sight is often marked at the bottom of the wide, shallow V with a white line, sometimes with a white triangle. It is always used with a bead front sight. It was developed for very fast shots at dangerous African game. It may well be the fastest system of all for emergency shots.

A friend of mine in south Louisiana mounted such a system on a 45-70 Mauser. He says it is very fast. Since, however, charging rhinos are rare there, it has not really been put to the test.

Open sights do have some advantages. They are relatively cheap, fairly rugged and adequate for plinking or short- to medium-range hunting. The disadvantages, however, are serious ones. Use of open sights puts a real burden on the human eye. It gives the shooter three things to look at—the target, the front sight and the rear sight. The eye can only focus on one thing at a time. A young shooter with good eyes may think he can focus on all three, but in reality he is rapidly and constantly changing focus from one to the other. As we get older, we don't even pretend we can do it. Because something is always out of focus, open sights cannot give us the consistency we need for the best possible accuracy.

There is another serious drawback to open sights—they are not easy to adjust. The most common types of open sights are dovetailed into the rifle barrel. Windage (side-to-side) adjustments must be made by tapping the sights, either front or rear, laterally in their dovetails.

Elevation (up-and-down) adjustments are made by moving the stepped elevator to raise or lower the sight leaf that holds the notch. Often, one step will be too low; the next too high. In such a case, careful filing of the elevator can make it right. With a post front sight, the top of the blade can be filed down.

Now, all this tapping and filing is a trial-and-error procedure. It takes a lot of time and, more importantly, a lot of shooting. Several shots must be fired at each change; the number of cartridges and their cost add up. I have used up well over a box of fifty rounds of ammunition before I was satisfied with the sight adjustment of a little 22 rifle. I have also taken an open-sighted 30-30 to the range, used up a box of twenty rounds (all I had with me) and gone home disgusted because the rifle was still not quite right.

All is not doom and gloom, of course. I have used, and still use, open-sighted rifles that are very satisfactory for their purposes. Some have held their adjustment for decades without attention.

Open sights with accurate adjustments can be made. However, if a company is going to go to the expense of making an open sight with precision adjustments, it will be expensive. It is more logical to put that precision into a better type of sight.

Aperture Sights

Aperture sights, often called "peep" sights, are considered a better type of sight for several reasons.

Some big centerfire rifles, used for fast shots on dangerous game, have only open sights. This is a Winchester Model 70 African in 458 Winchester Magnum.

Some rifles are adequate for their ordinary use with open sights. This is a 22-caliber Remington Model 514, a bolt-action single shot.

Focus on the front sight. Even if the rear sight and bullseye seem a bit fuzzy, they can still be aligned if the front sight is in focus. Here, the camera lens duplicates what your eye will see when using a post front sight and a square notch rear sight.

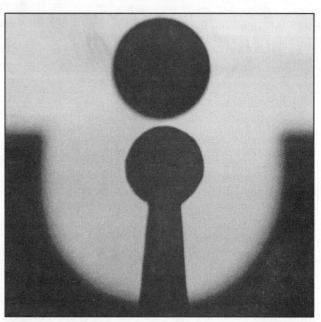

Again looking through the camera lens, here is a sight picture with bead front and U-notch rear sights.

Let's consider adjustment. We've just seen that most open sights are not precisely adjustable. While not all aperture sights have micrometer adjustments, the better ones do. Adjustments are made by turning threaded shafts to move the aperture for windage and elevation. If, for example, the screw threads are forty to the inch, and the adjustments are twenty-five "clicks" to a full turn of the knob, then each click moves the sight $1/1000$-inch. This is very precise adjustment. Some target sights are made to these specifications, or very close to them.

There are other advantages to aperture sights independent of adjustment.

Sight Radius

Aperture sights are mounted farther back on the rifle, generally on the receiver. This rearward mounting results in a greater distance between the sights, or as it is generally termed, a longer sight radius. The farther the sights are apart, the greater will be

the precision of aiming because the effect of small misalignments between the two sights will be less.

How to Use an Aperture Sight

A big difference with the aperture sight is the fact that you look *through* the aperture, not *at* it—sort of "peeping" through a hole at something, which may well be how the term "peep sight" came about.

How can you align the peep hole with the front sight if you don't look at it? The strongest light through a small hole is in the center, and your eye naturally seeks out the strongest light, therefore, the center.

Also, you probably know that when you peer through a small hole, the sharpness of what you see improves. This is the principle of the pinhole camera—everything is in focus through a pinhole.

Target shooters often use sight discs with tiny holes in their aperture sights. The hunter, however, will do better with a large

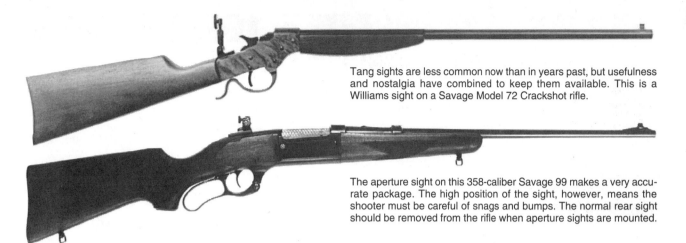

Tang sights are less common now than in years past, but usefulness and nostalgia have combined to keep them available. This is a Williams sight on a Savage Model 72 Crackshot rifle.

The aperture sight on this 358-caliber Savage 99 makes a very accurate package. The high position of the sight, however, means the shooter must be careful of snags and bumps. The normal rear sight should be removed from the rifle when aperture sights are mounted.

Look through, not at, an aperture rear sight and focus on the front sight, even if the target is fuzzy.

The small hole in an aperture rear sight looks much larger to the shooter because it is close to his eye. The shooter simply looks through the aperture, not at it.

hole in the disk, or no disk at all. The loss of sharpness is more than made up by being able to see more through the hole, and see it more quickly. Many believe that a very large aperture, which is seen only as a "ghost" of a circle, is the fastest sight of all. With such a system, no thought at all is given to the rear sight. Attention is all on the front sight, which looks more prominent by contrast.

The front sight used with an aperture rear on a hunting rifle may be either a bead or post. For military-style target matches, the post rules. For many types of target shooting, an aperture front sight is used. One places the circular bullseye on the target inside the circle of the front sight, which is seen through the fuzzy circle of the rear sight. This is a very effective target sight system—circles within circles.

Actually, most target rifles now have front sights that accept interchangeable inserts. Apertures of different diameters and posts of different widths can be put in to suit the individual shooter.

Mounting Aperture Sights

Aperture sights are often called receiver sights because they are most commonly mounted on the receiver of the rifle.

Tang sights, another type of aperture sight, put the sight behind the receiver on the tang of the rifle. Such sights were popular in decades past on single shot and lever-action rifles (and some are still in use), but they are seldom seen today.

There have been other mounting locations. The cocking-piece sight was a peep attached to the cocking piece of a bolt-action rifle. It was generally used where bolt movement prevented a mount on the receiver. Aperture sights were also made to mount on the breechbolt of the Winchester Model 71 and other Winchester lever-action rifles. Because there is always some play in striker and bolt mechanisms, one would not expect the finest accuracy. However, such sights did well in the hunting fields and were used for many years.

Any disadvantages? Well, of course. You don't get something for nothing. Aperture sights stick up into the air more than

WHAT IS SIGHT RADIUS?

For years I wondered why the distance between the front and rear sight was called sight radius. Why not call it sight distance and be done with it? After all, firearms publications define sight radius as the distance between the front and rear sights. Obviously, a radius is a measurable distance, but does not the term refer to the distance from the center to the periphery of a circle or sphere?

For years I puzzled over this. However, not wanting anyone to know that I didn't know something I thought they thought I should know, I never asked. Later, I found out they didn't know either.

Let's think about it this way:

Consider the rear sight a fixed point at the center of a circle. The front sight then may be considered as being a point on the outside of the circle. Now, the term "radius" makes more sense.

Let us think of an open sight rifle, with the sights 18 inches ($1\frac{1}{2}$ feet) apart. The sight radius is, thus, $1\frac{1}{2}$ feet. Our imaginary circle is also, then, one with a radius of $1\frac{1}{2}$ feet. Now, think of a misalignment of the sights of $\frac{1}{100}$-inch (.01-inch). This will give us a new line at a very small angle to the original sight radius.

If we increase the distance 100 times, to get to the target, the error will increase 100 times. Therefore, when you multiply 100 by $1\frac{1}{2}$ feet (150 feet, or 50 yards) the error is 100 times .01-inch, or 1-inch.

So, with an 18-inch sight radius, a sight misalignment of .01-inch will give us an error of 1-inch on a 50-yard target. Neat how we got that to come out even, isn't it?

Now, let's look at what happens if we double the sight radius by mounting an aperture sight on the receiver. Our hypothetical rifle now has a distance between sights (sight radius) of 36 inches, or 3 feet, or 1 yard.

Let us use the exact same misalignment of .01-inch. The error at 1 yard in front of the rear sight is now .01-inch. We are still shooting at the same target 50 yards away. The error now at 50 yards is simply 50 times .01-inch, or $\frac{1}{2}$-inch.

Thus, by doubling the sight radius, we have cut our error due to the same misalignment exactly in half.

Can it really be that simple? Well, obviously, we can't just move the same sight farther back on the rifle, because sights are made to be used in different ways, at different distances from the eye. Once we change the type of sight, we introduce other variables that can make more difference than the sight radius.

However, the physical principles of the situation do not change. A longer sight radius always gives a theoretical advantage in precision. Just be aware that other factors can easily overshadow the effect of sight radius.

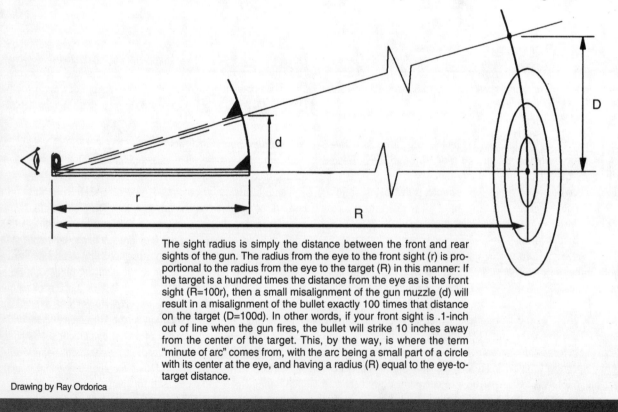

The sight radius is simply the distance between the front and rear sights of the gun. The radius from the eye to the front sight (r) is proportional to the radius from the eye to the target (R) in this manner: If the target is a hundred times the distance from the eye as is the front sight (R=100r), then a small misalignment of the gun muzzle (d) will result in a misalignment of the bullet exactly 100 times that distance on the target (D=100d). In other words, if your front sight is .1-inch out of line when the gun fires, the bullet will strike 10 inches away from the center of the target. This, by the way, is where the term "minute of arc" comes from, with the arc being a small part of a circle with its center at the eye, and having a radius (R) equal to the eye-to-target distance.

Drawing by Ray Ordorica

Scope Reticle Styles

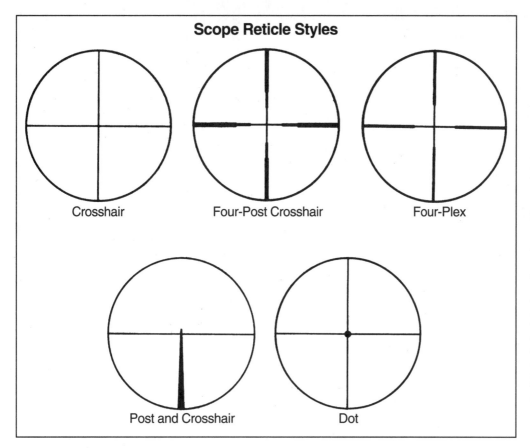

Crosshair

Four-Post Crosshair

Four-Plex

Post and Crosshair

Dot

Simple crosshairs (top left) are seldom seen these days, though they work for many applications. Today's shooters want a more clearly defined heavy edge to the crosshair, such as the double-thickness or four-post crosshair. Today's most popular and probably most useful reticle has fine crosshairs in the center, plus heavy posts directing the eye to the center. This is useful when hunting in marginal light, as is the post and crosshair at bottom left. With this system you place the target on top of the post, and the crosswire prevents canting. The old dot reticle (bottom right) was popular on early hunting and target scopes. The wires are nearly invisible. So is the dot in dim light!

open sights and so are more exposed to possible damage. This is generally not a problem, but a rifle can be dropped or bumped by accident, and it is something to consider.

Optical Sights

Optical sights are generally called telescopic sights. This always seemed a misnomer to some, because the scopes did not "telescope" like the old draw-tube versions of yesteryear. Recently, some companies have begun calling their products riflescopes instead of telescopes.

Optical sights for rifles had been used at least as far back as the Civil War. During that conflict, some scope-equipped rifles were used by snipers, some with great effect. After that conflict, scopes were used on some of the big blackpowder rifles of the buffalo hunters.

In the early decades of the 20th century, rifles with optical sights were being used for target shooting, and some hunters took them into the field.

During World War II, the importance of long-range sniping was again recognized. Specially made M1903A4 Springfield rifles and some M1 Garands were fitted with Weaver and Lyman telescope sights.

As was the case with semi-automatic rifles after World War II, the use of optical sights may have grown naturally in the sporting world. However, a breakthrough in optics during the war essentially assured the increased popularity of optical sights. This was the development of coated lenses.

When light strikes a glass surface, it is bent. Most of it passes through the glass, but some is reflected and lost. This loss of light is in the neighborhood of 3 percent. The loss happens at every air/glass surface. In a scope with five separate lenses, there were ten air/glass surfaces, for a possible loss of 30 percent of the total light.

It was discovered that a transparent coating of magnesium fluoride on each lens would minimize reflection, allowing almost all the available light to pass through the lens. Scope systems that previously passed about 65 percent of the available light now could let more than 90 percent through.

The improved performance of these brighter scopes gave a great boost to the popularity of riflescopes in the postwar years. The sporting use of optical sights grew tremendously. Today, some rifles are made and sold without sights, because it is taken for granted that the owner will scope it.

In the past, scope alignment was changed by adjusting the mount, and some target scopes still use that system. However, most of today's hunting and target scopes have internal adjustments. These features may be just as precise as those of a good micrometer sight, making the optical sight very accurate and easy to adjust.

Some think the advantage of an optical sight is in its magnification, which may be as low as $1^1/_2$x for close-range woods hunting or as high as 6x to 20x for open-country, varmint, target and silhouette shooting. The highest power scope I have seen mounted on a rifle was 30x. The spotting scope I was using that day was a 20x. I was impressed.

Magnification is not the whole story. With a scope, all the different things you are looking at are in focus. The target and sighting device, or scope reticle, are both in the same optical plane of a properly adjusted optical sight. This is a very important factor. The new shooter can look into the scope and everything is aligned optically. Because of this, scope sights may be good choices for beginners. They may shoot better with a scope, not because a scoped rifle is more accurate, but because it frees their concentration for the other fundamentals of shooting.

For hunting, optical sights make it easier to see the target. This allows more accurate shooting. It also allows the hunter to distinguish between legal game and non-legal game, and other things that should not be shot.

This is not to say that optical sights have no disadvantages. Good as they are, we must remember that, as the saying goes, "There ain't no free lunch."

The tubular framework, the adjusting devices and the optics that provide the advantages also add weight and bulk. Hardly anything is handier to take for a walk in the woods than a Winchester 94 carbine. Hardly anything is more awkward for woods-walking than a scoped 94.

Although the cost of good optics has been coming down, scope sights still add expense to the cost of a hunter's gear. And the magnification that lets you tell a buck from a doe also magnifies your wobble by the same amount when your heart starts pumping fast.

Optical sights may also be damaged or put out of action by a hard fall or a good soaking. This does not mean that today's riflescopes are fragile. They are not. However, there are conditions under which open or aperture sights are still useful.

Although we have gone over the three primary types of

Rifles with heavy recoil should have a scope set well forward, so the rear of the scope is not driven into contact with the shooter's face. This Sako Finnbear, in 338 Winchester Magnum, has its Weaver K4 scope set well forward.

Optical sights are very common on bolt-action big game rifles. This 30-06 Winchester Model 70 has a Tasco variable scope.

Optical sights are popular for a number of uses. This Bushnell scope on a 22 bolt-action rifle makes a satisfactory squirrel outfit.

If your sights are canted (tipped) to the right, your shot will hit low and to the right.

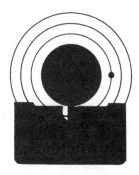

If the front sight blade is too far right, your shot will go right.

By raising the front sight blade too high, your shot will go high.

Canting your sights to the left will make your shot go low and left.

When the front sight blade is too far left, your shot will go left.

If you hold the front sight too low, the shot will go low.

sights—open, aperture and optical—be aware that other types exist. Electronic "dot" sights and laser sights are offered. More often used on handguns, they are also available for rifles. Although I've seldom seen them on longarms, keep them in mind. They may be important in the future.

Sight Alignment

Sight alignment is the proper alignment of the eye with the sights themselves.

The optical sight, the most complex of the sights, is actually the simplest to use. The riflescope puts the target and sighting system all in one optical plane. The reticles (sighting devices) may be crosshairs, or combinations of crosshairs and dots or posts, possibly more creative combinations. Almost invariably, the aiming takes place in the center of the scope's field. To achieve correct sight alignment, you simply look through the center of the scope and place the crosshairs on the spot you want the bullet to hit.

For the aperture sight, alignment of eye and sight is also easy. We look through the rear aperture, not at it, and our eye automatically finds its center. We don't really see the rear sight. Therefore, sight alignment merely consists of looking at the front sight through the rear.

Now we come to the simplest of sights, open sights, and we find the greatest complexity of alignment. There are other combinations, but we will stick with the two most common: bead front with U-notch rear; or post front with square-notch rear.

Remember the human eye can only focus on one thing at a time. The sights may be anywhere from 1 to 2 feet apart. You cannot focus on them both at the same time, so do not frustrate yourself by trying. So, where to focus? *Always focus on the front sight.*

With your eye focused on the front sight, the rear sight will be a bit fuzzy. Don't worry about it. You can still accurately align a sharp front sight in a fuzzy notch.

With the bead front sight in the U-notch, align the top of the bead with the top of the horizontal portion of the rear sight, and center the front sight inside the notch. That's all there is to it.

Now, at this point, you must be warned of a terrible danger. Somewhere, sometime, someone will tell you that under certain circumstances you should use a "fine bead" (draw the bead down into the bottom of the notch) or a "coarse bead" (hold the bead up out of the notch.) This explanation will seem very logical, and your only salvation will be to ask yourself this question: When has lack of consistency ever improved anyone's shooting? Forget the idea of fine and coarse beads.

With the post front sight in the square-notch, the top of the front sight should be aligned with the top of the horizontal portion of the rear notch. The post should be centered in the notch, with an equal amount of light on both sides. Because we are dealing with straight lines in both horizontal and vertical directions, alignment can be somewhat more precise than with the bead-and-U system.

The center hold is useful if you want your shots to hit exactly where your gun looks. It tends to disappear in the center of a big black bullseye, but is right at home in the field.

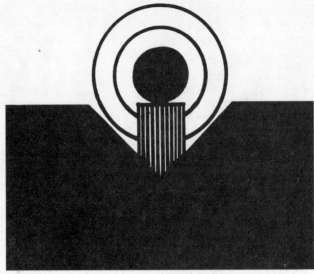

The 6 o'clock hold is fine for fixed-range shooting, as on the target range, but it makes hits uncertain at uncertain ranges.

Sight Picture

Sight picture is the proper alingment of the sights with the target. For optical sights, sight picture is easy—just place the crosshairs where you want the bullet to strike. For iron sights, using either open or aperture sights, the sight alignment is made as we've just discussed. Now, the only new thing we need to get our sight picture is to add the relationship of the target to the front sight.

With an aperture front sight, the target should be in the center of the aperture. Aperture front sights are used almost exclusively for target shooting, and it is not surprising that their round holes work well with round bullseye targets.

With the post or bead front sights found on most rifles, two common options for sight picture are used: 6 o'clock hold and center hold.

The *6 o'clock hold* gets its name from the face of the clock, with 6 being the bottom position. A round bullseye is seen as a clock face, and the top of the post or bead is held at its bottom position. It may appear to be just touching, or with a thin line of white between the bull and the sight.

The greatest advantage of the 6 o'clock hold is that the dark front sight is slways distinct from the dark bullseye, allowing for a more precise sight picture. The greatest disadvantage is that the sight adjustment must be changed for targets of different sizes. Also, point of impact is more difficult to estimate if shots are made at targets encountered at unknown ranges.

The *center hold* is known by that name because the sights are adjusted with the top of the front sight, post or bead held to the exact center of the bullseye.

The greatest advantage of the center hold is that the point of aim and the point of impact are the same. The strike of the bullet is at the top of the front sight, so the same sight picture can be used with different targets, always simply holding to the center. The greatest disadvantage is that it is hard to tell where center really is. Slightly high or slightly low may look pretty much the same, and some precision is lost.

In general, a rifle used for target shooting may be sighted in for either the 6 o'clock or center holds, depending on the preference of the shooter or coach.

For hunting rifles, the center hold is generally deemed best. The front sight is placed on the game so that the bullet strikes to the top center of the bead or post.

If you are not sure what might suit you best, try both methods as you sight-in.

Sighting-In

Some people are lucky. We may know a friend who buys a rifle, new or used, gets a box of ammunition, heads to the range, sets up a target, and immediately shoots good groups exactly where he wants them. If this fortunate friend were going to hunt only with that ammunition and expected all his shots at that range, he needs to do nothing more. However, most of us need to sight-in our rifles.

Sighting-in is the process of adjusting the sights of a rifle so the bullet strikes the target at the same spot at which the sights are pointing. A rifle must have its sights adjusted so the shooter can place his shots in the target he wants to shoot, at the range he wants to shoot, with the ammunition he wants to shoot.

How to begin?

I have seen people get a new rifle, set up a target at 100 or 200 yards, fix a solid rest at the firing line, and start shooting. I hate to admit it, but in days gone by, I was one of those people. I know from experience this is not a good way to start.

An old coach once said that sighting-in a rifle that way was like "fishing for the bullseye." It is possible to fire a string of shots and see no hits on the paper. At that point, you (or I) have wasted good ammunition and know no more than before we started.

There is a better way.

It is possible to make an approximate alignment of the sights without even shooting. This is called boresighting. Set the rifle securely on a sandbag or other solid rest. Remove the bolt and center the bullseye in the bore. Note that with rifles other than bolt actions, it is possible to look through the bore. You may need to use a tiny mirror inserted into the open breech. (Or it just may not be worth the trouble, so wait for the next step.)

With the bull centered, and without disturbing the rifle's alignment, raise your head and check your sights. They also should be pointing at the bull. If not, your sights need adjustment.

Now, we have made some progress without even firing a shot. Next, it is time to do some shooting. If your rifle was one that did not lend itself to boresighting, this will be the starting point.

The initial shooting should be done at short range, no more than 25 yards. The bullseye should be small, and the target paper should be large. The bullets will hit the paper somewhere, and that will give you an idea as to where the rifle is shooting.

The rifle should be fired from a solid rest. A benchrest with sandbags or a rolled sleeping bag is great. Shooting prone with a rest is just about as steady.

Now, shoot. Some experts suggest two shots, some three. (I always shoot three, unless I am low on ammunition.) Take the midpoint between the two shots or the center of the triangle as the point of impact.

Let us suppose the point of impact is 2 inches low and 4 inches to the right. Obviously, to move the shots where we want them, we must bring them 2 inches up and 4 inches to the left.

No matter what type of rear sight your rifle wears, the rule for adjustment is always the same: **Move the rear sight in the direction you want the shots to go.**

Sometimes it is necessary to move the front sight to make an adjustment. The rule for front sight adjustment: **Move the front sight in the opposite direction you want the shots to go.**

The method of adjustment you use will depend on the type of sight you have. If you are shooting a new rifle, or have a new scope or sight, refer to the directions that came with it. Many riflescopes and micrometer receiver sights are marked to indicate how they should be adjusted to move the point of bullet impact. With non-adjustable open sights, you may have to resort to the tap-and-file methods mentioned earlier.

At any rate, our hypothetical rear sight needs to come up and left. Make the adjustments and shoot again. Suppose your point of impact now is 3 inches low and 5 inches right. Whoops! You've moved the sights the wrong way! Come back to your starting point, and continue your adjustments. Make notes of the changes you make for reference. Shoot again. Now you are 1-inch low and 2 inches right. You have moved the sight exactly half the distance you needed from the original point of impact. Make the additional adjustments. Some people prefer to make only windage or only elevation adjustments between shots. This takes more ammunition, but helps them to keep better track of the adjustments.

When the sights are right for short range, they should be on the paper at longer ranges. Put up a new target at your desired (longer) range and make your final adjustments.

Eye Dominance

An eye must see the sights, so let us give a little attention to this important factor. Just as most people are right-handed or left-handed, most people are either right-eyed or left-eyed. That is, one dominant eye wants to take over when both eyes look at something.

There is an easy way to determine your dominant eye. Extend your arms in front of you. Put your hands together so a small opening shows. Keep both eyes open, and look through the hole at a distant object. Move your hands back to your face while continuing to look at the object. One eye will be blocked out by your hand. The eye you are still using to see the object is your dominant eye.

The presence of a master eye has been noted in shooting publications at least since the beginning of the 20th century. It is primarily a concern only when the dominant eye does not cor-

Optical sights are common on hunting rifles. Here, Robert Malloy, the writer's brother, sights-in his rifle, a Winchester Model 70 in 30-06, prior to the deer season.

These High Power rifle shooters use blinders on their aperture rear sights to eliminate any distracting images from the left eye.

respond to the dominant hand. Previous solutions have ranged from closing the offending master eye, to putting a blinder in front of it, to shooting from the opposite shoulder.

Note that a left-hander with a dominant right eye is in better shape to switch shoulders, because most rifles are made for right-handed use. I have known a number of left-handed shooters who shot right-handed, and enjoyed using the guns the "right" way.

The latest advice offered in the NRA and Boy Scout handbooks is to shoot from the same shoulder as the master eye. If

SIGHTING-IN TIP

Let's mention it again, so it is fresh in your mind. The primary rule for sight adjustment: **Move the rear sight in the direction you want the shots to go!**

If you forget this rule, you can recall it by imagining an extreme condition. For example, how will moving the rear sight to the right affect the impact on the target? Imagine the rear sight moved 1 foot to the right and hanging out in space. Moving the rifle to bring the front sight into alignment with this phantom rear sight would make the barrel point well to the right. If a shot were fired from this extreme position, it would hit far to the right of the target. By this method, you have reminded yourself which way to move the sight.

you are taking a shooting course, by all means do this if the instructor wants you to. In many cases, improvement in your shooting can be immediate.

There are, however, some difficulties with this approach. Hand-eye coordination may be better for a right-hander with his right hand and right eye, even if his left eye is dominant. Shooting a right-handed bolt-action rifle from the left side may not be much of a problem for Smallbore shooters, with their leisurely time limits. Shooting a right-handed bolt-action rifle from the left shoulder during the rapid-fire stages of a High Power match would be extremely difficult.

Many target shooters attach a translucent blinder to their rear sights to suppress distracting images from the other eye, even if their hand/eye dominance coincides.

Some people have better vision in the eye that is not dominant; some have undergone a long-term change in dominance from one eye to the other; some seem to cross over from one eye to another in different situations. It would seem that there is still much to be learned about eye dominance and its application to shooting.

If I seem a little wishy-washy about eye dominance, it is because I am not sure just where I belong. If I do ten of the eye dominance tests I've described on myself, I'll average six or seven left eye, and three or four right eye. At one time, on the basis of a single test, I was instructed to shoot left-handed. I shot about as well as I had before, but it felt awkward. I soon switched back to shooting right-handed.

As you've probably noticed by now, it is often difficult to put what we know about guns and shooting into nice neat pigeon-holes. Benefit from the knowledge of others, but keep an open mind. Your personal shooting experiences may be the ones that will best help you and other shooters down the road.

CHAPTER SIX

SHOOTING THE RIFLE

IN ORDER TO shoot a rifle well, you must have certain skills. These skills must be used every time you fire a shot—shot after shot. They are essential, or fundamental, to being a successful rifle shot. Perhaps that is why they are generally called the fundamentals.

The fundamentals have been described in a number of different ways over the years. They remain pretty much the same no matter the description, boiling down to about five: position; aiming; breathing; trigger control; follow-through.

Position

Before we discuss the five basic rifle shooting positions, it is important to understand there are steps that will allow you to master any position: study the position; practice the position without the rifle; practice the position with the rifle; align the position. Carefully following these steps will lead to an improved shooting position.

The purpose of any shooting position is to provide a stable platform from which to shoot. There are a few things that are common to all positions.

1. A good position is comfortable, relaxed and balanced. The head is up, and the rifle is fully supported.
2. Bones support better than muscles. The rifle should be supported by the shooter's bone structure, not by muscle tension.
3. The shooter's position should naturally align the rifle with the target. If the rifle does not point naturally toward the target, the entire body position (not just the rifle) must be shifted to align the rifle with the target.

As we study positions, keep these things in mind.

A number of positions have been used over time. Today, five are in common use—a supported position called benchrest and four unsupported positions called prone, sitting, kneeling and standing.

Benchrest Position

The benchrest position gives the greatest possible support to the rifle. This support allows the shooter to devote less attention to holding the rifle steady and more attention to concentrating on the fundamentals.

There are special setups for competitive benchrest shooting, but we won't go into them here. However, for the simple bench-

Use of a benchrest gives good support to the rifle and allows concentration on the fundamentals of getting off a perfect shot. These Boy Scouts are at a summer camp near Quincy, Florida.

es or tables that most of us will use, there are two basic benchrest positions. We separate them by the position of the hand that does not control the trigger.

In the first variation, the forend of the rifle is rested on some firm but yielding surface. A stack of sandbags is the traditional rest. In the absence of sandbags, a rolled sleeping bag or mat can serve well. In all our examples, we will be describing methods for a right-handed shooter. The right hand then con-

trols the trigger. The left hand curls underneath the buttstock near the toe. By moving the stock with the left hand, the orientation of the rifle is changed. Another variation is to rest the left hand on the sandbag. The rifle then lies in the supported hand instead of in direct contact with the bags. This may be the preferred final sight-in position for a hunting rifle, as it is close to the way the rifle will be held in the field. This hand-forward position is also useful because some rifles shoot to a

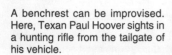

A benchrest can be improvised. Here, Texan Paul Hoover sights in a hunting rifle from the tailgate of his vehicle.

(Above) This is the prone position as used by a High Power shooter practicing for a match, using a military-type rifle with an extended magazine.

This shooter has a comfortable prone position, with his right leg drawn up somewhat more than most.

slightly different point of impact if the forend of the rifle is not held in the hand.

Prone Position

There are four generally used field or target-shooting positions. They are prone, standing, kneeling and sitting. Most target shooting courses now seem to teach them in this order, so we will use the same sequence. As we consider each position, we will assume that the shooter is shooting right-handed. Lefties, I apologize, but you will have to reverse the directions. Let us begin with the most stable, the prone position.

Without using a benchrest, the prone position is the steadiest of the field positions. Both elbows and a large area of the body are in contact with the ground. In fact, prone position with a support for the forend is almost as steady as the benchrest position. This position is used in precision target shooting, both Smallbore and High Power. It is also used in open-country hunting situations when there is adequate time to assume the position, and when ground cover does not block the view.

In a modern prone position, the shooter lies facing about 20 degrees to the right of the target. The left leg is parallel to the spine with the foot pointing back, or to the right. The right knee is drawn up somewhat, shifting some of the body weight to the left. The left elbow is extended forward and is just slightly to the left of the rifle. The left hand supports the rifle without putting pressure on it.

The right hand holds the pistol grip with firm pressure. The right elbow seeks a natural position, and the arm is relaxed. The head is as erect as possible, and the shooter should look straight forward through the sights.

Adjustments to the natural point of aim should be made by pivoting on the left elbow for windage, and by moving the left hand forward or backward on the rifle for elevation.

Many older shooters still use a prone position in which the body is at a 45-degree angle to the target, the left elbow is directly under the rifle and the legs are spread apart. It is little used now for target shooting, but a lot of records were set by people using it in days gone by. It is still widely used for prone shooting in the hunting field.

Here, the standing position is used by two High Power rifle shooters. Note the differences in the position of the left hand with the different rifles.

(Below) The standing position should be practiced by hunters, as it is often the only position that can be quickly assumed when game is spotted. The writer is practicing with a scoped Marlin 45-70 rifle.

Standing Position

The standing position is the least steady but perhaps the most-used of the field positions. Only the feet touch the ground, but the position is comfortable and feels natural. It is used for much target-shooting competition. It is the favorite position of the plinker and rabbit hunter. Many deer hunters have no other option.

Actually, there are two significant variations of the standing position. In the olden days they were called the "NRA" and "Military" positions. Let's call their modern counterparts the "Arm Rest Standing" and the "Free Arm Standing" positions. The basic difference is that the left arm receives support for the rifle from the shooter's body in the arm rest standing position.

Arm Rest Standing Position: To assume this position, the legs should be straight but not locked, about shoulder width apart. The weight should be about even on both feet.

The body bends slightly backward, but the head is erect. The left arm rests on the shooter's side or hip. The left forearm and wrist are straight. The left hand should support the rifle just forward of the trigger guard. There are a number of ways to position the fingers and fist to obtain this support, but in all variations the wrist is straight.

The right arm holds the butt firmly into the shoulder, with the index finger free to control the trigger. Natural point of aim is adjusted by moving the feet slightly for horizontal alignment. Vertical alignment is by changing the position of the fingers or fist of the left hand under the rifle.

Free Arm Standing Position: Almost everything is the same for this position, except the left arm is held away from the body, and the stance is upright, without the slight bend backward. The free arm standing position allows quick changes in direction and is

The writer demonstrates an arm rest standing position, using a 1917 Enfield rifle. The left arm is against the body, wrist is straight and, in this variation, the fingertips support the rifle.

generally the position of the hunter. The arm-rest position is generally the standing position most favored by target shooters.

Kneeling Position

Kneeling position is used in both American and International rifle competition. It is also a good field position, quick to assume, when ground cover does not allow a lower position.

To assume the kneeling position, the shooter sits on the right heel. For target shooting, a kneeling roll is placed under the right foot. As much body weight as possible should be balanced over the right foot. The right knee will be pointed 30 to 45 degrees to the right of the target. The lower part of the left leg should be vertical or forward, and the left elbow should rest on the left knee.

The back is bowed forward a bit, and the shoulders slump down. Remember, the body should be balanced over the right heel. The head stays upright. The right arm is relaxed, and the right hand grips the stock with the index finger free to control the trigger.

Find your natural point of aim by looking away from the sights for a few seconds, then looking back. If the position is not properly aligned, pivot the body around the right foot. Ver-

The writer demonstrates the free arm standing position, using a 1917 Enfield rifle. His left arm is free of any contact with the body.

tical adjustments are made by the left hand position on the stock.

The kneeling position can be very stable. Most new shooters do not find it so. When I began shooting on a rifle team back in the long ago, my kneeling scores were my worst! Even my standing scores came in higher. Other shooters shot decent kneeling scores, so I became determined to learn how to shoot that position. I had to practice a lot, but by the end of the season, my kneeling average had come up to only one point behind my prone average. The moral: don't give up on the kneeling position, even if you're not doing well with it.

(Above) A kneeling pad under the right foot allows the shooter's weight to be placed comfortably on the heel when using the kneeling position.

Sitting Position

Although International shooting events do not use the sitting position, in this country it is used in High Power shooting and in a number of Smallbore events. It is a very stable and very useful position for hunters, being slightly lower and slower to get into than the kneeling position, but steadier. The rest of the world will just have to eat its collective heart out. We have the sitting position and they don't.

In days gone by, the sitting position was assumed with the legs extended outward from the body. As time went on, better and better scores were shot with crossed-leg or crossed-ankle sitting positions. Although the old open position is often used for hunting, the crossed-leg and crossed-ankle positions are now considered standard.

If the legs are extended and crossed at the ankles, the position is called the *extended* sitting position. If the legs are crossed close to the body, the position is called the *closed* sitting position. There are some differences to consider in assuming the two positions.

To assume the extended sitting position, sit facing about 30 degrees to the right of the target. The left leg is crossed over the right at the ankles and the legs are extended away from the body.

This is important: no muscle tension should be used to hold the legs up. The legs should be relaxed and sag down as far as they will comfortably go. The body leans forward, and the elbows rest below the knees. The head position drops down, but only slightly.

I hate to admit it, but I have trouble getting into this extended position. I seem to be in a minority, though, as many shooters seem to prefer it. If you are just starting to use the sitting position, try the extended position first.

To assume the closed sitting position, sit facing at a greater angle away from the target, about 45 to 60 degrees to the right. Cross the left leg over the right and draw in the crossed legs

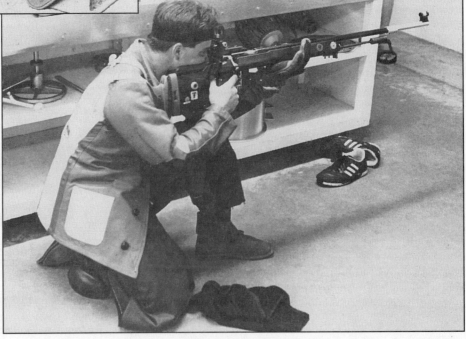

Championship Smallbore shooter Vincent Pestilli practices his kneeling position. Pestilli took time after his instructor duties at a Florida Junior Olympic Shooting Camp to practice in the camp kitchen.

close to the body. Lean forward and rest the elbows on the insides of the knees. The head must drop down, but as little as possible.

An upright head position is very desirable, as it lets you look through the sights, instead of straining to peek through them at an angle. If both positions seem equally comfortable to you, choose the one that allows the best head position.

Aiming

When you have a stable position with a natural point of aim, the next fundamental is aiming, which consists of:

1. Sight alignment—the proper relationship of the front and the rear sight, relative to your eye.
2. Sight picture—the relationship of the aligned front and rear sights and the aiming point on the target, again as seen by your eye.

These things were covered in some detail in Chapter 5: "Rifle Sights and Sighting-In." If something is unclear, go back and review, because proper sight alignment and sight picture are crucial to good shooting.

Keep both eyes open when aiming, even though only one is

HOW TO PRACTICE SHOOTING FROM ANY POSITION

1. Study the position. Look at the pictures of people in the positions in this book, other books, other shooting publications. Note especially those showing people who have won some sort of recognition while shooting from these positions. The position of a world champion may be worthy of more study than that of an occassional plinker.

You will soon note, however, that different people assume somewhat different positions. Positions have evolved over the years, and the results of decades of competitive target shooting have brought some subtle and some not-so-subtle changes in standard shooting positions. Hence older shooters may use slightly different positions from those used by younger shooters.

Another is that people are different. A short, stocky person cannot assume the exact same position as a tall, skinny one. Also, older shooters can't force their bodies into all the positions that younger shooters can. Flexibility diminishes with age.

2. Practice the position without the rifle. You may ask what is the point of getting into a shooting position without the gun. The reason is that you are thus forced to be aware of the orientation of the parts of your body. When you have the rifle in your hands, your attention focuses on the rifle. Without the rifle, you can note the position of your hands, arms, shoulders, torso, legs and feet, dealing with these aspects of a good position as you practice.

3. Practice the position with the rifle. Remember all the aspects of the position without the rifle. Now, with the rifle in position, make sure that the position is comfortable, balanced and stable, and that your bones support the weight of the rifle.

4. Align your position with the target. Until now, you have developed your position without reference to a target. Now we want to achieve a natural point of

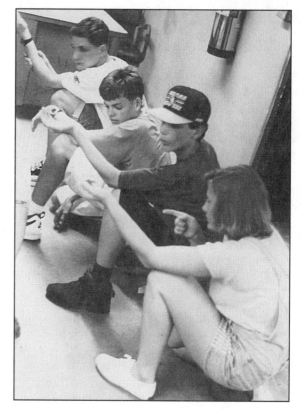

Practice a position without a rifle before you begin practicing it with one. These Florida Junior Olympic Camp shooters are getting their kneeling position oriented. Note the forearm is in direct line with the upper leg when the position is correct.

aim with the rifle directed at the target. Assume the position and aim at the target. Now, look away from the sights for a few seconds. Look back at the sights. Are they still pointing directly at the target? If not, do not "muscle" the rifle back to the target. Instead, shift your entire body position until the rifle naturally points to the target. You have now achieved your natural point of aim.

North Florida High Power shooters use a variety of crossed and open leg positions. Even experienced shooters may profit by reviewing the fundamentals and comparing notes with other shooters.

aligning the sights. To close the other eye adds muscular strain that we can do without. Most shooters automatically supress the image seen by the other eye. If what the other eye sees becomes a problem, many target shooters use a translucent blinder in front of it. The blinder allows the other eye to see light, but not a distracting image.

NRA FUNDAMENTALS OF SHOOTING

While we catagorize the five fundamentals somewhat differently, the basic handbooks of the National Rifle Association and the Boy Scouts list them this way:

1. Shooting Position is the posture of the body and how the rifle is held in relation to the target. Five positions are standard, benchrest, standing, prone, kneeling and sitting.

2. Shot Preparation refers to preparing to fire by aiming, and includes breath control.

3. Sight Picture Control is the (somewhat strange) term used to describe holding the rifle as steadily as possible while keeping the sights aligned.

4. Trigger Control means that the trigger must be squeezed to fire the shot without disturbing the alignment of the rifle with the target.

5. Follow-Through refers to continuing to maintain everything necessary for firing the shot for a short time after the shot is fired.

Breathing

If you breathe during the time you are trying to fire a shot, your body will move and the rifle will move. So, it is logical that you should not breathe at that time.

When getting ready to shoot, breathe normally. When everything settles into place, stop breathing. In the past, shooters were given instructions such as this: take a breath, let out half, then stop breathing while you fire the shot.

Recent studies of competitive shooters have shown that they all remembered the last part. When everything was right, they simply exhaled and stopped breathing for a few seconds while they fired the shot.

Don't stop breathing for more than about eight or ten seconds. If things aren't right to get off the shot within that time, just relax, resume breathing for a while, then try again.

Trigger Control

Once you have a stable position, good sight alignment and picture, and have momentarily stopped breathing, you only want one physical motion to take place. The trigger finger must move the trigger just enough to fire the shot. We are only talking about a tiny fraction of an inch of movement, but that movement is important, and it must be controlled.

Some call the control of the trigger a "squeeze"; some call it a "pull." It doesn't matter to me, as long as the pressure is *straight back* without disturbing the alignment of the rifle. It must also be a *smooth* movement (not a jerk) that does not disturb the alignment of the rifle.

Grasp the grip of the rifle and place your index finger on the trigger. The preferred contact point of the finger is the pad of the first segment, or the fleshy part of the finger just ahead of the first joint. However, people vary and rifles vary. The best spot for you is probably what we've just described, but it's possible it may be different.

The best way to tell is by *dry-firing*. This practice, a form of

To get into the hasty sling, give the strap a half-turn, insert the left arm, bring the arms around and place the left hand between forend and sling. The sling should lie flat across the back of the hand.

Many people feel the hasty sling helps support the rifle in the standing position. Note that no pressure from the left hand is needed to hold the forend.

shooting without ammunition, consists of preparing yourself as if you were about to fire a shot, but without loading a cartridge. When your stable position is aligned with the target, your sight picture and sight alignment are good, then stop breathing and squeeze the trigger.

Click! You notice that the sights jumped to one side as the firing pin fell. You have either jerked the trigger, or the placement of your trigger finger did not move the trigger straight back. This sideways movement of the sights would not be so obvious had you fired a cartridge, because the recoil would mask it.

Try again. When you know you've made a smooth squeeze, but the sights still jump to the side, your finger placement is probably the culprit. Try another part of your finger. Now, when the firing pin falls, the sights no longer jump. Use the position that allows you the best trigger control.

Even the most stable position is not perfectly steady. The sights, although they are perfectly aligned, seem to wobble across the target from time to time. The temptation is to jerk the trigger when the sights are right.

There is no excuse for jerking the trigger. No good shot fires at the *instant* his sight picture is correct. That is what a poor shot does, and that may be one of the reasons he is a poor shot.

The good shot understands that the rifle will move. He puts pressure on the trigger when the sight picture is pretty good, then holds it as the rifle moves away from the bullseye. When it comes back, he adds more pressure. Thus, the shot will always fire when the sight picture is at least "pretty good."

Remember: The trigger must come straight back without disturbing the rifle, and it must be squeezed smoothly, without disturbing the rifle.

Follow-Through

Follow-through is simply continuing to do what you were doing. In many sports, it means the continuation of a movement. In shooting, it is, well, the continuation of non-movement after a shot is fired.

Remember, back in Chapter 4, how we gave some thought to all the things that happen between the squeeze of the trigger and the exit of the bullet? The bullet doesn't take much time to leave the gun, but it does take *some* time. If you move during that time, the shot will be a bad one.

To prevent rifle movement while the bullet travels through the bore, maintain your position, sight picture, breath control and trigger control until the shot is long gone. Use the time to think about what you did right and what needs attention before the next shot.

Now that we have gone through the five fundamentals, let us back up and look at "Sight Picture Control," which is one of the original fundamentals listed in the NRA Basic Rifle Handbook. In other times, and in other publications, this factor has been called "Hold Control" or "Minimum Arc of Movement." Whatever the name, it means to hold as steady as possible. And this was a consideration in each of our five fundamentals.

Is holding steady important? Yes, but I'm not sure it deserves the same status as the other factors we've discussed. We know the rifle will move. We adjust our trigger control to compensate for that movement. Proper trigger control improves our shooting. Practice allows us to hold steadier.

We are all influenced by our experiences. I remember a youngster shooting standing for the first time. The boy was gamely trying to coordinate his new position, aiming, breathing and trigger control. I pointed out that he didn't look very steady. "Mr. Malloy," he said in frustration, "I'm not *trying* to wobble!"

Movement of the rifle will always be with us. We want it to be minimal while firing the shot. Practice over a period of time will minimize it. In the meantime, understanding the fundamentals will allow us to do good shooting.

Use of the Sling

We've just talked about the movement of the rifle during shooting. I think everyone will agree that anything that will help hold the rifle steady is good. Therefore, every rifle shooter should be familiar with the rifle sling.

Use of the sling is essentially universal for target shooting in the prone, sitting and kneeling positions. The sling supports the weight of the rifle so that the shooter's muscles do not have to. The sling is useful on a hunting rifle, too. Not only will it steady a shot at game, but it is a handy way to carry a rifle. The hunter's hands are thus free to do other things.

Hasty Sling

The drawback to a hunting sling is that, in many cases, there is not time to use it. When time permits, the standard loop sling

may be put on. More often, there will only be time for the "hasty" sling. As the name implies, it can be brought into use very quickly.

With the sling already adjusted (by previous trial and error) to proper length, place the upper left arm between the sling and the rifle. Swing the left hand in an arc outward, then over the sling to grip the forend. When the rifle is brought up to the

(Above) A shooting sling can also serve as a carrying strap, leaving the hands free for other things.

When using a loop sling, the loop is given a half-turn, the arm inserted, and the loop placed high on the left arm. The keepers are placed to hold it there. The sling lies flat across the back of the left hand. The rear segment of the sling serves no purpose with the loop sling and can be removed if desired.

FIRING THE PERFECT SHOT

Now, it is time to put everything together. You will now take everything you know, and you will use it to fire the perfect shot. Your rifle has been sighted-in, and you have complete confidence in it.

You approach the firing line. Let's say you will shoot prone.

You give the sling loop a half turn, put your arm through, tighten the sling and assume the prone position. The position and the sling are both just right, and the rifle is very steady. Your head is upright, and your eye quickly aligns the sights.

The aligned sights form a good sight picture on the target. You look down for a moment, then look back at the sights.

Your sights now point to the left of the bullseye. You move your body slightly, pivoting on your left elbow. Perfect sight picture. Look away again, then back at the sights. Still perfect. You have achieved your natural point of aim.

The range command to commence firing has been given, and you have chambered a cartridge. You concentrate on your sight picture, minimizing movement as you prepare to squeeze the trigger. Almost unconsciously, you exhale slightly and hold your breath. The pad of your index finger begins to squeeze the trigger straight back.

The sights wobble off a bit and you hold your pressure on the trigger. Back to the correct sight picture, and apply more smooth steady pressure on the trigger. The shot fires.

You remain motionless, maintaining follow-through for two seconds. Time to think. Where were the sights when the shot went off? It looked like a perfect sight picture, didn't it? You call the shot a center "ten."

You take a breath and look into your spotting scope. There it is—a "ten" right in the center! You have done it. You have fired the perfect shot.

Now, if you can fire one, why not two? If you can fire two....

Careful attention to the fundamentals of rifle shooting will produce good groups and good scores. This Boy Scout is pleased with his target, fired at a summer camp rifle range.

shoulder, the sling lies across the chest, outside the upper arm and across the outside of the left hand.

Loop Sling

The loop sling is the sling of the target shooter. It can be used by the hunter if time is available. It provides substantially more support, but it does take longer to put on. The loop sling is the type used by U.S. military forces since the beginning of the 20th century.

To use the loop sling, disconnect it from the rear swivel (if attached) and open up the loop. Give the loop a half-turn counter-clockwise and insert your arm. Slide the loop high on the arm and tighten the keepers. Swing the left hand over the sling and grip the forend. The half-turn you gave the loop allows the sling to lie flat against the back of your hand.

When properly adjusted, the sling and the bones of your left arm form a stable triangle that easily supports the weight of the rifle.

CHAPTER SEVEN

RIFLE SHOOTING ACTIVITIES

SOME PEOPLE love rifles and are content to stay at home and admire them. Most of us, however, want to use them. And we are fortunate there are a number of rifle shooting sports in which we can participate.

Joe Bowman, the great exhibition shooter from Texas, once said that all sports involve a target, a projectile, and some sort of power to get the projectile to the target.

Obviously, for a sport such as basketball, the basket is the target, the ball is the projectile, and muscle power gets it to the desired place.

With the rifle, the burning powder provides the power to get our projectile to the target. As we discussed in Chapter 6, we control the rifle so that the projectile gets to the desired place.

When considering the rifle shooting sports, what a variety of projectiles and targets we have! And, there's a vast array of rifles and ways of using them, for getting that projectile to the target.

One thing that sets rifle shooting apart from many other sports is that it can be a lifetime sport. I know a number of regular shooters who are in their seventies, but it is hard to recall any active football players that old. Because it does not require large physical size or great strength, rifle shooting is an equal opportunity sport. Men and women can compete on equal footing; an American woman, Margaret Murdock, has won several Olympic medals for rifle shooting. Shooting is also a participant sport. In most cases, shooters outnumber onlookers.

Let's put the rifle shooting sports into these convenient categories: plinking; hunting; silhouette shooting; target shooting (Smallbore, High Power, Benchrest).

Plinking

Almost everyone knows what it is, but plinking is hard to define. I usually think of it as informal shooting at informal targets. A friend thinks that definition is too formal; he calls it shooting at things that go "plink." Whatever the definition—targets move, things break, and it's lots of fun.

The 22 rifle is the king of the plinkers. Of course, any type of rifle can be used, but the low cost of 22 ammunition makes it especially suitable.

Glass bottles and "tin" cans were once the prime targets of plinkers. They broke and bounced satisfactorily, and hits were easy to see, but they left a residue of sharp shards of glass and

An afternoon of shooting fun called plinking can be provided by a few targets such as drink cans, water-filled balloons, or Life Savers, plus a good rifle and some ammo. Be sure to clean up your range when you're done.

Beverage cans make fun targets because they jump when hit. Plinking is fun for new and experienced shooters alike.

ragged rusty metal. If you own your own land, have set aside a special plinking area and don't mind cut feet or tetanus, I guess glass bottles and steel cans are still OK. However, better targets exist.

Charcoal briquettes, candy wafers, balloons, clay pigeons, aluminum cans, crackers and plastic bottles are all good targets. They either leave little objectionable residue or can be easily (and safely) picked up and carried away.

When plinking, the shooting is informal, but safe gun handling is never relaxed. All the safety rules you know must be strictly followed. If you have a bit of trouble remembering them, consider going back to Chapter 2 to refresh your memory about the rules of firearms safety.

Plinking is fun alone, but most people enjoy it more with family or friends. Several people can play informal games with the targets, and new games can be invented as the shooting progresses. Stationary targets, swinging targets and rolling targets can be used. Shooting simultaneously, shooting in sequence, or miss-and-out techniques can be used to add interest and competition.

A single shot 22 and a box of cartridges has been a traditional way to provide plenty of plinking fun for a couple of boys. When plinking, make sure of a safe location and adult supervision.

A safe location is an absolute requirement for plinking. Some shooting ranges allow plinking at certain types of targets in specific areas. One local range permits shooting at plastic, but not at glass or metal containers. Even when such targets are permitted, you must think about your target and what is beyond. Every bullet must go into a safe backstop. Shooting on private land, with permission, is great. Some state and national forests and other tracts of public land allow informal shooting; some don't. You must check with the appropriate authorities before you go out to shoot on public land.

Most of us are aware that fewer places to plink exist now than in decades past. You can keep your plinking areas open by being a safe, responsible shooter. Don't allow an area to become trashed out, even if you must pick up other people's targets as well as your own.

The point of plinking is to have fun. It is a wonderful sport that deserves to continue.

Hunting

Hunting with a rifle is an American tradition. From the earliest days of our country, people hunted. The rifle came to be the standard firearm of the skilled woodsman. Whether hunting small game or the largest game on earth, Americans have always used appropriate hunting rifles. Varmint hunting, which grew from the need to eliminate destructive pests or vermin, is a challenging sport in itself.

Over time, today's rifle hunter gains some of the characteris-

Big game hunting in America usually means deer hunting. Mule deer such as this buck provide good eating as well as a fine challenge.

(Above) Millions of Americans enjoy the sport of hunting. Wildlife Management Areas are set up in many parts of the country. Be sure you understand and obey all game laws and license requirements.

North America is home to some of the biggest bears on the face of the earth. Hunting them requires a powerful rifle and is one of the greatest challenges for the rifleman.

(Left and above) Varmint hunting provides a tremendous challenge. It's a test of both hunting and marksmanship skills.

tics that made legends of the early frontiersmen. A love of the outdoors, knowledge of the environment and deep respect for nature grow to be part of the good hunter. Such people support sensible conservation and wildlife management practices, and wildlife has thrived as a result.

People who don't hunt have trouble understanding this. They seem to feel that hunting is somehow unnatural and detrimental to the animals. I have been asked if I couldn't just enjoy the outdoors without hunting. My answer is, "Sure!" I enjoy hiking and backpacking, too, and sometimes just taking a stroll in the woods. But there is a difference. When I am hiking, I am a visitor to the woods. When I am hunting, I am a part of the environment.

Because hunters are generally not a pretentious or vocal lot, it is difficult for some to realize how many of us there are. In a recent survey by the National Sporting Goods Association, hunting, with about 18 million participants, ranked above tennis. Target shooting, with about 13 million, outnumbers skiing and backpacking by several million.

At any rate, if you hunt with a rifle, you should know and practice all the rules of safety, choose a rifle appropriate for the game hunted, know it well, and know how to shoot it well. Before going afield after game, spend time studying your quarry and its habits. And, of course, check with your state's game and fish commission and become familiar with the game laws and license requirements of your area.

Perhaps I've wandered a bit off the subject of rifles, but you should know that when you pick up your rifle to go hunting you become part of a very large group of sportsmen, both past and present.

Silhouette Shooting

Silhouette shooting is target shooting, but many people equate target shooting with firing at paper targets. Silhouette shooting combines elements of both plinking and hunting.

Steel silhouettes in the shapes of animals and birds are the targets. The sport came into the southwestern United States from Mexico. Animal target shooting apparently began there about the time Pancho Villa was operating in nothern Mexico during the World War I period.

Legend has it that one of Villa's leaders settled a dispute between two men who were about to duel to the death. He let the two compete by taking long-range shots at two steers scheduled for butchering. As the story goes, the men became so engrossed in the competition, they forgot their argument.

Before long, the tradition of a shooting match prior to a fiesta sprung up. The targets were the animals that would be eaten later that day. As more shooters became interested in such shooting, steel (reusable) silhouettes of the animals were gradually substituted for the animals themselves.

In the early 1960s, Americans in the states bordering Mexico learned of such matches and began to participate and hold their own competitions. The wide-open spaces of Mexico and the American West permitted ranges out to 500 meters (about 550 yards).

The sport, of course, appealed to other Americans, and as silhouette popularity spread across our country, matches were begun for pistols and 22-caliber rifles (at reduced ranges), as well as airguns.

Four animals are represented in metal. Chickens are shot at the shortest range. Then, as distance increases, shooters try for pigs, turkeys and rams.

For High Power (centerfire) rifles, these chicken-pig-turkey-ram distances are 200, 300, 385 and 500 meters. For 22-caliber rifles, the ranges are 40, 60, 77 and 100 meters.

The High Power silhouettes are approximately life-size, and the metal rams weigh about fifty pounds. Substantial power is needed to knock down a ram. Smallbore rifle targets are much smaller, ranging in size from a chicken less than three inches long to a ram of slightly over six inches long. Since not all ranges

Smallbore silhouette shooting requires only short ranges and low-cost ammunition. Numerous 22-caliber rifles of many varieties can compete.

(Below) High Power silhouette shooting is a long-range sport, and many shooters now use special rifles with target-type scopes.

have 500 meters available, there are also reduced-scale targets for shorter distances.

All shots are taken from the standing position. When the competition began, hunting rifles with iron sights were used. Gradually, specially designed silhouette rifles appeared, and today, almost all are equipped with optical sights.

Restrictions are few, pertaining primarily to rifle weight limits and the use of special clothing. Almost any 22-caliber rifle can be used in the rimfire matches. Special silhouette rifles are available, but in small local matches, most shooters just use their hunting rifles.

High Power shooters seem to favor cartridges of the 308 Winchester class as a good compromise between knock-down power and recoil. Scope power is not limited, but I have found that too much power magnifies my lack of steadiness. Scopes of 6x to 12x are common. Almost any big game or varmint rifle can be used, allowing a shooter to give the sport a try with what he already has.

Here are the weight limits, including sights:

High Power (6mm or larger)
High Power Silhouette Rifle—10 lbs., 2 oz.
High Power Hunting Silhouette Rifle—9 lbs.
Open High Power Silhouette Rifle—11 lbs.

Smallbore (22 Rimfire only)
Smallbore Silhouette Rifle—10 lbs., 2 oz.
Smallbore Hunting Silhouette Rifle—7½ lbs.
Open Smallbore Silhouette Rifle—11 lbs.

Silhouette matches are generally casual, friendly affairs. Coaching is allowed on the firing line, and a coach may spot a

shooter's hits or misses as the shooting progresses. Targets are engaged in groups of five at a time. A total of forty shots are fired at each match, one at each of ten silhouettes of the four different animals. Score is the number of animals knocked completely off their pedestals.

There is a lot of spectator appeal to these matches, because there is no question as to the result of every shot fired. At each shot, a well-hit silhouette responds with a satisfying clang and (usually) topples off its stand. A missed target just continues to stand there! A great deal of good-natured kidding can occur when all a shooter's silhouettes remain standing. Attention really focuses on a shooter when four animals are down and the rifle is ready for the last shot of that five.

Target Shooting

All the sports we've just discussed involve shooting at targets, but most people think of target shooting as just punching

Smallbore silhouette shooting is offered for both rifle and pistol at approximately the same ranges. Here's the difference. The small targets are rifle targets; the large ones are for pistols.

These steel silhouette targets don't need to be reset each time they're hit because they are mounted to swing, not drop.

holes in paper targets. Target shooting can be in competition, shooting shoulder-to-shoulder against other competitors for best score; or, it can be for qualification when shooting against a fixed score, trying to equal or surpass it.

There are basically three categories: Smallbore, High Power and Benchrest.

Smallbore

Smallbore rifle shooters use the 22 Long Rifle rimfire cartridge. This cartridge was introduced shortly before 1890, but modern Smallbore target shooting with it didn't begin until after World War I, in 1919. Such shooting was originally planned as training for military big bore rifles.

The famous Winchester Model 52, Savage Model 19 NRA Match Rifle and Springfield M1922 were the first 22s that can be considered match rifles. They were all superbly accurate rifles for their day, all—even the Springfield—available to

civilians, and the interest in precision Smallbore shooting grew.

By 1925, Smallbore target shooting began to shape into a new sport, entirely independent of the original military training procedures. The 22 rifles could be used indoors as well as out, and indoor gallery shooting at 50 feet became popular.

Today, Smallbore rifle shooting is fired using a precision 22-caliber match rifle. Competition is conducted in one or more of the four standard positions—prone, sitting, kneeling and standing.

In the United States, matches may be prone only, all four positions, or three-position matches (omitting sitting). International matches generally recognize only prone, kneeling and standing positions. After World War II, interest in International shooting increased in this country. Rifles with different stocks and accessories became generally available that permitted a shooter to specialize in prone shooting, position shooting or International free-rifle competition.

Smallbore matches may be held indoors or out, and at distances ranging from 50 feet to 100 yards. Time limits are generous. The shortest time limit is one minute per shot, for prone stages in all Smallbore matches. Time is not checked for each shot, however. If a stage of fire calls for twenty shots, the total allowed time is twenty minutes. The longest time limit is for the standing position of the NRA Three-Position Course—two minutes per shot.

What do you need to get started? A rifle with sights, ammunition, a sling, glove, jacket and spotting scope are the essentials. Other items are gradually acquired with time and as experience dictates.

Are you a little afraid of getting into competition without knowing what you're getting into? A number of qualification

Junior shooters at a Florida Junior Olympic Shooting Camp shoot for record from the kneeling position. These types of events are held nationwide.

Smallbore rifle shooting is among the more popular target activities for those with a competitive edge, as evidenced by the crowd on this firing line.

Targets come in many shapes and sizes. The diamond shape here is preferred by many for precise holding with scopes. Big bullseyes can obscure crosshairs. Benchrest shooters use hollow squares.

High Power rifle matches are shot at long ranges, but at least the targets are big. Here, range officials double-check target scores during a High Power match.

courses may be fired with a Smallbore rifle. They range from the long-popular 50-foot course to outdoor courses at 50 and 100 yards. Light rifle (under 7 pounds) and Sport Shooting courses are also available for those who want to use field-type rifles. You shoot for certain scores at a number of levels. When you qualify for one level, you can receive an award for that accomplishment and go on to the next level. Information on qualification courses is available from the NRA.

High Power

In 1903, two things happened that affected rifle shooting in the United States. First, the M1903 Springfield was adopted, and second, the annual National Matches were established. These two items combined to establish the basic form of High Power rifle competition.

A course of fire was set up for military training to make use of the accuracy and rapid reloading potential of the Springfield. The National Match Course is still the basic course of High Power competition today.

The course begins with ten shots standing, slow-fire (10 minutes). The second stage is ten shots-rapid fire (60 seconds), dropping from standing to sitting (or kneeling). These two stages are fired at 200 yards.

The third stage is ten shots rapid-fire at 300 yards, standing to

prone, in 70 seconds. Reloading the rifle during the rapid-fire stages must be done within the time limit.

The final stage is twenty shots slow-fire, prone, in 20 minutes, at 600 yards. The National Match Course thus requires fifty shots.

Different combinations of these stages are used for various match programs. By doubling the first three stages, we have an eighty-round match. By doubling the entire course, we have a 100-round match.

Because few areas now have 600-yard ranges available, reduced-size targets are made for shorter ranges. It is possible to shoot the entire match at 200 or even 100 yards.

Both bolt-action and semi-automatic rifles are used, but only with metallic sights.

Other courses of fire still exist that involve shooting at up to 1000 yards. However, few ranges in this country can host this type of match any more.

When preparing to fire the rapid-fire stages of the National Match Course, a shooter will generally establish his shooting position, then rise to standing, with his feet in approximately the same positions they had in the shooting position. This technique allows him to quickly assume the firing position again.

On command, the rifle is loaded. On another command, the timing begins, and the shooter must then drop into firing position, fire, reload, and fire the additional rounds within the 60- or 70-second time limit.

Although the rules permit either sitting or kneeling for 200-yard rapid-fire, almost all shooters choose the steadier sitting position.

As in Smallbore, High Power qualification courses are available. There is also a High Power qualification course (introduced in 1985) that allows hunting rifles with optical sights. Details are available from the NRA.

Benchrest

In the mid-1800s, benchrests and very heavy muzzle-loading rifles appeared. They allowed experiments with sights, bullets and loads, and a lot was learned from them. The heavy guns faded away, but the benchrests remained and were used by many riflemen for testing purposes.

During the 1930s, competition in shooting from the bench began. The new discipline was considered the ultimate precision shooting sport. After World War II, benchrest shooting as a sport became formalized, and the National Benchrest Shooters Association was formed to be the governing organization.

Benchrest shooting appeals to a relatively small but highly dedicated group of shooters who strive for the finest possible accuracy. They are fascinated by accuracy and the equipment that can produce it.

There are four classes: Benchrest (sometimes called unrestricted); Heavy Varmint; Light Varmint; Sporter.

The Benchrest rifle has few restrictions, and some do not even look much like conventional rifles. A typical one may weigh 35 pounds. Heavy Varmint rifles may weigh no more than 13 pounds, with sights, and there are barrel size limitations. It is probably the most popular class. The Light Varmint rifle

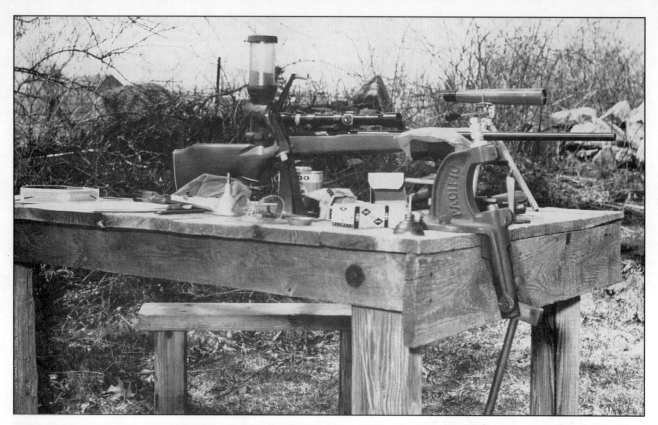

Benchrest shooters load at the range for maximum consistency and accuracy. Shooters use only a few cases that are reloaded again and again, on the spot as required.

has a weight limit of $10^1/2$ pounds. The Sporter rifle is similar, but must be larger than 22-caliber.

Ammunition is, of course, critical. Shooters will go to the utmost lengths to produce ammunition that is as perfect as possible. They use specialized loading tools and generally load all their ammunition on the range. Because consistency of components is so important, most competitors load just a few selected cartridge cases over and over.

Benchrest matches tend to be relaxed, friendly affairs. Shooting is generally done at 100 or 200 yards, and though 300-yard matches are sanctioned, relatively few are held. Time limits are fairly long here. Varmint and Sporter classes get seven minutes to shoot five record shots, while Benchrest shooters are allowed twelve minutes to shoot ten record shots.

Shooters reload their ammunition behind the firing line and exchange information. Targets are scored by the center-to-center size of the shot group, not by the position in the scoring rings.

Benchrest shooters approach the rifle shooting sports from the standpoint of maximum precision of both rifle and ammunition. This sport has greatly advanced our knowledge of rifle accuracy, and it appeals to those who would like to add to that knowledge.

Olympic Shooting

Competing in the Olympics is the ultimate dream for many athletes, shooters included. In actual fact, shooting is one of the most popular Olympic sports. In recent games, only track has attracted more participating nations than shooting. However, where many athletes find the rules of their sport at home the same as at the Olympics, American shooters are not so lucky.

America may or may not have had the greatest interest in shooting in years past, but our country still has only one vote on the International Olympic Committee. Most of the shooting events at the Olympics are patterned after those developed in Europe.

Actually, former shooters would consider us pretty lucky just to know what the events are. Our earliest Olympic shooters went to the games without even knowing what guns or what courses of fire they would be shooting!

The modern Olympics began in 1896. The site of the original Olympic Games in Greece had been buried until the 1880s, when archeologists began excavating the area. The work inspired a Frenchman, Baron Pierre de Coubertin, who conceived the idea that the Games could be revived.

The 1896 Olympics were held in Athens with the support of the Greek government and were surprisingly well-organized. The games were opened with a shot fired by the Queen. Rifle matches were fired at 200 and 300 meters, but American shooters had entered only the pistol matches.

The early Olympics let the *host* country select the shooting events to suit itself. Officials would naturally schedule events familiar to their own shooters. The practice made it difficult for other nations to plan ahead. Shooters showed up confused about the courses of fire, the correct equipment and the ground rules.

A combined listing from the early Games had a bewildering

Rifle shooting sports appeal to young people. At the 1992 Florida Junior Olympic Shooting Camp, Camp Blanding base commander Col. Norman Redding congratulates Smallbore Rifle winners Rob Given, J. Van Deusen and Char Fosmoe.

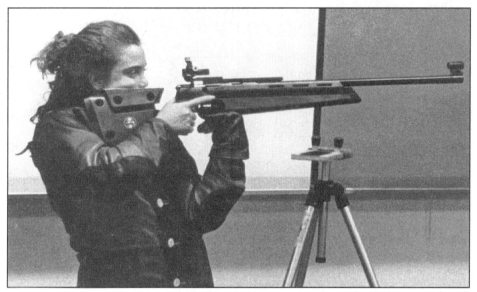

Shelby George, 1994 Smallbore winner for the Florida Junior Olympic Shooting Camp, gives other shooters the benefit of her knowledge at an indoor training session. Notice that the bolt is open and her finger is off the trigger.

Smallbore rifle shooting has been a popular sport since its organization during the 1920s. This group of Smallbore shooters is firing a standing stage at the Florida Junior Olympic Shooting Camp.

State Games are held in most states, and shooting events are included. At Florida's 1994 Games, Junior Smallbore winner Ben Rubin is congratulated by NRA's Bud Eyman, referee of the shooting events.

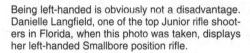

Being left-handed is obviously not a disadvantage. Danielle Langfield, one of the top Junior rifle shooters in Florida, when this photo was taken, displays her left-handed Smallbore position rifle.

array of events. They included contests for rifles, military rifles, miniature rifles, carbines, pistols, revolvers, dueling pistols, shotguns, bow and arrow, crossbows and cannons. Some matches were for individuals only, some for teams only. Host countries might decide on a large number of shooting events or practically none at all.

After World War II, International shooting was reorganized, and the events are now governed by rules of the International Shooting Union. Even though the events are those popular in Europe, American shooters now know exactly what the courses of fire will be.

Rifle shooting events currently fired in the Olympics are primarily for the Smallbore rifle, with metallic sights.

Smallbore Free Rifle, Three-Position, is fired at 50 meters, with a rifle that is "free" of most restrictions. Weight can be up to 17.6 pounds (8 kilograms). For record, 120 shots are fired, 40 each from prone (60 minutes), standing (90 minutes), and kneeling (75 minutes).

Smallbore Free Rifle, Prone, fires 60 shots at 50 meters, and the total time allowed is 1¹/₂ hours.

There is also a course for the Smallbore standard rifle. It is basically the same course as the Free Rifle, but shooters use a lighter rifle of 12.1 pounds (5.5 kilograms) and fire 20 shots from each position. At present, this course is open to women only.

Also included in the Olympic events are Air Rifle and Running Game courses. Biathlon (skiing combined with shooting) is held at the Winter Olympics.

The 300-meter Free Rifle courses have been very popular Olympic events in the past, but are not included in the latest list-

ing. They are still widely used as International shooting events and have been part of the World Championships and the Pan American Games. Similar to the 50-meter course, they use a centerfire rifle no larger than 8mm. Both prone and three-position courses are fired.

So, looking back, what are the opportunities for a rifle shooter?

Let's see...we can go out and plink with friends on an informal basis. We can sharpen up our rifle skills and enjoy small game or big game hunting. If we are very good and work very hard, we can shoot in the Olympics. I believe we've already mentioned the World Championships and the Pan American games. There are also State Games (held in most states), Senior Games (open to older shooters) and Junior Olympic programs for young shooters. Shooting events are held by shooting clubs, the Boy Scouts, 4-H, Jaycees, military and veterans units, and a number of other organizations.

There are local matches, postal matches, school matches, league matches, state matches, regional matches, and the National Matches. Some matches are formal; some are informal. If true competition doesn't appeal to you at this time, qualification courses are available.

We can shoot at things that break and bounce, at legal game both large and small, at silhouettes of animals, and at a multitude of types of paper targets.

Whether you are an experienced expert or a newcomer, I'll bet that there is an exciting rifle shooting sport that is just right for you!

CHAPTER EIGHT

UNDERSTANDING THE MODERN HANDGUN

IF YOU ARE reading this book from cover to cover, you may wonder why the handgun section follows the rifle section.

The fundamentals of shooting a handgun are actually closer to those of shooting a rifle than they are to those needed for shotguns. So, while the techniques of rifle shooting are fresh in our minds, let's consider handguns.

Handguns hold a special place in the hearts of Americans. True, there were pistols in use in all sorts of countries since matchlock days, probably dating back to at least the 15th century. However, in America, myriad events unfolded during the 1800s that made the one-hand firearm a part of our heritage forever.

The Colt revolver was invented in 1836. The Seminole Wars, which lasted until 1842, showed the advantages of the new handgun. Then came the Mexican War of 1846-1848, the California Gold Rush of 1849, the move west during the 1850s, the Civil War of 1861-1865, and the western expansion and settlement following that conflict.

All these events showed the value of a handgun that could fire a number of times. They also showed the value of a man who could shoot such a firearm well.

Consider that throughout history, men who were mounted and armed were agents of the government, always to be feared by the common man. In America, in the period after the Civil War, this changed. For the first time ever, in all of history, an ordinary workingman—the American cowboy—was mounted and armed. Small wonder that the cowboy and his six-shooter became the stuff of legends!

Handguns in the hands of Americans helped tame the Western frontier. Handguns played a role in the Spanish-American War and the Philippine insurrection that followed. During the early years of the 20th century, the United States conducted the most extensive tests of handguns that had ever been done.

The result was a sidearm, the Colt Model 1911 45 Automatic, that is still considered by many to be the best pistol in the world. It was used in two World Wars, finally superseded only a relatively short time ago by the Beretta 9mm.

The handgun has been used as a military pistol, a police sidearm, a gun for target shooting, an effective hunting firearm, and a choice for personal protection. In the past, handguns have been all these things to Americans, and they remain so today.

Recently, semi-automatic pistols have been widely accepted for law-enforcement use, but revolvers are still used as well. Officer Wayne Joyner wears an S&W 357 Magnum revolver as he writes up a report.

Parts of a Handgun

When we were discussing rifles, we agreed that the basic parts of a rifle—derived from the old lock, stock and barrel of muzzle-loading days—were the action, stock and barrel. It isn't quite so simple with handguns, but we can still use a basic breakdown of *action, frame* and *barrel.*

The Barrel

As with a rifle, the barrel is the metal tube through which the bullet passes. The hole inside the barrel is the *bore*. Spiral grooves are cut into the bore to give a rotation or spin to the bullet as it travels toward the target. The cuts are called, logically, *grooves*. The high areas between the grooves are called *lands,* and the combination of lands and grooves is called *rifling.* It is obvious that in this way, handguns are closely related to rifles.

The rifling generally consists of four to six sets of lands and grooves. (Some British revolvers have seven, just to make things hard to classify.) The rifling curves either to the left or to the right, but it doesn't seem to make any difference, except for purposes of description.

If the barrel were long enough, a bullet engaged in the rifling would make one full rotation while passing through the bore.

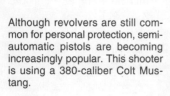

Although revolvers are still common for personal protection, semi-automatic pistols are becoming increasingly popular. This shooter is using a 380-caliber Colt Mustang.

Handgun barrels are often not long enough for a complete turn, but the *rate of twist* is still the same. Thus we talk of the twist of the rifling, for example, as one turn in 10 inches or one turn in 16 inches. These are usually abbreviated as 1 in 10 or 1 in 16, and sometimes as 1:10, etc.

As with rifles, the front of the barrel is the *muzzle,* but the rear end can be different for various types of handguns. We'll get into these differences in some detail as we discuss the basic types of handguns.

The Frame

The frame is the basic structural component of a handgun. It is essentially the part to which all the other parts are attached. The parts of the action are installed in or on the frame. The *grip*, which lets the gun be grasped and held, is generally part of the frame. *Grip panels* of wood, plastic or other material ordinarily are attached to cover the sides of the grip frame to offer a comfortable hold. In some cases, a protusion from the frame allows a completely separate grip to be installed.

The Action

The action of a handgun is the mechanism used to load, fire and unload. For most practical purposes, the action consists of the moving parts that make up the handgun. We'll take up actions in more detail as we cover the different types of handguns.

Types of Handguns

There are two common types of handguns in use today: *revolver* and *semi-automatic.* Single shot pistols are used extensively in some areas of sport, and there are also other types that we'll cover later.

Revolvers

A revolver is a handgun that has a rotating *cylinder* with a number of chambers that hold the cartridges. Cylinders have been designed with from four to ten chambers, but the usual number is six.

The cylinder is rotated by parts linked to either the trigger or hammer.

The barrel of a revolver thus has no integral chamber at the rear of the bore—the cartridges are loaded into the chambers of the cylinder. When a cartridge is fired, the bullet passes through the front of the chamber, across a tiny gap and into the rear of the barrel. There is generally a slight taper within the rear end of the barrel at this point, called the *forcing cone.* Its job is to take care of any slight misalignment between cylinder and barrel and force the bullet into proper alignment with the bore.

A cartridge is fired by the forward movement of a *hammer,* which is powered by a spring called the *mainspring* or, sometimes, hammer spring. The hammer can have a *firing pin* at its

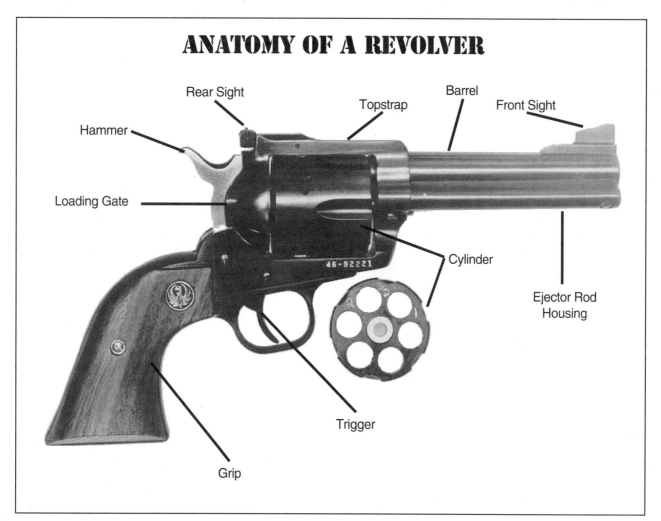

ANATOMY OF A REVOLVER

Rear Sight

Topstrap

Barrel

Front Sight

Hammer

Loading Gate

46-92221

Cylinder

Ejector Rod Housing

Trigger

Grip

UNCOCKING A REVOLVER

Sometimes a revolver is cocked for a shot and the shot is not taken. This may happen while hunting, on a range when a cease fire is called, or in other situations.

It is important to be able to uncock a loaded revolver safely.

Uncocking a single-action revolver:
1. Place the left thumb in front of the hammer, between the hammer and the frame.
2. Place the right thumb firmly on the spur of the cocked hammer.
3. Control the hammer, press the trigger and gently lower the hammer until it contacts the left thumb.
4. Carefully remove the left thumb and ease the hammer all the way forward.

5. For Colt-type single actions, after the hammer is all the way down, pull it back one click to the first notch.

Uncocking a double-action revolver:
1. Place the left thumb in front of the hammer.
2. Place the right thumb firmly on the hammer spur of the cocked revolver.
3. Press the trigger and ease the hammer forward until it contacts the left thumb.
4. Release the trigger. (Note that this is different than for the single action, in which the trigger stayed pressed.)
5. Ease out your left thumb and carefully lower the hammer all the way down.

(Below) The strange-looking Japanese Type 26 revolver is double-action-only—the hammer cannot be cocked. It was the Japanese military sidearm during the Russo-Japanese War of 1904-1905.

(Above) The British Enfield No. 2 Mark 1* is a double-action-only revolver. Earlier versions could be cocked for single-action shooting, but this variant cannot. This was the standard British revolver of WWII.

Nattily attired in his stylish flying-duck tie, the writer squeezes off some single-action shots from a double-action Webley Mark VI. The big Webleys are perhaps the largest breakopen revolvers still seen in common use.

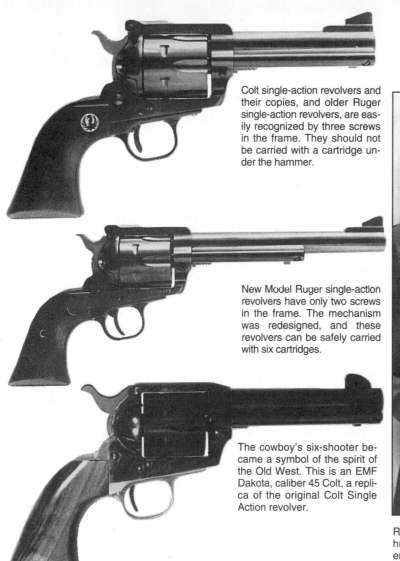

Colt single-action revolvers and their copies, and older Ruger single-action revolvers, are easily recognized by three screws in the frame. They should not be carried with a cartridge under the hammer.

New Model Ruger single-action revolvers have only two screws in the frame. The mechanism was redesigned, and these revolvers can be safely carried with six cartridges.

The cowboy's six-shooter became a symbol of the spirit of the Old West. This is an EMF Dakota, caliber 45 Colt, a replica of the original Colt Single Action revolver.

Revolvers come in all sizes. Robert Malloy examines a huge one built in traditional single-action style, but enlarged and chambered for rifle cartridges such as the 45-70.

front face, or it can strike a separate firing pin mounted in the frame.

The hammer is released by a *trigger*, a (usually curved) lever protruding from the underside of the frame.

All the foregoing is basic to how revolvers of all types work. Now, let's group revolvers into two basic types: single action and double action.

If you listen to enough revolver shooters long enough, you will be exposed to the fact there is some dispute as to the exact definition of these terms. As you can imagine, no one sat down before revolvers were introduced and worked out a terminology that they must follow. After the revolvers appeared, the terminology evolved.

What I present to you here is based on the meager historical information I have been able to uncover. The use of the terms is consistent with that presented in the NRA's *Pistol Shooting Handbook*.

With a *single-action* revolver, the trigger performs the "single action" of releasing the hammer. The hammer must be cocked with the thumb, and it stays cocked until it is released by pulling the trigger. Perhaps the best-known example is the Colt Single Action Army revolver of 1873, which actually incorporated the phrase "Single Action" into its official designation.

In a *double-action* revolver, the trigger performs the "double action" of cocking the hammer back and then releasing the hammer.

Most double-action revolvers can also be fired in the single-action mode by thumb-cocking the hammer and then pressing the trigger. Most modern revolvers—as made by Colt, Smith & Wesson, Ruger, Wesson, Harrington & Richardson and others—are double actions. The term "double-and-single-action" is not incorrect, just unnecessary. A modern double-action revolver is assumed to have single-action capability unless otherwise specified.

So far, so good. But, as we know, there are always some oddballs that refuse to be shoved into our nice categories. Some revolvers have been made (and have recently become more popular) in which the hammer cannot be cocked, but can be fired only by the double-action pull of the trigger mechanism. Historical examples of this type are the Smith & Wesson Centennial, British Enfield No. 2 Mark 1* and Japanese Type 26. The term "double-action-only," often shown as DAO, is legitimately applied to such revolvers.

You will sometimes run across the term "trigger-cocking" used for such revolvers. At first, this seems logical, but you should be aware that some obsolete Iver Johnson (and possibly

SOLID-FRAME REVOLVER WITH OR WITHOUT EJECTOR ROD

Both single- and double-action revolvers of this type may be encountered. Some examples are the Colt Single Action Army and all its copies and modifications, Ruger single-action revolvers, some early European military revolvers and some H&R double-action 22 revolvers made with "frontier" styling and features.

To load:

1. Put the hammer in loading position. For the Colt and its copies, including Old Model Rugers with three screws in the frame, this is the second notch back. For some other types, it will be the first notch or the rebound position. The New Model Ruger single-action revolvers (with two screws in the frame) can be left with the hammer down.
2. Open the loading gate. The cylinder should turn freely.
3. Align the chambers with the loading port and load the cartridges, turning the cylinder to index each chamber.
4. Close the loading gate.

This is a good time to note that, unless you are going to load and immediately shoot six shots, the Colt-type six-shooter should carry only five cartridges. Because the half-cock hammer notch is not a particularly strong one, old-timers got in the habit of carrying their Colts with

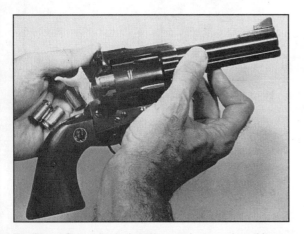

Traditional Colt-style single-action revolvers, such as this early Ruger, must have the hammer drawn back two clicks in order to load or unload. This one is being unloaded with the ejector rod.

New Model Ruger single-action revolvers can be loaded or unloaded with the loading gate open and the hammer forward. Six cartridges can be safely loaded in this redesigned model.

other) revolvers were made that are really trigger-cockers. One pull of the trigger cocked the hammer, and the second pull released it. The term "trigger cocking" is properly reserved for these rare revolvers and should not be used for any double-action-only arms.

There are three basic revolver frame types: solid; swing-out; breakopen.

The *solid-frame* revolver is our oldest type, dating back before cartridge use. It brings to mind the famous Colt Single Action Army again, but a large number of other revolvers are of solid-frame type.

The design is strong and sturdy. In manufacturing, one dispenses with some of the machine work needed to produce the other types. In a solid-frame revolver, the cylinder turns on a separate central pin that aligns the cylinder in the frame at front and rear. Loading and unloading can be accomplished

This Smith & Wesson target revolver, a Model 25-2, has a typical double-action trigger mechanism. It may be fired double action by just pulling the trigger or single action by cocking the hammer first.

five loaded chambers and the hammer down on the empty one.

It is possible to accomplish this by trial and error, but here is a dependable way to do it: Beginning with an empty cylinder, load one chamber, skip one, and then load four more rounds. Bring the hammer all the way back, then press the trigger and ease the hammer all the way forward. The hammer will now be down on the empty chamber.

To unload with an ejector rod:
1. Put the hammer in proper position, as when loading.
2. Open the loading gate.
3. Rotate the cylinder to bring each chamber into line with the loading port, and push a cartridge or empty case out with the ejector rod.
4. While manually rotating the cylinder slowly, visually check to make sure the revolver's chambers are completely empty.
5. Control the hammer with the thumb, press the trigger and ease the hammer forward.

To unload without an ejector rod:
1. Put the hammer in proper position, as when loading.
2. If the revolver has a loading port, it is usually possible to align each chamber with the port and push the cartridge cases out with a convenient rod. If there is no port, press the latch holding the cylinder pin. Draw the cylinder pin forward, out of the frame, and remove the cylinder. If cases do not drop out of the chambers, they may be pushed out with the cylinder pin.
3. Replace the cylinder and pin.
4. While rotating the cylinder, visually check to make sure the revolver is completely empty.

Many foreign revolvers have a solid frame and use a rod ejector system. This is a double-action Russian 1895 Nagant revolver.

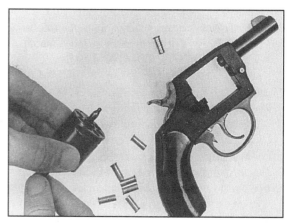

The simplest solid-frame revolvers, such as this Iver Johnson 22-caliber Cadet revolver, ordinarily have the cylinder removed for unloading. Empty cases are simply poked out with the cylinder pin.

This 1917 Colt 45-caliber revolver leaves no doubt that it is a double-action revolver by the "D.A." on its barrel. It was produced for use in WWI.

Like their Colt counterparts, S&W Model 1917 revolvers indicated that they were indeed double action by their "D.A." barrel marking. Such revolvers were substitute standard sidearms for U.S. troops during WWI.

SWING-OUT REVOLVER

To open a typical S&W swing-out revolver, push the latch forward and rock the cylinder out with the two middle fingers of the left hand.

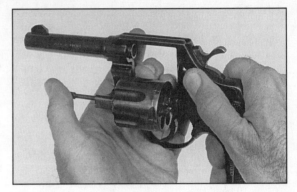

To open a typical Colt swing-out revolver, pull the latch rearward and rock the cylinder out.

Modern swing-out revolvers are all double action. Also, most of them have a hammer block, transfer bar or rebound device, so that the hammer at rest is automatically in a safe position for loading or unloading.

To load:
1. Operate the cylinder release latch with the right thumb, and gently push the cylinder out of the frame with the two middle fingers of the left hand.
2. Load cartridges into the chambers.
3. Gently push the cylinder closed until the latch clicks into place. (*Never* slam the cylinder closed, no matter how impressive it looks on TV.)

To unload:
1. Operate the cylinder release latch with the right thumb and swing the cylinder out with the middle two fingers of the left hand.
2. With the left thumb, push the end of the ejector rod as far as it will go. The cartridges or empty cases will be pushed out of the chambers.
3. Visually inspect the chambers to be sure they are empty.
4. *Gently* close the cylinder until the latch clicks.

Note that the latches on different makes of swing-out revolvers may function differently. The Colt latch is on the frame at the rear of the cylinder and is pulled rearward to release the cylinder. The Smith & Wesson and Charter Arms latches move forward. The Ruger latch goes inward, toward the inside of the frame. The Wesson Arms latch is on the crane in front of the cylinder and moves down to release the cylinder. The method used by H&R and some others is to pull forward on the ejector rod to release the cylinder.

Other than the location of the cylinder latch, the method of operation of all double-action, swing-out revolvers is much the same.

To open a typical Wesson swing-out revolver, depress the latch in the crane downward and rock the cylinder out.

To open a typical Harrington & Richardson swing-out revolver, pull the cylinder pin forward and swing out the cylinder.

through a port in the frame (if one is provided) or by removing the cylinder.

The *swing-out* revolver was in use before 1890 and today is our most common type. The cylinder swings out of the frame on a pivoted *crane* for loading and unloading. In almost all cases, it swings open to the left, but there has been, of course, at least one nonconformist that opened to the right.

Breakopen revolvers were in common use before 1880. The frame is hinged at its lower forward portion so that the barrel can be tipped down—and the cylinder simultaneously tipped up—for loading/unloading.

This type is also called hinged frame or tip-up. Harrington & Richardson, the only American producer of this type now, calls it a top-break. I am not sure if there is any convention for describing this type. I suppose I should use the H&R term, but all my life, my friends and I have called it breakopen. I'm open on the subject, but for now, please let me use my old familiar term.

Breakopen revolvers have been pretty much ignored in the shooting press in recent years, but there are a lot of these interesting guns out there, and a lot are still shot pretty regularly. The nice H&R Model 999 Sportsman 22 revolver is the only American breakopen revolver in production at the time of this writing.

Breakopen revolvers have a poor reputation among many people. It is true that many of the early breakopens had a rather weak latch system, and the steel used long ago was not up to today's standards. Still, breakopen revolvers were for decades the mainstay of Smith & Wesson. That company produced large heavy-duty models for calibers such as 44 Russian and 44-40 Winchester. Many smaller companies offered the breakopen as their top-of-the-line model, considering it superior to their solid-frame revolvers.

Post-WWII revolvers made by H&R and Iver Johnson had much stronger latches than their earlier models. The British Webleys and Enfields with their stirrup latches are even stronger. They may be considered equal in strength to equivalent swing-out types.

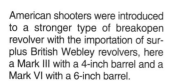

American shooters were introduced to a stronger type of breakopen revolver with the importation of surplus British Webley revolvers, here a Mark III with a 4-inch barrel and a Mark VI with a 6-inch barrel.

The big 455 Webley Mark VI was considered by many the strongest of the breakopen revolvers, and many were converted to 45 ACP.

Breakopen revolvers are not held in high regard by some people, but they have been around for a long time. This beautiful U.S. Revolver Company 38 was the writer's first revolver. The grips are custom-made from yellow pine.

BREAKOPEN REVOLVER

To open a typical breakopen revolver, lift the latch and pivot the barrel/cylinder forward. This is an H&R 22-caliber Model 999 Sportsman.

Opening the stirrup latch on the Webley breakopen revolver allows the cylinder to be swung forward for loading.

It is wise to have older breakopens checked out by a gunsmith before using them. Some early ones had to be manually thumbed to half-cock, although most later guns have rebounding hammers, hammer blocks or transfer bars. Just learn as much as possible about the revolver.

To load:
1. Open the latch.
2. Pivot the barrel/cylinder up and forward.
3. Load the chambers
4. Slowly pivot the barrel/cylinder back and *ease* the latch shut. (Snapping the latch shut is a cause of wear that will loosen this type of revolver.)

To unload:
1. Open the latch.
2. Pivot the barrel/cylinder up and forward. The extractor star will extend and drop automatically to eject the cases or unfired cartridges in the cylinder. With some Iver Johnson and H&R revolvers of post-WWII manufacture, a separate ejector rod lies under the barrel. Pivot the barrel/cylinder forward, then press this rod back to eject.
3. Check visually to make sure all chambers are unloaded.
4. Pivot the barrel/cylinder back slowly and ease the latch shut.

Some breakopen revolvers, such as this 38-caliber H&R Model 925, have a separate ejector rod under the barrel.

To prevent excessive wear, breakopen revolvers should never be snapped shot. Hold the latch open, ease the gun closed, and close the latch.

Semi-Automatic Pistols

A semi-automatic pistol is a handgun that uses the energy of one shot to get itself ready for the next shot. This energy is generally from recoil, but may come from the gas generated by the previous shot.

Semi-automatic pistols are sometimes called self-loaders or autoloaders. More commonly, they are just called automatics, although they do not fit the definition of a true automatic firearm.

The semi-automatic pistol has the same three basic parts as the revolver: frame, barrel and action. However, the operation is very different.

In a revolver, the multiple cartridge chambers were in the cylinder. The barrel of a semi-automatic has a single chamber in the rear of the bore.

The frame of a semi-automatic generally has a hollow grip which contains the *magazine*, a storage device to hold cartridges to be fed into the chamber. The frame may also contain a *magazine release*, *slide stop* (also called a slide lock or slide release) to hold the action open, and *safety*, a mechanical device to reduce the chance of accidental firing.

The details of semi-automatic pistol actions vary greatly. Some have a hammer (similar to that of revolvers) that strikes a firing pin. Some are striker-fired, that is, the firing pin is spring-loaded and released to strike the primer, firing the cartridge. Such pistols are often called hammerless. However, some "hammerless" guns have hammers that are not visible, but which are concealed in the mechanism of the pistol.

The earliest semi-automatics, such as the Borchardt, Mauser and Luger, had exposed barrels with a breechblock behind the chamber. In the late 1890s, John M. Browning came up with a marvelous invention, the *slide*. It rode atop the frame and covered the barrel, recoil spring and other mechanisms, allowing a very compact pistol. You may hear the term "slide" used generically for any kind of semi-automatic pistol mechanism. When you hear the command "Slides Back" on a pistol range, you open the action of your semi-automatic pistol, no matter what the design.

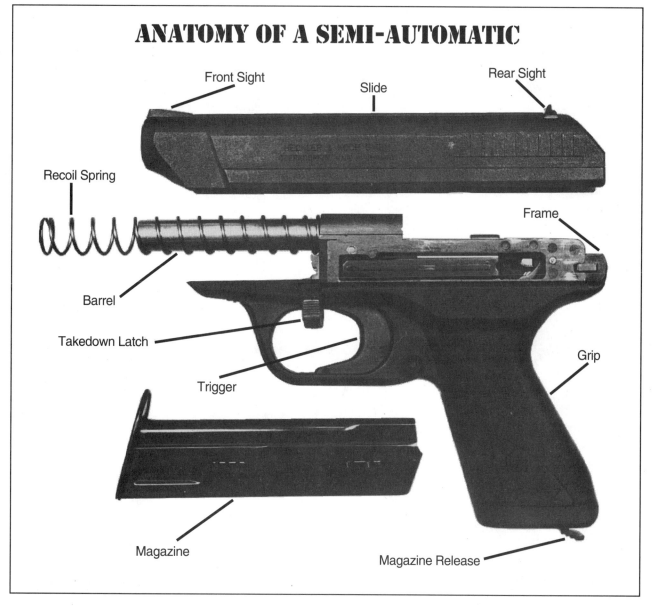

ANATOMY OF A SEMI-AUTOMATIC

Front Sight

Slide

Rear Sight

Recoil Spring

Frame

Barrel

Takedown Latch

Grip

Trigger

Magazine

Magazine Release

(Left) The 1911 Colt, a single-action pistol, is considered by many to be the best semi-automatic pistol ever designed. It was adopted by the U.S. Army in 1911 and is still in limited military service.

(Above) During WWII, Model 1911A1 pistols were made in large quantities by different manufacturers. This one was made by Ithaca. This specimen has the distinction of being the first semi-automatic pistol ever owned by the writer.

(Left) The Colt 1911 design is still one of the world's most popular pistols. It has remained in commercial production as the Colt Government Model.

(Right) The Walther P-38 introduced many Americans to the double-action semi-automatic pistol during WWII. This one is a wartime model, made by Walther in 1941.

The Ruger 22 semi-automatic pistol, introduced in America in 1949, became one of the most popular 22-caliber pistols of all time.

A DAO 9mm pistol, the Sardius was introduced in the late 1980s and imported from Israel.

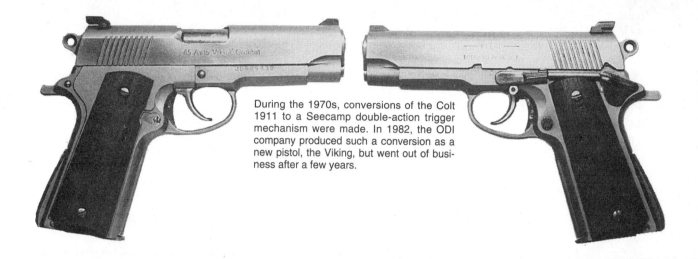

During the 1970s, conversions of the Colt 1911 to a Seecamp double-action trigger mechanism were made. In 1982, the ODI company produced such a conversion as a new pistol, the Viking, but went out of business after a few years.

SEMI-AUTOMATIC PISTOL

Most of the semi-automatic pistols you will encounter will be be either single action (the most numerous type), conventional double action (next most), or double-action-only. You still need to know how the one in your hand works, but the basic procedures are the same.

These steps are generally correct for all semi-automatic pistols. Keep in mind, though, that there are many different mechanical designs.

To load:
1. Remove the magazine.
2. Pull the slide to the rear and lock it open with the slide stop (if the pistol has one).
3. Visually inspect the chamber to make sure it is empty.
4. Lay the pistol down (pointing in a safe direction, of course).
5. Load the magazine. Push cartridges into it, down and to the rear.
6. Pick up the pistol and insert the loaded magazine.
7. Release the slide stop. The slide will move forward, stripping the top cartridge from the magazine and loading it into the chamber. For pistols that do not have a slide stop, pull the slide all the way back and release it so that it can move forward and chamber a cartridge.

To unload:
1. Remove the magazine.
2. Pull the slide all the way to the rear. This will eject the cartridge from the chamber.
3. Visually check the chamber to make sure it is empty.

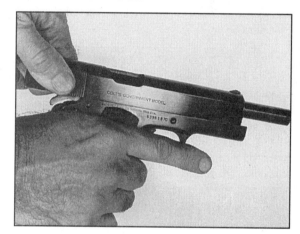

When operating the slide on a semi-automatic pistol, keep your finger off the trigger. This Colt Government Model is a 45 ACP.

Open the Ruger pistol by pulling the internal "slide," or bolt, rearward.

Here is how a semi-automatic pistol works: When a shot is fired, the energy of that shot pushes the slide to the rear. The empty cartridge case is extracted from the chamber and ejected from the pistol at the end of the rearward movement of the slide. As the slide moves backward, it compresses a recoil spring. When the rearward travel is completed, the spring pushes the slide forward again. As the slide moves forward, it strips a cartridge from the magazine and pushes it into the chamber. The hammer or striker was recocked during the rearward movement, and the pistol is ready to fire another shot.

Early semi-automatic pistols were single action. From our discussion of revolvers, remember that the trigger thus performs the single action of releasing the hammer or striker.

Double-action semi-automatics were being tested as early as 1907, when the Knoble pistol was given a trial by the U.S. Army. The German Walther PP pistol was a commercially successful double-action design in the early 1930s. Then, during World War II, the double-action Walther P-38 became familiar to American GIs.

These pistols were double action for the first shot, then the recoiling slide cocked the hammer, and succeeding shots were single action.

Some of the early double-action designs had a decocking lever. If the pistol were cocked for single-action shooting, depressing the lever would safely lower the hammer without firing the cartridge. A decocking lever is featured on most traditional double-action semi-automatics made today.

Other early designs were double-action-only. That is, every shot was fired by a long pull on the trigger which first cocks the hammer and then releases it. The slide chambers a new round for each shot, but does not cock the hammer or striker. Primarily, these early pistols were small pocket pistols carried for personal protection. Examples are the Little Tom and Le Francais pistols.

In recent times, as liability lawsuits became common, some law enforcement units required officers to carry pistols that could not be cocked. The thinking was that they could not be sued for a nervous officer's twitching off a shot from a cocked pistol if it couldn't be cocked.

Double-action-only (DAO) pistols have become more common because of this. Also, the popular Glock pistol, a modified form of DAO, is widely used. Glock, however, calls their design "Safe Action."

Because it might provide an advantage to be able to fire precise single-action shots, Browning introduced the BDM (Browning Double Mode) pistol. An external adjustment with a screwdriver can make the pistol operate in either of the two different manners.

This Semmerling LM4 is one of the few manually operated repeating pistols produced in recent times. It is in 45 ACP and must be cycled by hand for each shot.

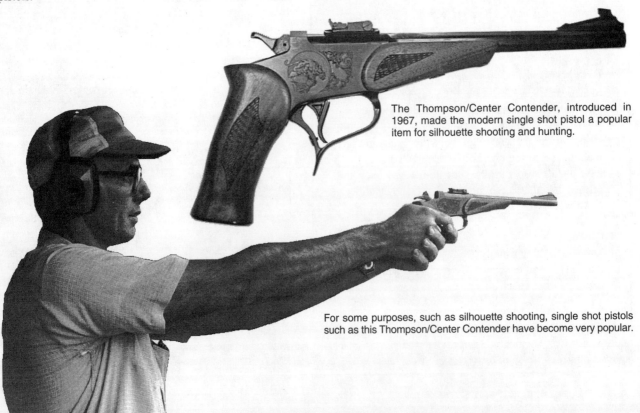

The Thompson/Center Contender, introduced in 1967, made the modern single shot pistol a popular item for silhouette shooting and hunting.

For some purposes, such as silhouette shooting, single shot pistols such as this Thompson/Center Contender have become very popular.

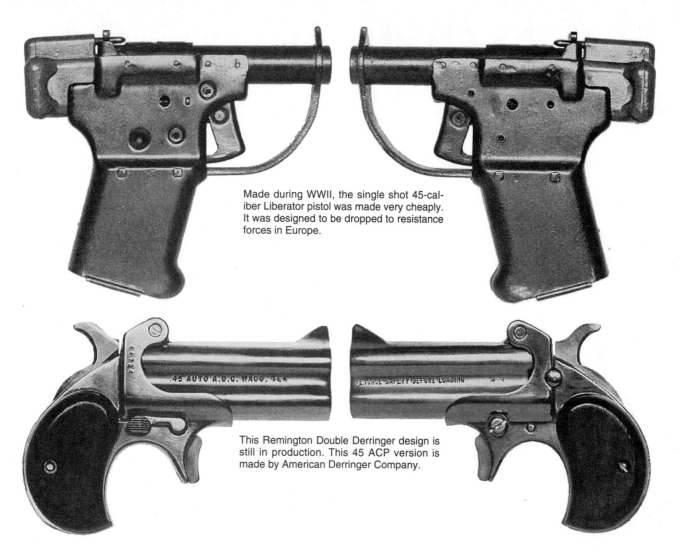

Made during WWII, the single shot 45-caliber Liberator pistol was made very cheaply. It was designed to be dropped to resistance forces in Europe.

This Remington Double Derringer design is still in production. This 45 ACP version is made by American Derringer Company.

If you are planning to try out a pistol, better be sure you have the instruction manual or knowledgeable advice handy. Instruction manuals may usually be obtained from the manufacturer for free.

Single Shot Handguns

At one time, long ago, all handguns were single shots. The revolver replaced the single shot as a military sidearm rather quickly, and eventually the single shot faded from the hunting and target shooting scenes, too.

Almost.

Only the 22-caliber single shot pistol continued in service in the highest echelons of target shooting, and a few diehards hunted with single shots of various kinds. There had been single shot derringers, cartridge equivalents of Henry Deringer's original muzzle-loading pocket pistol. During World War II, a single shot 45-caliber pistol, nicknamed the Liberator, was dropped to the French Underground behind enemy lines. A brief flurry of single shot pistols was seen after World War II, as Savage, Sheridan and Mendoza introduced inexpensive 22-caliber pistols suitable for the trail or tackle box.

However, if anything can claim to have reintroduced the single shot pistol to America, it is probably the silhouette shooting sport. Long-range pistol shooting at steel silhouettes favors accuracy and power, not cartridge capacity or rapidity of fire. Single shot handguns increased in popularity. Shooters soon learned that anything suitable for silhouettes also served as a pretty good hunting pistol, too.

Although the Thompson/Center Contender is likely to be the single shot pistol most commonly encountered today, others have been made in some quantities. In production at the time of this writing are pistols by Remington, Anschutz, Ithaca, Maximum, Merrill (now RPM), Wichita and others.

Other Handgun Types

There are also double-barrel derringers in production today. Most are copies or modifications of the old Remington Double Derringer. Their popularity today is really no surprise, as the original reportedly remained in production from 1866 to 1935. One manual repeating pistol, the compact 45-caliber Semmerling, remains in very limited production. Four-barrel pistols have been made, and sometimes copies or new designs have been put into production for a while.

Such handguns are generally small, usually bought for protection and fired only a few times for familiarity. We will not spend further time on them, but they are interesting arms, as are all handguns, in my opinion.

CHAPTER NINE

HANDGUN AMMUNITION

WE BRIEFLY DISCUSSED handgun ammunition a bit earlier in Chapter 1, but it is worth refreshing our memories now. Recall that handgun cartridges have four components: cartridge case; primer; powder; bullet.

The cartridge case is the container that packages the other three components into a nice compact unit. The case is generally made of brass, but aluminum and mild steel cases are also made. The primer is the impact-sensitive chemical compound that detonates on impact to ignite the powder. The powder burns and, as a result, a large volume of high-pressure gas is generated very rapidly. The bullet is the projectile pushed by the expanding gas through the bore and toward the target. Handgun bullets are generally made of lead, sometimes covered (jacketed) with a layer of a copper alloy or other metal.

Cartridges may be classed as rimfire or centerfire. Rimfire ammunition has the priming compound inside the hollow rim at the base of the cartridge case. The metal of the case is soft enough so that when the firing pin hits it, the metal dents and crushes the priming compound. The priming compound then detonates, and the flash ignites the powder charge.

In centerfire cartridges, the primer is a separate component in the center of the base of the cartridge case. A centerfire case is much stronger than a rimfire case, which permits much higher pressure and hence more powerful loads.

The proper identification of handgun ammunition is important because many pistol and revolver cartridges are similar in size and shape.

The primary designation of handgun ammunition is caliber. In firearms usage, caliber refers to the diameter of the bore.

In days of old, single shot muzzle-loading pistols were often of the same caliber as muzzle-loading muskets, sometimes approaching three-quarters of an inch. The pistols just used smaller charges of powder. The widespread acceptance of the revolver meant smaller calibers for handguns, for the cylinder had to hold a number of shots, yet be of reasonable diameter to be carried and shot easily. Although it was not the first Colt revolver produced, the Walker model revolver was introduced in 1846 in 44-caliber and saw service in the Mexican War. The 44 soon became a standard military caliber.

For a muzzle-loading revolver, the lead ball had to be oversize to be able to seal the chamber. If the chambers were not sealed, flash from one shot could set off loads in other chambers. This was definitely something to be avoided. Thus, a 44-caliber revolver used a ball of slightly over 45-caliber.

The Colt Walker revolver of 1846, shown here in replica form, began the American tradition of handguns in the 44- to 45-caliber range.

Some cartridges exist for only a short time. The U.S. 1909 45-caliber cartridge was developed for the Colt Model 1909 Army revolver. When the Model 1911 45 Automatic pistol was adopted two years later, the cartridge became obsolete.

Although many types of handguns were used during the Civil War, revolvers of 44-caliber were the standard sidearms. After the war, by the early 1870s, cartridge revolvers were coming into common use, and 44 and 45 were the most popular calibers.

Revolver Cartridges

Whereas rifle cartridges of the blackpowder cartridge period might be offered in several different loadings (for example, the 45-70-500 and 45-70-405), the revolvers with their non-adjustable sights generally were designed to shoot a single load.

Blackpowder rifle cartridges ordinarily were identified by a set of two or three numbers. We've just mentioned two 45-70 loads. The cartridge was 45-caliber, loaded with 70 grains of powder, and was offered with either 500-grain or 405-grain bullets.

Winchester introduced the 44-40 Winchester cartridge with their 1873 lever-action rifle. It was about 44-caliber and loaded with 40 grains of blackpowder. Before long, Colt and Smith & Wesson (as well as others now departed) chambered revolvers for the popular new cartridge. Revolvers were also made for Winchester's later 38-40 and 32-20 rounds as well.

However, when Colt designed a new cartridge in 1871, it was just called the 44 Colt. Then, for its new 1873 revolver, adopted as the U.S. Army sidearm, its new cartridge was, in like fashion, simply called the 45 Colt.

At that point, Smith & Wesson had already brought out a number of proprietary cartridges. The 44 S&W American round was introduced in 1869, followed by the 44 S&W Russian in 1870.

These big 44 and 45 revolvers were obviously well suited to the frontier and military use by virtue of their simplicity and ruggedness. By 1890, the Army had decided that a smaller revolver would be just as good. They adopted the new swing-out cylinder Colt double-action in 38 Long Colt caliber. The smaller caliber did not prove effective during the Philippine insurrection that followed the Spanish-American War. The old Colt single-action 45s were called back into service, and a new double-action 45, the 1909 Colt, with a powerful new smokeless-powder version of the 45 Colt cartridge, was adopted. It had a short life as our official military handgun, for it was superseded by the famous Colt 1911 45 automatic.

So, at least in America, handguns of 45-caliber dominated the military scene for a long time. They were obviously not suited for all purposes. By the end of the 1870s, handguns of 32, 38 and 41 calibers had also become common. Many of these old-time cartridges survived the transition from blackpowder to smokeless loadings. Today, we still have a number of revolver cartridges in at least limited production from that time period: 32 Short Colt (1875); 32 Long Colt (1875); 32 Smith & Wesson (1878); 32 Smith & Wesson Long (1896); 32-20 Winchester (1882); 38 Short Colt (1874); 38 Smith & Wesson (1877); 38 Special (1899); 38-40 Winchester (1874); 44-40 Winchester (1873); 45 Colt (1873).

Many revolver cartridges developed during the blackpowder days are still in production at the time of this writing. Some are barely hanging on, while others are some of our most popular handgun loads: (Top photo, from left) 32 Short Colt, 32 Long Colt, 32 Smith & Wesson, 32 S&W Long, 32-20, 38 Short Colt; (Bottom photo, from left) 38 Smith & Wesson, 38 Special, 38-40, 44-40 and 45 Colt.

The 44 S&W Special at the left was originally introduced as a blackpowder cartridge (1907), but the other three were factory-loaded only with smokeless: 357 Magnum (1935) and 44 and 41 Remington Magnums (1956 and 1964).

The recent popularity of handguns for hunting and long-range silhouette shooting has given rise to a new breed of powerful handgun cartridges: 44 Auto Mag, 45 Winchester Magnum, 454 Casull, 445 SuperMag and 357 Maximum.

The 44 Magnum has plenty of power for most shooters. This experienced shooter's two-hand grip is coming apart as his Smith & Wesson Model 29 begins recoiling from a full-house load.

These cartridges, and some others now gone, filled most of the available niches for some time.

The 44 Russian was lengthened by Smith & Wesson in 1907 to form the more powerful 44 S&W Special, but it was not until 1935 that a really new development appeared, the 357 Magnum. In developing the new load, Smith & Wesson just lengthened the 38 Special case by 1/10-inch to form the new cartridge. However, the pressure level was greatly increased, putting the new 357 into an entirely different power category. For two decades, it was rated the most powerful handgun cartridge in the world.

It was bumped from that lofty position by the same company's 1956 development, the 44 Remington Magnum. Smith & Wesson, in conjunction with Remington, created the 44 Magnum by lengthening the 44 Special case 1/10-inch and increasing its power level substantially.

Because these new cases were formed by a simple increase in length, 38 Special ammunition may be fired in a 357 Magnum revolver, and 44 Special loads may be used in a 44 Magnum revolver. (Not the other way around, of course, and this is the reason for the lengthened cases.) Many people practice with the milder loads and save the full-power magnum loads, with their heavy recoil, for serious hunting, silhouette or defense purposes.

In 1964, the 41 Magnum was introduced to fill the gap between the 357 and 44, but it never achieved the popularity of either of its predecessors. Recently, other high-intensity cartridges have been introduced for long-range silhouette and hunting uses. They include the 357 Maximum, 445 Super Mag and 454 Casull. Really powerful hunting cartridges include the 475 and 500 Linebaughs.

Departing slightly from this trend is the 32 H&R Magnum, a relatively recent introduction that is based on a lengthened 32 S&W Long case. It is loaded to substantially more power than the older cartridge and has gained some popularity as a smaller-bore defense and small game round. The shorter 32 S&W and 32 S&W Long cartridges may be fired in 32 H&R Magnum revolvers if lighter loads are desired.

Semi-Automatic Pistol Cartridges

Smokeless powder made a new type of handgun feasible—the semi-automatic pistol. The first successful semi-automatic pistol was the Borchardt, invented by a naturalized American citizen, Hugo Borchardt, and offered for sale in Germany in 1893. It is difficult for me to think of semi-automatic pistols as old-timers, in use that long ago. Now, over a century later, Borchardt's pistol is a collector's item. However, the cartridge he developed is still in production, and new pistols for that cartridge are still being made in China. Today, the cartridge is known as the 30 Mauser or 7.62mm Tokarev.

There was a real flurry of development for semi-automatic pistols and cartridges in the 1890s and early 1900s. Mauser, the German company, brought out a pistol in 1896 (affectionately known now as the "broomhandle") that used the Borchardt cartridge, but loaded to a higher power level.

In 1894, the German Bergmann firm introduced a line of blowback and locked-breech pistols of various calibers. The cartridges are all obsolete but one, the 9mm Bergmann-Bayard, which is still used in Spain and a few other countries.

American firearms genius John M. Browning was not idle during this period. Belgian manufacturer Fabrique Nationale (FN) introduced the first Browning-designed 32 Automatic pistol in 1899. In 1900, another John M. Browning design, the 38 Automatic, was put into production by Colt.

Also introduced in 1900 was the famous Luger pistol, in caliber 30 Luger. Georg Luger was an associate of Hugo Borchardt. The Luger pistol was a compact modification of the Borchardt design, and the 30 Luger cartridge was a shorter version of the 30 Borchardt round.

The original 30-caliber cartridges were modified to become 9mms. The 30 Luger was followed by the 9mm Luger in 1902. The 30 Mauser evolved into the 9mm Mauser in 1908. The 30 Mauser has long outlived its 9mm offspring, while the 30 Luger was soon overshadowed by the 9mm Luger. The 9mm Luger,

Introduced for commercial markets in 1905, Colt's first semi-automatic 45 was soon considered for military use. This model was the first pistol chambered for the 45 ACP (Automatic Colt Pistol) cartridge and was marked "Calibre 45 Rimless Smokeless" on the slide.

The recent importation of 9mm Makarov pistols into the U.S. from former Iron Curtain countries has created a demand for this ammunition. The 9mm Makarov is not a true 9mm, but is slightly larger in diameter, about a 9.2mm, and is intermediate in length between the 9mm Luger and the 380 Automatic.

Some pistols are forever associated with the ammunition they introduced. The 9mm cartridge for the famous P.08 pistol is still called "9mm Luger."

(Above) Semi-automatic handgun cartridges that have stood the test of time and are still popular: 25 Automatic (1906); 30 Mauser (1893, as 30 Borchardt); 32 Automatic (1899); 380 Automatic (1908); 9mm Luger (1902); 38 Super (1900, as 38 ACP); and 45 Automatic (1905).

Relative newcomers to the lineup of American semi-automatic pistol cartridges: 9mm Makarov, 41 Action Express, 10mm Automatic, 40 Smith & Wesson and 45 Winchester Magnum.

known also as the 9mm Parabellum, is the most widely used 9mm cartridge in the world.

It is hard to imagine the tremendous amount of semi-automatic pistol and cartridge development that took place during the 1890s and early 1900s. Most of our current semi-automatic pistol cartridges date from the period before 1910: 25 Automatic (1906); 30 Mauser/7.62mm Tokarev (1893, as 30 Borchardt); 32 Automatic (1899); 380 Automatic (1908); 38 Super (1900, as 38 ACP); 9mm Luger (1902); 45 Automatic (1905).

We see other semi-automatic pistol cartridges in use, of course. The 9mm Makarov was developed in the Communist Bloc after World War II, but only in recent years has it been generally imported and seen common use in America. During the 1980s, the 40/41-caliber niche gained attention with the introduction of the 10mm Automatic, 41 Action Express and 40 Smith & Wesson.

We have also seen some big boomers added to the market, with the appearance of the 44 Auto Mag, 45 Winchester Magnum, 50 Action Express and others. Such offerings were made to appeal to long-range silhouette shooters and handgun hunters. But for the most part, most of our semi-automatic pistol cartridges are the tried-and-true old-timers, with only a handful of new offerings.

Metric Conversion

There is an easy way to switch back and forth between inches and millimeters: Multiply the metric caliber designation by four to get the inch designation.

It's pretty close, anyway. Using this guide, a 9mm cartridge has a bullet diameter of about 36-caliber. The actual measurement is about .355-inch, but the 1=4 system is close enough for most purposes.

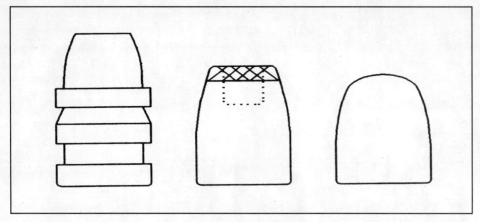

Typical pistol bullets include (from left) semi-wadcutter (SWC), flat-nose, and round-nose. The SWC is usually a cast lead-alloy boullet. Its grooves are for holding lubricating grease and for crimping the brass case into it to hold the bullet in place against recoil. The jacketed flat-nose design is often hollowpointed and is used for self-defense and hunting. The round-nose bullet is commonly used in autoloaders. Its full metal jacket and smooth nose shape ensure reliable feeding.

Rimmed cartridges are commonly used in revolvers and in single shot pistols. The rim positions the case in the gun and permits extraction. Semi-rimmed and rimless cases are usually used with autoloaders.

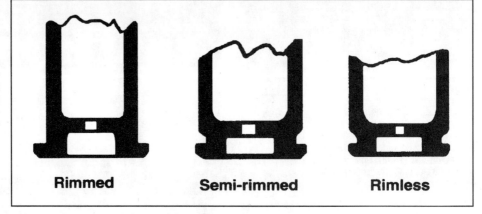

Rimmed   **Semi-rimmed**   **Rimless**

Cartridge Identification

We've seen two basic systems of naming cartridges. For want of better names, let's call one the American system, the other the metric system. In the American system, the caliber and a descriptive name identify the cartridge. Common examples are 38 Special and 45 Automatic.

Note that this system is not completely precise. A 38 Special is not really a 38, for its diameter is actually .357-inch, more of a 36. That's OK, though, because the name is for a definite cartridge and we all agree on what it is to be called.

Now, for semi-automatic pistol cartridges, we often use terms such as 45 Automatic or 45 ACP. In this case, both refer to the same cartridge, the one developed for Colt's 1905 semi-automatic pistol, which was the first in 45-caliber. ACP simply represents Automatic Colt Pistol.

In the metric system, we identify cartridges by the diameter of the bullet, then by either a descriptive name or the length of the cartridge case.

The 9mm Luger (or 9mm Parabellum) cartridge is also referred to as the 9x19mm. In like fashion, the 380 Automatic (which is also known as 9mm Browning Short, Corto or Kurz) is the 9x17mm. The 9mm Makarov is the 9x18. This last round indicates that metric designations, alas, are not completely precise, either. The Makarov bullet is actually about .365-inch, or about 9.2mm. However, it doesn't really matter, as long as we all call it the same thing.

Besides naming cartridges by measuring the bullet diame-ter and case length, we can also describe cartridges by the shape of the case. There are fewer varieties than with rifle cartridges.

Rimmed cases have a rim, or flange, at the rear which allows positioning in the chamber. The rim also allows extraction from the chamber.

Rimless cases have no flange, and position themselves in the chamber either on the mouth of the cartridge case or on a shoulder near the front of the case. Extraction is accomplished by an extraction groove near the base of the case.

Semi-rimmed cases have an extractor groove and look very much like rimless cases at first glance. However, on close inspection, they are seen to have a slight flange for positioning and extraction. There are only three semi-rimmed cartridges in general handgun use, so they are easy to keep straight.

Generally, rimmed cases are used for revolvers, and very often for single shot pistols. Semi-rimmed and rimless cases are most often used for semi-automatic pistol cartridges.

Here are some examples:

EXAMPLES OF CASE TYPES

Case	Type	Cartridge Examples
Rimmed	Straight	38 Special, 44 Magnum
Rimmed	Bottleneck	256 Winchester
Rimless	Straight	45 ACP, 9mm Luger
Rimless	Bottleneck	30 Mauser, 30 Luger
Semi-rimmed	Straight	25 ACP, 32 ACP, 38 Super

Bullets started off being made of lead. When semi-auto pistols came into being, it was felt they required a harder bullet to keep from being deformed during the operation of the pistol. For a long time, bullets then were made of lead for revolvers and were metal cased (lead with a covering of a copper-alloy metal) for semi-automatics.

Today, we might encounter lead, metal cased, softpoints or hollowpoints for many types of handgun cartridges, designed for revolver, semi-automatic or single shot.

With the increased use of handguns for hunting and self-protection, a number of new bullet designs feature greatly increased, controlled expansion and stay intact after expanding.

Caution: Before we leave cartridge identification, we must note that identification of the cartridge by dimensions or name may not be enough.

The 38 Super was designed in 1929 as a high-pressure load for a new Colt pistol. The case and the bullet were *identical* to those of the older 1900-era 38 ACP. All cartridges for both the 38 Super and the 38 ACP carried the same 38 ACP headstamp. The only distinction between the ammunition produced at that time was that the 38 Super cases were nickel plated. Not much of a distinction, but it seems to have been understood by shooters of the time. The 38 ACP can be safely fired in the 38 Super pistol, but the Super cartridges should never be used in the older guns.

Recently, +P (Plus P) or +P+ (Plus P Plus) designations have been applied to some handgun cartridges. These are loaded to *higher pressures than standard ammunition* for that caliber.

These cartridges may be identified on the box or the cases may be headstamped +P or +P+ on the base. These high-pressure loads will chamber in any handgun made for that cartridge, but ought to be fired only in guns designed for them. For example, 38 Special revolvers run a great range, from massive revolvers built on 45-caliber frames down to lightweight snubbies that weigh less than a pound. Not all are suitable for the +P loads.

Play it safe. Check the manual that came with the handgun to see if it is approved for +P or +P+ use. If it is not clear as to what should be used, check with the manufacturer or a knowledgeable person.

If you are still not sure, *do not use* the hotter ammunition. Trade it to a friend whose pistol can definitely use it, start a cartridge collection, or hold it as an excuse to get another pistol. Under no circumstances should you try ammunition that might injure you or your pistol.

The Wonderful 22

It seems as if we've ignored the 22 rimfire. True, the larger-bore handgun cartridges, with their many varieties, take attention away from the 22.

In a way, that is not fair, because the first successful handgun cartridge developed in this country was the 22 Short, introduced by Smith & Wesson back in 1857 for their first revolver. Development was pretty rapid after that, and rimfire cartridges for rifles—the 44 Henry and 56-56 and 56-50 Spencer—were used with great effect during the Civil War.

Revolvers for rimfire cartridges became popular after that

An assortment of 22-caliber cartridges, past and present: (from left) 22 BB Cap, 22 CB Cap, 22 Short, 22 Long, 22 Extra Long, 22 Long Rifle, 22 Long Rifle Stinger, 22 Winchester Rim Fire (WRF) and 22 Winchester Magnum Rimfire (WMR). The 22 Short was our first handgun cartridge, and the 22 Long Rifle is probably the most popular.

Revolvers commonly have been fitted with cylinders for two different cartridges, if the required bore diameter is the same for both. This Ruger Single-Six has cylinders for both 22 Long Rifle and 22 Magnum.

conflict, and by 1900, something like seventy-five different rimfire calibers for both rifles and revolvers had been loaded by American companies. Some of these niches were better filled by centerfire cartridges, so most of the rimfires faded away. The ones that still remain—the 22s—have established such a secure spot in the shooting world they will probably be with us as long as guns are made.

The 22 Long was introduced about 1871, and the 22 Extra Long in about 1880. These were all blackpowder rounds, and were used in rifles, revolvers and single shot pistols. The 22 Extra Long, with its 40-grain bullet and 6 grains of blackpowder, proved to be not particularly accurate. The case was shortened to the same length as the 22 Long, the powder charge reduced, and a wonderful new cartridge, the 22 Long Rifle, was born in 1887. The Long Rifle has proven to be one of the most useful, most accurate cartridges ever made.

The more powerful 22 Winchester Rim Fire (22 WRF) was developed for rifles in 1890. It became obsolete, but in 1959, Winchester lengthened the case, gave it an increased-pressure load and a thinly jacketed bullet. The new cartridge was the useful 22 Winchester Magnum Rimfire (22 WMR.) The case was not only longer but also larger in diameter, so rifles could not interchange the new round with the 22 Long Rifle.

However, the bore diameter is the same for both, so revolvers could use both rounds by having two interchangeable cylinders. A number of companies made such *convertible* revolvers. At least one semi-automatic pistol is made for the 22 WMR.

By 1977, CCI in Lewiston, Idaho, had brought out a new cartridge to bridge the gap between the 22 Long Rifle and the 22 WMR. The new Stinger would fit in a Long Rifle chamber, but used a lighter bullet and gave increased velocity. Soon, other companies followed with their own hyper-velocity loads. Such cartridges are useful, but seem to give their best results in rifles rather than in handguns.

Other 22 RF cartridges of interest are the reduced-velocity loads for indoor shooting and very quiet outdoor shooting. Originally made in tiny little cases as 22 BB (Bulleted Breech) Cap and 22 CB (Conical Bullet) Cap, they are now made by CCI in the same length as the 22 Short and 22 Long. They are wonderful for quiet practice.

However, unless you own a handgun specifically chambered for 22 Short or 22 WMR, the 22 Long Rifle will be the cartridge you probably will use the most. At the few cents a round they cost, they are incredibly reliable and amazingly accurate. The 22 Long Rifle is truly a marvel of manufacturing precision.

There are enough handgun cartridges in existence now that it seems there should be enough to fill every need. However, inventive minds keep coming up with new designs, and each decade seems to see some interesting new developments. Many of these don't gain much acceptance, but some do.

There is enough innovation going on in the field of handgun ammunition—new cartridges, loads, bullets, etc.—that it would be interesting to follow its progress even if one were not a shooter.

CHAPTER TEN

HANDGUN
SIGHTS AND SIGHTING IN

HANDGUNS OF ALMOST any type are capable of accurate shooting. But to bring out this inherent accuracy, they need proper ammunition. And, they need sights of some sort.

Sights on handguns were probably an afterthought. Early firearms such as hand cannons—simple small tubes with a handle of some sort to hold—were just pointed at the target. They were used at very short range, and little thought was given to sighting, except in a general sense.

Muskets eventually acquired a bead on the front to help in aiming them at targets at longer ranges, although handguns were still just pointed at short range. At the time of the Revolutionary War, military handguns were mostly sightless.

Rifles, however, were capable of much greater accuracy than smoothbore muskets, so they made better sighting worthwhile. American frontiersmen who used both rifles and pistols wanted rifles with good sights, and they wanted rifled pistols with equally good sights.

In early America, sight systems for both rifles and pistols took the form of an upright front and a flat rear that contained some sort of notch in which to align the front sight. Sights were generally adjusted by being tapped back and forth in dovetail cuts, and filed for height. By careful adjustment, the owner was eventually able to put a bullet where he wanted it, using a certain load, when shooting at a certain range.

This simple sighting arrangement remained in general use for generations, and it might be said this is still the type in general use. In days gone by, bead front sights and U-notch rears were as popular for handguns as they were for rifles, but they are essentially gone now. Most handguns come from the factory today with blade or post front sights and square-notch rears. To use rifle terminology, they come with open sights. However, there are other types of sights seen on handguns today, and we can group them into five categories: open; aperture; optical; electronic; laser.

Open Sights

Let's break these sights into two slightly different categories, fixed and adjustable. The sight picture is essentially the same for both. The primary *mechanical* difference is that fixed sights are immovable and adjustable sights are, of course, movable. They allow easy lateral (windage) and vertical (elevation) adjustments.

The primary *practical* difference is that the fixed-sight handgun has a sight picture that is correct for only one load at one

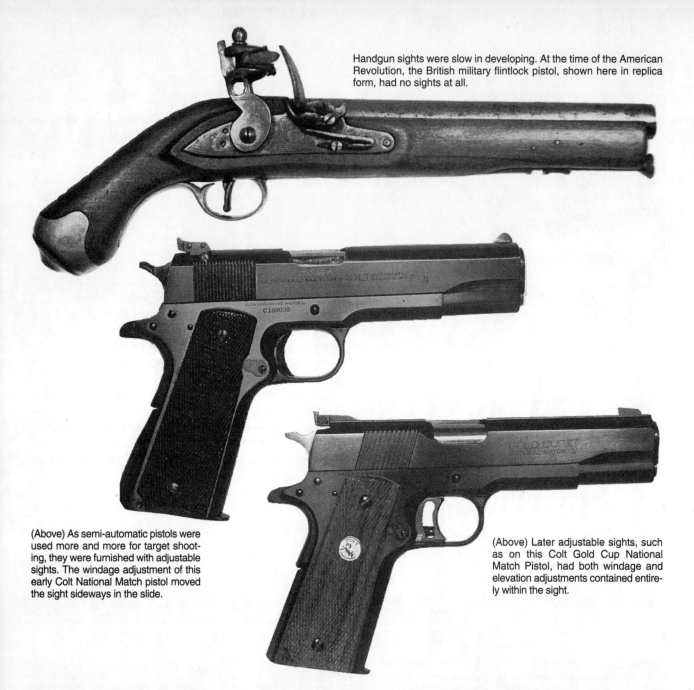

Handgun sights were slow in developing. At the time of the American Revolution, the British military flintlock pistol, shown here in replica form, had no sights at all.

(Above) As semi-automatic pistols were used more and more for target shooting, they were furnished with adjustable sights. The windage adjustment of this early Colt National Match pistol moved the sight sideways in the slide.

(Above) Later adjustable sights, such as on this Colt Gold Cup National Match Pistol, had both windage and elevation adjustments contained entirely within the sight.

distance. The adjustable-sight handgun can be adjusted for a number of different loads and ranges.

There is a place for both. Because fixed sights are not easily adjusted, they are not easily knocked *out* of adjustment. This ruggedness can be a plus for a military, police or self-defense handgun. The load may be a standard one, and the range will be assumed to be short. Under these conditions, fixed-sight pistols and revolvers have served very well for many decades. Adjustable sights allow the hunter or target shooter to sight-in his handgun for his choice of loads at any desired range.

Both types will probably be with us for some time.

Aperture Sights

Aperture sights, common on rifles, are seldom seen on handguns. The reason, obviously, is that handgun sights are generally not used very close to the face. The whole theory of the aperture sight involves looking *through*, not at, the aperture. Yet, there are positions for hunting and silhouette shooting that allow the proper use of an aperture sight, and some guns are so equipped by their owners. Note that the aperture sight on a handgun may allow an advantage in sight picture, but it probably offers no advantage in sight radius. Generally, pistol sights are already about as far apart as they can practically be.

Optical Sights

Optical sights, often called telescopic sights, or just scopes, have been used on rifles at least as far back as the Civil War. The *common* use of optical sights on handguns dates back just a few decades. Thus, they did not have to go through the long development process that riflescopes did. Proper mounts to get the scope solidly attached to the handgun were the biggest problem. Things have now been pretty

More optical sights are seen on revolvers as time goes by. Big revolvers, too. Jenny Lynn Moore tries out her scoped Colt Anaconda.

Mounts for electronic and optical sights can adapt such sights to almost any pistol now. This shooter has a bridge mount on his 45.

well standardized, and there are a number of mounts and scope/mount combinations that can be used on just about any handgun today.

The magnification of handgun scopes is generally somewhat lower than that of rifle optics. This is as would be expected, because it's more difficult to hold a pistol steady than a rifle. Remember, magnification magnifies the wobble as well as the target.

Magnification is not the whole story with optical sights. With a scope, no decision needs to be made about whether to focus on the front sight, the rear sight, or the target. Everything you are looking at is in focus! The target and the sighting device in the scope—the reticle—are both in the same optical plane. The shooter can look into the scope and everything is optically aligned for him.

New shooters may get better results with a scope—not because a scoped handgun is more accurate, but because it allows the beginner to concentrate on the other fundamentals of shooting. For oldsters with vision problems, a scoped handgun may allow them to continue with the handgun shooting sports.

For handgun hunters, optical sights make it easier to see the target. This factor may allow more accurate shooting and certainly aids in identifying legal game.

Eye relief varies somewhat with handgun scopes. Eye relief is the distance between the ocular (rear) lens of the scope and the shooter's eye when the shooter clearly sees the entire field of view. Each type of scope sight has a specific range of eye relief. For rifles, the scope is generally mounted over the receiver, and the primary concern with eye relief is not getting hit above the eye by the scope when shooting a rifle of heavy recoil.

The handgun shooter must determine his shooting position and then get a scope suited to it. Eye relief for different hunting, silhouette, action and bullseye shooting positions may vary from a number of inches to several feet.

As with scoped rifles, scoped handguns are not a perfect solution for every shooting situation. The scope adds bulk and weight. Although the cost of good optical products has come down, scopes are still quite an added expense. A scoped handgun severely restricts portability, and the types of holsters that may be used are few. Severe weather or a fall could put an optical sight out of commission when iron sights might survive.

You will notice, however, there are more and more scoped handguns in the field and on the range. As with scoped rifles, many shooters have weighed the good and bad points of scoped handguns and have decided that the advantages outweigh the disadvantages.

Electronic Sights

Often known as *red-dot* sights, these are becoming more popular. A dot (not always red) appears to be projected onto the target. When the dot is on the target, the handgun is aligned with the target.

There is no magnification, but this simplicity of aiming, along with the everything-in-focus aspect similar to that of optical sights, makes the electronic sight a feasible choice for beginners and those with vision problems. An interesting variation is found in the addition of an electronic dot to a conventional scope. It is used as a regular scope, but in reduced light conditions, the dot can be switched on.

The disadvantages for electronic sights are the same as those of scopes: weight, bulk, expense and portability. Add to this the fact that a battery provides the energy to produce the dot. If the battery goes dead, no dot. I knew I had entered a new phase in the history of handgun shooting when I heard this alibi at a bullseye pistol match some years ago: "My light went out."

Laser Sights

Innovation continues, and a type of handgun sight we see more and more often is the laser sight. The laser sight actually projects a beam of intense red light onto the target. You simply put the spot on the target and squeeze off the shot, knowing that the shot is properly aligned.

You know it can't really be that easy. For one thing, the beam generator and the power source add weight, bulk and expense to a handgun. In bright light, the spot is less readily visible at a distance. In dim light, it is very visible, but the target is less so.

If the shooter's eyes are not perfect, the laser sight will not compensate. If the target appears sharp to the shooter's eyes, the laser spot will be sharp. If the target is blurry, the laser spot will appear blurry, too.

A big advantage of the laser sight is that it does not require precise alignment of the eye, the sights and the target. It also does not preclude the use of open sights (in most mountings). They are still not very common, but more people are noticing laser sights. Keep your eye on them.

Handgun sight radius is generally fixed by the placement of the sights and the barrel length. Note how the longer barrel of the Ruger Mark I target pistol increases the sight radius over the Ruger Standard Model.

In an attempt to increase sight radius, some match shooters use pistols with ribs that extend the front sight forward of the slide.

Sight Radius

We mentioned sight radius a short while ago, and we went into the topic in some detail in Chapter Five: "Rifle Sights and Sighting-In."

A quick review is worthwhile here, for sight radius is far more critical for handgunners than for rifle shooters.

Very generally, sight radius is the distance between the front and rear sights. The greater this distance, the less the effect of small misalignments, and the greater the precision of aiming.

Most handgun sights are very close together relative to most rifle sights. A small misalignment will mean a much greater error at the target than that same misalignment with a rifle. Thus, sight radius is critical to handgun shooters. Critical, but is it important?

There is generally little we can do about sight radius. Front sights are already mounted quite close to the front of the pistol, and rear sights are already mounted near the rear. Some target shooters order longer barrels. Some install extended front sights which extend forward of the muzzles of their pistols. These extended sights do indeed increase sight radius, but they can be banged more easily and do not lend themselves to holster carry.

Another factor is that handguns most often are not held as steadily as rifles. A pistol or revolver with a short sight radius looks rock steady. One with the sights far apart looks pretty wobbly. Consider a 38 Special snubbie with a 2-inch barrel. The sights are only a bit over 3 inches apart, and few ordinary men can shoot the little revolvers well. Yet, there is no mechanical reason these guns cannot shoot well, and some people can shoot them pretty well. The one thing on which we all seem to agree is that the sights look steady because they are so close together.

Now, think about an Olympic Free Pistol. Such pistols are free of most restrictions and have long barrels and extended sights. Barrels are often close to a foot in length and sight radius may be near 18 inches. Holding one at arm's length is a disheartening experience for most people, because the sights seem to wobble and lurch constantly. Yet we know these pistols are incredibly accurate, and Olympic shooters are able to punch amazingly small groups with them.

So, there is a human psychological factor involved with handgun sight radius.

Back about 1930, 22-caliber single shot target pistols were more or less standard with 10-inch barrels. Harrington & Richardson, during velocity experiments, made up several target pistols with different barrel lengths, thus giving different sight radii. It was found that a pistol with an 8-inch barrel shot almost as well as the standard 10-inch version. A number of shooters commented that the shorter pistol was actually easier to shoot because the sights seemed clearer and appeared to move less. In 1931, Major Julian S. Hatcher won the 20-yard match at Bisley, England, with a perfect score (only the second perfect score ever fired there), using the 8-inch pistol. He surmised that the psychological effect of seeing the sights with less perceived motion more than made up for the theoretical precision of the longer sight radius.

So, for all practical purposes, we can ignore handgun sight radius. The distance between sights on most standard pistols is suitable for most people. Besides, there is not much we can do to change the radius on the handgun we have. About all we can do is consider different barrel lengths when getting the next gun.

It may have seemed like a long way around to come to this conclusion, but the question will come up for you sooner or later, and you should have this background. Remember that individual preferences concerning sight radius on handguns vary. You must come to a conclusion that is satisfactory for you.

Sight Alignment

Sight alignment is the relationship between the shooter's eye, the rear sight and the front sight.

Very quickly, now: Optical and electronic sights combine the target and sighting device into a single plane. We simply place the crosshairs or the dot on the target. More simply said than done, it is true. However, because of the single optical plane, we need pay them little attention. Same with the laser sight, for there is nothing to be aligned.

However, the vast majority of handguns have front sights and rear sights. Properly aligning them is one of the most important aspects of good shooting.

Handguns today are almost exclusively equipped with a square-topped front post and square-notch rear sight. These are called Patridge sights, named after their inventor, E.E. Patridge, who developed them in 1898.

Remember that the human eye can only focus on one thing at a time. A shorter sight radius may make both the sights look almost in focus, but you can't focus on them both. You must make a decision as to which sight to focus on. *Always focus on the front sight.* With a good focus on the front sight, the rear will be a bit fuzzy. Keep the front sight in sharp focus, and you can align the sharp front sight in the slightly fuzzy rear notch.

With the square front sight properly aligned in the square notch, the top of the front post should be level with the top of the rear sight. The post should be centered in the notch, with an equal amount of light on both sides. Because we are dealing with straight lines in both the horizontal and vertical directions, alignment is substantially more precise than with the old Paine bead-and-U-notch system, named after Ira Paine, a famous marksman of the 1880s.

In order to stress the importance of sight alignment, many pistol coaches start students by shooting at a completely blank target. With no bullseye to distract their attention, shooters concentrate completely on sight alignment, and some spectacularly good groups have been fired this way.

Sight Picture

Sight alignment, we said, was the proper alignment of the eye with the sights themselves. Sight picture is the alignment of the sights with the target.

We'll quickly dispose of the sight picture for optical and electronic sights: Put the crosshairs (or dot) where you want the bullet to strike. That's easy to say, but those sighting devices will wobble around, particularly when associated with a scope of some magnification. The sight picture itself, however, is very simple, because all elements are in the same optical plane.

Sight picture with iron sights involves the post and notch of the sights and their relationship to the target. The sight alignment—the relationship of the sights alone—is very, very critical with a handgun. Because of the shorter sight radius of the handgun, sight alignment must be very precise to avoid wild shots. Make sure you have your sight alignment down pat before pointing those sights at a target.

When you have mastered sight alignment and are ready to

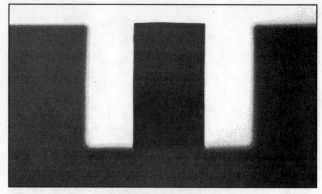

Sight alignment—the relationship of the front and rear sight—is extremely important to a pistol shooter. Looking through the camera lens, we're trying to duplicate what you might see. Focus on the front sight, even if the rear sight is somewhat fuzzy.

When the aligned sights are oriented to the target, the focus is still on the front sight, even if the rear sight and target are both fuzzy.

consider a relationship between the aligned sights and the target, you have two options: the 6 o'clock hold and the center hold.

The *6 o'clock hold* gets its name from the face of the clock. The round bullseye is seen as a clock face. The top of the front post is held just below the 6 o'clock position, tangent to the circle. The sights should be adjusted so that the strike of the bullet is in the center of the bullseye. The focus of the eye, never forget, is on the front sight, looking at the front sight, *really seeing* the front sight. And when doing so, the bullseye will be somewhat fuzzy.

The 6 o'clock hold has been used successfully for a long time. Its great advantage is the dark front post is always distinct from the dark bullseye. Young shooters and new shooters generally do well with it, as there is no confusing overlap of front sight and target. Most experienced competitive shooters use the 6 o'clock hold for precision shooting.

With the *center hold*, the top of the front post is placed directly in the center of the black bullseye. The sights should be adjusted so that the strike of the bullet is exactly in the center of the bullseye. An advantage of the center hold is that very

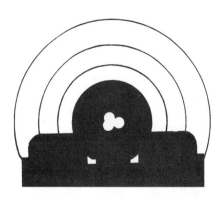

6 O'Clock vs. Center Hold

The 6 o'clock hold (left) allows precise alignment, but bullets strike above the point of aim. The center hold (right) obscures part of the target, but bullets strike where the gun looks. Pick the method that suits you best.

young shooters may have difficulty understanding the 6 o'clock hold. The concept of holding below the bull to make the bullets strike the center of the bull may be too abstract; they want to hit where they aim. The disadvantage of the center hold is that it's often hard to tell where center really is. Slightly high or slightly low may seem pretty much the same with a dark post and dark circle.

Note, too, that with the sights properly aligned, the rear sight takes up an awful lot of space in front of your eye. A great deal more target area is covered with the center hold than with the 6 o'clock hold. For many people, it is comforting to see a lot of target, so it is more natural for them to use the 6 o'clock hold.

I use the 6 o'clock hold almost exclusively. At the risk of seeming wishy-washy, then, I must say that the center hold is not without advantages. It is easy to understand, and it allows the same hold on targets of different sizes. For hunting, a strike of the bullet to the top of the post is prefered, and sighting with a center hold will accomplish this.

Sighting-In

Sighting-in a handgun is essentially the same procedure as with a rifle, but there are some differences. The range is generally shorter. Also, most revolvers and semi-automatic pistols do not allow easy bore-sighting.

To sight in our handgun we should have a solid rest. Seated at a bench with the pistol firmly clasped in both hands, the wrists should be resting on sandbags, a special pistol rest or a rolled sleeping bag. The range should be short. Twenty-five yards is about right, because this is the range at which most pistol target shooting is done.

The bullseye should be small and the target paper should be large. This way, the bullets should hit the paper somewhere. Shoot three to five shots to get a group. Three shots will let you take the center of the triangle as the center of the group.

If the center of your first group is low and to the left, you need to move your shots and the rear sight up and to the right. The basic rule for sight adjustment is always the same: *Move the rear sight in the direction you want the shots to go!*

Sometimes, it is necessary to move the front sight to make an adjustment. The rule for front sight adjustment: *move the front sight in the opposite direction of the way you want the shots to go!*

The method of adjustment you use will depend on the type of sight. Modern micrometer sights are screwdriver-adjustable for both windage (lateral) and elevation (vertical). Some older guns have a windage adjustment on the rear sight and an elevation adjustment on the front sight. Fixed sights may sometimes permit a windage adjustment by tapping the sight sideways in its dovetail slot. Elevation is adjusted by installing higher or lower fixed sights, or by filing, in the primitive manner of our forefathers. *Do not file sights until you are sure you understand what you are doing!* Metal once removed is not easily replaced.

With scope and electronic sights, just follow the directions that come with the sight; adjusting systems can vary.

SIGHTING-IN TIP

The basic rule of sight adjustment is move the rear sight in the direction you want the shots to go.

You don't really need to memorize this. You can recall it by imagining an extreme situation. Imagine a great big rear sight with its big square notch moved 3 inches to the right, hanging out in space. Moving the muzzle of the pistol to the right to bring the front sight into alignment with this imaginary rear sight would make the gun point far to the right. If a shot were fired with the gun in this extreme position, the bullet would hit far to the right of the target.

With this little trick, you can easily remind yourself which way to move the rear sight. No matter who on the range may be watching, you can pick up your screwdriver and confidently make your adjustment, knowing that moving the rear sight to the right will move the shots to the right.

Eye Dominance

Just as most people are right- or left-handed, they are also either right- or left-eyed. That is, the dominant eye wants to take over when both eyes look at something.

There is a subconscious misconception, even among people who should know better, that the dominant eye sees better than the other eye. While this might certainly be true in some situations, there is really no connection between visual acuity and eye dominance.

Not sure which is your dominant eye? Put your hands together so that only a small opening remains. Extend your arms and look through the hole at a distant object, keeping both eyes open. While continuing to look at the object, bring your hands back toward your face. The opening will now be in front of only one of your eyes, the one looking at the object. That eye is your dominant eye.

The presence of a master eye has been mentioned in shooting publications since at least the beginning of the 20th century. It becomes a concern when the dominant eye does not correspond to the dominant hand. No one who has shot for some time wants to find out he is doing it wrong, but it generally is a problem only when a right-handed person has a left master eye.

Previous solutions have ranged from closing (or partially closing) the offending left dominant eye, to putting a blinder in front of it, to shooting with the left hand.

Keep in mind that a left-hander with a right dominant eye might be more willing to switch hands, because most handguns were designed for right-hand use. Many semi-automatics are now made with ambidextrous controls, but even so, most of them still eject to the right. A rapid reload of a revolver during a PPC or IPSC pistol match is a matter of practice for a person shooting right-handed. It is a matter of frustration for one shooting left-handed. I knew some lefties who shot right-handed so that they could use revolvers the "right" way.

The advice offered by the NRA's basic pistol handbook says the dominant eye should always be used for aiming, and it is recommended that the shooter grip the pistol with the hand on the same side of the body as the dominant eye.

There are several other possibilities, one of which is shooting with one hand and the opposite eye. I have known shooters who did this. Apparently, their manual dexterity was better one way, but the dominant eye was on the other side.

Many pistol shooters are already accustomed to shooting with both left and right hands, because PPC and some NRA Action Pistol matches require firing with the weak hand.

If you are taking a shooting instruction course and a question is asked about eye dominance, the expected answer is to use the same hand as on the side of your dominant eye. If your instructor wants you to use your dominant eye, by all means do so, even if it is the one you are not used to. In some cases, improvement in shooting performance has been immediate and dramatic.

I am not certain we know all we need to about eye dominance. Just switching hands on the basis of a single factor ignores others, such as hand-eye coordination.

Determining your dominant eye can be done by the simple test of looking at a distant object, then raising your hands, leaving a small opening.

Add in that some people have better vision in the eye that is dominant, some have better vision in the eye that is not; some have undergone a long-term change in dominance from one eye to another, and some people seem to cross over from one eye to another in different situations. I seem to be in this latter group, which is why the subject is of such interest to me.

It would seem that there is still much to be learned about eye dominance. However, I want to make clear that eye dominance—the tendency of one eye to take over—is an established fact. Many shooters have benefitted from understanding this and modifying their shooting techniques to suit their eye dominance.

You may have noticed by now that it is sometimes difficult to put what we know about guns and shooting into nice neat categories. Equipment develops, knowledge increases, and experience grows. Handgun sights and sighting are areas that have changed dramatically within the past few decades. As a shooter, plan to benefit from the knowledge of others, but keep an open mind and share your experiences. What you pass on may help other shooters coming along down the road.

CHAPTER ELEVEN

SHOOTING THE
HANDGUN

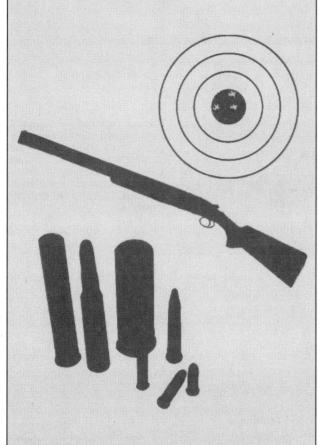

IN ORDER TO shoot a handgun well, a shooter must learn and understand certain basic skills. These skills must be used each and every time you fire a shot. They are essential, or fundamental, to being a successful handgun shooter.

The fundamentals of handgun shooting have been described by different people over the years in a number of different ways. The skills they describe remain pretty much the same. I'll present them here in the same general order as they are presented in the basic pistol handbook offered by the National Rifle Association: grip; position; breath control; sight alignment; trigger squeeze; follow-through.

Grip

The grip of the hand or hands on the handgun is probably the most important part of any of the shooting fundamentals. As before, we will assume a right-handed shooter. Again, my apologies to you southpaws.

One-Hand Grip

These points are important to achieving a proper one-hand grip on a handgun:

- Place the pistol in the right (shooting) hand with the left hand. Note that this is a lot different from just picking up the pistol with the right hand. As always, keep the gun pointed in a safe direction, and keep your finger off the trigger.
- Fit the pistol into the "V" formed by the thumb and forefinger of the right hand, high on the rear part of the frame or grip backstrap.
- Align the pistol so that the pistol, wrist and forearm form a continuous line.
- Grip the pistol between the lower three fingers and heel of the hand (base of the thumb). Grip pressure is straight back, without any sideways movement. Your hold should be firm, but not a white-knuckle death grip. Think of squeezing the handles of a pair of pliers.
- The thumb of the shooting hand should be alongside the frame, exerting no sideways pressure.
- The trigger finger, or index finger (which you have kept off the trigger until now), may now contact the trigger, but it must not touch the frame of the gun. More about this when we get to "trigger squeeze."

Handguns don't weigh much, compared to rifles, and if they move in a different direction each time a shot is fired, groups will not be good. To prevent this, your grip must be

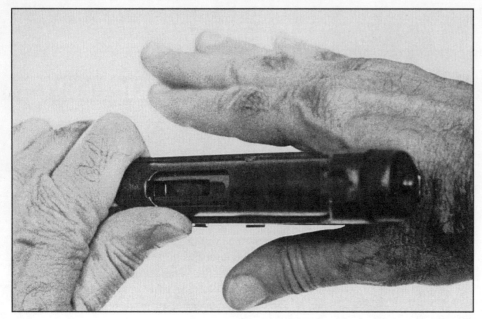

Use the left hand to place the pistol in the "V" of your right hand. The pistol, wrist and forearm should form a line.

This is the one-hand grip on a semi-automatic pistol. The pistol is in line with the wrist and forearm, and neither thumb nor index finger puts sideways pressure on the pistol. The first pad of the finger controls the trigger.

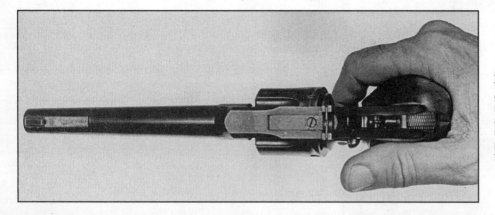

Although the target revolver has a very different configuration, the grip is essentially the same. The revolver is in line with the wrist and forearm, and neither thumb nor index finger exerts sideways pressure. The first pad controls the trigger.

uniform. The grip must be exactly the same for every shot fired.

Two-Hand Grip

Once we have a good one-hand hold, it is easy to progress to a good two-hand hold. Here's how:

- Grip the pistol in a firm one-hand hold (with finger off the trigger again) and bring the left hand to the pistol.
- Touch the heel of your left hand to the heel of your right hand already gripping the pistol.
- Wrap the four fingers of the left hand firmly around the three fingers of the right hand. The left thumb should be on top of your right thumb.
- Notice that now the entire "handle" of the pistol is clasped between your hands and completely surrounded. In theory and in practice, this seems to be the best two-hand grip.

There are others, of course. These things evolve. Old methods give way to new, and shooters are constantly experimenting with new ways to do things better.

Grip Variations

Some shooters take the basic two-hand grip I have just

HOW TO MASTER ANY POSITION

Study the position. Look at pictures of people using the various positions in this book and other shooting publications. Pay particular attention to those who have won some special recognition while shooting from those positions. Pay more attention to the position of a national champion than that of an occasional shooter.

You will soon notice, however, that different people use somewhat different positions. There are reasons for this. One is that positions have evolved and changed over the years. The results of different types of competitive pistol shooting have changed our ideas of what a standard shooting position should be.

Another is that people are different. Body structure and age are some of the factors that influence the positions we can comfortably assume.

So, study the position in order to understand what makes a shooting position as stable and steady as possible.

Practice the position without the gun. At this point, you may well ask just what is the point of getting into a shooting position without something to shoot? It seems a little silly, doesn't it? However, without the gun you are forced to be aware of the orientation of the various parts of your body. When you are holding the pistol, your attention focuses on it. Without it, it is easier to think about the positioning of the feet, legs, torso, shoulders, arms and hands.

Practice the position with the gun. Remember all the aspects of the position you assumed without the gun in your hand. Now, with the handgun, take the position. Are bones supporting the position as much as possible? Is it comfortable? Relatively stable?

Align the position with the target. Until now, you have developed the position without any reference to a target. Now, we want to establish a natural point of aim, directly at the target. Assume the position and look at the target. Now, close your eyes or look away from the sights for a second or two. Look back at the sights. Are they still pointing at the target? If not, *do not* use muscle power to swing the pistol back to the target!

Instead, shift your entire body until the pistol points directly at the target. Look away again, then back at the sights. Not quite right? Shift your body again until the pistol points naturally at the target. Check again. If the gun remains on target you have now achieved your natural point of aim.

In days gone by, the standard way of shooting a

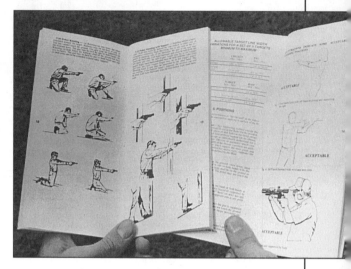

To get an idea of what positions are allowed for some of the handgun shooting sports, get the rule books for those sports and study them.

These students, during a basic pistol shooting course, use variations of the basic two-hand hold and isosceles standing position. Instructor Pete Henderson watches carefully during the shooting.

handgun was standing erect with the pistol held in one hand, the gun extended at arm's length. This is still the position for conventional bullseye competitive shooting and much casual shooting. However, newer shooting sports of the past several decades have made other positions common.

Pressure to hold the pistol is between the lower three fingers and the heel of the hand. Neither thumb nor index finger exerts pressure on the frame of the pistol. The pistol wrist and forearm are in a straight line. Robert Malloy shows how to do it.

described, but only wrap three fingers of the left hand over the right, extending the left index finger around the front of the trigger guard. This was quite the fad for a while, and many pistols have trigger guards with curves or hooks or checkering to accommodate this hold. For me, it tends to pull the pistol to the side. Try it and see if it works for you.

Another minor variation is placing the left thumb over the right wrist. If you try this method with a semi-automatic pistol, be absolutely sure that your thumb is out of the path of the recoiling slide.

Another variation has been called the "cup-and-saucer" method. A proper one-hand hold is taken, and then the butt of the pistol is placed into the cupped palm of the left hand. This grip adds steadiness but does not offer much control of the pistol during recoil.

The basic two-hand grip is useful for both single- and double-action shooting. The basic one-hand grip can also be used for both, but most shooters curl the thumb down onto the grip for more control when shooting double action with one hand.

Position

Before we go into the individual positions, it is important to understand the four basic steps that will allow you to master any position: study the position; practice the position without the gun; practice the position with the gun; align the position with the target. Following these practice steps will help any shooter to improve when using any of the numerous shooting positions.

The purpose of any of the basic positions is to provide a structure, as stable as possible, from which to shoot the gun.

Let us consider these handgun shooting positions: benchrest; one-hand standing; two-hand standing; kneeling; sitting; prone; freestyle.

Benchrest

While many shooters don't really think of it as a "position," the benchrest gives the greatest possible support to the handgun. This allows the shooter to devote less attention to holding the gun steady, and more to concentrating on the fundamentals.

There is no organized benchrest competition for handgun shooters as there is for rifle shooters. The benchrest postion for pistol shooting has its main uses in assisting new shooters, sighting-in, and testing a new pistol.

To take the benchrest position, sit behind a bench or table, facing the target. Sandbags or other support, such as a rolled sleeping bag, should be on the bench.

Grip the pistol in both hands, in the manner we previously discussed. As always, keep the gun pointed in a safe direction and keep your finger off the trigger. Extend both arms in front of the body and rest the hands on the sandbags. The hands can be directly over the sandbags, or the gun can be forward a bit so that the wrists rest directly on the supporting surface. I like this better in most cases, because the pistol can recoil in about the same manner as if it were being hand-held without support.

One-Hand Standing

Poking the pistol toward the target with one hand while standing on your hind legs has always been the traditional way of shooting a handgun. It is still the position used for competitive bullseye shooting. The popularity of other handgun sports in recent decades has made the two-hand hold common now. Some folks feel the one-hand position is not accurate. If you watch a top pistol shooter put bullet after bullet into a 50-yard 10-ring that measures only slightly over 3 inches in diameter, you will soon get rid of that feeling.

To assume the one-hand standing position, stand facing about 45 degrees to the left of the target. (Remember, we are assuming you are right-handed.) Feet should be about shoulder width apart with the weight evenly distributed. Legs should be straight, but not locked. Body and head should be comfortably erect.

The pistol is gripped firmly in the right hand, and the right arm is extended—and it *is* locked. Establish a natural point of aim.

Because you are using only one hand to hold the gun, you have to do something with the other hand so that it will not be a distraction to you. Stick it in your side pocket or into your waist-

(Left) The writer uses a firm two-hand grip on a 45-caliber Ruger Blackhawk during a silhouette match.

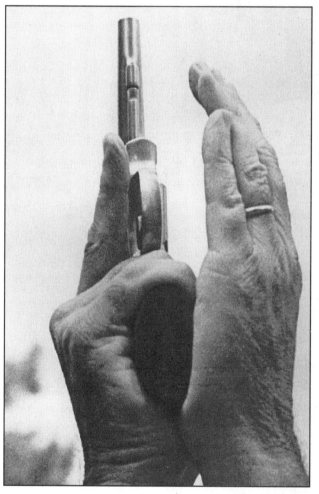

(Below) For a two-hand grip, take a good one-hand grip, put the heels of your hands together, and wrap the four fingers of the left hand around the three of the right hand. The finger stays off the trigger until ready to shoot.

band, but don't let it swing free. Do not use muscle tension to hold it in an unnatural position.

Two-Hand Standing

This position is useful for hunting, silhouette shooting, and some of the action and practical pistol sports.

This one is somewhat steadier than the one-hand position, especially, it seems, for new shooters. Steadiness, however, is not the greatest advantage of the two-hand position. Control is.

With a two-hand hold, control of the pistol is much better, and therefore the trigger finger is able to make a better squeeze. Control allows more rapid recovery from recoil, permitting faster and more accurate shooting. Control of movement allows changing the direction the gun is pointing very quickly, and one can therefore engage multiple targets within a short period of time.

To assume the two-hand standing position, face the target squarely, head on. The feet should be about shoulder width apart, with your weight distributed evenly. The legs are straight, but not locked. The head is erect, and the arms are fully extended. If natural-point-of-aim adjustments need to be made, the pivot point is halfway between your feet.

This is the dominant two-hand position used now and is generally referred to as the isosceles position. This refers, of course, to the isosceles triangle, in which the two long arms are of equal length.

There is another two-hand standing position, generally called the Weaver stance. This was developed by Sheriff Jack Weaver of Lancaster, California, in the late 1950s. It came into wide use during the 1960s, remained very popular for some time, and is still in use.

In the Weaver stance, the body faces the target angled slightly to the right. The right hand pushes the pistol forward with a right arm that is straight or almost straight. The left arm is bent, and the left hand joins the right hand to grasp the pistol in a firm two-hand grip. The left arm actually exerts a "pull" against the "push" of the right arm. The opposing muscle pressure allows a great deal of control of the pistol. Very accurate and very rapid shooting can be done from the Weaver stance.

Its strength, it seems, is also its weakness. The Weaver stance cannot be maintained for more than short periods of time without tiring the shooter. For handgun practice and action match courses with short time limits, the Weaver stance is still used. For long matches and silhouette shooting, the isosceles position seems to have taken over.

(Above) When learning the fundamentals or trying out a new pistol, the benchrest position is useful. Here young Kenneth McDaniel sights in a 9mm Tokarev over a sleeping bag. If you place your left thumb over your right wrist when using a semi-automatic pistol, make sure the slide will not contact it during recoil.

Ann Sayers uses a firm two-hand grip and a Weaver stance while practicing with several different types of pistols.

The isosceles standing position is the two-arm position used by most shooters today. A young Patrick Malloy uses it to try out a 9mm Stallard pistol.

Other Positions

Other positions are not as easily defined for handgun shooting as for rifle shooting. For hunting, the handgunner will avail himself of any support he can. A large number of positions may be assumed, and they may be unique to particular situations. For silhouette, PPC and Action Pistol courses, the rule books indicate a number of allowable positions, or at least do not restrict positions. If you are interested in such sports, get the rulebooks and check the various positions that are permitted.

These are often-used hangun shooting positions:

Kneeling is quick to assume and can be reasonably steady. The shooter kneels with his right knee on the ground and sits on his right heel. The left elbow is on the upright left knee. The right arm extends straight from the shoulder, gripping the pistol in the manner we've studied. The left hand then completes the two-hand grip, and the pistol is supported by the body through the elbow and knee. The final result has notable similarities to the kneeling position used in rifle shooting.

Sitting is the most-used position. The shooter faces directly toward the target with his legs spread into a slight "V," knees drawn up. The shooter leans forward so that his extended arms can place his elbows on or just inside his knees.

A modification of this position involves leaning back against a tree or other stable object. Instead of leaning forward, the shooter draws his knees back toward his body until the elbows have a secure rest. This position, because of the back support, is a very stable field position.

In the *prone* position, the shooter lies on the ground facing the target, arms extended toward the target. The gun may be held with both hands in the basic two-hand grip, or the left fist may be placed on the ground to support the shooting hand, which holds the pistol with a firm one-hand grip. Some shooters roll slightly and rest their head on their shooting arm.

Freestyle shooting is included here just to make sure we cover all the possibilities. There is a provision for freestyle positions in silhouette shooting that allows any safe position in which the gun is supported only by the body, does not touch the ground, and does not endanger any competitors or range personnel. Freestyle positions often involve lying on the back and supporting the handgun against a leg.

Hanguns are relatively small and can be held in a number of ways that rifles cannot. The positions, therefore, have an astounding number of variations. Try the traditional ones first. However, remember that they have gradually evolved, and something new may be in favor in years to come.

Breath Control

If you breathe during the time you are trying to fire a shot, your body will move and the gun will move. In order to minimize body movement, you must hold your breath while firing.

When you're getting ready to shoot, breathe normally. When you are actually preparing to fire a shot, stop breathing. Take a breath, let a little air out, then hold the rest while firing the shot.

Studies of competitive shooters have shown that most of them don't control their breathing in that manner. They just simply don't breathe during the time they make the shot. There are other things to think about, so they just stop breathing without doing it in any particular sequence.

If you hold your breath too long, you will run out of oxygen and muscle tremors will start. If things aren't right for you to get off a shot, relax, take a few breaths, and try again.

Sight Alignment

We covered sight alignment in Chapter 10: "Handgun Sights and Sighting-In," but we need to stress it here as one of the fundamentals. It is one of the most important fundamentals of all shooting.

Sight alignment is the proper relationship of the front sight and the rear sight, as seen by your eye. For most handgun sights, this means the front post is centered in the rear notch, and the top of the front sight is even with the top of the rear sight.

Recall, also, that you must focus on the front sight—really see it. The rear sight will be slightly out of focus and the target even more so. No matter. Concentrate on the front sight!

The sight picture is the relationship of the aligned sights and the target, as seen by the eye. This is not as important for pistol shooters as it is for rifle shooters. Handguns wobble around a lot more, so the relationship of the sights to the target changes rapidly. Don't let this bother you—continue to concentrate on the front sight and maintain sight alignment.

If your sights are perfectly aligned, and the pistol wobbles to the edge of the black, your shot will still be in the black. If your sights are under the black, but are not aligned (your front sight is somewhere other than in its proper place in the notch), your shot will be wild—almost certainly out in the white, perhaps off the target. This is why sight alignment is so important.

If you have been shooting handguns for any length of time, you already know you can't hold one perfectly still. With practice you can minimize this movement, but seldom can anyone hold a pistol as steadily as he can a rifle. We overcome this lack of steadiness (we hope) by special attention to two of the fundamentals. One is sight alignment, which we've just discussed. The second is trigger control, coming up next.

Trigger Squeeze

When you have the best possible grip and position, excellent sight alignment and at least a pretty good sight picture, and have momentarily stopped breathing, you only want one physical motion to take place. The trigger finger must move the trigger just enough to fire the shot.

We are concerned with only a tiny fraction of an inch of movement, but that movement is critically important and must be carefully controlled.

Some people call the control of the trigger a pull or a press. Because we have to call it something, let's call it trigger squeeze. I like this term because it emphasizes the gradual increase of pressure applied.

It doesn't really matter what you call it as long as the pressure is straight back without disturbing the alignment of the sights. It must also be a *smooth* movement that will not disturb the alignment of the sights.

Grip the handgun and place your index finger on the trigger. The preferred contact point is the pad of the first segment, about halfway between the fingertip and the first joint. The trigger finger should not touch the frame of the gun.

It is possible that this first-segment pad may not be the best contact point for every person and every pistol. Double-action triggers, in particular, may be difficult to operate. Many shoot-

FUNDAMENTALS OF HANDGUN SHOOTING

Grip is the manner of holding or grasping the handgun.

Position is the shooter's body posture while holding the handgun, and involves the relation of the body to the target. It is sometimes called stance.

Breath Control neccessitates altering the breathing to minimize body movement.

Sight Alignment is the relationship of the front and rear sights.

Trigger Squeeze is the manner in which pressure is applied to the trigger so as not to disturb the sight alignment.

Follow-Through is the condition of continuing to maintain everything necessary to fire the shot for a short time after the shot has been fired.

ers use the first joint for both single action and double action, and some seem to do quite well that way. However, long experience by a lot of very good shooters indicates that the pad of the first segment is generally the best contact point. Our objective is not to make everyone do everything the same way, but to make sure that everybody *smoothly* presses the trigger straight back.

Are you smoothly pressing the trigger straight back? The best way to tell is by dry-firing. This practice is a form of shooting without ammunition. Prepare yourself as if you were about to fire a shot, but with your gun unloaded. When you have the sights properly aligned, squeeze the trigger.

Click! The sights jumped to one side as the hammer fell! You either jerked the trigger or the position of your trigger finger did not move the trigger straight back. The movement of the sights would not be obvious when actually shooting, because recoil would mask it.

Dry-fire again. If you know you made a smooth squeeze, but the sights still jumped to the side, your finger placement is probably the culprit. Try using another part of your finger. You might even try using the pad of the first segment, as your instructor recommended. Now, when the hammer falls, the sights no longer jump. Make a note of the correct finger position that allows this correct trigger control.

It is embarrassing, but I must tell you a story so you will not make the same mistake that I did. Many years ago I began shooting outdoor pistol matches. The only handgun I owned suitable for the centerfire and 45 stages was a 1917 Colt revolver. The old Colt shot groups that were good enough for our local matches, but placed its shots all to one side.

I was sure the sights were off. After all, I was a competitive target shooter, wasn't I? And I was shooting groups, wasn't I?

Because the sights were not adjustable, I spent a lot of time carefully putting a slight bend into the front sight and filing the rear sight notch. I finally got the groups more or less centered. Time passed, and I graduated to other and better target pistols, learned more about pistol shooting, fired a lot of matches...but still kept the old 1917. Many years later, I took it out to the range again. Strange. It was shooting off to the other side, now. Slowly, the horrible truth dawned.

The sights had never been off! I have long, skinny fingers, and my early method of trigger placement had been cramming my finger into the trigger guard as far as I could and squeezing the trigger wherever the finger happened to land. I had unknowingly put sideways pressure on the trigger and frame, and the muzzle shifted slightly to the side each time the hammer fell. I did it consistently enough so that the revolver still more or less grouped all right, but off to one side.

The lesson to be learned from this story is that I know what I'm talking about when I tell you that the trigger must come straight back. Spare yourself embarrassment.

Also, you must not jerk the trigger. Note how wobbly that pistol looks when you point it at the target. You know your sight alignment is good, and there is a real temptation to get a shot off the instant the sight picture is just right. Don't succumb to that temptation, or you will almost certainly jerk the trigger and get a wild shot.

Your hold will become steadier with practice, but you know the pistol will always move around. Put pressure on the trigger when the sight picture is pretty good and hold it as it wobbles away. When it comes back, add more pressure. Thus, the shot will always fire when the sight picture is at least pretty good.

Pistol champion Frank Higginson used to tell beginners they could become good pistol shots if they remembered three

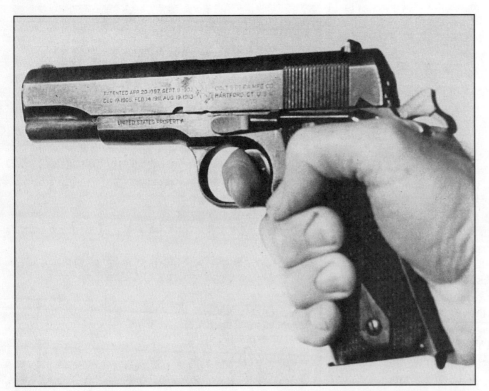

Although the writer shot fairly well for some years using the first joint for squeezing the trigger, he is now convinced that the pad of the first segment gives better results.

FIRING THE PERFECT SHOT

Now it is time to put everything together. You will take everything you know, and you will use it to fire one perfect shot.

Your handgun is perfectly sighted-in for the ammunition and for the range. You have complete confidence in it.

You approach the firing line. Let us say that you will fire your one shot single action, from the one-hand standing position at a 50-yard bullseye target.

You take your position. With your left hand, you place the gun into your right hand; the backstrap fits into the "V" of the shooting hand. The lower three fingers of your right hand and the base of the thumb firmly grip the pistol. Your thumb lies to the left of the frame. You are not ready to shoot yet, so your trigger finger is still outside the trigger guard.

You face about 45 degrees to the left of the target and extend your right arm, holding the pistol toward the target. The pistol, your wrist, and your forearm form a straight line. Your head and body are comfortably erect.

The perfectly aligned sights form a good sight picture with the target. You look down for a moment, then back at the sights. The sights now point slightly to the left of the bullseye. You move your entire body slightly to the right, pivoting on the right foot. Perfect sight picture. Look away again, then back at the sights. Still perfect. You have achieved your natural point of aim.

The command to fire has been given, and you have a cartridge loaded. You place the pad of the first segment of your index finger on the trigger.

You concentrate on your sight alignment, minimizing movement as you prepare to squeeze the trigger. Almost unconsciously, you exhale slightly and hold your breath. The pad between your fingertip and the first joint begins to squeeze the trigger straight back.

Amy Clare demonstrates her knowledge of the fundamentals at the 1992 Florida Junior Olympic Shooting Camp. Coaches Frank Higginson and Choy Soliz observe.

The sights wobble off a bit, and you maintain your pressure on the trigger. Still in perfect alignment, they wobble back to a 6 o'clock position. More smooth, steady pressure on the trigger, and the shot fires.

You remain motionless, maintaining follow-through for two seconds. Time to think. Where were the sights when the shot fired? It looked like a perfect sight picture, didn't it? With perhaps a bit more "white" than normal? You call the shot a "ten," possibly slightly low.

Take a breath and look into the spotting scope. There it is—a beautiful "ten" just below the center "x" mark on the target! You have done it, you have fired the perfect shot!

Now, if you can fire one perfect shot, surely you can fire another one. If you can fire two...

things: look at the front sight; bring the trigger straight back; and do the first two things at the same time!

Follow-Through

Follow-through is simply continuing to do what you were just doing. In many sports, it means the continuation of a movement. In shooting, it means continuing to do everything that was being done when the shot was fired. Essentially, it is a short period of nonmovement.

When we were discussing handgun ammunition, we gave some thought to all the things that happen between the squeeze of the trigger and the exit of the bullet. It doesn't take much time, but it does take *some* time. If the pistol moves during that time, the shot will be a bad one.

To minimize movement during the time the bullet passes through the barrel, simply extend the time of the shot for a second or two. Maintain your grip and position, and your sight alignment. Do not take another breath. Maintain your trigger squeeze. Continue to do all this after the shot is long gone. Use those few seconds to "call" the shot, to think about what you did right, and what needs attention before the next shot.

CHAPTER TWELVE

HANDGUN SHOOTING ACTIVITIES

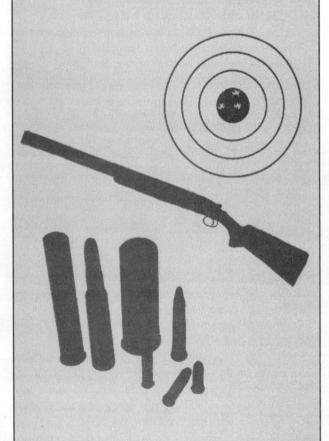

HANDGUNS ARE FASCINATING things. Many people collect them and are content to admire them without ever firing a shot. Most of us, however, want to shoot them, and we're fortunate that there are many handgun shooting sports in which we can participate.

Shooting the handgun can be a lifetime sport, as well as an equal-opportunity sport. Young people and old, men and women, folks from all walks of life, can participate. "Participate" is the key word. It is a common thing to find more participants than spectators at shooting matches.

Great size or strength is not needed. The handguns used may be either simple or sophisticated, and the list of equipment needed for most handgun matches is relatively short. In other words, just about anyone who is interested can participate in the various pistol shooting sports. Often, the same equipment will allow a person to participate in several of these sports.

Let's put the most popular handgun shooting activities into convenient categories: plinking; hunting; practicing; silhouette; action/combat/practical; bullseye; international and Olympic.

Plinking

Everyone knows what plinking is. It is. . .well, it is a bit hard to define, isn't it? Back in the rifle section of this book, I said I usually thought of it as informal shooting at informal targets. A friend thought even that loose definition was too formal. He called it shooting at things that go "plink" when hit. Whatever the definition, things move, break and bounce, and it is a lot of fun.

A 22 handgun of just about any type is excellent for plinking. The low cost of ammunition makes a 22 especially suitable. However, many different calibers of centerfire handguns also make good plinkers. Handgun ammunition is generally less expensive than centerfire rifle ammunition. Reloads, military surplus and special lower-cost cartridges such as CCI's Blazer line bring the cost of many centerfire handgun cartridges down to plinking levels.

It is fun (and easy) to shoot up a lot of ammunition while plinking. However, lots of ammo isn't necessary. One of the most memorable plinking sessions I ever had was with a friend many years ago, with only a partial box of 22s between us. We had an unlimited supply of targets, a K-22 Smith & Wesson revolver and that small supply of cartridges. Normal

At almost any pistol range, you'll see people engaged in informal practice. The writer's brother, Robert Malloy, was part of a group getting in a little practice with their 45s.

shooting would have ended the fun quickly. We hit upon a modified form of "Russian Roulette."

One of us would load a single cartridge, turn the cylinder without looking at it, close the revolver, and pass it over. The other would cock it and try a shot. If the hammer dropped on an empty chamber, any flinch or twitch was very noticeable. The gun was then passed over and the next chamber was tried. Eventually, one of us got off a shot. The lucky shooter would then load one cartridge and the procedure would start anew. We stretched less than a box of ammunition into a long afternoon of fun. And we learned a lot about shooting, because we knew the other guy was always watching to gleefully point out a bad trigger squeeze.

However, most plinking is at a much faster pace than that. Most handgun plinkers use revolvers or semi-automatic pistols capable of quick shooting, and a fast pace is exciting.

In years gone by, glass bottles and tin cans were the major targets. They broke and bounced satisfactorily, and hits were easy to see. Unfortunately, they left a residue—sharp shards of glass and rusty ragged metal—that could be a danger to others and were difficult to pick up. Broken glass especially was bound to be a problem to someone, somewhere along the line.

Better targets exist. Charcoal briquettes, candy wafers, balloons, clay pigeons, crackers and plastic bottles all are good handgun plinking targets. They either leave little objectionable residue or can be easily—and safely—picked up and taken away.

When you are plinking, the shooting is informal, but you must not relax safe gun handling. All the safety rules you know must be strictly followed. Here's a quick refresher of the main three:

1. Always keep the gun pointed in a safe direction.
2. Always keep your finger off the trigger until ready to shoot.
3. Always keep the gun open and unloaded until ready to shoot.

Plinking is fun alone, but most people enjoy it more with family and friends. Several people can have informal games with the targets, and new games can be invented as the shooting progresses. Stationary targets, swinging targets, rolling targets—all can be used in appropriate safe locations. Shooting simultaneously, shooting in sequence, miss-and-out—all these different ways of shooting may be tried.

A safe location is an absolute necessity. Some organized shooting ranges allow plinking in certain areas or at certain types of targets.

A range near my home permits shooting at plastic containers, but not glass or metal. Even when shooting at plinking targets is permitted, you must be aware of what lies beyond your target. Every bullet must go into a safe backstop.

Private land, used with permission, of course, is great for plinking. Some state and national forests allow informal shooting, but some do not. The same holds for other tracts of public land. It is vitally important to check before you go out to shoot.

To most of us older shooters, it is painfully obvious that fewer places to plink exist now than in decades past. You can help keep plinking areas open by being a safe, responsible shooter. Don't allow an area to become trashy with old targets. Pick up other shooters' debris as well as your own targets when you finish.

The whole point of plinking is to have fun with your handgun. It's a wonderful sport that deserves to continue.

J.D. Jones, handgun hunter and wildcat developer extraordinaire, took this South African springbok at about 300 yards with his Thompson/Center Contender single shot pistol.

Hunting

Hunting with a rifle is an old tradition, but hunting with a handgun is a newer aspect of the shooting sports. Hunters back in the muzzle-loading days often carried a pistol as a backup firearm, in case they needed a second shot. Hunting solely with a handgun seems to have evolved in the frontier days after the Civil War, when hunting from horseback required one hand to control the mount and the other could use a handgun, usually a large revolver.

The Grand Duke Alexis of Russia visited the United States and hunted buffalo from horseback in the area of the North Platte River in 1872. He used a 44 Smith & Wesson revolver and was so impressed that Russian contracts for the gun took most of that firm's revolver production for several years.

Later generations of hunters just liked the challenge of pursuing game with the handgun. Backpackers and other wilderness travelers found that they could take along a pistol for small game hunting when there was no room for a rifle.

What can you hunt with a handgun? Small game with a 22 pistol, definitely. I can still remember how proud I was whenever I got a rabbit in my younger days. Hunting without a dog, I would jump up a bunny and could—sometimes—"whistle" him to a stop as I drew my revolver. Then—sometimes—I'd bag him with a 22 bullet as he sat wondering what that sound was.

For small game, the 22 rimfire is the first choice. However, any of the centerfire pistols will do. Even cartridges considered marginal or barely adequate for personal defense have plenty of power for small game hunting. Such sport is a good chance to get some practice with your handgun. Just about any 32, 380, 9mm or 38 handgun will do. Just be sure you know exactly where it shoots, and make sure it is legal for hunting in your area.

For deer and even larger animals, the 357 Magnum has been used a lot, but some consider it marginal in power. The 44 Magnum holds special attraction for this sort of hunting. It is readily available, compact, controllable and powerful enough. A number of even more powerful pistol and revolver cartridges are also available. Now that single shot pistols are chambered for powerful rifle cartridges—and for wildcat cartridges often more powerful than standard rifle cartridges—there are hardly any limits on handgun hunting. African elephant and Cape buffalo have been hunted and killed with handguns.

Handgun hunters must be good hunters. They must get close to the game and have the skill to make clean kills with the "small" gun they are using. Some people, however, don't seem to understand handgun hunting. All we can do, I guess, is show them that we are good people who know what we are doing. Know and practice all the rules of safety. Choose a gun/cartridge suitable for the game hunted, and practice so you know how to shoot it well. Study the game and its habits. And, of course, check with your state's game commission; be familiar with the game laws and the license requirements of your area.

Practicing

When I am on a range doing some shooting, I often take a break and chat with other shooters. We exchange pleasantries about what we're shooting, how we're shooting and why we're shooting.

Shotgun shooters may be getting ready for dove season, or duck season, or quail season. They may be getting in a little practice before the next trap match.

Rifle shooters could be getting ready for deer or squirrel season. They may be preparing for the next Smallbore, silhouette or High Power match.

On the pistol range, most of the shooters are practicing. For the next match? For the hunting season? No, just practicing. A typical conversation may bring out something like, "I bought this pistol for protection, and I kinda' enjoy shooting it, so I came here to do some practicing."

Practicing has recently become one of the major handgun activities.

All right, I'm sure there is a better term for it. Perhaps familiarization or skill development. But that's not what they say. What they say is, "I'm practicing."

Some of these people may have had little shooting experience or previous interest in shooting as a sport. They may have bought handguns for protection and, being prudent people, understood that they needed to have skill in the use of their guns. So, they go to the range and practice.

Handgun practice, in this sense, is informal, non-organized shooting at paper targets. It is generally done at 50 feet or 25 yards, because most ranges can accommodate targets at those distances. Targets may be bullseye targets of any size, silhouette targets, or homemade targets. Scores are almost never recorded. The object of the people who participate in this type of shooting is to develop enough skill so they can keep their shots as close together as possible in an area that is smaller than the vital area of a man.

Pistol practice doesn't require any special targets, and scores are rarely kept. Here, a shooter tries his skill at keeping his shots in the center of a Colt silhouette target.

As shooters, we are missing a bet if we do not cultivate such people. They are usually receptive to ideas for improving their shooting skills. Many are quick to see that participating in a pistol match (of any kind) could help them shoot better. Knowing little about the handgun sports, they may be hesitant about competing; most, however, would be pleased to be invited to watch a match to see what it is all about.

And, if the truth be known, it should be easy to make contact. Often I've noticed some of our top local competitive shooters trying out guns I'd never seen before, shooting along with me at odd-size targets. What was I doing there with them? Just practicing, of course.

What is the difference in size between rifle and pistol silhouette targets? Bob Durham holds a smallbore pistol turkey. Smallbore rifle turkeys are above.

Here is a standard silhouette layout. Chickens are the closest metal targets, followed by pigs, turkeys and rams.

Silhouette Shooting

Handgun shooting sports, as we've said before, are really participant sports, not spectator events. One handgun sport that does have substantial spectator appeal is silhouette shooting.

Silhouette shooting is target shooting, of course, but many people reserve the term "target shooting" for firing at paper targets. Silhouette shooting combines some of the elements of both plinking and hunting. The targets are steel silhouettes in the shapes of animals and birds. They must be hit and knocked off their stands to be scored as hits.

The sport came into the southwestern United States from Mexico, a modification of what was originally a rifle sport. In decades past, many Mexican fiestas began with a rifle match. The targets were the animals that would be eaten later that same day.

As more shooters became interested in such shooting, steel silhouettes of the animals were substituted for the animals themselves. By the 1960s, rifle silhouette competition was established in some of our southwestern states. The long ranges (up to 500 meters) of the rifle matches were not for everyone. In 1975, a match for pistol enthusiasts, with ranges to 200 meters, was held in Arizona.

Today, pistol silhouette matches are staged by both the National Rifle Association (NRA) and the International Handgun Metallic Silhouette Association (IHMSA). The primary difference in the past has been that IHMSA matches were restricted to iron sights, while NRA matches allowed optical sights. As we know, sports change with time, and IHMSA is phasing in some scope matches.

Each silhouette course consists of forty shots at forty silhouettes. One shot is fired at each of ten chickens, ten pigs, ten turkeys and ten rams. A match may be Long Range, with the chickens at 50 meters, pigs at 100, turkeys at 150 and rams at 200 meters. Hunter's Pistol matches are fired at half-size targets at 40, 60, 75 and 100 yards, distances which may be more easily accommodated at many ranges. Smallbore Hunter's Pistol matches use 22 rimfire pistols and lighter targets at 40, 60, 75 and 100 yards.

Silhouette matches are generally casual, friendly gatherings with a lot of spectator appeal. There is no question as to the result of each shot. A hit silhouette topples off its stand as the clang of the bullet strike comes back to the line. A missed silhouette just stands there for all the world to see.

Ann Durham uses a Ruger 22-caliber revolver as her smallbore silhouette handgun.

All the modern action or practical handgun sports probably can trace their origins back to police revolver training during the period between the World Wars.

Action/Combat/Practical Shooting

Although the courses may be very different, we can consider action, combat, and practical shooting together, for they can be thought of as the speed sports of pistol shooting. Two-hand grips and several different positions are usually used. The shooter is either timed or must perform within a fairly short time limit.

Courses that combine accuracy and speed with a handgun have long been realized to be of value in training police offi-cers. In the period between the World Wars, Colt developed a man-size silhouette target with areas marked off that award points for hits in various places. It is still widely used by police units for training.

PPC

The FBI used the Colt silhouette target to develop what was probably the first widely used standardized combat course. Called the Practical Police Course (PPC), it originally had stages at 7, 25, 50 and 60 yards. Over the years, it evolved into

"Where did these come from?" During a North Florida practi-cal event match, Action Pistol shooters seem perplexed that all the shots are not clustered neatly in the center.

Hugh Owen assumes the ready position, with hands above shoulder level, for the start of the 25-yard stage of the practical event in an NRA Action Pistol match.

Upon the signal to commence fire, Owen draws his revolver. His finger is well away from the trigger.

The revolver is brought up to eye level and clasped in a firm two-hand grip as he begins firing.

what is now called the Police Pistol Combat course, retaining the same PPC initials.

Designed for police officers, it has an appeal to civilians, and matches are often open to civilians, although scores may not count for more than local record. There are several optional courses, perhaps the most popular being the National Police Course (7-, 25- and 50-yard stages) and the National Police Course B (7-, 15-, 25- and 50-yard stages.) These are sixty-shot matches with separate time limits for each stage. Reloading is required within the time limit in some stages. The handguns used are usually semi-automatic pistols or revolvers of 35-caliber or larger. Optical sights and high-speed or magnum ammunition are not permitted. Several position changes are required during the course of the match.

PPC has been around a long time. The rules are fairly simple, and the time limits are pretty generous. The course has a lot of appeal to new shooters who want to get into the pistol speed sports. Not much equipment is required; you need a handgun, a holster, and four magazines or speedloaders, and, of course, eye and ear protection.

Practical Shooting (USPSA)

In contrast to the PPC stress on not using ammunition of power greater than standard loads, matches under the guidelines of the United States Practical Shooting Association consider greater power something to be rewarded.

Practical shooting grew in the southwestern United States during the 1950s. The experiences of World War II and the resurgence of interest in the American West had created a new interest in pistol shooting. Instead of being satisfied with traditional bullseye shooting, some wanted pistol events that included movement of both targets and shooters, plus speed and the use of powerful handguns.

Marine officer and author Jeff Cooper, through his writing, brought such events to the attention of shooters throughout the world. By 1976, combat shooting sports were popular in a number of countries. An organization called the International Practical Shooting Confederation (IPSC) was formed. The term "Practical" in the name was the term used by Cooper, who was elected the first president of IPSC. Although some would prefer the term "combat shooting," the word "practical" accords well with the public image we would prefer for such shooting. Each country in the IPSC has a national organization. The United States Practical Shooting Association (USPSA) administers matches here.

The concept of practical shooting is to improve defensive shooting skills with a handgun in a sporting atmosphere. There are no standard courses. However, every course stresses accuracy, speed and power.

How much power? Loads are chronographed and this factor is applied: bullet weight multiplied by velocity, divided by 1000. If the power factor is 175 or higher, the load is consid-

132

ered a major caliber. If it is between 175 and 125, it is a minor caliber. Hits with a major caliber are awarded a greater value. If the power factor is below 125, it isn't even scored. As a rule, full 45 ACP loads are major, and full 9mm loads are minor.

A combination of score, time and power factor, then, compose the final score. Because of a great deal of motion by both shooters and targets in some courses, safety is heavily stressed. There are no restrictions on sights, and optical or electronic sights are commonly used.

Practical matches have a big following. They are exciting to watch and have a considerable amount of spectator and commercial appeal.

Action Pistol

Some shooters wanted more standardized courses, and NRA Action Pistol Shooting answers this need. There are about sixteen different courses of fire described in the rule book. A competitor needs only to know which course is being offered and is then able to prepare for it, even without having seen the location.

Very generally, USPSA matches are somewhat more involved, requiring reloading within the time allowed to the shooter. Very generally, NRA Action matches are somewhat more straightforward, and many courses allow for reloading the handgun outside of the time limits.

Sight restrictions are at the discretion of the match sponsor. The sponsor must clearly state that either there are no restrictions on sights or, conversely, that optical sights are not allowed.

A certain level of power is required, but it is less than in USPSA matches. Bullet weight times velocity must equal at least 120,000 to qualify. Note that this would equate to a power factor of 120, which is slightly less than the lower limit of minor for USPSA or IPSC matches.

Action pistol matches can be held at most club ranges and are lots of fun, both to shoot and watch.

Richard Hill, a regular winner at both bullseye and silhouette matches in southeast Texas, poses beside one of his 45 targets at a Houston bullseye match. He seems pleased, as most shooters would be, with a score of 100-9x.

The writer checks the positioning of the 8-inch metal plates and their return mechanism, prior to the falling plate event at an Action Pistol match.

Local bullseye pistol matches bring out a wide variety of both shooters and handguns.

Bullseye Shooting

Conventional pistol matches, commonly known as bullseye shooting, is the sport most people think of when pistol competition is mentioned. Small wonder. Bullseye shooting has been around longer and has had more participation than any other pistol shooting sport. All shots are fired from the traditional one-hand standing position. Perhaps this is why many people think of the one-hand position as the "correct" way to shoot a pistol.

Bullseye target shooting was strongly, if haphazardly, developed around 1880. Matches of a sort were held at the first modern Olympics in Athens in 1896. Although two Americans did well, there was considerable confusion about the course of fire. There was an obvious need to organize and standardize pistol target shooting, and also to keep records.

The United States Revolver Association was formed in 1900 and coordinated pistol shooting in this country until the National Rifle Association began running pistol matches about the time of World War I. The USRA still conducts postal matches, in which teams shoot before witnesses and mail in the results. Most bullseye matches now, however, are NRA-sanctioned events.

There are a number of different bullseye matches, but they all boil down to three basic elements:

1. Slow-Fire - ten shots
2. Timed-Fire - ten shots
3. Rapid-Fire - ten shots

These three elements make up what is known as the National Match Course (NMC). Possible score is 300 points. There are

Freestyle position is permitted for some silhouette matches. Someone once described freestyle positions as those that cannot be described any other way. This one seems to fit the description.

134

other courses, but they are essentially just modifications of the National Match Course. Let's look at the elements of this course of fire:

Slow-Fire: Fired at 50 yards on the NRA B-6 target, this stage allows 10 minutes for the competitor to fire ten shots. The target has an 8-inch black aiming bull which contains the 8, 9, 10 and X rings. The 10 ring is 3.36 inches in diameter. The X ring is used as a tie-breaker. A lot can happen to a bullet going 50 yards, and this is a very demanding stage of fire. The shooter fires five shots, reloads five more without command and finishes his ten-shot record group.

Timed-Fire: Shooting for timed- and rapid-fire stages is done at 25 yards. The target is essentially the same as that used at 50 yards, but only the 9, 10 and X rings are black, so the aiming bull is smaller. Because the range is cut in half, the aiming bull appears to be about the same size over the sights.

Timed-fire consists of two five-shot strings, each fired in 20 seconds. Reloading is done outside the time limits. When shooters have all reloaded after the first string, a separate time limit of 20 seconds begins for the second five-shot string. Thus, a record group consists of ten shots.

Rapid-Fire: Similar to timed-fire, five shots plus five shots, fired at 25 yards, this stage's time limit is reduced to 10 seconds per string.

Many ranges have turning targets at the 25-yard line which are mechanically turned away, then turned to face the shooters for either 20 seconds or 10 seconds, depending on the stage, timed- or rapid-fire. Ranges without turning targets generally use whistle or voice commands to begin and end the time periods.

Other matches beside the NMC are fired. The NRA Short Course is fired all at 25 yards, using a reduced target for slow-fire.

Other courses for 25 and 15 yards, all at 20 yards, and all at 50 feet, may be better suited to some ranges, particularly indoor types. In all cases, all matches fire the basic thirty shots, ten each in slow-, timed- and rapid-fire.

Handguns used here fall into three categories: 22, centerfire and 45. A 45-caliber revolver or semi-auto can be used for both centerfire and 45 matches, so two guns (22 and 45) can serve for all three-gun matches.

Multiples of the basic thirty-shot match (300 possible points) may be combined to suit a club's needs. Thus, a bullseye match may be described as a 900, 1200, 1800 or 2700. A full match is a 2700 (270 shots), which is three times over the 300-point course, with each of the three pistol categories.

The highly accurate target revolver was the principal handgun of bullseye pistol matches for many decades. However, in the post-World War I period, accurate 22-caliber semi-automatic pistols showed a real advantage in timed- and rapid-fire, because they cocked themselves automatically. In the early 1930s, Colt introduced the Match Target 45 semi-automatic. Within a decade or two after World War II, the accuracy of semi-automatic pistols had improved to the point that one seldom saw a revolver in serious competition during the 1970s.

It is interesting, though, to watch a good revolver shooter go through the timed- and rapid-fire stages. As the revolver recoils, his thumb comes up to the hammer spur and draws it back. On the way down, the revolver is cocked and the thumb returns to its position alongside the frame. The gun can be back on target, cocked, in about the same time as a 45 auto. However, it required considerable practice to be smooth, and the revolver offers no accuracy advantage over the semi-automatic any more.

Still, strangely enough, I see more revolvers at bullseye matches lately. I think a number of shooters who participate in the speed (combat) matches with revolvers want to use them for the bullseye matches to gain the extra familiarity.

Bullseye shooting has been called the basic training for any of the other handgun shooting sports. The idea is that if you master the fundamentals to the point where you can do pretty well in a bullseye match, it is easier to get the hang of the other handgun sports.

It certainly is the way to start if you have an eye on international or Olympic competition.

Olympic and International Shooting

Handgun shooting events have been part of most of the modern Olympics since they began in 1896. Although handgun shooting was not well organized within most countries and was certainly not coordinated between countries back then.

A group of fourteen American athletes attended the 1896 Olympics. Two brothers, John and Sumner Paine, both pistol shooters, formed the entire U.S. shooting team. There was a great deal of confusion about the courses of fire and the guns required. Because of this, the Paine brothers brought along everything they could think of. Packed in their steamer trunks were several Colt Single Action Army revolvers, a Smith & Wesson 44 Russian revolver, several single shot 22-caliber target pistols, some smaller pistols, and 3500 rounds of ammunition.

The brothers arrived in Athens to find a strange Greek target, a small black bullseye with a huge white center, and an even stranger scoring system, which multiplied the score by the number of hits on the target. The range was not that for which any of their handguns had been sighted.

The Colt revolvers were accepted for the first event, the Military Revolver Match, and it was clear that the Paines far outclassed the other competitors. John won first place, and Sumner took second.

As the winner of the first day's shooting, John did not shoot in the next event, the Any Revolver match. Sumner used the Smith & Wesson 44 Russian and easily took first place.

The brothers would have been eligible to fire in the next match, but they had brought nothing that the officials would accept. Although the match was scheduled for "pistols of usual caliber," only 11mm muzzle-loading pistols were allowed. The Paines each had won a first place, so they just watched from then on. Having arrived in Greece with 3500 rounds of ammunition, they returned to America with 3404. So ended America's first participation in Olympic pistol competition—a strange mixture of competence and confusion.

Shooters from other countries had many of the same problems. The early Olympics permitted the host country to

Bullseye shooting appeals to young people. Here, the pistol competition winners of the 1992 Florida Junior Olympic Shooting Camp are congratulated by Col. Norman Redding, Commander of Camp Blanding, a Florida National Guard base. The winners: (from left) Ephraim "Flip" Caangay, Erin Lynch and Greg McDade.

select the shooting events. Officials would naturally schedule events familiar to the shooters of that country. The practice made it difficult to plan ahead. Shooters showed up confused about the courses of fire, the correct equipment and the local rules.

After World War II, international shooting was reorganized. Even though American shooting programs were well developed, our country had only one vote on the International Olympic Committee. Most of the shooting events are, therefore, those developed in Europe. The International Shooting Union, with headquarters in Germany, governs international shooting now.

Pistol events fired at the Olympics include Free Pistol and Rapid Fire Pistol. The courses are now standard, and anyone in the world may prepare for them.

The Free Pistol is "free" of most restrictions, but it must be a 22-caliber pistol with iron sights. Shooters fire sixty shots for record in 120 minutes. The bullseye target is placed at 50 meters, with a ten-ring that measures about 2 inches in diameter. This is a very difficult course, more so than the slow-fire stage of the National Match course. Only the finest single shot target pistols are used.

Rapid Fire Pistol is fired at 25 meters at a bank of five targets. Shooters fire five shots, one shot at each target, in successive courses of 8, 6 and 4 seconds, repeating until 60 record shots are fired. Targets are roughly man-size, with oval scoring rings centered above the target's midpoint. Pistols used are semi-automatics chambered for the 22 Short cartridge. The low recoil allows rapid movement from target to target.

Besides the Olympics, international pistol matches are held at the World Games, the Pan American Games and the Championships of the Americas.

Now, then, what are the opportunities for someone interested in handgun shooting? Let's see—we can go out and plink with friends on an informal basis. We can develop our skills and enjoy small game or big game hunting. Although we don't like to think of the need to use a handgun in self-defense, we should certainly practice with our handguns.

Competition? If we are very good, we can shoot in the Olympics or other international competitions. There are also State Games, Senior Games for older shooters and Junior Olympic programs for young shooters. Shooting events are held by shooting clubs, the Explorers, military units, veterans units, law enforcement units and a number of other organizations.

As for matches, there are local, postal, school, league, state, regional, and the National Matches.

If competition is not for you at this time, the NRA has a number of qualification courses available. You shoot against fixed scores for different awards. Check them out.

We can plink at things that break and bounce. We can hunt legal game. We can shoot at metal silhouettes of animals. We can shoot at a multitude of types of paper targets. In speed matches, we can also shoot at steel plates and bowling pins.

Whether you are an expert or a newcomer, I'll bet that there is an exciting handgun shooting sport that will interest you!

CHAPTER THIRTEEN

UNDERSTANDING THE MODERN SHOTGUN

MANY SETTLERS IN Colonial America relied on shotguns to provide both food and protection. Colonists were heavily dependent on Europe for both guns and gun parts, but by the early 1700s, an American influence on shotguns was beginning to be felt.

Americans preferred small bores in order to conserve hard-to-get powder and shot. Many of the shotguns made in America had the style of the Kentucky or Pennsylvania rifles. Indeed, some of the Kentuckys identified as rifles are actually small-bore shotguns.

Smoothbore muskets and European fowling pieces, although their large bores were wasteful of powder and lead, made very effective shotguns. Small shot could bag small game. For large game or protection against marauding Indians or Redcoats, large buckshot or a single round ball could be used. Often the combination of a round ball and three pellets of buckshot—buck and ball—was found to be very effective.

By the second decade of the 1800s, the percussion cap had been perfected and was making the flintlock obsolete. However, in America, percussion caps were difficult to obtain, but getting flint was easy. Flint only had to be found, picked up and shaped, so flintlocks were used in America well into the percussion era. For rifles, the "poof-bang" delay of the flintlock was still acceptable, but in wingshooting, the delayed ignition often meant missed birds. Perhaps as much as any other factor, shotgun use hastened the acceptance of the percussion system in America.

By the 1840s, Remington and other companies were making muzzle-loading shotguns of mostly single-barrel and some double-barrel types. Muzzleloaders were made long after the advent of breechloaders. By 1880, the double-barrel breechloader had become America's favorite shotgun. However, it was soon challenged by repeaters and, in the early 1900s, semi-automatic designs.

For most Americans, hunting put meat on the table, and the quick firing, multi-shot pumps and autoloaders eventually became the most popular guns in America.

The usual way of classifying shotguns is by action type. Let's define the action of a shotgun as that mechanism that allows the shooter to load, fire and unload the gun.

The three major parts of a muzzle-loading shotgun (or rifle) are the "lock, stock and barrel," which gave rise to that common expression, which means the entirety of anything.

In modern shotguns, the action takes the place of the lock.

137

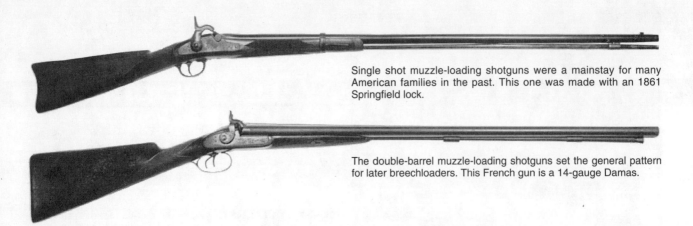

Single shot muzzle-loading shotguns were a mainstay for many American families in the past. This one was made with an 1861 Springfield lock.

The double-barrel muzzle-loading shotguns set the general pattern for later breechloaders. This French gun is a 14-gauge Damas.

The three primary components of a modern shotgun thus are action, stock and barrel. Shotguns are usually the same general size and shape as rifles, and you will notice many similarities in parts and functions of the actions.

Parts of a Shotgun

Let's go over all the basic parts of a shotgun. In most cases, the stock is the simplest part, so we'll consider that first.

The Stock

More stocks are made of synthetic materials now than in the past, but the traditional stock is still made of wood. We'll assume a wood stock, but the terminology is really the same.

Beginning at the rear, the *butt* is the end portion, generally flat or slightly curved, that fits against the shoulder. The top of the butt is the *heel*, and the bottom is the *toe*. The shooter's cheek rests on the *comb*. Continuing forward, the stock reaches its smallest point, the small, or more commonly, the *grip*. If the bottom and top lines are straight, and parallel to each other, it is a *straight grip*. If the bottom line curves down somewhat like the grip of a pistol, it is called a *pistol grip*.

Continuing forward, we come to the *forend* or *forearm*. In some cases, it is a continuation of the same piece of wood as the butt. In most cases, with shotguns, it is separate.

A number of different parts may be attached to the stock. A *buttplate* or a *recoil pad* generally covers the butt. A *grip cap* may be at the end of a gracefully curved pistol grip—perhaps for protection of the wood, perhaps for appearance. *Sling swivels* are sometimes installed on hunting guns; carrying the gun by a sling or carrying strap leaves the hands free for other things.

The Barrel

The barrel is the hollow steel tube through which the shot charge passes. The cartridge, called the shotgun shell or shotshell, is inserted into the *breech* or back end. On firing, the shot charge is propelled through the *bore*, the hole through the barrel, until it passes the *muzzle*, or front end, and goes on to the outside world.

Because the shot charge contains numerous projectiles and is pushed straight out the bore, the bore of a shotgun is smooth, without rifling. Can it be that simple? Of course not. In recent years, a number of shotguns have been offered with rifled bar-

To learn how a shotgun operates, you should understand its parts. Here, instructor Hank Sorensen explains the parts and functions of various shotguns to a group of attentive Boy Scouts.

ANATOMY OF A SHOTGUN

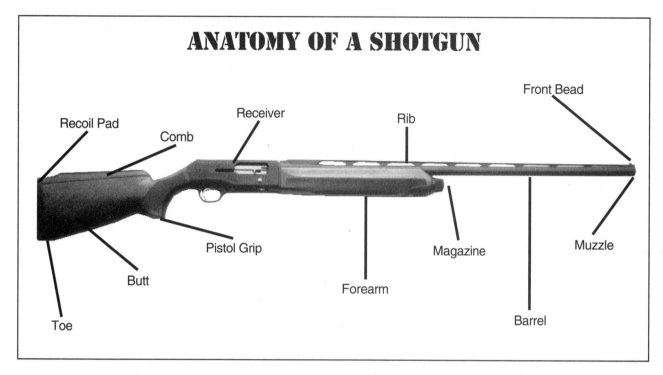

rels for use solely with slugs, which are single projectiles used for big game hunting. We'll discuss these special shotguns later, but for the purposes of demonstration, let us assume that all shotguns have smooth bores.

The Action

The action of a modern shotgun is the combination of moving parts that allow the shooter to load, fire and unload the gun. All shotguns have a *receiver*, a metal frame into which all the other parts are inserted or fastened. Common to all are a way to

open the action, insert a shell into the chamber, and close the action. When the gun is thus loaded, a trigger mechanism can release the hammer or striker, causing the firing pin to strike the primer of the cartridge.

In addition, some shotguns have a *magazine*, a device to store ammunition and allow cartridges to be fed into the chamber. Every shotgun has some sort of mechanical safety device. It should be used, if the design permits, whenever the gun is loaded or unloaded. Many repeaters also have an *action release* to allow opening the action when the shotgun is loaded and cocked.

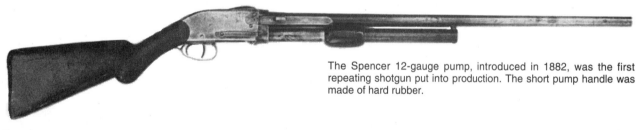

The Spencer 12-gauge pump, introduced in 1882, was the first repeating shotgun put into production. The short pump handle was made of hard rubber.

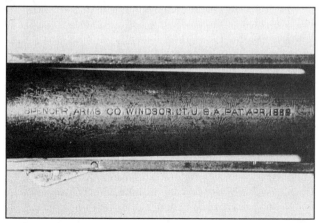

The barrel of the Spencer shotgun carries the earliest patent date of all repeating shotguns.

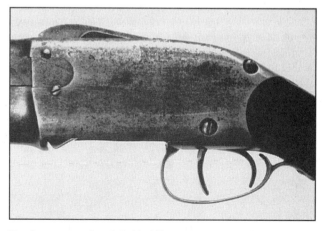

The Spencer receiver, left side. What appears to be a forward trigger is actually an upside-down hammer spur.

139

Shotgun Types

The actions of shotguns are the primary things generally used to classify them. We are going to consider modern shotguns by these four action types: slide action (pump); hinge action (single- and double-barrel types); semi-automatic; bolt action.

Slide Action

The actions of these guns are opened and closed by sliding or pumping the forend back and forth. The movement resembles the operation of an old-fashioned water pump in use in the late 1800s. The name "pump gun" has been commonly used since then. The term "trombone action" is also used to describe these guns. The rearward movement of the forend, or slide handle, unlocks the action and opens it, ejecting the fired cartridge case at the end of the stroke. The forward movement chambers a new cartridge and leaves the gun cocked, ready to fire.

The first successful pump shotgun was the Spencer of 1882. It was invented by Christopher Spencer, who had invented the Spencer repeating rifle used so effectively during the Civil War. Winchester followed in 1893 with a design by John M. Browning. An improved version in 1897 became the famous Winchester '97 pump gun. This one found great favor with hunters and was used by the U.S. Army during World War I.

The Winchester '97 trench guns, loaded with six buckshot rounds, proved so effective that the German high command issued a warning that any Americans caught with the guns would be summarily executed. The U.S. response was twofold: First, American leaders got off a blistering message to the Germans that they had better not try to carry out that threat; and second, they ordered more pump guns to be sent to the front.

Since then, slide-action shotguns have always been used by military forces. They proved especially effective in close-range jungle fighting in Vietnam.

But it is as a hunting gun that the slide-action shotgun has made its reputation. Throughout the world, the slide-action smoothbore is recognized as the American choice of hunting shotguns.

Slide-action shotguns have been made in large numbers by Winchester, Remington, Mossberg, Savage, Stevens, Ithaca, Marlin, High Standard, Noble, Harrington & Richardson, Smith & Wesson and others.

Mossberg, the largest maker of bolt-action shotguns, had never made a pump gun before 1955. The company used its experience in bolt-action manufacturing to create a new type of pump shotgun. The Mossberg Model 200 had a full-length wood stock and a box magazine. This gun, which was similar in appearance to their bolt-action shotguns, was soon replaced by the company's Model 500. The new Mossberg 500 was a more conventional-looking slide action which went on to become the country's best-selling pump gun.

I haven't kept count, but I'll bet most of the shotguns I've seen in the hunting field are pumps. No one hunting with a pump ever seems to feel he needs anything else. The action seems to begin opening when a shot is fired. Pushing the slide handle closed seems to automatically point the gun for its next shot.

They keep on working. In the rain, wind, dust, heat and cold, in any sort of bad conditions, pump guns, both old and new, keep satisfying their owners.

Some of the old-timers we've mentioned—the Spencer and Winchester Models '93 and '97—and some Marlin hammer guns are still seen shooting occassionally, but for the most part, the hammerless pump gun is the standard form.

A slide-action shotgun has a two-piece stock and forearm, and a tubular magazine below the barrel. It is hammerless (actually, they have concealed hammers inside the receiver) and has an action release that allows the action to be opened when the gun is cocked. A mechanical safety device prevents the trigger from being pulled when it is set to "safe." Such guns are loaded from the bottom of the receiver directly into the tubular magazine. The number of shells held in the magazine ranges from two to five.

Differences in operating the guns of different manufacturers lie mainly in the location of the safeties and action releases. Some may have a magazine release for easy unloading of the magazine. If possible, refer to the operating instruction manual that came with the gun. Most manufacturers will provide one at no charge.

The Winchester Model '97 was the first really successful repeater and stayed in production for sixty years. Here, the writer, somewhat younger and leaner, looks over the woods while carrying a 12-gauge '97, his favorite gun for many years.

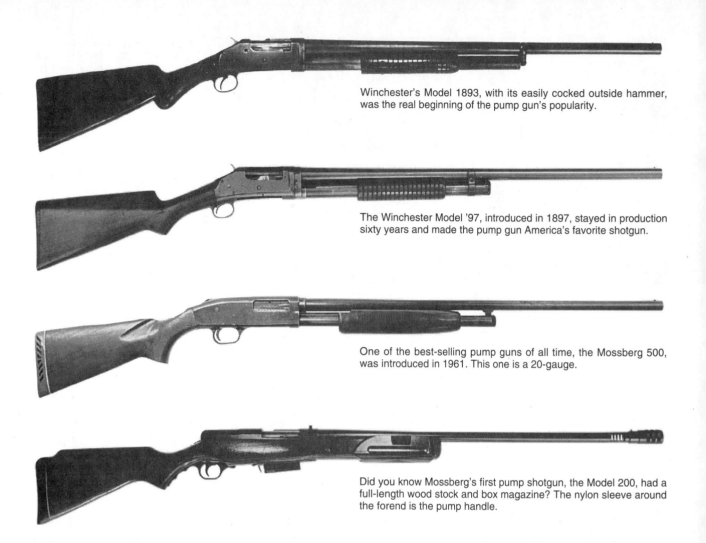

Winchester's Model 1893, with its easily cocked outside hammer, was the real beginning of the pump gun's popularity.

The Winchester Model '97, introduced in 1897, stayed in production sixty years and made the pump gun America's favorite shotgun.

One of the best-selling pump guns of all time, the Mossberg 500, was introduced in 1961. This one is a 20-gauge.

Did you know Mossberg's first pump shotgun, the Model 200, had a full-length wood stock and box magazine? The nylon sleeve around the forend is the pump handle.

SLIDE ACTION

To load:
1. Put the safety on.
2. Open the action by sliding the forend to the rear.
3. Drop one shell into the open port on the right side and close the action. The chamber is now loaded.
4. Insert additional shotshells into the loading port on the bottom and push them forward into the magazine.

To unload:
1. Put the safety on.
2. Depress the cartridge stop or activate the magazine release. Unload shells from magazine.
3. Press the action release and open the action, ejecting the shell from the chamber.
4. Visually inspect the chamber and magazine to be sure the gun is empty.

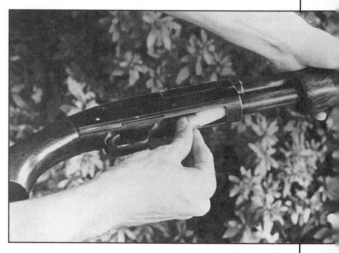

Loading the magazine of most pump guns is accomplished by pushing a cartridge forward into the magazine tube from the bottom loading port. This is a Mossberg Model 500.

Loading a side-by-side shotgun is accomplished by opening it and putting two shells into the chambers. The writer is loading a Stevens 311 in 20-gauge.

Not all hinge single shots are inexpensive utility guns. This trapshooter is using a special single-barrel trap gun.

Hinge Action

These shotguns date back to our earliest breech-loading shotguns. French gunsmith Lefaucheux brought out a double-barrel hinge-action shotgun for pinfire cartridges in 1836. For perspective, 1836 was the year the first cap-and-ball Colt revolver was patented.

The remarkable Lefaucheux shotgun was the ancestor of all modern double-barrel shotguns. Its pinfire cartridge was far ahead of its time and was the first self-contained shotshell. Not only did it have all the components modern shotshells have, but each cartridge also contained its own firing pin! The Lefaucheux hinge-action two-barrel gun was the general pattern used when muzzle-loading double shotguns were replaced by modern cartridge shotguns.

All hinge-action guns are constructed so the barrel or barrels pivot open on a hinge pin set several inches ahead of what is commonly called the standing breech or, more properly, the standing breechblock. When closed, the breech end of the barrels are locked against this fixed breechblock, which is a part of the frame of the gun.

In America, the end of the Civil War marked the beginning of the switch from muzzle-loading shotguns to breechloaders. The earliest were single shots.

This is not so strange. Hunters were used to single shot muzzle-loading shotguns, and although repeating rifles dominated rifle development, new developments in shotguns were slower coming. Sharps had already offered a single shot breech-loading shotgun, similar to the rifle design, before the war. Remington soon offered a rolling block action in single shot shotgun form in 1867.

By the early 1870s, Stevens had offered hinge-action break-open rifles, pistols and shotguns. The hinge-type shotgun caught on. Other makers saw the popularity of this type, and because such guns were ordinarily the least expensive types offered, the competition quickly became intense. Almost every firearms manufacturer offered a single shot hinge-type shotgun at one time or another. The variations in design and construction are staggering, yet most look and work pretty much the same.

Along with the low-priced single shots, a relatively few high-grade single shot hinge guns have been made for trap shooting. Most single shots, however, have been the low-priced utility guns. For over a century, such guns have stood ready behind farmhouse doors and have been used by innumerable young boys to bag their first game.

Currently, a full line of hinge-action single shot shotguns is

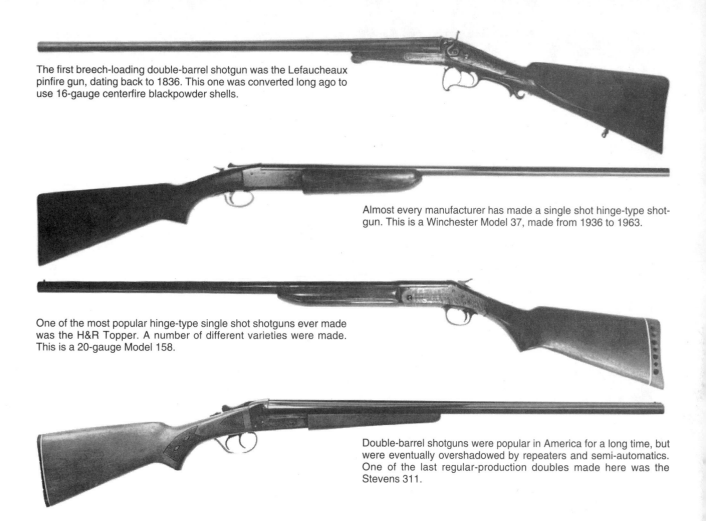

The first breech-loading double-barrel shotgun was the Lefaucheaux pinfire gun, dating back to 1836. This one was converted long ago to use 16-gauge centerfire blackpowder shells.

Almost every manufacturer has made a single shot hinge-type shotgun. This is a Winchester Model 37, made from 1936 to 1963.

One of the most popular hinge-type single shot shotguns ever made was the H&R Topper. A number of different varieties were made. This is a 20-gauge Model 158.

Double-barrel shotguns were popular in America for a long time, but were eventually overshadowed by repeaters and semi-automatics. One of the last regular-production doubles made here was the Stevens 311.

made in the United States and marketed by Harrington & Richardson and New England Firearms. A number of other brands are imported. They are generally considered good starter and utility guns.

By 1880, the double-barrel hinge-action shotgun was fast becoming the most popular type in the world. In America, this style dominated the scene well into the 20th century. A quick second shot and two different chokes were options that a single shot could not offer.

Great American gunmakers such as Parker, Remington, Baker, L.C. Smith, Ithaca, Lefever, Stevens, Fox, Savage and Winchester produced double-barrel hinge-action guns that were, in some cases, superb shotguns.

The doubles gradually gave way to the popularity of slide-action and semi-automatic guns. At the time of this writing, no regular-production side-by-side doubles are made in this country, although a number are imported.

Somewhat strangely, as the side-by-side double faded away from the American scene, another hinge-type two-barrel gun began to grow in popularity. This was the over/under, having one barrel mounted above the other.

The Browning Superposed over/under was designed by John M. Browning after World War I. Manufacture was to take place at the Fabrique Nationale (FN) plant in Belgium, and Browning went to Belgium in 1926 to be present when the first over/unders

came out of the plant. Unfortunately, the Superposed was his last design because he died in Belgium of a heart attack. In his seventy-one years, John Moses Browning had invented more different types of firearms than any other gun designer in history.

Other prewar over/unders soon followed. In America, we had the Remington Model 32 and Marlin Model 90. Then, production of most sporting guns was stopped during World War II. The Morrone gun was made after the war, but soon went out of production. Neither Remington nor Marlin resumed O/U production after the war.

Until the 1960s, the only over/under that had been on the American market continuously was the Belgian-made Browning. American shooters were now becoming quite enamored of such guns. In 1963, Winchester announced their Model 101, a Japanese-made over/under. Then in 1973, Remington introduced the Model 3200, which resembled their earlier Model 32.

Perhaps because the top barrel offers a single sighting plane similar to that of a repeater or automatic, American shooters adopted the over/under and lost interest in the side-by-side double. After all, they still had the fast second shot and two-choke option that had made the double the first choice for so long. Whatever the reason, over/under shotguns are imported in great numbers by many companies, and Ruger manufactures several versions here. They are widely used for both competition and hunting.

SINGLE SHOT HINGE ACTION

To load:

1. Operate the opening latch to pivot the barrel open.
2. Load a shell into the chamber.
3. Gently pivot the action closed until the barrel latches into place.

To unload:

1. Press the opening latch. The barrel will open and the ejector will eject the case or unfired shell. (In some designs, the shell will only be lifted from the chamber and must be removed by hand.)

Loading most hinge-type single shots is done by simply opening the gun and placing a shell into the chamber. This is a Harrington & Richardson 20-gauge.

DOUBLE-BARREL HINGE ACTION

Both side-by-side and over/under shotguns operate in the same general way.

To load:

1. Apply the safety.
2. Open the action by rotating the barrel latch to the side.
3. Load two shells into the chambers.
4. Gently close the action until it latches.

To unload:

1. Apply the safety.
2. Open the action by moving the barrel latch to the side.
3. Empty cases or unfired cartridges will be ejected or lifted from the chambers.

The over/under must swing open more than a side-by-side double, but loading is accomplished in the same way, by opening it and placing shells into the chambers.

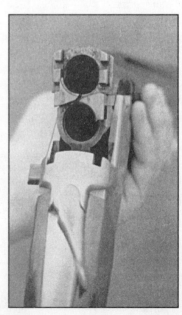

The hinge-type over/under shotgun has one barrel in line above the other.

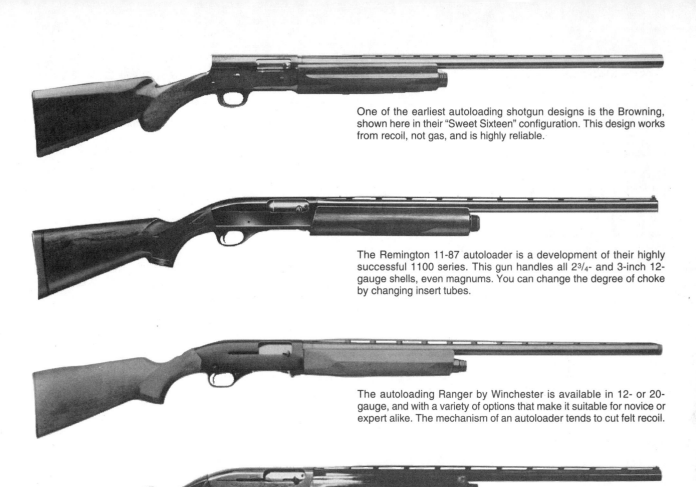

One of the earliest autoloading shotgun designs is the Browning, shown here in their "Sweet Sixteen" configuration. This design works from recoil, not gas, and is highly reliable.

The Remington 11-87 autoloader is a development of their highly successful 1100 series. This gun handles all 2³/₄- and 3-inch 12-gauge shells, even magnums. You can change the degree of choke by changing insert tubes.

The autoloading Ranger by Winchester is available in 12- or 20-gauge, and with a variety of options that make it suitable for novice or expert alike. The mechanism of an autoloader tends to cut felt recoil.

Semi-automatic shotguns are very popular in America today, and the Remington Model 1100 has been one of the most popular. This one is a 12-gauge with a ventilated rib barrel.

Semi-automatic shotguns have become very popular in recent decades. These Texas Skeet shooters are both using semi-autos—a Remington 1100 on the left and a Winchester 1300 on the right.

Semi-Automatic

Semi-automatic shotguns use the energy of one shot to get the gun ready for the next shot. This energy comes from either recoil or the gas generated by the shot just fired. Semi-automatic guns are sometimes called autoloaders or self-loaders, or, even more commonly, automatics.

Semi-automatic shotguns seem very modern, but have actually been around for quite some time. John M. Browning worked out the basic design for an autoloading shotgun at the end of the 1890s. By 1902, it was ready to be put into production. Unable to get a committment from Winchester—the company that had bought all his previous rifle and shotgun designs—Browning went to Belgium. The gun was produced there by the FN plant starting in 1904.

Soon, Remington and Savage made guns based on the Browning principles, and beginning in 1911, Winchester was forced to bring out competing models. After World War II, Americans were used to semi-automatic firearms, and the demand for the type increased. A number of new designs appeared, and huge numbers of modern gas-operated shotguns, primarily the Remington 1100, have been made and sold. It is interesting to note that the original Browning design, made as the Browning Auto 5, has remained in continuous production to this day.

A number of different semi-automatic shotguns have been made over the years, and you should obtain an operating manual for the one you plan to use. The location of safeties, bolt releases and magazine controls vary, but the general principles of operation are similar for many models.

Bolt Action

By the end of World War I, American soldiers had become used to the bolt-action rifle. When they returned home, they were interested in obtaining similar arms for hunting, and bolt-action rifles became very popular. Winchester, faced with wartime manufacturing capacity far beyond its peacetime needs, expanded into new products and new types of guns.

Two of Winchester's offerings were guns of a new type—single shot, bolt-action shotguns. The small, light guns were the Model 41, the company's first 410 shotgun, and the Model 36, a 9mm rimfire. The 9mm did not sell well in this country, but the little 410 became fairly popular and made Americans aware of the small bore shotgun.

The new Winchesters were not really the first bolt-action shotguns ever made. Obsolete military rifles had been converted to bolt-action shotguns in Europe before and after World War I. However, Winchester was the first company to actually manufacture bolt actions as new guns.

When America entered the Great Depression, inexpensive guns for hunting were in great demand. Mossberg and Stevens made bolt-action 410 repeaters in 1933. As time went by, 20-gauge versions were added. Then, production was suspended during World War II.

By the end of that war, large numbers of young men had experience with guns and shooting. They were glad to be done with war, but many of them wanted to continue shooting when they returned and became interested in hunting. A joke of the post-war period was that returning GIs were interested in two things—and the second one was hunting.

SEMI-AUTOMATIC

To load:
1. Apply the safety.
2. Open the action by pulling the cocking handle back until the bolt locks open.
3. Load the chamber by placing one shell inside the ejection port and then operate the bolt release, allowing the bolt to spring forward.
4. Load the magazine by inserting cartridges through the bottom port and pushing them forward into the magazine.

To unload:
1. Apply the safety.
2. Unload the magazine by pressing the release and removing the cartridges. Be aware that release mechanisms vary greatly among the different designs.
3. Open the action to eject the shell from the chamber.
4. Visually inspect the chamber and magazine to make sure the gun is empty.

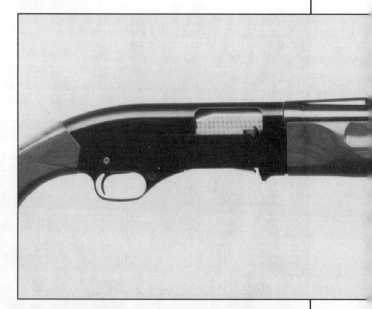

This is the action of a semi-automatic shotgun, closed. To open, pull back the cocking handle near the loading part.

In days gone by, a 410 was considered a good beginner's gun. We no longer think so, but when this photo was taken, Jo Ann Malloy, the writer's wife, was practicing with a Stevens bolt-action 410.

This unprecedented demand for hunting guns caused an increase of production for all types of firearms. However, guns that could be made quickly and cheaply were needed immediately, and bolt-action shotguns fit that description.

In the decades following World War II, bolt-action shotguns were made by Mossberg, Stevens, H&R, High Standard (first for Sears, Roebuck & Co., later under their own name) and Kessler. The Kessler bolt-actions might have earned the title of the least attractive shotgun ever made. One of them was my first shotgun. I still have a soft spot in my heart for the clumsy looking Kesslers.

During the 1970s and 1980s, labor costs and new manufacturing techniques combined to bring the prices of bolt-action and slide-action shotguns closer together. Few people chose bolt-action shotguns when they could have a pump gun for a few dollars more.

By 1986, all bolt-action shotguns had been discontinued except for the long-barreled Marlin Model 55 Goose Gun. It looked as if the bolt action would pass into shotgun history.

Then, with the development of sabot slugs in the early 1990s, people began taking a look at the potential accuracy of a bolt-action shotgun equipped with a rifled barrel.

At the time of this writing, two bolt-action shotguns, the Marlin 512 and the Tar-Hunt, are offered with rifled barrels for use with slugs. Two others, the Marlin Model 55 Goose Gun and a new Browning bolt action, have traditional smoothbore barrels.

It is difficult to predict the future of the bolt-action shotgun. However, one thing is certain: Huge quantities have been made, and many of the rugged guns are still in service. Therefore, it is worth understanding how they operate.

All bolt-action shotguns operate like bolt-action rifles, with an up-and-back, forward-and-down movement of the bolt to load cartridges for firing. There have been a number of mechanical variations, but the magazine arrangements have been the greatest differences. Although a number of different types have been made, two of them predominate: tube magazine (as offered by Harrington & Richardson, Sears and High Standard); and removable box (clip) magazine (as offered by Mossberg, Stevens, Marlin and Kessler).

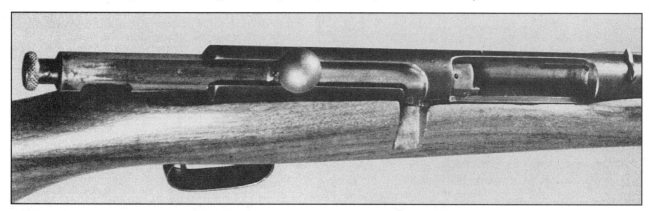

The Winchester Model 41 has a very simple action.

After WWI, a number of German 8mm Mauser rifles were converted into bolt-action shotguns.

Introduced in 1920, the Winchester Model 41 was Winchester's first 410 and America's first successful bolt-action shotgun.

Large quantities of J.C. Higgins bolt-action shotguns, made for Sears by High Standard, were sold after WWII. This Model 10 is a six-shot 12-gauge repeater.

By the late 1980s, all bolt actions had been discontinued except for the Marlin Model 55 Goose Gun. With its long 36-inch barrel and 3-inch chamber, it is a useful gun for a number of situations. On impulse, the writer used this gun for trapshooting and fired his highest score.

BOLT ACTION REPEATER WITH BOX MAGAZINE

To load:
1. Apply the safety.
2. Remove the box magazine and load two rounds into it.
3. Place one round in the chamber of the gun and close the bolt.
4. Insert the magazine. The gun is now loaded with three shots.

To unload:
1. Open the bolt to eject the shell from chamber.
2. Remove the magazine from the gun.
3. Inspect visually to be sure the gun is empty.

BOLT ACTION REPEATER WITH TUBE MAGAZINE

To load:
1. Apply the safety.
2. Open the bolt.
3. Insert cartridges through the port in the bottom of the stock and push them forward into the magazine.
4. Close the bolt, then open it again. A cartridge is now in the carrier, ready to chamber. With the bolt still open, one more round may be added to the magazine, if desired.
5. Close the bolt.

To unload:
1. Apply the safety.
2. Open and close the bolt to work shells through the action until the gun is empty.
3. Visually check the magazine and chamber to be sure the gun is empty.

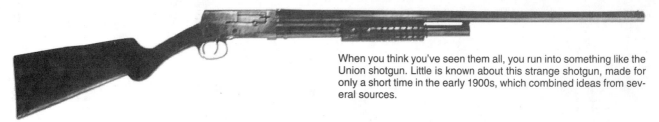

When you think you've seen them all, you run into something like the Union shotgun. Little is known about this strange shotgun, made for only a short time in the early 1900s, which combined ideas from several sources.

Not all shotgun stocks are conventional in shape. This lady's Remington 870 pump gun is fitted with a folding stock. Such stocks make compact units for traveling, but it is difficult to shoot flying targets with them.

Miscellaneous

Have we covered them all? If you have been reading right from the beginning of the book, you know it is never that simple. Some guns exist, it might seem, solely to defy whatever classification system we can set up.

Back in 1893, the same year Winchester introduced its Model 1893 pump gun, inventor Andrew Burgess designed a novel shotgun that operated by means of a pistol grip sliding backward and forward. Only a relatively small number were made. In 1899, Winchester bought the struggling company and discontinued the Burgess gun.

The Spencer had, of course, been the first slide-action shotgun, and it used an interesting vertically moving breechblock instead of the horizontal style of the later Winchester pumps. In the early 1900s, the Union Arms Company of Toledo, Ohio, brought out a pump shotgun with a strange action of both horizontally and vertically moving components. Only a few Union guns were made.

Also in the early 1900s, the Young shotgun was made in Columbus, Ohio. The action was the exact opposite of a traditional pump gun. To open the action, the shooter pumped the forearm (and barrel) forward, instead of backward. The gun was closed by pulling the forearm rearward. Very few of the nicely made Young guns were produced.

You probably won't see guns such as these when you're out shooting, but you should know they exist. Somewhere along the line, you will get into a discussion on shotgun types with your friends, and you don't really want to say that you know all the possible types. You can be sure that there is something out there that you never thought was possible.

We didn't mention lever-action shotguns in the general discussion because they haven't been made for many years, but quite a few have been made. Winchester made thousands of 12- and 10-gauge lever-actions as their Models 1887 and 1901. Marlin modified its lever-action rifle design in the early 1900s and marketed it as a 410-bore lever-action shotgun. In the 1950s, Kessler Arms Company of Silver Creek, New York, made a modern design of a short-stroke lever-action shotgun. The small company failed after three years.

The lever gun never really caught on as a shotgun action. Most specimens are now in collections, rather than in the field.

So, sooner or later, you are bound to see a gun that does not fit the categories we've discussed. There is not much point in spending a great deal of time on these oddballs, interesting as they are. The guns in common use today are here because they do their jobs well. They are the ones you should know how to handle.

CHAPTER FOURTEEN

SHOTGUN
AMMUNITION, CHOKES AND SIGHTS

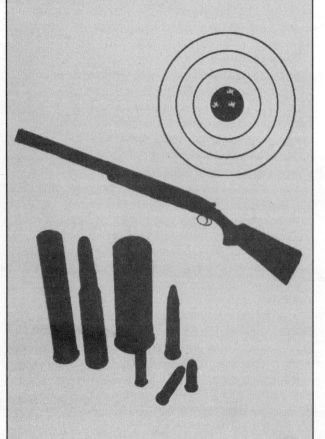

UNLIKE RIFLES AND handguns, which are designed to put a single projectile in a specific place, shotguns are designed to throw a pattern of shot pellets at relatively short range. Because the use of a shotgun is very much different from that of a rifle, we would expect the ammunition to be different, and it is.

We briefly touched on shotgun ammunition way back in Chapter 1, but let's spend just a little time on the subject now. As a quick review, remember that a modern shotgun cartridge, or shell, has five components: cartridge case; primer; powder; wad; shot.

The *cartridge case*, or shell, is the outer container into which all the other components are assembled. Today, it is typically made of plastic. In years past, most shotshells had cases of rolled paper. Such cases are still made, but only in limited quantities. The terminology of shotgun ammunition is a bit strange, because both the empty cartridge cases and the loaded cartridges are commonly called shells. The practice has been going on so long there seems no hope of changing it, so just be aware of this.

The *primer* contains a chemical compound that detonates on impact. The shotshell primer, often called a battery cup, is installed in the center of the flat base of the shell. When struck by the firing pin, the priming compound detonates to ignite the powder charge.

The *powder* is a chemical compound that burns rapidly when ignited to form a large volume of gas which pushes the other components out of the gun. Logically, the powder charge is placed just above the primer when the shell is loaded.

The *wad* sits between the powder and the shot, separating them and forming a seal. Today, most wads are made of moulded plastic. In days gone by, they were made of fiber. Several different thicknesses of fiber wads could be placed in the shell to adjust for different loads of powder and shot. Now, we adjust by using plastic wads specifically designed for specific loads.

The *shot* charge is in the front part of the shell and is composed of round pellets of shot. Shot is usually made of lead, but we also use steel or bismuth these days, because federal regulations require non-toxic shot for waterfowl hunting.

Shot is identified by a number. The smaller the number, the larger the shot; conversely, the larger the number the smaller the shot.

LEAD SHOT

1. TUBE
2. SHOT
3. WAD
4. POWDER

5. PRIMER
6. BASE WAD
7. HEAD
8. CUSHION
(lead only)

STEEL SHOT

Note that there is a progression in the shot sizes. If every number had been included (some are not made now), the sizes would all be .01-inch apart.

Want to impress your friends? If you know the shot number, subtract from seventeen and you will have the diameter in hundredths of an inch. If you know the diameter, subtract from seventeen and you will have the shot number.

In hunting, small shot is used for smaller game and large shot is used for larger game. We don't need a chart for this, but it stands to reason that small game can fit between the spaces in the shot pattern if the pellets are too far apart. We can leave fewer spaces by using a smaller size of shot. For a 1-ounce load, we have only 220 pellets of #6 shot. If we switch to #8 shot, we have 401 pellets in a 1-ounce load. Therefore, very generally, we choose shot of about #8 size for the small dove and quail, and #6 for rabbit and pheasant.

Why not just use small shot for everything? Well, you never get something for nothing. Small shot pellets lose velocity and energy much faster than large pellets, so for larger game you must use shot large enough so that it will retain its energy and give a clean, humane kill. For longer ranges, you also need shot large enough to retain its energy at the desired range.

The figures just discussed are for lead shot. The situation is somewhat different for steel, which is less dense than lead. Therefore, a pellet of steel shot will lose energy much faster than a lead one of the same size. The only way we can provide equal energy when using steel shot is to use shot of much greater diameter, but larger shot diameter means fewer pellets fit into the shell. Because of these conditions, steel shot is believed by many to cause more duck deaths by crippling than

Modern shotguns of recent manufacture, like this Remington 11-87, are safe for steel shot loads, but older guns might not be suitable for use with steel.

LEAD SHOT SPECIFICATIONS

Size	#9	#8	#7½	#6	#5	#4	#2	BB
Diameter (in.)	.080	.090	.095	.110	.120	.130	.150	.180
Wt. (grs.)	0.77	1.09	1.28	1.99	2.57	3.37	5.03	8.75
Charge Wt. (oz.)				Pellet Count				
½	284	200	170	110	85	65	43	25
11/16	390	275	234	151	116	89	59	34
¾	426	300	255	165	126	97	65	37
7/8	497	350	298	192	148	113	76	43
1	568	401	341	220	170	130	87	50
1⅛	639	451	383	247	191	146	97	56
1¼	710	501	426	275	212	162	108	62
1⅜	781	551	468	302	233	178	119	68
1½	853	601	511	330	255	195	130	75
1⅝	923	651	554	357	276	211	141	81
1⅞	1065	751	639	412	318	243	163	93
2	1136	802	682	440	340	260	174	100
2¼	1278	902	767	495	382	292	195	112

Assumes 0.5 percent antimony content. Harder shot will be less dense, and hence weigh less, but will have more pellets in a given charge weight. Softer pellets would weigh more and have fewer pellets per given charge weight.

LEAD VS. STEEL

	Lead Pellet			Steel Pellet	
Size	# Per Oz.	Wgt. Grs.	Size	# Per Oz.	Wgt. Grs.
BBB	42	10.4	F (TTT)	39	11.0
BB	50	8.8	TT	46	9.6
			T	52	8.3
B	60	7.3	BBB	62	7.1
1	72	6.1	BB	72	6.1
2	87	5.0	B	87	5.0
3	106	4.1	1	103	4.3
4	130	3.2	2	125	3.5
5	170	2.6	3	154	2.9
			4	192	2.3
6	220	1.9	5	243	1.8
7½	341	1.3	6	317	1.4
8	401	1.1			
9	568	0.8			

might be saved from lead poisoning. The possibility of waterfowl deaths caused by ingesting lead pellets was the reason given for requiring the use of steel shot. Steel shot for waterfowl is the law of the land, and manufacturers have addressed its poor ballistic features with ammunition that holds more steel shot. We'll touch on this shortly, in our discussion of gauges.

Buckshot is simply bigger spherical shot for bigger game, including deer. In some places, it is widely used for this purpose. It is also commonly used in shotguns for law enforcement and defense purposes.

STANDARD BUCKSHOT SIZES

U.S. Buckshot	Dia. (in.)	No. Pellets per lb.
000	0.36	98
00	0.33	115
0	0.32	140
1 Buck	0.30	173
2 Buck	0.27	232
3 Buck	0.25	284
4 Buck	0.24	344
FF	0.23	400
F	0.22	464
TT	0.21	560
T	0.20	672

Now, back to the cartridge we put together just a while ago. The cartridge is loaded in your gun and you are ready to shoot. Your finger presses the trigger. The firing mechanism is released, and the firing pin strikes the primer. The primer detonates, ignites the powder and the powder burns, forming expanding gas.

The gas pushes the wad and shot through the barrel and out the muzzle. The light plastic wad catches the air and drops behind, while the shot continues on its way to the target.

Gauge

Shotguns and their appropriate ammunition are distinguished by *gauge*. Today, 12- and 20-gauge shotguns are the most popular, but 10-, 16- and 28-gauge are also used. There is also a 410, but that is designated by its bore diameter and is not really a gauge. If it were given a gauge designation, it would be about 67.

"Gauge" is simply an old term for the number of round balls of that bore size that could be made from a pound of lead. Thus, the smaller the gauge *number*, the larger the bore size.

410-Bore

The little 410 is really a 41-caliber. In times past, the 410 was thought to be an ideal beginner's gun because it didn't kick much. However, beginners get discouraged very fast if they don't hit anything, and the 410 doesn't throw much shot. It is a useful size, because the guns are generally light and the shells are easy to carry. But the occasions for a 410 are limited. For sitting game, such as early-season squirrels in the leafy treetops, a 410 can be justified.

It can also be used for wingshooting, but the results are disappointing to most hunters. My only real wingshooting triumph with a 410 was on a Texas dove hunt. My companion used a 12-gauge semi-automatic and I used a bolt-action 410, because that was all I had along. There was nothing to concentrate the birds in that spot, and they were all just passing through. He missed all his doves, but I got one.

The 410 is a standard bore for Skeet shooting. It is fascinating to watch good shooters shoot a round of Skeet with the little guns. You begin to wonder, how do they do it?

Ammunition for the 410 is made in 2½- and 3-inch lengths. The 3-inch shells are all high-velocity loads with $^{11}/_{16}$-ounce of shot, with sizes from #9 to #4. The 2½-inch loads can be target or hunting loads, both with ½-ounce of shot. A $^1/_5$-

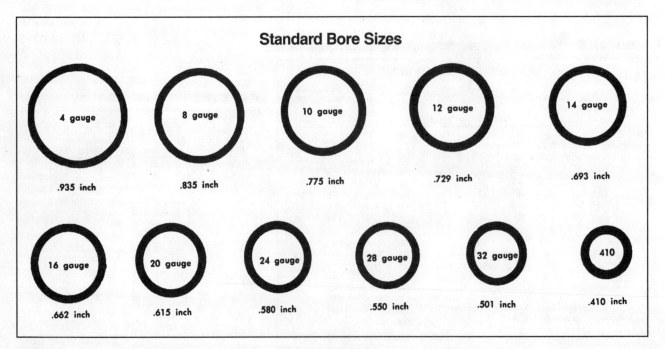

Standard Bore Sizes

4 gauge .935 inch
8 gauge .835 inch
10 gauge .775 inch
12 gauge .729 inch
14 gauge .693 inch
16 gauge .662 inch
20 gauge .615 inch
24 gauge .580 inch
28 gauge .550 inch
32 gauge .501 inch
410 .410 inch

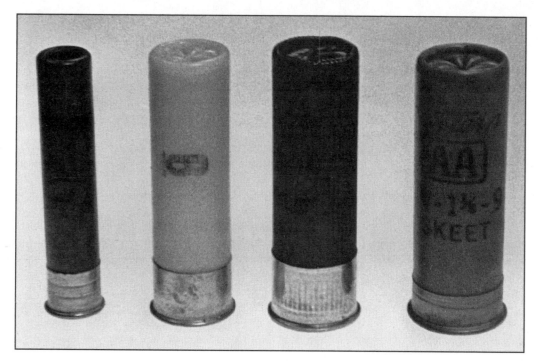

The most common shotgun ammunition sizes generally encountered in the field are (from left) 410-bore, 20-, 16- and 12-gauge. The 28-gauge is used primarily for Skeet, and the 10-gauge is often the choice for long-range waterfowl hunting.

ounce slug load is also available. This is only about 88 grains of lead, so it isn't recommended for anything but small to medium game.

28-Gauge

Stepping up from the 410 is the cute little 28-gauge, which is also a standard gauge for four-gun Skeet shooting. It is a useful size for close shots on small game, such as quail rising in front of dogs. In most quail hunting endeavors, a hunter walks miles carrying a gun for just a few shots. On a recent quail hunt, I watched a friend effortlessly carry his little over/under, and I had to agree that a lightweight 28 does indeed have a place in the world.

However, it is not really a popular size, and shells may be hard to locate. From a dealer's point of view, these shells may be slow selling. A friend of mine said his family was the only one in his area that hunted regularly during World War II, because they had a 28-gauge. The ammunition companies switched to wartime production, and no new shotshells were available. Local stores quickly sold out their prewar stock, all except their 28-gauge shells. No one else nearby had a 28, so my friend was able to get shells for hunting throughout the war.

Today's 28-gauge shells are all 2¾ inches and are loaded with ¾- to 1-ounce of shot.

20-Gauge

During the 1960s, the 20-gauge took the lead over the 16-gauge in popularity. Some said that with 3-inch Magnum 20-gauge shells available, there was really no longer a need for the 16. I don't know if that was the reason, but there is no denying the popularity of the 20. It, too, is a standard gauge for four-gun Skeet. Most 20s are probably taken hunting. The 2¾- and 3-inch loads are offered in a variety second only to that for the 12-gauge. Loads from ¾-ounce to 1¼ ounces of shot are available.

The 20 is the smallest gauge in which steel shot is factory loaded. Steel shot, lead shot, buckshot, rifled slugs, sabot slugs, target loads, high-velocity loads—everything is available for a 20-gauge shotgun. It is probably safe to say that the 20-gauge will be around for a long time.

16-Gauge

The 16-gauge has always puzzled me. My first shotgun, a bolt-action Kessler, was a 16, and it did everything I needed a shotgun to do for years. Even back then, though, the 16 played second fiddle to the 12-gauge. It always seemed to me that the 16-gauge guns would be the first choice of countries that were on the pound/ounce system. However, the 16 has its greatest popularity in Europe, which has been on the metric system for centuries.

At any rate, the 16 began to fade away in America some decades back. As the demand decreased, costs of manufacture went up. By dropping the 16, gun makers were able to make just two frames, 12 and 20, and dispense with the in-between size that wasn't selling so well. Today, as far as I know, no American manufacturer makes a 16, although some imported doubles offer that option.

Strangely, I see more 16-gauge shells on the dealers' shelves lately. Even steel shot loads, too. Steel shot was another thing that helped put the 16 to pasture. When lead shot was banned

PRACTICAL HUNTING BALLISTICS FOR LEAD SHOT

Shot Size	Maximum Charge Wgt. (oz.)	Normal Velocity (fps)	Maximum Range (yds.)
BB	1½	1260	60
#2	1⅜	1260	55
#4	1¼	1330	50
#6	1⅛	1165	45
#7½	1	1165	40
#9	⅞	1135	35

and steel shot became the law for all waterfowl hunting, steel was not loaded in 16-gauge shells. This meant that a hunter with only a 16 was barred from duck hunting. A friend of mine was in that position. He had hunted all his life with one shotgun, a Winchester Model 12 in 16-gauge, bought brand-new back in the 1930s. He gave up duck hunting. If he is still interested, 16-gauge steel loads are now available.

Apparently, some people have pulled their old 16s out of the closet, and I'm glad. It is a nice in-between size when you would like more than a 20 but don't need a 12.

Rifled slugs and buckshot are now also available in 16-gauge. Loads between $7/8$-ounce and $1^1/4$ ounces are offered, in shot sizes from #8 to #2. That's not as wide a selection as for the 12 or 20, but not bad.

I don't use a 16 as much as I have in the past, and I now load my own ammunition for this gauge. However, I still buy a couple of boxes of 16s now and then. I want the manufacturers to think somebody is still interested.

12-Gauge

The 12-gauge is the undisputed king of the hill of American shotgunning. It is the first choice for hunting, Skeet, trap, Sporting Clays, law enforcement and home defense. It seems it was always that way.

America's first repeating shotgun, the Spencer pump gun, was available in 12-gauge only. So was the first Winchester slide action, the Model 1893. Its successor, the famous Winchester '97, was available only in 12-gauge for many years, and then the 16 was added. With that sort of a start, it is small wonder that the 12-gauge has been considered the American standard.

Ammunition for the 12? What a variety!

Today, we can get $2^3/4$-, 3- and $3^1/2$-inch shells in 12-gauge. There are more different loads available for the 12 than all the other gauges combined. Lead shot, steel shot, rifled slugs, sabot slugs, buckshot, target loads, mid-velocity loads, high-velocity loads, magnum loads—all are available. Shot loads weighing from 1 ounce (the old standard 16-gauge load) to 2 ounces (the old 10-gauge magnum load) are available.

Needless to say, if you do all your shotgunning with one gun, the greatest choice of loads, and therefore the greatest versatility, is with the 12-gauge.

10-Gauge

The 10-gauge was standard back in the blackpowder days. When smokeless powder arrived, the 10 seemed always to be around, but hardly anybody knew shooters who actually used one. Today the 10-gauge seems to be making a comeback.

Steel shot loses its energy much more rapidly than lead shot. Some waterfowling situations that were well handled by heavy duck loads of lead shot only crippled ducks with steel shot. In order to approach the effectiveness of lead, bigger shot sizes and bigger volumes of steel shot were needed.

The answer to this dilemma has come in two ways—the introduction of the $3^1/2$-inch magnum 12-gauge, and renewed interest in the 10-gauge. Both provide greater volume for large loads of large-diameter steel shot.

Ten-gauge guns are mostly used for waterfowl hunting. This is probably just as well, for heavy clothing worn by most duck and goose hunters helps absorb recoil. The 10-gauge can kick. I'll have to admit, though, that my experience may have colored my outlook a bit.

The first 10-gauge shotgun I ever fired was on a duck hunt in Louisiana long before the steel shot days. My hunting companion, B.A. Bordelon, had just bought a used Spanish 10-gauge double. He had never fired it, but everything seemed to check out all right, so he brought it along "to shoot cripples."

We made a blind around his flatboat and used my pirogue to retrieve downed birds. He shot a duck and went out in the little boat. While he was still out picking up his bird, another flitted over the decoys on my side, and I downed it.

SUGGESTED GUN/LOAD COMBO FOR HUNTING

Game	Gauge	Shot size	Choke
Ducks	10, 12,16, 20	BB, 2, 4 ,5, 6 (steel)	Full to Mod.
Crows	10, 12,16, 20	2, 4, 5, 6	Full
Geese	10 or 12	BB, 2, 4, 5 (steel)	Full
Pheasant	12, 16 or 20	5, 6, $7^1/2$	Full to Mod.
Partridge or Grouse	12, 16 or 20	6, $7^1/2$, 8	Mod. to Imp. Cyl.
Quail	12, 16, 20, 28 or 410	6, $7^1/2$, 8, 9	Mod. to Imp. Cyl.
Doves/pigeons	12, 16, 20, 28 or 410	6, $7^1/2$, 8	Mod.
Woodcock	12, 16, 20, 28 or 410	6, $7^1/2$, 8	Mod. to Imp. Cyl.
Rabbits	12, 16, 20, 28 or 410	4, 5, 6, $7^1/2$	Full to Imp. Cyl.
Squirrels	12, 16, 20, 28 or 410	4, 5, 6	Full to Imp. Cyl.
Rail	12, 16, 20, 28 or 410	$7^1/2$, 8, 9	Mod. to Imp. Cyl.
Turkeys	12, 16 or 20 3" mag.	BB, 2, 4, 5	Full
Fox	12, 16 or 20	BB, 2 buck	Full
Coyotes	12, 16 or 20 3" mag.	3 or 4 buck	Full
Deer or black bear	12 or 16	Rifled Slug	Cyl.

Large size steel shot—like BB, #2, #4, #5 or #6—should be used when hunting ducks.

But it wasn't dead. It got its head up and slowly began swimming off. "Use the 10-gauge!" Bordelon called from the decoys. I picked up the big double, slid two of the big 3½-inch shells into the chambers, walked to the end of the flatboat, put the bead on the duck and pressed the rear trigger.

Wham! I had never been kicked so hard in my life! I found myself hopping and dancing backward, trying to stay upright and not fall over anything. I regained my balance just short of going into the water at the other end of the boat.

I looked back at the duck, and could hardly believe my eyes. The water had been churned into a froth, but the duck's head was still up.

I staggered back, leaned way forward, braced myself, put the bead back on the duck and pressed the front trigger.

Nothing happened.

Slowly the truth dawned, and I confirmed it by opening the gun. Both shells had gone off! I had just fired two 10-gauge magnum shells—4 ounces of lead—simultaneously!

My friend gave me his perspective. He had been watching, wondering how shooting the big gun would be. "I was really impressed when the gun jolted you back the entire length of the boat," he said. "But what impressed me *most* was seeing you reach for that other trigger!"

We learned later that the sear for the front trigger was worn. Pressing the front trigger first, everything worked OK. However, pressing them back trigger first, as I had, jarred the bad sear loose and both barrels went off together.

At any rate, call it psychological or what, I've never really been comfortable with a 10-gauge since. By the way, I eventually *did* get the duck.

The 10-gauge ammunition available today reflects the serious use of the big guns. No small shot, no target loads are available just heavy loads of large shot, either steel or lead, and buckshot and slugs. The maximum lead load has been stepped up from 2 to 2¼ ounces of shot. The rifled slug weighs a full 1¾ ounces. That's 765 grains of lead!

Choke

Most shotguns have a slight constriction near the muzzle, called choke. The bore reduction may be less than .010- to over .030-inch. The purpose of choke is to control the pattern of the shot. Think of it this way: If the inside of the shotgun barrel were a true cylinder, the diameter of the shot load upon leaving the muzzle would be the same as the diameter of the bore. Because of sideways movement of the individual pellets, the diameter of the pattern would increase as it moved forward. The pellets would move in random fashion, some going toward the center, some moving out. However, because the center is filled with other pellets, movement tends to be out.

The result would be a fairly rapid enlargement of the shot pattern. Let us think of shooting at a 30-inch circle at 40 yards. Starting from the muzzle, which is less than an inch in diameter, the shot would spread to the point where only about 25-35 percent of the pellets would be inside the 30-inch circle.

Now, think of that same barrel with a constriction or choke near the muzzle. As the shot load passes through this constriction, its inertia changes. The pellets, instead of just moving forward, are forced to move inward as well. In a split second, they are past the choke, but what a difference!

Instead of immediate random movement of the pellets, they now have a movement toward the center, which tends to hold the shot load together. Soon this inertia wears off, and the pellets begin to spread, of course.

The effect of the choke is to hold the shot together longer. Our 30-inch circle at 40 yards might now contain 65-75 percent of the pellets. The greater the degree of constriction, the tighter the choke, and the greater the range at which the gun will throw a dense pattern.

There is another, perhaps a simpler, way of thinking about choke. Assume that an optimum pattern of shot for any of our shooting will have all the pellets inside a 42-inch circle. Then, with an Improved Cylinder gun, this optimum pattern will

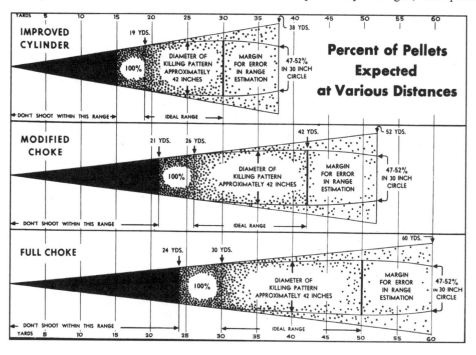

155

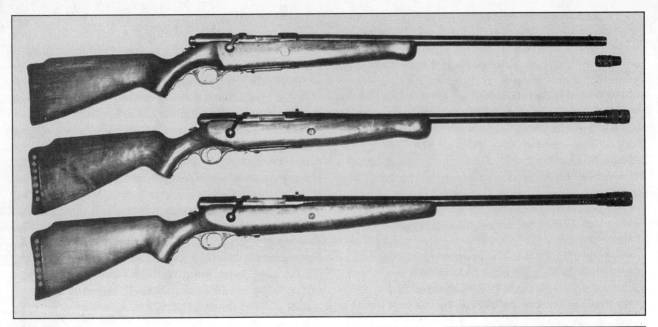

Three Mossberg bolt-action shotguns with factory choke devices. The upper is a Model 185-D with an external choke tube (shown detached.) The lower two are variants of the Model 185-K with adjustable chokes.

CHOKE VS. PATTERN	
Choke	% of Pellets
Cylinder (no choke)	25-35
Improved Cylinder	35-45
Modified	45-55
Improved Modified	55-65
Full	65-75

In 30-inch circle at 40 yards

(Above) With an adjustable choke device, simply turn the outside collet to the desired setting.

(Right) Under the collet, steel "fingers" squeeze inward, providing the choke constriction.

(Left) External choke tubes are simply screwed onto a threaded muzzle. This is the earliest type of choke device, dating back to the 1860s, and is no longer made.

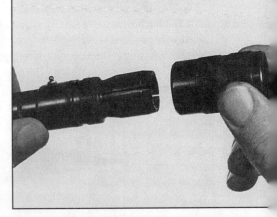

(Left) Internal choke tubes screw into threads inside the muzzle. It requires more complex machining, but does not change the profile of the barrel. Special wrenches are used to switch tubes.

(Right) The Poly-Choke was one of the first adjustable choke devices, allowing different chokes by turning the outside collet. This one has slots at the muzzle to reduce recoil.

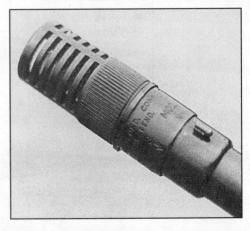

occur at about 25 yards from the muzzle. With a Modified choke, it will be a little farther out, about 35 yards; and with a Full choke, about 45 yards.

Either one of these methods of looking at choke gives us an idea of what to expect. If quail are exploding up in front of us about twenty yards away, we don't want a tight choke; we probably don't want any choke tighter than Improved Cylinder. If ducks are decoying cooperatively, dropping in at 30-35 yards, a Modified choke will do just fine. Uncooperative ducks that pass by at 45-50 yards may call for a Full choke.

Note that the power of a single pellet is unchanged by the degree of choke through which it passed. Our purpose in selecting the proper choke is to put those pellets into the correct density of pattern for the shooting we are doing. But, the pellet size must be selected to give adequate power at the range it contacts the target.

Simple, isn't it? Just remember what we discussed about shot sizes, too. Longer ranges require larger pellets in order to

USEFUL CHOKE RANGES

Choke	Ideal Range (yds.)	Useful Range (yds.)
Cylinder (no choke)	15 to 20	10 to 27
Skeet (Also called Skeet #1)	20 to 27	15 to 32
Improved Cylinder	25 to 32	20 to 37
Skeet #2	30 to 37	25 to 42
Modified	35 to 42	30 to 47
Improved Modified	40 to 47	35 to 52
Full	45 to 52	40 to 57
Extra Full	50 to 57	45 to 62

maintain sufficient downrange energy for game shooting. Also, larger pellets require heavier shot loads to maintain sufficient pattern density. When everything is right, the choke, shot size and charge weight all work together to give us the results we want.

There are, of course, other factors to be considered. Older guns, made before plastic wads came into use, generally shoot modern ammo tighter than the choke marked on them. This is because the plastic cup holds the shot together for a short time, adding to the effect of the choke.

New guns take this into account, and the amount of choke constriction is ordinarily a bit less than in days past. However, you should be aware that many guns, old and new, do not shoot the pattern marked on the barrel. Patterning the gun will prove to be one of the most useful and informative things a shotgun shooter can do.

Even knowing all about choke, most people can't just carry several different guns, with different chokes for various ranges, every time they go hunting. It has been said that if you want one gun for all kinds of shooting, the best one is a 12-gauge with a Modified choke. If a person only wants one gun at the lowest possible price, this is probably still good advice.

Obviously, there are other ways of looking at the problem. One solution is to use a different gun for every type of shooting. Another is to change chokes.

Choke Devices

The whole history of shotgun chokes and choke devices is a bit cloudy. Choke boring for shotguns may well have been discovered, forgotten and rediscovered several times. The first patent for a choke device was granted to American inventor Sylvester Roper, who later worked with Christopher Spencer in the development of the Spencer pump shotgun. Roper's patent was granted on April 10, 1866, thus edging out a British patent to a man named Pape by about six weeks.

The Roper choke device consisted simply of having the muzzle of the gun threaded on the outside, so a collar with a tapered constriction could be screwed onto it. This system was used later by Mossberg with great success.

Despite the development, little was published about choke until the 1870s.

Old-time Illinois market hunter Fred Kimble probably was the person who brought the advantages of choke to public attention. In the early 1870s he developed, mostly by trial-and-error, a 6-gauge muzzleloader that would shoot extremely tight patterns at long range. By the mid-1870s, W.W. Greener, the English gunmaker, was offering choke-bored shotguns on a regular basis.

The options for a choked shotgun are these:

1. A *fixed choke* in a shotgun with a single barrel. For many situations, such as Skeet, trap and many types of hunting, this is perfectly satisfactory for a great many shooters.

2. A double with *two chokes*, a different one in each barrel. This has proven to be a very popular solution when shots may be required at different ranges. It applies to both side-by-side and over/under guns.

3. *External choke tubes*. Like Roper's original choke attachment, these screw on the outside of the barrel. Different tubes can offer different degrees of choke. Mossberg shotguns of the post-World War II period offered such interchangeable chokes. The Cutts Compensator tubes, although they screw into the compensator body, can be considered of this type.

4. *Adjustable chokes* may be installed on single-barrel guns. Turning the choke's outer collar offers different degrees of constriction by squeezing steel "fingers" together inside the collar. The Poly-Choke is perhaps the best-known example of this type. They are easily adjusted and perhaps the most useful of all choke devices, but some shooters do not like the extra bulk at the end of the muzzle.

5. *Internal choke tubes* fit inside the muzzle of the gun. Although much more expensive, they have two features that make many shooters favor them over external tubes: they do not change the profile of the gun (important to many people), and they may be used in double barrel guns. Most over/under guns used for Sporting Clays competition are fitted with internal tubes in both barrels. They are the slowest way to change choke, but this is of no consequence in competition.

Shotgun Sights

Shotguns are usually pointed, not aimed, so the sights on shotguns are different from those on rifles.

The standard sighting arrangement for a shotgun is a simple bead near the muzzle. That is almost the whole story. The shot-

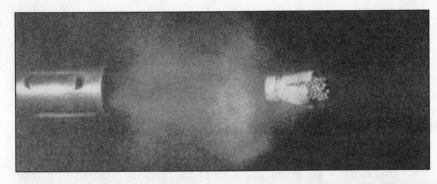

(Left) Upon leaving the muzzle, the wad helps contain the shot charge, promoting a tighter pattern. (Below) Eventually, the wad meets air resistance and falls away from the shot charge, which slowly begins to disperse.

gun shooter looks at the target, not at the sights. The bead is just a reference point to keep the gun aligned between the eye and the target.

Ah, keeping the gun aligned! The face must be properly placed on the stock, various body parts must be in their correct positions and the eye must be looking straight down the barrel. All this must be uniform, every time, shot after shot. Consisten-cy is not easy for most shooters. Therefore, many guns have sighting aids other than just a simple bead. All these things must serve the purpose of aiding alignment without taking the shooter's attention away from the target.

Ribs, sometimes ventilated, sometimes solid, may be mounted atop the barrel. A second small bead is sometimes placed on a rib about midway down the barrel, improving sight alignment.

PATTERNING A SHOTGUN

The following steps show hunters how to pattern their shotguns.

- Select an area that provides a safe backdrop.
- Set up patterning paper at least 40 inches square and mark an aiming point near the center of the paper.
- Select the shotgun/load combination to be tested and measure the distance from the patterning paper that approximates the typical range the load will be used at while hunting.
- Wear a good set of shooting glasses and hearing protectors.
- Shoot at least five test patterns, each on a separate pattern sheet.
- Outline a 30-inch circle around the densest portion of the pattern and count the "hits."

The number of shot holes in a 30-inch circle will give you pattern density. This is an important factor in making clean kills. Minimum densities differ with the size of the game and shot size.

You'll never know the potential of your specific gun/load unless you pattern.

The shooter should see the front bead sitting atop the middle bead, roughly forming a figure-eight pattern.

Some beads are bright red, orange or other colors, to catch the eye. Others are designed in an elongated fashion so they look noticeably different if the face is out of position.

If a certain type of sight works for you, then use it. If one type of sight system were obviously better than all others, everyone would use it. Some people seem to use some types better than others.

To find out how yours suits you, nothing beats patterning your shotgun. You probably want to do this anyway to check your choke, if nothing else. Some ranges have patterning boards for shotguns. If not, blank newsprint paper or wide butcher paper can be hung on a simple frame. Mark a black aiming spot about the size of a clay pigeon and shoot at it. Is your pattern perfectly centered? High? Low? If the pattern is not centered, is it the gun's fault or yours? Try it again, paying attention to align the gun properly between your eye and the target. Some sights or choke devices will make the gun shoot high or low, so be aware of this. Patterning your gun is a simple procedure that will let you learn a lot about your gun—and about yourself.

The Shotgun as a Rifle

Shotgun sights take on new meaning when we use a shotgun as a rifle. In some areas, only shotguns are allowed for hunting deer and other large game. This means using either buckshot or slugs. Buckshot use is similar to using any shot; the gun is pointed rather than aimed. However, slug use takes the shotgun into another world. A single projectile, the shotgun slug requires precision placement. Sights, then, must be similar to rifle sights.

Slugs may be of several types, but only two are in common use in this country—the rifled slug and the saboted slug.

Although a type of rifled slug had been used in Germany before 1900, the common rifled slug—known in this country as the Foster slug—was introduced by Winchester in 1936. Rifled slugs are cup-shaped projectiles with a deep hollow base and with ridges and grooves on the outer surface. This "rifling" probably contributes only a little to stability in flight. The greatest stability of a rifled slug comes because the nose end is heavier than the hollow back end, so it flies nose forward.

Such slugs are used in smoothbore shotguns and may have an effective range of about 75 yards. Because the slug is of soft lead, it can be safely fired through any degree of choke. The slug simply squeezes down while passing through a tight choke. Best accuracy, however, has been reported with guns that are choked either Cylinder or Improved Cylinder.

Rifled slugs are made for 20-gauge ($5/8$- or $3/4$-ounce), 16-gauge ($4/5$-ounce), 12-gauge (1 or $11/4$ ounces) and 10-gauge ($13/4$ ounces). A 410 rifled slug is also available, but weighs only $1/5$-ounce, and is only recommended for smaller game.

Saboted slugs are contained in a sabot, or carrier, of another material, generally plastic. Only the sabot touches the bore, so the slug itself can be smaller in diameter and made of harder material, such as solid copper. When the saboted slug leaves the

Rifled slugs come in many varieties. The shooter should try several to obtain the best possible accuracy in a specific shotgun.

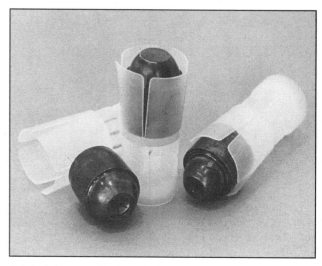

Saboted slugs are shot through rifled barrels. The sabot engages the rifling, then drops away after leaving the muzzle.

muzzle, the light sabot meets air resistance and falls behind, while the slug continues on its way alone.

Because these slugs are like rifle bullets, they must be spun in order to be stable. They are best shot from special rifled shotgun barrels. However, rifled choke tubes are available to spin the slugs as they near the muzzle. Saboted slugs may be considered effective to 100 yards or more.

To deliver this effectiveness, the shotguns must have sights that are similar to rifle sights. Many shotguns designed for slugs already have rifle sights. Most have open sights, but some have aperture sights. Aftermarket sights may be readily installed on most shotguns. Marlin bolt-action shotguns have always been drilled and tapped for a Lyman receiver sight. A number of companies make mounts to install optical sights on shotguns.

In order to use a shotgun effectively as a rifle, you must use the same procedures as you would when shooting a rifle. So, if you are going to shoot slugs with rifle sights, you may want to go back now and brush up on the rifle shooting fundamentals in Chapter 6.

If you are going to use your shotgun as a shotgun, please continue ahead to the next chapter.

CHAPTER FIFTEEN

SHOOTING THE
SHOTGUN

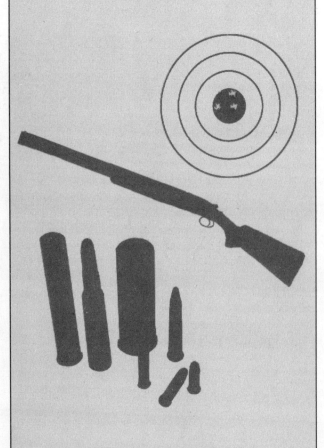

SHOOTING THE HANDGUN, we have seen, is similar to shooting the rifle. We try to minimize the movement of the gun in order to place a single projectile into a stationary target.

Shotgun shooting is very different, though it also requires self-discipline, self-control, coordination and practice. The differences are the target and the ammunition. In shotgun shooting, we are trying to hit a moving target with a large number of small projectiles fired from a moving gun.

To shoot a shotgun well, you must know, understand and practice the basic points or fundamentals.

Let us consider five fundamentals: stance; gun-ready position; swing to target; trigger pull; follow-through.

Note that these fundamentals are a bit different from those for rifle and pistol shooting.

Stance

When we discussed rifle and pistol shooting, we talked about position. We thought of it as the proper orientation of the body necessary for a stable structure. A stable structure was necessary in order to fire the most accurate shot possible at a stationary target.

The stance of a shotgun shooter is also the proper orientation of the body, or the position of the body and its relationship to the target while shooting. However, the shotgunner's stance is designed to allow movement. Two general aspects make up a good shotgun stance: The stance must be comfortable and relaxed; the stance must be aligned with the spot in which you expect to contact the target.

A comfortable, relaxed stance should have the body balanced, with the feet about shoulder-width apart. Stance is as important to a shotgunner as to a boxer, and for the same reasons. You must be in a good position to move, yet retain your balance and control.

The body ought to have a slight forward lean. The left knee should have a slight bend to it. (We're again assuming a right-handed shooter.) The right knee may be straight or also have a slight bend.

An easy way to understand this is just to assume a boxer's stance. Stand without the gun and "put up your dukes." Your left hand will be punching forward, about where it will grasp the forend, and your right hand will be back close to your face, about where you will grasp the pistol grip. Your body feels limber and relaxed, and ready to move. Your position with the shotgun will be very similar to this.

Foot position is vital to a proper stance. The left foot should be out front and pointing at where the target will be shot.

Your body must be ready to move. Move where? Ah, that is where the alignment of your stance comes in.

Try this: Assume your comfortable, relaxed stance. Look straight ahead and pick an object as your target. Put the empty gun to your shoulder and swing it to your left and right several times with your eyes closed. Let the swinging come to a complete stop in a natural, relaxed position. Open your eyes. Is the gun pointed straight ahead toward your intended target? If not, look down at your feet and note their location. Shift them slightly until the gun points where you expect to hit the target.

Does this sound suspiciously like the "natural point of aim" we discussed for both rifle and handgun shooting? Yes, it is basically the same thing, with one difference.

For rifle and handgun shooting, the natural point of aim allowed us to align the gun with a definite target. With the shotgun, our natural point of aim aligns us with the area in which we expect to hit the target we cannot yet see. If the target appears to the left or right of where we expect, we can move our body to the left or right without running out of swing.

Each time you are about to shoot, ask yourself, "Where do I expect to hit this target?" Then position your feet in the proper places to naturally align your stance with that area.

There are additional things you will pick up with practice, of course. Right-handed shooters can swing farther left than right, so they might establish a stance that points farther to the right for some shots.

Ultimately, the basic conditions of a good stance should be considered every time you intend to fire a shot.

Gun-Ready Position

The gun-ready position is the posture assumed before moving the gun to fire the shot. Should not the gun-ready position be established with the gun already at the shoulder? A fair question.

American Skeet and trap rules allow the gun to be shouldered before the target appears. Most shooters at these events do shoulder their guns before calling for the target, because it takes a finite amount of time to raise the gun. Some shooters, however, start with the gun off their shoulder. There are some good reasons for this. One of them is the tendency to focus on the barrel and bead of a shouldered gun, instead of focusing on the target. There is a tendency to aim the gun, rather than point it. Some shotgun sports—Sporting Clays and International Skeet—require the gun to be well below the shoulder until the target appears. Also, many shotgunners are hunters. There are few instances in hunting where the gun is shouldered in advance of the shot.

For all these reasons, let us consider the gun-ready position to be the gun butt held low, along the front portion of the rib cage. The basic stance is assumed, and the gun is pointed toward the general area where the target will be hit.

The right hand firmly holds the grip of the stock. The left hand firmly holds the forearm. The left-hand position can be varied with the type of gun, size of the shooter, and other factors.

Before we leave the subject of the left hand, I must address a question that is sure to be asked. Should the index finger lie

The writer assumes the gun-ready position, with stock down, looking over the muzzle to the area in which the target will be hit. The gun is a 20-gauge Stevens.

along the forearm pointing toward the target, as some do, or should it be used to grip the forearm? I wish I knew.

I do not point my finger, for two reasons. Most of my shotgunning is done with pump guns, and I seem to need all the fingers I can get to operate the slide handle. Perhaps more to the point, I have long arms, and my left hand is always at the very front of the forearm. If I pointed, my pointing finger would either be hanging out in space or touching a hot barrel. I have studied a great number of pictures of good shotgun shooters in action—some point, some don't.

The gun itself is pointed where we expect to hit the target. The muzzle is slightly below our line of sight. Where do we look? Don't focus on the front sight bead. With both eyes open, we focus on the area *in which we expect the target to first appear.*

Swing to Target

Imagine we have a shooter in the gun-ready position. Let's look him over. He could be on a trap field, Skeet field or cornfield. His gun-ready position will be about the same. He stands in a relaxed stance, the gun aligned with the area in which he expects to hit the target. He holds the gun stock lightly at about the level of his rib cage. His eyes look over the muzzle to where he expects to first see the target. For this shot, he expects his target to be a straightaway one, so he looks straight ahead.

On seeing the target, our shooter moves the shotgun and his body together as a single unit toward the target. The gun is simultaneously raised into the correct firing position.

Let's go over a couple of very important points here. As the shooter mounts the gun, he brings the stock up to his face, not his face down to the stock. When his right elbow comes up, his right shoulder automatically rises and allows the high placement of the stock against his face. However, the butt does not come sliding *up* to the shoulder, it comes *back* against the shoulder after the stock is raised.

This does not all happen as separate jerky motions. The idea is to mount the gun in a smooth, fluid movement. The muzzle should already be tracking the target, and the barrel will be in alignment between your dominant eye and the target. With practice, the shooter should be ready to fire the shot just after the butt touches his shoulder.

Trigger Pull

We'll assume your swing to the target on a straightaway shot has been a good one. You are still focused on the climbing target, but you can see the shotgun muzzle coming up toward it. At the instant the muzzle seems to touch the target, pull the trigger.

The trigger pull should be a quick, crisp backward motion of your finger against the trigger. It should almost be an instinctive reflex movement when the muzzle aligns with the target.

You may hear shotgun trigger control referred to as trigger

The writer swings up to the target on a straightaway shot. The stock has been brought up to the face, not the face down to the stock. The gun is a 12-gauge Marlin Model 49.

slap by some older shooters. This term does convey the idea of a very quick motion, but it implies that the finger is not contacting the trigger before the motion. It's better to think of it as trigger pull, not slap.

Follow-Through

Follow-through is continuing to do what you were doing before. In rifle and handgun shooting, follow-through essentially was remaining as motionless as possible for a short time after the shot. The shotgun, however, is moving, so it is essential that the follow-through keep it moving just as it was before the shot was fired.

Remember that the mechanical action of the firing pin against the primer, the detonation of the primer, the burning of the powder and the travel of the shot charge through the bore all take some time. While all this is going on, the target continues to move.

If the movement of the gun stops before the shot load leaves the muzzle, the shot will not hit the target. Instead, it will pass behind as the target sails by. Make sure you hit the target by continuing your gun movement longer than necessary. During follow-through, the stock must stay firmly against the cheek and the butt must stay firmly against the shoulder. The movement of the gun must continue exactly as it was before the shot was fired. Probably the greatest cause of misses by beginning shooters is stopping the swing too soon and not following through.

How to Begin

Most shotgun shooters probably start by getting hold of a shotgun and some shells, and then going out to do some shooting. After all, that is how I started, although it is not a particularly good way. Without adequate instruction, you may develop some bad habits that may be hard to unlearn. With some instruction, such as this book provides, you have exposure to good techniques put together by some very knowledgeable people.

But, wow, there is an awful lot to remember when you get on station with a loaded shotgun! In only a few seconds things happen that take pages to describe. We will go through a number of these steps before you start shooting, possibly making your shotgunning life much easier.

Eye Dominance

This factor should be seriously considered in shotgun shooting, perhaps more so than in rifle and handgun shooting. In shotgunning, it is essential to be able to align the shotgun between your eye and the moving target while both eyes remain open; if the wrong eye tries to take over, shooting results can be poor and frustrating.

The good news is that most people have the dominant eye and the dominant hand on the same side. Eye dominance only becomes a problem when, say, a right-handed shooter has a dominant left eye.

Determining your dominant eye is important in shotgun shooting. It can be done simply by looking at a distant object with both eyes and then swinging up your arms with an opening in your hands. Then move your hands back toward your face. Your dominant eye will look through the opening. Try it several times.

Dry-firing is a useful technique for developing shotgun skills. These 1992 Florida Junior Olympic Shooting Camp shooters are all swinging to the same target. One fires as the others dry-fire.

In such cases, with both eyes open, the shooter sees the target and swings the muzzle to it. As the shotgun gets to his face, he may realize, in a panic, he is trying to align the image of the bird as seen by one eye with the image of the barrel as seen by the other eye. Some shooters don't realize this is happening. They see a target, see a bead, and shoot. The result is a crossfire shot and a wide miss.

The presence of a dominant or master eye has been noted in shotgunning literature since at least the early 1900s. Solutions proposed in the past have been closing one eye, squinting, blocking the vision of the offending eye, and special stocks with cast off. Some strange-looking stocks with obvious bends and crooks have been made. They allow a shooter to shoot from one shoulder while using the opposite eye.

The solution generally recommended today is to use the dominant eye and shoulder the gun on that side. In many cases, the improvement in shooting has been immediate and dramatic.

However, there is much we still do not know about eye dominance. Some people seem to have ambidextrous eyes; others seem to change back and forth, either on a long-term or short-term basis.

I have seen an instructor, on the basis of a single eye dominance test, direct a shooter to shoot from his weak side. Later,

it was found that the dominance seemed to have changed, and the shooter was then told to change back to his strong shoulder.

I would recommend that the simple eye dominance test described earlier in this book be done at least ten times, to make sure the shooter has a definite master eye.

If you have a definite dominant eye, you will almost certainly do your best shotgun shooting from the corresponding shoulder.

Pointing

It is often difficult for new shooters—or experienced rifle and handgun shooters, for that matter—who are used to carefully aiming a gun, to *point* a shotgun. Let's make it a bit easier by temporarily doing away with the shotgun and just pointing.

Have someone throw some targets for you. Assume the proper stance, with left arm forward, but just extend your left index finger. Focus on where the target will appear and call "Pull." As soon as you see the target, point at it, keeping your finger aligned with it for its entire flight.

Your focus should be on the target, not on your finger.

When you are comfortable with this, add the time necessary to fire a shot by putting in a sound effect. As your finger touches the climbing bird, say "bang" or "kaboom" or "blam," whatever appeals to you. Sounds silly, but it will forcibly demonstrate your control over the moment when the shot is fired.

Next, practice pointing with the shotgun. Go back and review the fundamentals. Practice your stance, gun-ready position and swing, then have some more targets thrown. Again, practice staying with the target all the way to the ground. Always focus your eyes on the target.

Dry-Firing

At this point, dry-firing can be added. With the gun unloaded, go through the entire routine again. Stance, gun-ready, swing to target, touch the target, trigger pull, follow-through. Only this time, pull the trigger instead of saying "bang," and add a follow-through of several seconds. Practice until it feels comfortable and natural. This is a good way of discovering any problems that might be masked by the actual shooting of the gun.

Now you are ready to shoot live ammunition. However, if one is available, some instructors add an extra step beforehand to build confidence—the BB gun!

A military program to teach instinctive shooting was begun during the Vietnam War, using Daisy BB guns that had no sights. Nicknamed "Quick Kill," the program worked so well that Daisy offered sightless guns as part of their shooting education program. The name was modified to "Quick Skill."

The special Daisys are nice, but any BB gun without sights can be used. Some start by swinging up the gun to hit stationary targets. Gallon-size milk jugs thrown by hand make good moving targets. Soon you will be hitting the milk jugs consistently—with a single pellet!

So after that, hitting a moving target should be no problem with the shotgun, right? True, the targets are smaller than a milk jug, and they go much faster, but the shooting principles are exactly the same. Plus, you have all those pellets in one shotgun shell!

FUNDAMENTALS OF SHOTGUN SHOOTING

Stance: Stand comfortable and relaxed, aligned with the area in which you will hit the target.

Gun Ready: The gun is controlled by both hands, ready to move to the target.

Swing to Target: While looking at the target, bring the gun to your face, right elbow up, butt back to shoulder.

Trigger Pull: At the instant the muzzle "touches" the target, quickly pull the trigger.

Follow-Through: Continue doing exactly what you did before the shot, after the shot has fired (keep swinging).

If you have gone through all the above procedures, you have learned quite a bit about shotgun shooting. At this stage, you may have wasted some targets, but you have not wasted any shotgun shells.

Leading a Moving Target

When a target is moving, we must take into account the distance and direction it moves. We know that when we shoot, there is a delay before the shot reaches the target area. We want the target and the shot to arrive at the same place at the same time. So, leading a moving target is simply forward allowance to compensate for the target's speed and direction.

There are three basic ways of leading a moving target: swing-through or fast swing; sustained lead; snap shooting.

Swing-Through

Although there is no real way to prove it, I'll bet most moving targets that are successfully hit are hit with the swing-through method. It has sometimes been called "painting the target out of the sky."

The method involves a swing that is faster than the movement of the target—a fast swing. The muzzle thus swings through the target and the trigger is pulled as the gun passes the target. Note that because you are swinging faster than the target, when you press the trigger the muzzle has passed in front of the target by the time the shot leaves the gun.

Does this sound vaguely familiar? You have actually been using this method already on what seemed to be straightaway shots. Those straightaways have been given a forward allowance without our thinking about it. Those targets were *rising* when we saw them. By swinging up to them, pressing the trigger and following through, we are actually swinging through the target with a fast swing.

So, leading a moving target is really nothing new. With a rising straightaway target, we start moving below the target in the same path as the target, swing rapidly to the target, press the trigger and keep swinging.

The fundamentals do not change when a target is crossing at an angle in front of us. For this crossing target, we start moving behind the target, swing through it, press the trigger and keep swinging.

We have painted it out of the sky in a lateral direction. Our straightaway shots have painted it out of the sky in a vertical direction.

Now, swing-through is not the only type of forward allowance used. However, the others are not used as much as they have been in the past. It is worth knowing about them, though, so let's spend just a brief time with them.

Sustained Lead

With a sustained lead, the shooter sees the target, then estimates how far ahead of it he must lead in order to hit it. He then points the muzzle that estimated distance ahead of the target and swings *at the same speed as the target.* He presses the trigger and follows through. If all goes well, the target flies into the shot.

Swing-through has often been called "painting the target out of the sky." It uses a swing faster than the moving target. The muzzle swings through the target, the trigger is pulled as the gun passes it, and a follow-through is maintained. The target is literally painted out of the sky.

The difficulties with sustained lead are obvious. The shooter must be able to judge by long practice how much lead to sustain in a number of different situations, and this is not easily done.

Snap Shooting

This poses even more difficulties than sustained lead. It is suitable for some types of hunting shots, and has been used, for example, for close-range quail hunting in heavy cover.

When the target appears, the shooter judges its speed and direction, and estimates the spot where it will be in another split-second. He then snaps a shot directly at that spot.

Both snap shooting and sustained lead methods require the benefit of substantial practice. Most shooters start hitting sooner, and make more hits, with the swing-through method.

Remember, not only the techniques of leading, but all the techniques of shotgun shooting have evolved over the years. You will see different experienced shooters use techniques that are somewhat different from each other. Learn what you can from them and find the details of technique that work best for you.

When using a sustained lead, the shooter estimates the lead in front of the target, points to that spot, continues to swing at the same speed as the target, and fires his shot. This method takes lots of practice.

Snap shooting involves guesstimating, almost instinctively, where to aim in front of the target. Very little swing or follow-through is needed. The shooter fires at a spot, believing the moving target will intersect the shot charge.

FIRING THE PERFECT SHOT

It is time now to call on everything you know, put it all together, and fire one perfect shot.

Let us say you will have a single clay target launched from the high house of a Skeet field. You will be on station four. We will discuss Skeet in the next chapter, but for now, it is sufficient to know that the target will cross almost directly in front of you from left to right.

You have complete confidence in your gun and your ammunition. You have patterned the gun. The choke and the shot size are right for this range, and the pattern is

and your left firmly holds the forearm in about the center.

With your feet firmly in place, you pivot your upper body to the left. You estimate the flight path of the target, and look at the area from which you expect the target to appear. The muzzle of your gun is just below the anticipated path of the target.

You call "Pull!"

The target appears, moving swiftly from left to right. Both of your eyes are focused on it. Your gun's muzzle

Allen Hoover swings to the target during a Skeet match. When this picture was taken in 1987, Hoover was one of the top 4-H Junior Shooters in Texas. His gun is a Browning Citori.

centered when your eye is properly aligned with the barrel.

You approach your station and assume your stance. You are comfortable and relaxed. You intend to break the target over the center marker, so you align your stance with the marker. You close your eyes for a moment and swing the gun sideways slightly to find a natural point of aim. Because you are right-handed, you decide to align your stance slightly to the right of the center marker. If you do not break the bird directly over the center marker, you will not run out of swing.

You have loaded the gun, and it is in the gun-ready position. The stock is lightly against your ribs and the butt is near your waist. Your right hand is on the grip,

begins to follow it as you bring the gun firmly to your face. Your right elbow is level with your shoulder. The butt comes back firmly against your shoulder.

The barrel is aligned with your dominant right eye and is already moving toward the target, on the same flight path. The muzzle very rapidly overtakes the target, and as it passes, you quickly press the trigger.

You do not stop your swing, but follow-through, continuing to swing along the same path. You have not felt any recoil or noticed any noise, but out of the corner of your eye, you see the fragments of a cleanly broken target.

You have just fired the perfect shot! Now, if you can fire one, surely you can fire two. If you can fire two...

CHAPTER SIXTEEN

SHOTGUN
SHOOTING
ACTIVITIES

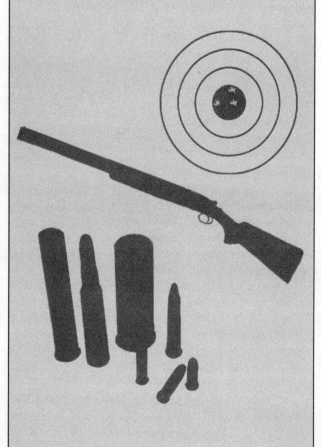

IT HAS BEEN said that a man with a shotgun could have a full life of sport. It was probably in reference to wingshooting in England in days gone by, but there is still some truth to it today. Certainly any person in America—man, woman or youngster—who has the use of a shotgun has a number of shotgun activities from which to choose. Here are a few: trap, Skeet, Sporting Clays, international shooting, informal clay targets, and hunting.

Trap

It would seem that the earliest mention of trapshooting is found in a 1793 edition of an old English publication called *Sporting Magazine*. It is mentioned as being well-established, so it would seem that it was developed during the late 1700s, when the use of flintlock shotguns was in vogue.

Trap probably originated as practice for field shooting. Live birds, generally pigeons, were kept in "traps" and then released when the shooter was ready. The first traps were holes in the ground covered by old hats or similar covers. Later, cage traps with sliding lids were used.

The first recorded trapshooting club apparently was the Hornsey Wood House Pigeon Club in England, formed in 1810. In 1831, the sport was introduced into the United States. The Sportsmen's Club of Cincinnati began shooting live pigeons from traps, and the sport slowly spread. It is probable that travelers returning from England helped promote it.

About the end of the Civil War, thought was given to replacing live birds with artificial targets. The introduction of a glass ball target by Charles Portlock of Boston, Massachusetts, in 1866, was probably the first attempt to duplicate the flight of a bird with an inanimate object. Portlock's traps were similar in design to a medieval catapult, but improved versions soon appeared.

Live and artificial bird shooting existed side-by-side for many years. Improvements were made in the inanimate targets. Some glass balls were formed around feathers. When the targets were broken, shooters could see the feathers fly.

In 1880, George Ligowsky of Cincinnati, Ohio, invented a clay bird and a trap to throw it. While the glass balls had simply been tossed into the air, Ligowsky's targets simulated the actual flight of a bird. The targets were formed of baked clay.

They were hard enough to resist breaking in transport and apparently were also hard enough to resist shot pellets. Never-

In a 16-Yard trap match, five shooters are all 16 yards behind the trap. Here, the middle shooter is ready to fire. The man to his right will shoot next. Each shooter fires five shots from each of the five stations.

theless, the form, which was essentially like our modern clay targets, was good.

Eventually, pure clay birds gave way to a mixture of clay and pitch, or ground limestone and pitch. They transported well, yet broke easily when shot. Trapshooting at artificial birds increased in popularity.

By the late 1800s, the sport had become so popular that the need for standard rules was seen. The first governing organization, established about 1893, was essentially a commercial organization. Called the Interstate Manufacturers and Dealers Association, it held annual Grand American shoots. In 1895, the name of the organization was shortened to The Interstate Association, although it was often called the Interstate Trapshooting Association.

By the end of the 1890s, public clamor against live bird contests brought about the first Grand American using clay targets in 1900. The last Grand using live birds was in 1902.

After World War I ended in 1918, the name of the organization was changed to the American Trapshooting Association. Though still under the control of the manufacturers, trap was becoming so popular that the shooters felt they should control the game, and in 1923, absolute control of the sport was turned over to amateurs. The name of the organization was changed slightly to the Amateur Trapshooting Association. The initials thus remained ATA. The following year, 1924, permanent home grounds were built in Vandalia, Ohio, and the Grand has been held there ever since.

Today's trapshooting range has a clay target launching machine, or trap, hidden in a trap house, the top of which is $2^1/_2$ feet above ground level. There are five shooting positions facing the trap house. The shooting positions are 3 yards apart and 16 yards from the trap.

Each shooter gets five shots from each of the five positions. This makes a total of twenty-five shots, which is referred to as a "round" of trap.

The trap is required to launch targets at different lateral angles for each shot. Clays may be thrown within a maximum angle 22 degrees to the left or right of trap center. From each shooting station, shooters may get targets that go left, right or straightaway.

The targets are thrown to land no less than 48 yards and no more than 52 yards from the trap. The vertical angle is kept constant at 8 to 12 feet above ground at 10 yards in front of the trap. Essentially, all trap shots are at rising targets.

There are three different events in trapshooting: 16-Yard, Handicap and Doubles. The *16-Yard* event is fired by all shooters at a distance of 16 yards from the trap. Shooters of differing ability are placed in different classes.

The *Handicap* event, instead of placing shooters in different classes, requires shooters with a better record to shoot from a greater distance. Distances extend back to 27 yards.

Note that both these events try to make shooters compete on an equal basis. One uses classes while the other handicaps better shooters with greater distance. Both events are single-target events in which only one bird is thrown at a time, although the shooter never knows the angle at which it will be thrown.

In *Doubles* events, two targets are thrown simultaneously. However, angles are always constant. The targets follow the paths of the extreme right and extreme left stations' straightaway angles of the 16-Yard event.

The guns used in trapshooting are generally 12-gauge guns with barrels 28 to 32 inches in length. Chokes are generally Full, Improved Modified or Modified. At many local matches,

Because targets in trapshooting are rising, many trap guns have elevated ribs and high, or adjustable, combs to make them shoot high. This shooter checks his gun at the trapshooting competition of the 1994 Florida Sunshine State Games.

shooters simply use the same gun they use for hunting. Indeed, the Grand American was once won with an ordinary field-grade semi-automatic.

I hate to admit it, but the best 16-Yard trap score I ever shot was with a 12-gauge bolt-action Marlin Goose Gun, with its 36-inch Full-choke barrel. The trap match was scheduled just after waterfowl season. The old Goose Gun was cleaned and ready to go, and on an impulse, I took it to the match. However, I only shot well with it that one time. I guess that proves two things. One, I am not a very consistent trapshooter; and two, if you are just starting out, you can shoot trap with almost anything you've got.

However, the particulars of the trapshooting game lend themselves to specialized trap guns. Because the bird is rising, high combs and high ribs are often used to assure a high shot pattern. Because the guns are shouldered before the bird is called, stocks may be longer than ordinary hunting stocks and may have special buttplates to position the gun uniformly each time you mount. Long barrels help maintain a steady and smooth swing.

Trap Doubles, of course, requires a gun that can shoot two shots in rapid succession. On the other hand, for 16-Yard and Handicap matches, any type of shotgun can be used. If you are new to the game, chat with other shooters and ask them about their guns. Trapshooters are generally a friendly bunch, and most will be glad for the opportunity to give you the benefit of their experience.

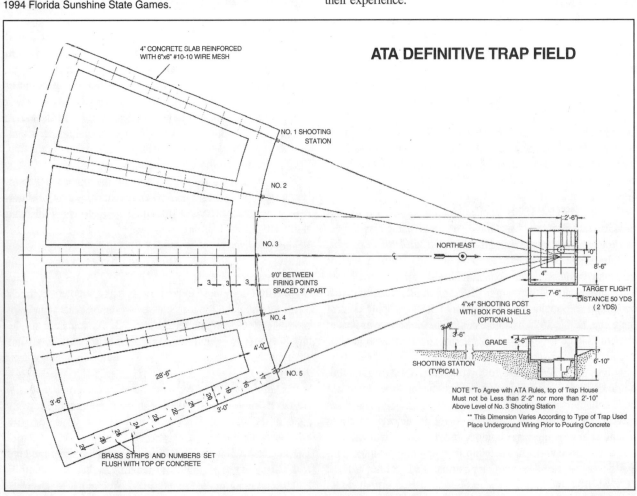

ATA DEFINITIVE TRAP FIELD

Skeet targets always travel the same paths. Coach Richard Gentry describes the path of a target to shooter Autumn Blum at the 1993 Florida Junior Olympic Shooting Camp.

Skeet

By 1910, clay targets and the traps to throw them were in common use. In Andover, Massachusetts, William H. Foster and Henry W. Davies were friends who shared a love of hunting. Henry's father, C.E. Davies, was the owner of Glen Rock Kennels and was an ardent hunter himself. The elder Davies had a reputation as a fast and smooth wingshot. After a day in the field, they would all sometimes return to the kennels, set up a trap and try to duplicate the shots they had missed during the hunt.

The shooting practice developed into a regular pattern. The pattern inevitably led to competition between them and, then, with other local shooters.

The shooting system they created involved shots at all angles. The original field was a complete circle with a radius of 25 yards. The outer edge was marked off like the face of a clock. The single trap was set at the 12 o'clock position, and threw the targets over the 6 o'clock position.

"Shooting around the clock" consisted of two shots at each position, which gave twenty-four shots at a great variety of angles. Then, as now, most shotgun shells came in boxes of twenty-five. The last shell was used, at first as a stunt, to shoot from the center of the circle at an incoming target. It was such an exciting shot that it was retained as a regular part of the game.

In shooting 'round the clock, shots were fired to all points of the compass. There was no "safe" area, and all shooters and spectators had to move around the circle together. One day, a neighbor started a chicken farm on the field adjoining the kennel land. Shots could no longer be fired in that direction.

Encroachment onto land that had previously gone unused gave us Skeet, much as it appears today. Because shots could not be fired toward the neighboring farm, the circle was simply cut in half, and a second trap installed at 6 o'clock. This gave the shooter the exact same shots he had encountered before, but now on one side nothing was fired in that direc-

tion and spectators could sit in one spot and watch the shooters progress.

William Foster, by then, had become editor of *National Sportsman* magazine. When he joined the magazine's staff, he had promoted "clock shooting." He realized that this modified semi-circle form could have national appeal.

He worked out a complete program for the new arrangement. The new game had seven shooting stations around the semi-circle, and an eighth in the center, midway between the two traps. He added doubles at stations one, two, six and seven. With singles from all stations, this gave a total of twenty-four shots. The twenty-fifth would be the first missed target. If none were missed, the shot was considered an optional shot and could be taken from any station. The radius had been reduced from 25 yards to 20 yards. The second trap was now elevated, to provide an even greater variety of shots.

The idea was introduced to the public in February of 1926, and a prize of $100 was offered for the best name for the new sport. Of the more than 10,000 suggestions sent in, the winning name, "Skeet," was submitted by Mrs. Gertrude Hurbutt, of Dayton, Montana. It was derived from an old Scandinavian word for "shoot." Short and catchy, it was a good choice.

The sport grew rapidly. Soon, the formation of a national organization seemed a good idea. In 1935, the first National Skeet Shooting Association was formed, and a National Championship shoot was held that year.

About that time, the original layout was altered slightly as a safety precaution. Originally, birds from the high house went straight over the low house, and vice versa. There was danger to the shooter, because he could be hit by fragments of a broken target. The traps were re-angled so that the flight paths of the targets crossed 6 yards out from station eight. The configuration was subtly modified so that every station except station eight was 21 yards from this crossing point. A Skeet field still looks like a semi-circle, but it is actually not.

The last championship under the original association was

DIAGRAM for SKEET STAND

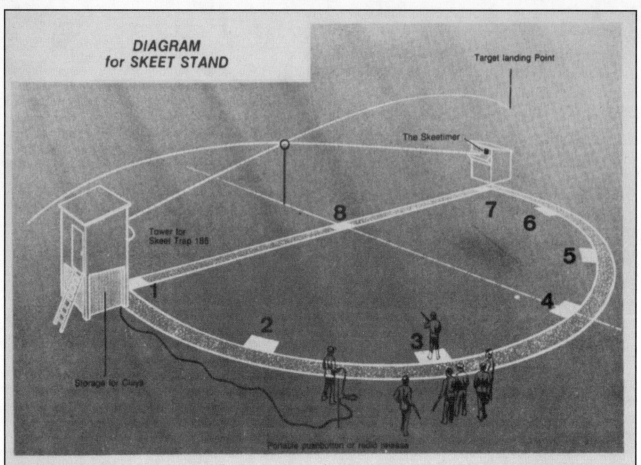

Target landing Point

The Skeetimer

8   7   6

5

Tower for
Skeet Trap 185   1   4

Storage for Clays   2   3

Portable pushbutton or radio release

COMBINATION SKEET AND TRAP FIELD

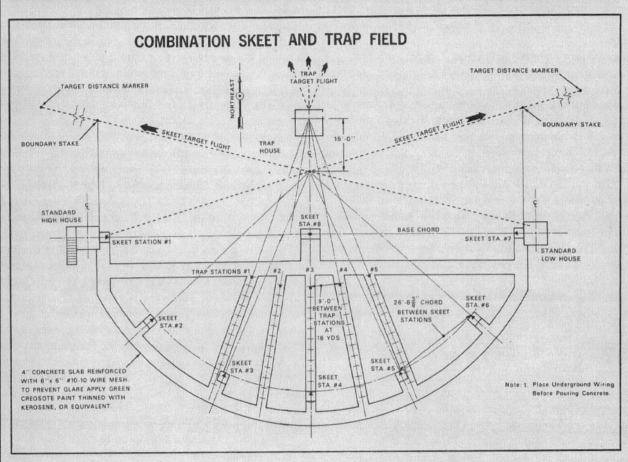

TARGET DISTANCE MARKER

TRAP
TARGET FLIGHT

TARGET DISTANCE MARKER

NORTHEAST

SKEET TARGET FLIGHT   TRAP HOUSE   SKEET TARGET FLIGHT   BOUNDARY STAKE

15'-0"

BOUNDARY STAKE

STANDARD
HIGH HOUSE

SKEET
STA. #8   BASE CHORD   SKEET STA. #7

SKEET STATION #1   STANDARD
LOW HOUSE

TRAP STATIONS #1   #2   #3   #4   #5   SKEET
STA. #6

SKEET
STA. #2   9'-0"
BETWEEN
TRAP
STATIONS
AT
16 YDS   26'-8 3/8" CHORD
BETWEEN SKEET
STATIONS

SKEET
STA. #3   SKEET
STA. #5

4" CONCRETE SLAB REINFORCED
WITH 6" x 6" #10-10 WIRE MESH.
TO PREVENT GLARE APPLY GREEN
CREOSOTE PAINT THINNED WITH
KEROSENE, OR EQUIVALENT.   SKEET
STA. #4   Note: 1. Place Underground Wiring
Before Pouring Concrete.

held in 1942. With United States involvement in World War II, civilian Skeet shooting completely shut down.

However, the military recognized the value of Skeet shooting in teaching men to hit moving targets and recruited many of the top Skeet shooters as instructors. All branches of the Armed Forces used Skeet as training. A friend of mine, who served in the 8th Air Force as a B-17 belly-turret gunner, told me of his Skeet shooting training, his group using Remington Model 11 semi-automatic shotguns. He enjoyed Skeet so much he shot it after the war.

With the war's end, a new National Skeet Shooting Association was formed in 1946, and the championships resumed in 1947. Perhaps because so many veterans had been introduced to the sport, Skeet shooting grew rapidly, far beyond its pre-war status. With so many new people entering the sport, the rules were changed in 1952 to allow the gun to be mounted to the shoulder before the bird was called. This rule change helped new shooters break at least a few targets the first time out, and Skeet's popularity increased.

Ironically, around this same time, Skeet became recognized as an international sport. The older American rules of a low gun position and variable-time target release were the ones adopted for international competition and International Skeet became a part of the Olympic Games in 1968.

Today, Skeet shooting in America follows the easier rules adopted in 1952 and, because of this, has great appeal to ordinary shooters. However, because International Skeet can be shot on ranges set up for American Skeet, all Skeet ranges are all built on the same plans. The differences are that International Skeet requires a low gun position, a variable target release, and the target is thrown to about 72 yards. The target for U.S. Skeet is thrown to about 60 yards.

A round of Skeet consists of twenty-five birds. The birds always fly the same paths. The field has eight shooting stations, seven equally spaced in what appears to be a semi-circle, and an eighth one in the "center." A high house, which launches the target about 10 feet above ground level, is behind station one. A low house, which introduces the target about 2½ feet above the ground, is behind station seven. The target paths are angled so that the clays cross 6 yards from the central station eight location. The other seven stations are all 21 yards from this crossing point. The crossing point is marked by a stake.

At each station, a shooter will fire at one target from the high house, then at one from the low house. Doubles are shot from stations one, two, six and seven; that is, the two stations closest to each trap house. On doubles, it is recommended that a shooter always try for the target going away from him first. After the doubles, twenty-four shots have been fired. The twenty-fifth, or optional, shot is not really optional any more. It is a repeat of the first miss. If the shooter does not miss, the optional shot is taken at the station eight low house target.

As with trapshooting, Skeet began with shooters using their hunting guns. Many people today shoot Skeet primarily to keep their shotgun skills sharp for the hunting season and just use the same shotgun they use for hunting. Others consider Skeet a primary sport in itself and use specialized shotguns for Skeet alone.

Any shotgun used for Skeet must be capable of firing two quick shots for the doubles. Experienced pump gun shooters are still occasionally seen on the Skeet field, but most shotguns used for Skeet now are either semi-automatics or over/unders. I began Skeet shooting with a Winchester '97 pump that had one of the old 26-inch Cylinder-bore "Brush Gun" barrels. That gun got me into the "20s" at Skeet, but would look very much out of place now.

Skeet shooting has targets thrown from both high and low house traps. Here a shooter prepares to take a high house target, which comes out about 10 feet above the ground.

Because the gun must swing fast, shorter barreled shotguns are generally used for Skeet than for trap. Barrel lengths seldom run over 26 inches. Most birds are broken near the crossing point at 21 yards so the range is short, and open chokes, noticeably Improved Cylinder, are the rule.

There are four classes of Skeet competition: 12-gauge, 20-gauge, 28-gauge and 410. Actually, smaller gauges can be used in any event, so a shooter with a 16-gauge shotgun can fire in the 12-gauge events. Matter of fact, the 12-gauge event is shown in some older publications as the "all-gauge" class. I have been to a small local club where the members shot for fun and everybody shot together with whatever they brought.

On the other hand, top shooters do not penalize themselves unnecessarily. They use what they consider to be the best allowable guns and ammunition. The maximum shot loads allowed for each gauge are these:

MAXIMUM SHOT LOADS	
Gauge	Charge (ozs.)
12	1 1/8
20	7/8
28	3/4
410	1/2

Shooters may use factory ammunition or reloaded shells, if the reloads meet the above standards. At a tournament, reloads may be weighed to make sure that they actually meet the maximum shot load standards.

Reloaded shells are a way of life for many dedicated shooters. A number of years ago I visited the home of Allen Hoover, who was at that time one of the top Texas 4-H junior Skeet shooters. One wall of his bedroom was dominated by a long reloading bench with four mounted reloading presses permanently set for 12, 20, 28 and 410 Skeet loads. After each tournament, the entire family would settle in and crank out enough loaded shells for the next weekend's event.

The best way to get started in Skeet is probably to visit a Skeet club and watch what is going on. Talk to the shooters and look at their guns. Skeet shooting is a fast, exciting sport. It requires very little in the way of equipment, and many hunters already have everything they need to get started.

Sporting Clays

Sporting Clays is a relative newcomer to the world of shotgun shooting sports. Some hunters wanted off-season practice that was less regimented than trap or Skeet. Small inexpensive clay traps had become readily available during the 1960s, and a few hunters could get together in a safe area and design their own games.

I participated in one of these informal courses in the early 1970s. Traps were set out of sight in bushes, up on towers and in trees. Everybody brought his hunting gun and gave it a try to see how well he could do.

Gradually, shooters learned that others around the country were doing the same thing. The informal name "Hunter's Clays" was sometimes used, and recommendations were swapped as to

safety precautions and special courses. Competition began and scores were kept at the local level.

Eventually, like trap and Skeet before, a need was felt for a national organization to coordinate events and keep records. The National Sporting Clays Association was formed in March, 1989, as a nonprofit organization owned and operated by its members.

Like golf, Sporting Clays courses are all different. Participants are placed into classes based on their shooting records. Though course layout is not standardized, the targets are. Targets may be used to simulate the flights of different birds or the bounding run of a rabbit. Participation is open to shooters using shotguns of 12-gauge or smaller. Commercial or reloaded ammunition may be used, with shot size not to exceed #7 1/2 (.095-inch diameter.) The permissible weights of shot loads are the same as for Skeet.

Targets are presented to the shooter in several ways: single target; report pair; following pair; simultaneous pair.

A *single* target is ordinarily attempted with a single shot, but some setups allow two shots at a single target.

A *report pair* initially releases one target to the shooter. When he shoots at that first target, the second one is launched at the sound, or report, of the shot.

A *following pair* consists of two targets in sequence, in which the second one is launched after the first, the timing to be at the discretion of the officials.

A *simultaneous pair* is two targets launched at the same time.

All shots are taken from the standing position. Before calling for a target, the shooter must hold his gun in a low position with the heel of the butt of the stock below the level of his armpit. The gun does not have to touch any part of the body. When the

A young shooter smokes a target during a Sporting Clays match. The "wings" of the station limit the arc through which the gun may swing.

shooter calls for a target, it can appear immediately or within 3 seconds. The gun cannot be mounted until the moving target is visible.

A recent offshoot of Sporting Clays is NRA Clays. This movable tower on wheels has mounted traps that throw a variety of targets. This permits setting up stations to the sides of the tower and throwing targets in several directions from a central location. This system has allowed clubs to begin a Sporting Clays program where only limited space is available.

Guns for Sporting Clays resemble hunting guns for the most part. However, as with trap and Skeet, competition has brought about the introduction of special guns for the sport. A gun must be capable of shooting two shots in rapid succession, so pumps, semi-automatics, over/unders and a few side-by-side doubles show up. Because shots may be near or far, the advantage goes to the shotgun with different degrees of choke. Shotguns with multiple barrels, of different chokes and lengths, are permitted, as are adjustable choke devices and interchangeable choke tubes.

Competitors may also enter a shoot with several different guns, if they want, attempting different targets at different fields with completely different guns. Or competitors can swap guns with each other for different targets. Needless to say, lively discussions about the best guns to use are often encountered. All this makes for a rather informal, relaxed game that is a lot of fun.

The NRA Clays tower has allowed clubs to offer Sporting Clays matches even with limited space. A variety of traps can be used to throw different targets in a number of directions.

Shotgun shooters often shoot several different shotgun sports. Florida Skeet champion Mary Beverly tries NRA Clays at a shoot near Thomasville, Georgia.

Most shotgun sports use standard clay targets. Carla Pararo looks over some that her daughter, Caroline, has picked up during a break at a Sporting Clays event.

International Shooting

Clay target events for international shotgun shooting are International Trap, Double Trap and International Skeet. All three events are fired in the Olympics and in other international competition.

International Trap

Sometimes called International Clay Pigeon shooting, this game differs in several ways from American trap. There are five shooting positions, but they are in line, with centers of the stations 4 meters (13 feet) apart. A long trap house extends the width of the field, with its roof at ground level. There are three trap machines in front of each shooter, fifteen in all. Distance from the firing line to the opening of the trap house is 15 meters (19.5 yards.)

A shooter may shoulder his gun, and immediately on his call, a target will be released from any one of the three traps in front of him. Also, the height of the bird at 10 meters (33 feet) from the trap may vary anywhere from 1 to 4 meters (40 inches to 13 feet). In some cases, a "wobble" trap is substituted for the three individual traps. This still gives variations of both horizontal and vertical angles for all shots and is very challenging.

Clay target shooting was introduced as an Olympic event back in 1908, and the course of fire was apparently very similar to that used today. Team matches were held in some of the early Olympics, but were dropped after 1924.

Olympic shooters today fire a 125-target match, but other international matches may be 200 or even 300 targets. Shooters fire five shots from each of the five stations for a round of twenty-five, but contrary to American practice, the station is changed after each shot. Also unique to International Trap is the provision for firing a second shot at a target if the first one is missed. There is no bonus for breaking a target on the first shot, and no penalty for using the second shot.

The international clay target is similar to the standard U.S. version, but is made of denser material since the target comes out fast and travels 70-75 meters (about 80 yards).

Double Trap

This event is a relatively recent one. It uses the same field as International Trap, but only the center traps are used, with two targets thrown simultaneously. Thankfully, they go slower, only about 50 mph, and achieve a distance of only about 50 meters.

Shotguns of 12-gauge are used and may be shouldered before calling for a target, and targets are thrown immediately when the shooter calls. Matches consist of 150 targets for men, but only 120 for women.

International Skeet

International Skeet was adopted directly from American Skeet and the field layouts are exactly the same. I get a chuckle when I think of them having to convert our dimensions into meters, instead of the other way around.

Adopted for the Olympics in 1968, International Skeet is more like the original American version of the game. Shooters must hold the 12-gauge shotgun at waist level until the target emerges; there is a variable delay of up to three seconds before the target appears; and the targets come out faster, about 60 mph compared to our 50 mph, and go farther, 72 yards instead of our 60 yards.

Informal Clay Targets

We have seen how each of the established shotgun sports grew out of informal shooting of clay targets. Such informal shooting is still going on.

A couple of friends with a mechanical trap, or even a hand trap, can have an afternoon of shooting fun. All that is required is a safe location, a shotgun, the trap, some clay targets, some ammunition and, of course, eye and ear protection.

Targets in informal shooting are generally straightaway shots that climb into the air after leaving the trap. This sort of shooting is perhaps the best for new shooters, as it allows hits early in the game and builds confidence.

Such informal shooting can be used to build skills or to earn NRA Shotgun Qualification awards. Boy Scouts can use such shooting as partial qualification for the Shotgun Shooting Merit Badge. If such shooting is not done on a regular trap or Skeet range, it should be recorded and witnessed.

Because most informal shooting is not done on a regular shooting range, even greater attention should be given to safety procedures. It is recommended that the operator of a hand or small mechanical trap be at least 5 feet to the right and 3 feet to the rear of the shooter.

This Outers FlightMaster Jr. is an example of a small mechanical trap that can be used for informal clay targets. Throwers like these can provide an afternoon of fun.

A shotgun allows participation in many types of hunting. This young hunter searches the sky for specks that may turn into ducks. He hold a 20-gauge Mossberg 500.

(Below) For many people, hunting is the prime shotgun sport. Here, the writer tries for a shot at an East Texas squirrel with a 16-gauge Mossberg Model 190.

Hunting

Probably more hunting is done with shotguns than with any other type of firearm. It also seems safe to say that more shots are fired by shotgun hunters.

A hunter may take his rifle deer hunting and plan on making a one-shot kill. The same hunter may take his shotgun after dove or squirrel, knowing that he can bring back a large bag limit and that he will probably miss some shots. So he brings plenty of ammunition and often uses up a lot of it.

Shotgun hunting is often broken into upland hunting, both birds and small game; waterfowl hunting; and large-game hunting. Entire books have been written on separate aspects of these sports.

In general, you should know the rules. You should have the proper hunting license, know the game laws and understand special regulations, such as the federal requirement of steel shot for waterfowl.

You should know your game. Understand the habits of the birds and animals you hunt. Know their food sources and their habitat. Know how the game is hunted in your area. Match the gun, choke and ammunition to the type of hunting you will be doing. Above all, develop skill with your shotgun. In fact, even if you consider yourself just a shotgun hunter, you might think about participating in some of the other shotgun sports we've covered.

We have discussed at least a few shotgun activities. You can shoot trap, Skeet and international variants of these sports. If you are good enough, you can work toward shooting in the Olympics. You can also shoot a round of Sporting Clays.

Or, you can just go out with family or friends and do some informal clay target shooting. You can hunt upland birds, small game, waterfowl or big game. Shotgun hunters have long seasons, and almost anything can be hunted with a shotgun.

With all these shooting opportunities, it seems almost impossible to really enjoy outdoor life without owning and using one or more shotguns.

CHAPTER SEVENTEEN

USING BLACK-POWDER GUNS

THE REVIVAL AND growth of blackpowder shooting was perhaps the least expected development in the history of the shooting sports.

Breechloaders had begun to supplant muzzleloaders by the time of the Civil War. In the decades following that conflict, developments in firearms proceeded rapidly. By the end of the 1870s, no more muzzle-loading firearms were being made in this country. By the end of the 1890s, smokeless powder had been accepted for both military and sporting use. Most major armies had machineguns before 1900. In the early 1900s, shooters were heading to ranges and hunting fields with semi-automatic pistols, rifles and shotguns. The world of firearms had become so modern, so fast, that the age of muzzleloaders seemed even further back in the past than it actually was.

Muzzleloaders never really went completely away, of course. A few people here and there still shot the old things. For most shooters, however, an obsolete, slow, smoky old muzzleloader was about the last thing they wanted.

However, time passed and a few people got interested again. By the early 1950s, Turner Kirkland of Dixie Gun Works was selling modern shooting replicas of Kentucky-style rifles. In the late 1950s, many people, especially those who lived in areas where dramatic Civil War battles had occurred, realized that the Civil War centennial was just around the corner.

Interest in the centennial grew, and commemoration of the Civil War would require Civil War guns. Some groups merely wanted displays of guns, some wanted shooting competitions to see what the old guns would do, others looked forward to reenactments of Civil War battles.

It became clear that the number of shootable original Civil War guns was insufficient. That is, there were not enough guns available that were absolutely safe and whose owners would permit them to be shot.

Replicas of the old guns, made of modern steel, would serve nicely, of course. However, American manufacturers were then discontinuing some models of modern guns because of the cost of production. It would be prohibitively expensive to duplicate the intricate parts of some of the old guns.

Val Forgett, owner of Navy Arms Co., arranged to have replicas made in Italy at reasonable cost. The first ones were replicas of the most common revolvers of the Civil War period. They were soon followed by replicas of the 1863 Remington contract rifle.

Civil War reenactments created a demand for replicas of Civil War firearms. Such events make history come alive for the spectators and are very popular. These reenactors represent the Confederate defenders at the Battle of Natural Bridge. The Confederate victory there saved Tallahasse from capture, the only Southern capital to escape such a fate.

Soon, replica Civil War revolvers and rifles were puffing smoke at shooting ranges across the country. Reenactments got other people interested, folks who had had little previous interest in any kind of shooting. Prices were reasonable, the guns looked historically correct, and many were bought strictly for decoration. Once they had them, many owners wondered what it would be like to shoot them, so they bought powder, balls and caps, and were soon added to the growing number of enthusiasts.

The 100th anniversary of the Civil War's end came and went in 1965, and reenactments have continued, an annual event in many places. By the end of the centennial, our country's Bicentennial was only a decade away, and Revolutionary War replicas became available. In 1976, there were a number of Revolutionary War reenactments, which added to the growing interest in the old guns.

As more hunters began shooting muzzleloaders, they petitioned state game commissions for muzzle-loading seasons, and most states now either have special seasons or allow frontloaders to be used during the regular gun or archery seasons.

Why Shoot Muzzleloaders?

There are a number of reasons why people shoot muzzleloaders today. A sense of history, possibly nostalgia, ranks high. It is hard to hold a blackpowder firearm without wondering what our forefathers experienced. Target shooting, reenactments and hunting with muzzleloaders all put us in closer touch with our heritage.

Hunting with a muzzleloader offers opportunities not available to other hunters. Areas of my home state, Florida, offer muzzle-loading seasons before and after regular season. I enjoy hunting with blackpowder before the regular season, switching

to modern guns during the regular season, then making another muzzleloader hunt during the post-season period.

One of the lesser reasons for the popularity of blackpowder guns is their unique status in the eyes of the law. In some localities, modern firearms and their use are restricted. In some of those areas, however, there is no legal restriction against possession of antique muzzleloaders or their replicas. Thus, blackpowder guns provide an opportunity for self-defense that would not otherwise exist. If you are considering such use, be sure you know the laws and regulations of your area.

Economy is certainly a consideration for many. A friend of mine in Louisiana does most of his hunting with a double-barrel muzzle-loading shotgun. He loads light or heavy shot loads for birds or small game, solid balls or buckshot for deer. He does all this at a fraction of the cost of buying factory ammunition or even reloading similar shells.

Just by varying the powder charge, the same gun, rifle, pistol or shotgun can be used for full-power hunting or mild-load target use.

Perhaps the greatest attraction of blackpowder shooting is simply that it is fun. The smoke and flash add to the enjoyment of shooting. Loading is slower, and the pace of shooting is slower. People chat with each other, look at each others' guns and exchange load information. Participants range from preteens to senior citizens. Reportedly, some people have been advised to take up muzzle-loading to combat stress. This topic was discussed at a recent North Florida muzzle-loading match. Perhaps one shooter summed it up best. "Well," he said with a laugh, "nobody here is in a rush to finish and leave."

The fundamentals of shooting a muzzle-loading rifle, shotgun or handgun are essentially the same as those for shooting their modern counterparts. Please consult the appropriate sections of this book for the basics of shooting these guns.

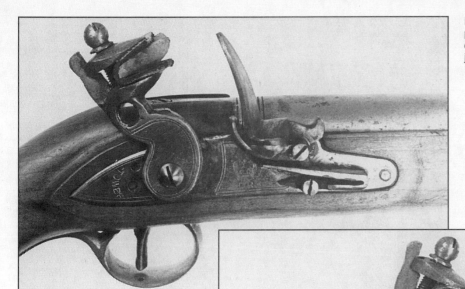

Ready to fire, a flintlock has fine priming powder in the pan, protected by the closed frizzen. The cock has a flint in its jaws and is at full-cock.

When the trigger is pressed, the flint strikes the frizzen and opens the pan. The resulting shower of sparks ignites the priming powder in the pan, shooting flame through the flash hole to fire the main charge.

Ignition Systems

Blackpowder guns in use today are mostly percussion, less commonly flintlock. These two options are not the only possibilities, however. Matchlocks, which used a glowing wick-like material to ignite the powder, were in limited use until about 1700. In Japan, they were actually used until the 1850s. Wheellocks used flint held against a spinning wheel to create sparks, which ignited the powder.

By the early 1600s, the flintlock had been developed, and its superiority to earlier types was evident. The main powder charge was in the barrel, as in the earlier types. A small hole through the barrel went from the main powder charge to the outside, as with the earlier types.

However, at the outer end of the hole was a *pan* filled with fine, easy-to-ignite powder. Covering this pan was a pivoting L-shaped part commonly called the *frizzen*. The horizontal portion of the frizzen covered the pan. The upright part stood in front of a *cock* (equivalent to a modern hammer). The cock had jaws to clamp a piece of flint. When the gun was fired, the flint struck the metal of the upright part of the frizzen, creating a shower of sparks. The frizzen pivoted forward, exposing the powder in the pan to the shower of sparks. The fine powder ignited, flashed flame through the flash hole, and ignited the main powder charge in the barrel.

If, as sometimes happened, the powder in the pan ignited, but the main charge did not, it was called a "flash in the pan." The long history of the flintlock has made this description of something that doesn't quite happen a part of our language.

When the flintlock fires, it does so with a "poof-boom" effect, as the pan and main charge fire a split-second apart. The gun must be held steady during this time. Follow-through, needless to say, is of the greatest importance when shooting the flintlock.

By the early 1800s, the percussion system had reached a useful form and was soon making the flintlock obsolete. The percussion guns still had the main charge in the barrel and a hole through the barrel for ignition. Now, however, the hole ended in a metal *drum*, into which was threaded a hollow *nipple*. A percussion cap was then placed on the nipple. The percussion cap was a small metal cup containing *fulminate of mercury*, a compound that detonated when struck. A hammer hit the cap, the flash of the detonation went through the ignition channel in the nipple and drum, and the powder was ignited.

This ignition was essentially instantaneous, eliminating the poof-boom delay of the flintlock. Also, percussion guns, with no powder exposed to the outside world, would fire in bad weather, like rain. The flintlock often would not.

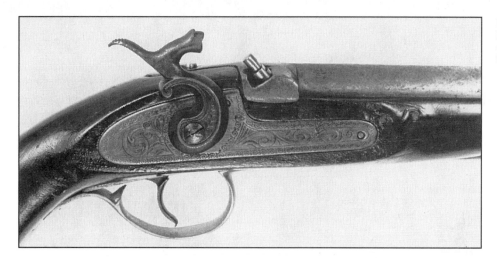
Ready to fire, a percussion lock has a cap of priming compound on the nipple. The hammer is at full-cock.

When the trigger is pressed, the hammer strikes the cap. The priming compound detonates, and a flash shoots through the hollow nipple to fire the main charge.

Components

To shoot a muzzleloader, we need a projectile to be fired, powder to provide the power, and an ignition source to ignite the powder. It would seem that except for a cartridge case, we have all the components of a modern cartridge. This is true in some ways, but there are differences. One is the powder.

Blackpowder

Modern cartridge arms use smokeless powder. All muzzleloaders, original and replicas, are designed for blackpowder. This powder dates back many centuries, and its composition and burning characteristics have remained essentially unchanged. It is a mixture of potassium nitrate (saltpeter), charcoal and sulfur. It is black in color and sold in four granulations. Coarser-grained powder burns slower and should be used in larger bores. When burned, blackpowder produces a cloud of dense white smoke with the unmistakable odor of sulfur.

The only safe substitutes for blackpowder now are Pyrodex, a registered trademark of the Hodgdon Powder Co., Inc., and Black-mag, made by Arco Powder. Both are different in chemical composition, but produce similar pressures and performance to blackpowder. Pyrodex is somewhat harder to ignite, and some consider this a benefit for safe storage. However, for the same reason, it is not recommended for flintlocks.

Blackpowder and Pyrodex are two powder options for muzzle-loading arms. Be sure to use the correct granulation for the gun you are shooting. Pyrodex P is for pistols, and FFg blackpowder is for large bore rifles, shotguns and pistols.

Muzzle-loading projectiles come in many shapes and sizes: (from left) 31, 36 and 44 balls for revolvers, with a heeled conical 36-caliber bullet in between the 36 and 44 round balls. For rifles, 45 ball, 45 Maxi-Ball, 45 Minie, 54 ball, two 58-caliber Civil War Minie balls (with one tipped to show hollow base), and 69-caliber Minie ball.

Replicas of 58-caliber Civil War rifles and rifle-muskets can use traditional Minie balls, bullets of modern design, or round balls.

Projectiles

Almost invariably, projectiles for blackpowder guns should be of pure lead. Round balls are perhaps the most-used projectiles for muzzleloaders. For rifles and single shot pistols, the ball will be slightly *undersize* (example: .440-inch for a 45-caliber). This is because the ball will be patched for loading, and the patch effectively enlarges the bullet. For revolvers, the ball will be slightly *oversize* (example: .451-inch for a 44-caliber). This is because the balls must be a tight fit into the chambers to prevent powder gas leakage.

Other shapes besides round balls can be used. Next to round balls, the hollow-base Minie balls are the most commonly used.

Civil War rifles were made to use Minie ball projectiles. The Minie ball, named for a French army captain who introduced the design in 1847, is a conical bullet slightly smaller than the diameter of the bore. It has a large hollow base; on firing, pressure from the powder gas inside this hollow expands the base of the bullet. Thus, the undersized Minie ball loads easily, but on firing fills the bore and gives good accuracy.

Loading a Muzzleloader

Loading a muzzleloader involves a number of steps which should always be done in exactly the same sequence. Knowledgeable shooters recommend eye protection while loading as well as firing. The steps presented in the NRA basic muzzleloading handbooks are well thought out, and the sequence here corresponds to those steps. Because the procedures for rifles

MUZZLELOADER POWDERS

Blackpowder comes in many different granulations for the many different opportunities presented to a muzzleloader shooter.

Fg—coarse-grained powder for use in rifles of 75-caliber or larger and shotguns of 10-gauge or larger.

FFg—medium-grained powder for rifles and pistols of 50-caliber or over and shotguns of about 12- to 20-gauge.

FFFg—fine-grained powder used in rifles under 50-caliber and shotguns under 20-gauge. This granulation is the most common handgun powder, used in revolvers of 31-, 36- and 44-caliber, and single shot pistols under 50-caliber.

FFFFg—extra-fine-grained powder that should be used *only* for priming the pan of flintlocks. It should *never* be used as a propellant charge because it will ignite too quickly and raise pressures inside the gun.

Black-mag is a new blackpowder substitute that is claimed to be cleaner burning and more water-resistant than blackpowder. It is sold in the same granulations as blackpowder.

Pyrodex is recommended for percussion muzzleloaders only, because it is more difficult to ignite in flintlocks. It comes in two easy-to-remember types:

RS—coarse-grained, for rifles and shotguns.

P—finer-grained, for pistols.

Specific loading data for different guns are available from various dealers and the manufacturers.

When withdrawing a rod, the hand can stay on the end, but when loading a ball, the rod should be held close to the muzzle (right) to prevent any chance of bending or breaking the rod.

and single shot pistols are essentially the same, let's consider them together. The procedure changes a bit for shotguns and revolvers, so we will consider them separately.

Priming

No matter what muzzle-loading gun you have loaded, priming it should not be done until all loads are securely in place. On a range, the gun should not be primed until you are on the firing line ready to fire. In the field, the gun should be primed only when it is legal to hunt and you are ready to begin hunting. At that point, the percussion cap may be placed on the nipple, or the pan of the flintlock may be primed. Some hunters prefer to cap their guns only after sighting game, ensuring the safest possible gun carry.

Failure to Fire

I hate to mention this, but sometimes muzzleloaders don't fire when the shooter pulls the trigger. The best way to avoid this problem is to load carefully, following the steps we've discussed. However, it does happen. Rest easy that there is always a reason, and we can always find it and correct it.

First, if you have a misfire, or failure to fire, keep the gun pointed securely in a safe direction for several moments. There is the possibility that your misfire is actually a hangfire, a delayed ignition from a smoldering spark rather than from the flash of the cap.

When a reasonable time has passed, take a look. The most common problem is a clogged ignition channel. Old-timers

(text continues on page 187)

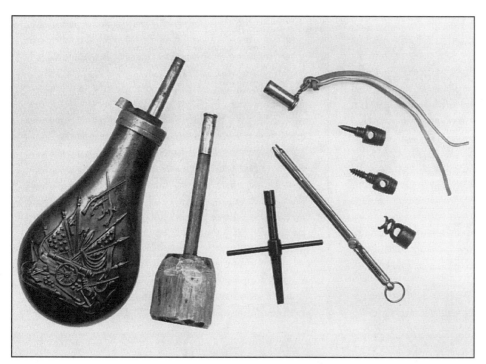

Some of these accessories will be useful during muzzle-loading shooting: (left) powder flask, short starter, nipple wrench, capping tool, a set of rod tools for unloading a stuck ball or wad—punch, ball screw and worm—and powder measure.

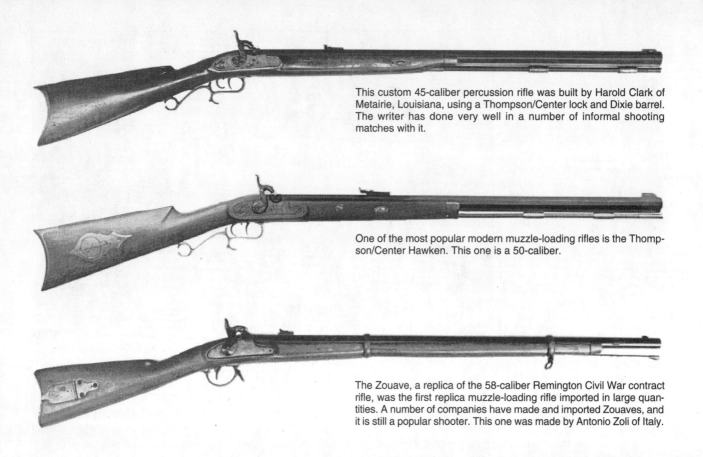

This custom 45-caliber percussion rifle was built by Harold Clark of Metairie, Louisiana, using a Thompson/Center lock and Dixie barrel. The writer has done very well in a number of informal shooting matches with it.

One of the most popular modern muzzle-loading rifles is the Thompson/Center Hawken. This one is a 50-caliber.

The Zouave, a replica of the 58-caliber Remington Civil War contract rifle, was the first replica muzzle-loading rifle imported in large quantities. A number of companies have made and imported Zouaves, and it is still a popular shooter. This one was made by Antonio Zoli of Italy.

LOADING BLACKPOWDER RIFLES AND SINGLE SHOT PISTOLS

1. Position the gun for loading. In the field, stand the rifle between your legs with the muzzle pointing up and forward, away from your body. For a pistol, kneel and stand the pistol between your knees. Percussion guns should have their hammers on half-cock; flintlocks should have the frizzens open. Some shooters bring special stands to the range to hold a pistol for loading, and some benches are notched to hold rifles for loading. If a bench is not notched, don't trust it. Don't lean your rifle against it and hope it'll stay put. It won't!

2. Check the bore for a load. Always, always do this when firing a gun for the first time. Even if you are the only one who shoots it, always check to made sure your gun is not loaded. This is cheap insurance. Insert the ramrod into the bore and mark the amount sticking out beyond the muzzle. Pull the rod out and place it alongside the barrel. If it reaches the flash hole or nipple drum, then that corresponding distance inside the bore is clear, and you can proceed.

3. Wipe and clean the bore. Oil or residue in the bore or flash hole can interfere with ignition. Run a clean patch into and out of the bore. For a flintlock, clean the pan and flash hole as well. A pipe cleaner works well to get inside the flash hole and clean it. For a percussion gun, fire a few caps on the nipple (keeping the muzzle in a safe direction, of course) to clear the ignition channel. When you fire the last cap, point the muzzle at a blade of grass. If it moves when you fire the cap, the ignition channel is clear.

4. Measure the powder charge. Pour the powder from its container into a separate powder measure. Measures may be purchased, or the shooter may want to make one for his particular gun. Never pour directly from the powder container into the muzzle, even if the container has a built-in measure. There may be a latent spark which could set off the entire container of powder. This is very dangerous. Such things seldom happen, but why take the chance?

Loading data for many guns are available from manufacturers and dealers. A safe rule of thumb is to start with a weight of powder equal to half the caliber. Thus, a 50-caliber rifle or pistol could use 25 grains of powder as a

A mixture of old and new parts, this muzzle-loading rifle began life as an 1863 Springfield and was used after the Civil War in cut-down form. A later owner rebarreled it with a modern 45-caliber barrel, and it is still shooting.

Most hunters still use muzzle-loading rifles of traditional appearance, but some of the new guns, like this Knight rifle, are of very modern design.

The Gonic rifle is another type of "straight-line" muzzleloader. It can be used for muzzle-loading hunts, but its lines and design are very modern.

starting load. For target shooting, light loads are generally the most accurate; they are certainly the most economical. For hunting, heavier loads are generally used.

Powder charges are expressed in grains, a unit of weight. There are 7000 grains in a pound. If you are using a charge of 25 grains for each shot, you will get 280 shots from a pound of powder.

5. Pour the powder into the bore. With the gun held firmly, and pointed in a safe direction, pour the powder into the bore. Tap the barrel lightly to make sure all the powder goes down all the way.

6. Prepare the patch. We're assuming you are loading a round ball at this stage. Round balls are patched with lubricated cotton cloth to clear fouling from the previous shot and seal the bore for this one. Pre-cut, pre-lubricated patches are available, but if you are not using them, then use a commercial patch lube made for the purpose.

7. Patch the ball. Center the lubricated patch over the muzzle. Place a pure lead ball on the patch. If the ball is a cast one, it will have a mark called a sprue at the point where the lead entered the bullet mould. It could cause a slight imbalance, so align it with the center of the bore. When I began shooting muzzleloaders, the advice I got was that the sprue should either be straight up or straight

down. Since the ball snuggles down into the patch, I never could figure how anyone could tell if it were straight down. So, always place the ball on the patch with the sprue facing straight up.

8. Start the ball and patch into the bore. You should have an accessory called a ball starter or short starter with you. It is just a very short ramrod. Most are made with two shafts, one just a fraction of an inch long and one several inches long. Place the shorter shaft over the ball and bop it with the heel of your hand. The force will push

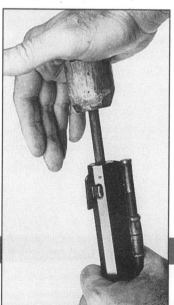

When a patched ball is inserted into the muzzle, use a short starter, striking it with the hand to push the bullet several inches into the bore.

Not very stylish, but it was the writer's first muzzle-loading pistol, built out of scraps when I was a kid. Only hand tools were used in its constuction—not for authenticity—because my family didn't have any power tools at the time.

Not very useful, but fun to shoot anyway, this replica derringer pistol is roughly of the style popularized by Henry Deringer (note the spelling) of Philadelphia in the mid-1800s. This replica's short barrel and single sight do not provide much accuracy, but it throws a ball and makes plenty of smoke.

the ball into the patch, pressing them both into the rifling. The ball should now be flush with the muzzle.

9. Trim the patch. If you are not using a pre-cut patch, there will be excess patch material sticking out of the muzzle. It should be trimmed away with a patch knife or any thin, sharp knife. Cut away from you, letting the blade ride across the muzzle. Be careful not to cut your fingers; blood is corrosive to steel.

10. Short-start the ball. Use the long shaft of the starter to force the patched ball several inches deeper into

the bore. Now it is in a good position for you to insert the loading rod or ramrod.

11. Seat the ball. Remove the starter. Insert the ramrod into the muzzle, gripping it a few inches above the muzzle and pushing it down. You do *not* want to grip it at the very end and shove, because you don't want to take the chance of breaking the rod. Push the ball all the way down, so that it is *firmly* seated against the powder. There must not be any air space between the powder and the ball.

In days past, some shooters used to bounce the rod to make sure the ball was firmly seated. If it were not seated, the rod would just go "thunk." If it were firmly seated, the rod would bounce an inch or two. Target shooters frown on this practice, because it can deform the ball. However, you might try it once. When you know the ball is firmly seated for a particular load, mark your rod at that point. Then you'll have a reference point for subsequent loadings.

If you are using a hollow-base Minie-type projectile, you do not have to patch it. The bullet base will expand on firing, so just follow steps 1 through 5 and then push the Minie ball down firmly against the powder. Some other modern types of muzzle-loading rifle bullets are also designed to be used without a patch.

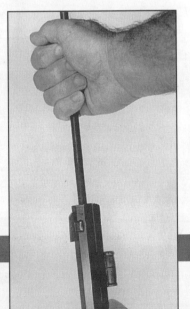

With the bullet started several inches into the bore, use a ramrod to seat it. Grasp the rod only a short distance above the muzzle, to avoid bending or breaking it.

LOADING BLACKPOWDER SHOTGUNS

Some of the initial procedures for loading muzzle-loading shotguns are also the same as for rifles. We will number them, but won't go into detail until we get to something new.

1. Position the gun for loading.

2. Check the bore for a previous load.

3. Wipe and clean the bore.

4. Measure the powder charge. At this point, we need to know that many recommended loads for blackpowder shotguns are given in drams. A dram equals 27.3 grains in weight. So, if a recommended load is 2½ drams, that equals 69 grains. Remembering that there are 7000 grains to a pound, you can get slightly more than 100 shots from a pound of powder if you use that load.

5. Pour the powder into the bore. Tap the barrel gently to make sure all the powder goes down. Many muzzle-loading shotguns are double-barrel guns. You definitely do *not* want to pour both charges into the same barrel. Work out some sort of system—left first, right second—so that never happens. An efficient method is after the first barrel is loaded, insert a card wad into that muzzle to signify it has been loaded. This will be a safety flag that's hard to miss. Once you decide on a system, use it *every time* you load.

6. Load the wad column. Since we are not shoot-ing a single projectile, we need a certain thickness of wadding to separate the powder and shot. Part of the wad column is a thin over-powder card wad, about ⅛-inch thick. If the shotgun is choked, you may have to start the wad at an angle. When it is in the bore, straighten it with the enlarged end of the ramrod and push it all the way down until it rests firmly on the powder.

Follow the over-powder wad with a thick fiber wad. This may be dampened slightly with commercial blackpowder lubricant if desired. It must be pushed down firmly against the card wad.

7. Load the shot. You should have selected a shot load that matches the powder charge. For the 2½-dram powder charge we discussed a moment ago, a charge of 1 ounce of shot is about right. Various types of dippers and shot flasks for measuring are available. With double-barrel shotguns, use the same system for loading the wads and shot as you used for loading the powder, to be sure you don't double-charge a barrel.

8. Load the over-shot wad. Something has to keep the shot in place, so we use another thin card wad and push it firmly in place over the shot. Again, it is a good idea to mark the ramrod with a reference point for the proper load.

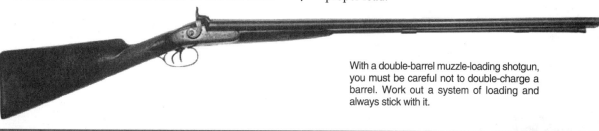

With a double-barrel muzzle-loading shotgun, you must be careful not to double-charge a barrel. Work out a system of loading and always stick with it.

(text continued from page 183)
used to carry a fine probe, called a vent pick, to clear this common problem. Use a small wire or pipe cleaner and make sure the nipple or flash hole is clear. Reprime and try again.

If this does not work, perhaps not enough powder (or no powder at all) has been loaded. It is sometimes possible to become distracted and forget to put in powder. For a percussion gun, remove the nipple with a nipple wrench and trickle in as much powder as possible through the nipple opening in the breech. With a flintlock, sometimes you can work powder in grain by grain through the flash hole. Reseat the ball down onto the powder, reprime and try again.

With a flintlock, the flint itself could be the problem. A dull flint may not produce enough sparks. You can remove the flint and knap (chip) it to sharpen the front edge.

If the gun just will not fire, the load will have to be pulled. A ball puller for balls or a wad puller for shotgun wads, attached to the end of a rod, can dig into the load and pull it back out. Often the ramrod is not sturdy enough for this, and a stronger rod, known as a work rod, must be used. I use a surplus 50-caliber machinegun cleaning rod as a work rod. Once the gun is completely unloaded, it should be thoroughly cleaned before trying to shoot it again.

All this is interesting, but not much fun. I've done it a number of times and can't remember ever enjoying it. It's much better to be very careful with your cleaning and loading procedures, and then you'll never have to worry about failures to fire.

We'll get into more detail in the general chapter on care and cleaning, but remember that blackpowder fouling is corrosive.

(text continues on page 190)

LOADING BLACKPOWDER REVOLVERS

The design of the muzzle-loading revolver is different from that of the guns we've discussed, so the loading procedure is different.

1. Check to be sure the revolver is unloaded. Check from the back end of the gun first! Put the hammer at half-cock and rotate the cylinder. No caps should be on the nipples. Now you can look into the chambers from the front and make sure they are empty.

2. Clean the chambers. Use a short rod and patch to remove oil and residue from the chambers.

3. Clear the ignition channels. Put caps on the nipples and fire them (keeping the gun pointed in a safe direction) to clear the holes in the nipples.

4. Position the revolver for loading. Stand the gun between your knees while kneeling or put it in a loading rack.

5. Measure the powder charge. Using the appropriate measure, fill it from the main powder container.

6. Pour powder into the chambers. Pour the proper amount of powder into each chamber separately. Rotate the cylinder until each chamber has been charged with powder.

7. Seat the balls. Balls for revolvers are slightly oversize and form their own seal without the need for

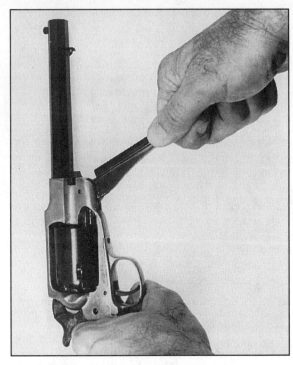

This Remington replica has a different style of rammer, but the loading procedure is the same.

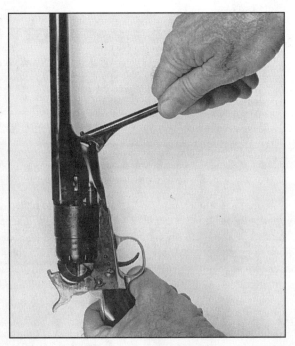

When charging the muzzle-loading revolver, here an 1860 Colt replica, put the hammer in the loading notch so that the cylinder will turn freely, load each chamber with powder, then push down the ball onto the powder with the revolver's rammer.

a patch. Unlatch the loading lever, swing it down and use the rammer to push the ball into the chamber. The ball should be seated firmly against the powder. A little lead will probably be shaved off during the seating, and that's OK. That shows you the ball was large enough to form a good gas seal.

Rotate the cylinder one chamber and repeat the process. Continue until the revolver is completely loaded.

8. Grease the chamber mouths. With balls in all chambers, fill the remainder of the space in each chamber with lubricant. Special lubricants are sold for this purpose, though products such as Crisco have been used with good results for a long time. The grease acts as both a lubricant and a seal. With each shot, it keeps the bore lubricated and softens powder fouling.

The grease also seals unfired chambers from the flash of the one that is firing. If the bullet alone does not make an adequate seal, the flash of firing can set off other chambers not aligned with the barrel. I have witnessed such a chain-fire one time, and I don't care to see it again. Greasing the chamber mouths helps to prevent this.

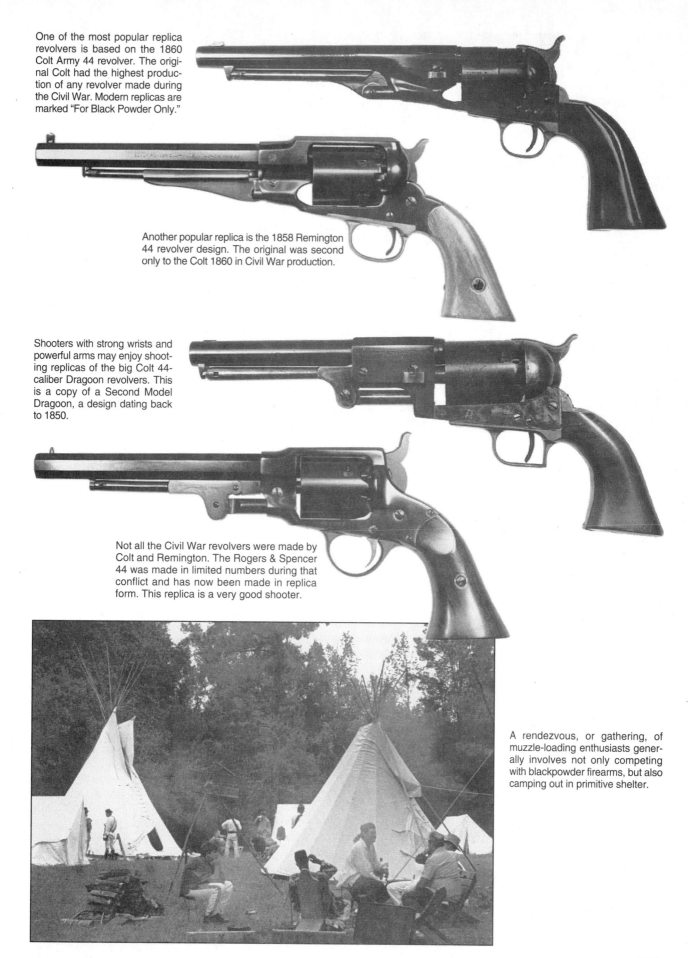

One of the most popular replica revolvers is based on the 1860 Colt Army 44 revolver. The original Colt had the highest production of any revolver made during the Civil War. Modern replicas are marked "For Black Powder Only."

Another popular replica is the 1858 Remington 44 revolver design. The original was second only to the Colt 1860 in Civil War production.

Shooters with strong wrists and powerful arms may enjoy shooting replicas of the big Colt 44-caliber Dragoon revolvers. This is a copy of a Second Model Dragoon, a design dating back to 1850.

Not all the Civil War revolvers were made by Colt and Remington. The Rogers & Spencer 44 was made in limited numbers during that conflict and has now been made in replica form. This replica is a very good shooter.

A rendezvous, or gathering, of muzzle-loading enthusiasts generally involves not only competing with blackpowder firearms, but also camping out in primitive shelter.

Serious hunting can be done with muzzleloaders, but the writer has found sometimes they also give him a good excuse to just get out into the woods.

(text continued from page 187)

Do not let your gun stay uncleaned for any length of time after firing. As in days gone by, the best cleaning solution is hot, soapy water. We are fortunate today to also have a number of commercial blackpowder cleaners. Most of my friends use such cleaners when hunting with a muzzleloader and use hot soapy water after a day on the range.

Be aware, corrosive powder fouling gets into other places besides the bore. It collects around the nipple or pan, inside the locks, and in the rammer mechanism of revolvers. All parts should be washed and dried thoroughly, then lightly oiled.

Muzzleloader Shooting Opportunities
Hunting

I'm not sure if anyone has kept records, but I've heard it said that most muzzle-loading shooters are hunters. Whether or not this is so, there certainly are a lot of opportunities for these hunters. As previously mentioned, many states have set up special muzzle-loading seasons or primitive weapons seasons (muzzleloader and archery combined). Big and small game may be taken, in some areas, with either rifle, pistol or shotgun.

The two-stage "poof-boom" firing sequence of the flintlock requires a steady and consistent hold. Here, Derek Anderson demonstrates good form as he touches off a shot from a 50-caliber mountain rifle.

190

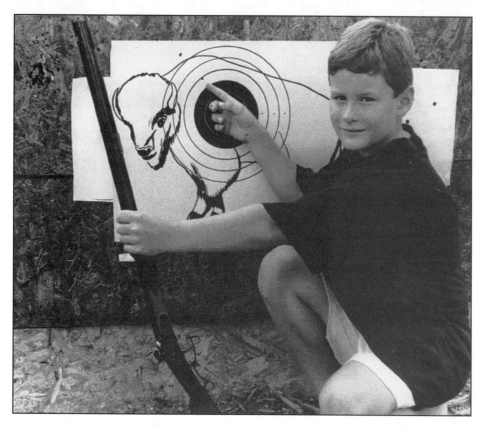

Muzzleloader shooting appeals to shooters of all ages. Josh Levy, nine years old, shows off his first shots from his new 31-caliber percussion rifle. Josh and his father, James, built the scaled-down rifle themselves.

(Below) Dave Anderson demonstrates the operation of a percussion rifle to a group of attentive Boy Scouts as Fred Bingham assists.

Competition

Local shooting clubs often have muzzle-loading matches for members and guests. These are generally relaxed, friendly affairs. National muzzle-loading matches are held annually in Friendship, Indiana, by the National Muzzle-loading Rifle Association.

Qualification

The NRA has a muzzle-loading firearms qualification program. Shooters fire against an established score, and when they have met the qualification for one level, they can move up and begin working toward the next level. Certificates and brassards can be earned at each qualification stage. Courses available are Rifle and Musket, Pistol and Revolver, and Shotgun.

Reenactments

Many reenactments of historic battles have target competition associated with them. The muzzle-loading firearms are generally restricted to originals or replicas of the type available at the time of the battle.

Participation in the reenactments themselves appeals to many people. Reenactments use only powder, without projectiles, in rifles and muskets. Pistols and revolvers use a tiny wad of toilet tissue over the powder to keep it from falling out. Safety rules are very strict. No one actually ever aims at another person, and organizers have reportedly stopped a reenactment just on the rumor of a safety violation.

Shooting the muzzleloader has been a wonderful opportunity to re-live part of our past in the present, and we have every reason to expect it to be a part of our future.

CHAPTER EIGHTEEN

USING
AIRGUNS

I'M NOT SURE anyone really knows how old airguns are. Some old writings, centuries and centuries old, mention weapons that could have been devices to propel projectiles by means of compressed air.

The oldest existing specimen that can be dated with any certainty is a gun in the Royal Danish arsenal. It dates back to before 1600. By the latter part of the 1700s, airguns had become effective military arms. Some Jaeger units of the Austrian army were issued powerful repeating airguns with a bore of about 13mm (52-caliber.) Compared to the flintlocks then commonly in use, they were relatively quiet, produced no smoke cloud, and could fire up to twenty shots per minute. They would shoot reliably in the rain, when flintlocks would not. Effective range was said to be about 100 to 200 meters.

These big airguns were used against the French after the French Revolution. They also saw service in Turkey and Hungary. With all their advantages, they were not without problems. Each soldier had to carry several high-pressure air reservoirs with him, and pump wagons to keep the reservoirs charged had to be assigned to each unit. These Austrian airguns were withdrawn from service about 1801. Apparently, the last official mention of them was in 1806 in a report on their removal to Hungary, as Napoleon's forces marched toward Vienna.

Americans interested in history are probably more familiar with the historical references to the airgun taken on the Lewis and Clark expedition of 1804-1806. The Lewis and Clark journals made at least eighteen references to the airgun without feeling that any detailed description was necessary. An airgun that is apparently the actual one used on that amazing expedition was located recently; it is about 36-caliber and has the air reservoir in its butt. It was used for hunting game and, perhaps unexpectedly, was a great benefit in establishing relations with the Indians along the route. The Indians were becoming familiar with firearms, and the flintlocks of the expedition did not impress them. The airgun was something new. It was able to hit targets yet have no smoke, no flash, and little sound. The Lewis and Clark party demonstrated the airgun on numerous occasions and had little trouble with the Indians.

However, it is obvious that relatively few airguns were being made back then. In those times, guns of any type were used for hunting, protection and military purposes. Airguns were large, powerful—and expensive!

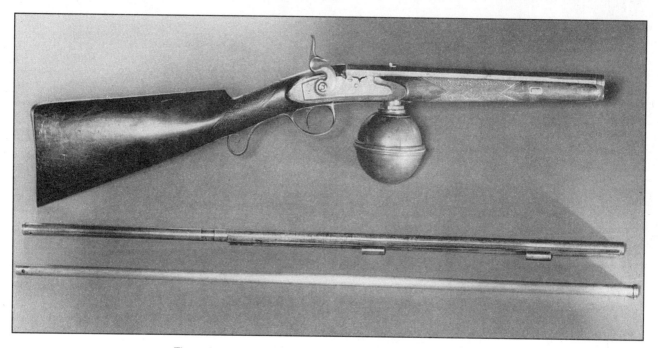

The antique shown here is typical of the airguns used in the early 1800s. This specimen is a ball-reservoir model, with compressed air stored under the forearm. This gun may have begun life as a muzzleloader, as evidenced by the serpentine.

Think about it—working flintlocks could be made with simple hand tools. If there were a question of strength, a part could just be made larger. It may not be true that almost any blacksmith shop could make a flintlock musket, but it is probably not far from wrong.

In contrast, airguns had rather intricate valve systems that required very skilled craftsmanship. They had to have some sort of complex pump system to build pressure. At a time when the knowledge of metallurgy was not well developed, they had to be strong because air pressures of 400 to 900 pounds per square inch (psi) were often stored in their reservoirs. All this had to be accomplished in a gun that was no larger and no heavier than a standard muzzle-loading rifle. Small wonder they were rare and expensive!

The reasons they were made at all were their relative lack of noise, absence of smoke, and—perhaps most important of all—the fact that they could function in bad weather.

When Lewis and Clark returned with their flintlocks and the airgun in 1806, people were already experimenting with a compound called fulminate of mercury. Within a decade or so, percussion caps were being used. By 1820, a percussion gun could be made more cheaply than a flintlock and was nearly as weatherproof as an airgun. Although the flintlock hung on stubbornly for a few decades, it was eventually replaced by the percussion gun. Construction of the big, powerful airguns probably stopped soon after the percussion system had become established.

Reportedly, some lower-powered airguns were made after the Civil War for use in shooting galleries. For use in the field, however, cartridge firearms in calibers from 22 to 58 became common after that conflict. There were really very few niches for airguns to fill.

With the coming of new mass-production techniques, airgun shooting in this country had a revival at the end of this century. The new guns were small and inexpensive. They found a new niche—short-range pest, target and recreational shooting.

By the mid-1880s, the Plymouth Iron Windmill Company of Plymouth, Michigan, was struggling, looking for new ways to attract customers in a collapsing windmill market. In 1886, a local inventor, Clarence Hamilton, showed the company an item that might make a good premium. It was a strange-looking little gun with a wire stock that fired a lead ball of BB shot size, using air pressure. As the story goes, L.C. Hough, the Plymouth president, tried it out and exclaimed, "It's a daisy!"

The name stuck. The Daisy BB gun went into production as a premium given to farmers who bought a windmill. Eventually, it became so popular that orders for the BB guns came in faster than orders for the windmills. More and more production space went to the airguns, and in 1895, the firm officially changed its name to the Daisy Manufacturing Company.

The dying windmill company became a growing airgun company. Daisy introduced a repeater in 1900, a lever action in 1901 and a pump gun in 1913.

The Daisy gun had hardly been introduced to the market when Walter Benjamin began making more complex pneumatic airguns at his home in Grand Tower, Illinois, in 1887. By 1899, sales were so good that he moved the small air rifle company to St. Louis, Missouri.

The Daisy and Benjamin names are still familiar to American shooters. Other companies came and went. Some, such as Crosman (1923) and Sheridan (1945) were formed, and their products still find favor with American shooters.

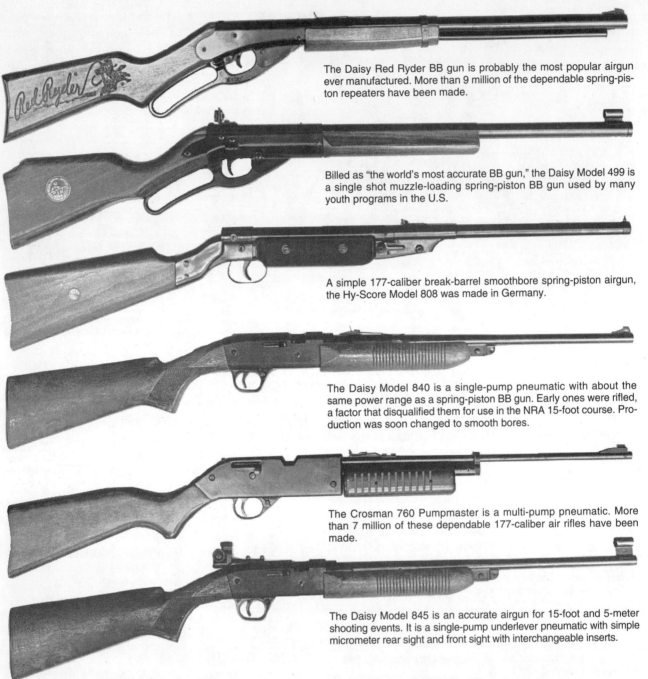

The Daisy Red Ryder BB gun is probably the most popular airgun ever manufactured. More than 9 million of the dependable spring-piston repeaters have been made.

Billed as "the world's most accurate BB gun," the Daisy Model 499 is a single shot muzzle-loading spring-piston BB gun used by many youth programs in the U.S.

A simple 177-caliber break-barrel smoothbore spring-piston airgun, the Hy-Score Model 808 was made in Germany.

The Daisy Model 840 is a single-pump pneumatic with about the same power range as a spring-piston BB gun. Early ones were rifled, a factor that disqualified them for use in the NRA 15-foot course. Production was soon changed to smooth bores.

The Crosman 760 Pumpmaster is a multi-pump pneumatic. More than 7 million of these dependable 177-caliber air rifles have been made.

The Daisy Model 845 is an accurate airgun for 15-foot and 5-meter shooting events. It is a single-pump underlever pneumatic with simple micrometer rear sight and front sight with interchangeable inserts.

Types of Air Guns

Both air pistols and air rifles are of two basic types—spring-piston and pneumatic.

Spring-Piston

These airguns use a manually operated lever of some sort (in some cases, it is the barrel itself) to compress a strong spring. The spring powers a piston that moves forward when released by the trigger. As it moves rapidly forward, the piston compresses air in front of it. The compressed air then forces the projectile out of the barrel.

Note that in a spring-piston airgun, the air is not stored in a compressed state before firing. The air is compressed by the movement of the piston *after* the trigger is pulled.

It is interesting to note that spring-piston airguns fall into some very different categories. Inexpensive smoothbore youth-type BB guns are spring-piston guns. So are the expensive precision air rifles used in international and Olympic competition.

Compression of air increases its temperature. Because the spring piston target guns do not compress air until the instant of firing, the temperature at the instant of firing is always constant, thus the pressure is always constant. By contrast, the theory goes, pneumatics will have different temperatures for shots taken at different times after pumping.

Pneumatic

This type of airgun uses compressed air also, but the air is compressed and stored *before* firing. Although CO_2 guns are

This low-powered Marksman pistol is one of the few examples of a slide-operated pistol. Suitable for short-range indoor shooting, it is fun to use and has remained popular for decades. Any resemblance to a 1911A1 Colt 45, I suspect, is purely intentional.

There were few true semi-automatic pellet pistols in years past, but this Benjamin 422, made back in the early 1960s, is one. Although the sights are only coarsely adjustable, the pistol was satisfactory for use in timed- and rapid-fire stages of the NRA Air Pistol course.

(Right) The Daisy Model 188 is a spring-piston air pistol that can use either BBs or pellets.

(Left) This Daisy Model 722, a 22-caliber, sidelever, single-stroke pneumatic, was one of a series of target pistols produced during Daisy's effort to make a "world class" air pistol. The 22 was dropped because all international shooting uses 177-caliber pistols. The micrometer sights are plastic, but it is a very accurate pistol.

The Crosman 38T is a CO_2-powered pneumatic 177-caliber revolver. In general appearance and feel, it is very similar to a Smith & Wesson revolver, and such airguns have been used for preliminary revolver training. With its adjustable sights, such an airgun would allow a shooter to begin the timed- and rapid-fire stages of the NRA 25-foot pistol qualification course.

sometimes considered separately from air guns that compress their own air, let us consider them here as pneumatics.

Pneumatics fall into three general categories—single stroke; multi-pump; CO_2.

In a *single-stroke* pneumatic, a manually operated lever of some sort is used to force air through valves to compress the air and store it in a reservoir. One stroke of the mechanism charges the reservoir with enough compressed air for one shot. After the single stroke, additional strokes should not be made. In some cases, they will have no effect; in others, additional strokes may actually damage the gun.

A *multi-pump* pneumatic also uses a lever and valve mechanism to compress and store air in the reservoir. However, the valve mechanism is more complex, allowing repeated pumps to increase the pressure in the reservoir. The pressure determines the velocity of the projectile, so the same gun can be used for different activities that require different power levels. Just vary the number of pumps for different situations.

In both single-stroke and multi-pump guns, the compressed air remains in the reservoir until the shooter releases it to fire the shot. Pulling the trigger releases all the stored air to propel the projectile through the barrel and on its way. For the next shot, the shooter begins the procedure by pumping more air into the reservoir.

CO_2 guns use metal cylinders of compressed carbon dioxide gas to provide power. Some guns have a reservoir that can be charged from a large CO_2 tank, a compressed-air tank or an external air pump. The valve system on these guns is such that a measured portion of the gas is released for each shot. Thus, once the gun's reservoir is charged, a number of shots can be fired before recharging is necessary.

Air Compression Mechanisms

There are a great number of mechanical designs to compress the air in airguns. Let us break these down into five categories, which are the ones used in the NRA's airgun handbook: break-barrel; overlever; underlever; sidelever; slide.

Break-barrel mechanisms are often called barrel-cocking. They use the barrel itself as a lever. The barrel is hinged near its rear portion to the frame or receiver. The mechanism is operated by pulling the forward portion of the barrel down. Linkage pivoted to the barrel operates the mechanism, either compressing a powerful mainspring on a spring-piston gun or pumping air into a pneumatic reservoir.

Break-barrel guns have good cocking leverage and are relatively simple. Because the precise alignment of the barrel and receiver is not constant, open sights—front and rear sights both mounted on the barrel—are generally used on such guns.

The *overlever* mechanism is a variation of the break-barrel design. It also uses a barrel hinged to the front of the frame or receiver, but the mechanism is operated by lifting the rear of the barrel upward. Overlever guns are not all that common, and they all seem to be pneumatics.

Underlever airguns use a lever located on the underside of the gun. To operate, the lever pulls downward. This category includes spring-piston BB guns such as the popular Daisy lever-action types. It also includes a large number of pneumatics such as those made by Crosman, Benjamin, Sheridan, Daisy and others. Such guns have the underlever pivoted near the front of the gun, and its handle is generally the forearm of the gun.

Underlever guns have the barrel and receiver in permanent alignment. This makes the installation of receiver or optical sights more practical.

Sidelever guns may be either spring-piston or pneumatic. They use a lever located either on the left or right side of the receiver. Sidelever mechanisms are favored for many target guns because they can be operated with a minimum of shifting of the shooter's position. Sidelever rifles also allow rigid mounting of receiver sights for precision target shooting.

A *slide* mechanism uses a movable part of the upper rear portion of the gun. The best-known example is probably the low-powered Marksman repeating pistol. This gun achieves half its compression on the rear stroke and the other half on the forward stroke.

The Marksman pistol achieves half its compression on the back stroke and half on the forward stroke, thus allowing a compact pistol. It can use BBs as a repeater or pellets as a single shot.

Multi-pump pneumatic rifles are generally underlever guns, with the pivot on a forward part of the gun. Here, the writer pumps a Daisy 880, a 177-caliber air rifle.

The power for the Crosman 38T comes from a CO_2 cylinder housed inside the grip. The revolver may be fired either double or single action.

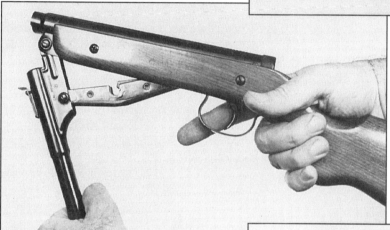

Spring-piston break-barrel guns, such as this 177-caliber Hy-Score, cock the spring by pivoting the barrel downward.

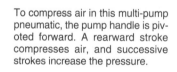

To compress air in this multi-pump pneumatic, the pump handle is pivoted forward. A rearward stroke compresses air, and successive strokes increase the pressure.

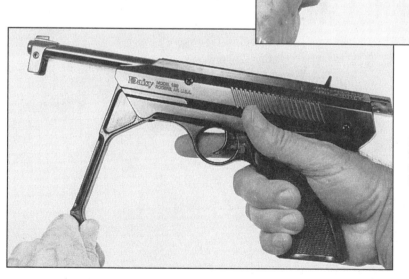

Pulling down the underlever on the Daisy Model 188 cocks the spring and opens the action for loading.

Airgun Ammunition

Airguns are designed to use a particular kind of ammunition, although some will use several kinds. Airguns fall generally into four common calibers: 177 (4.5mm), 20 (5mm), 22 (5.5mm), and 25 (6.35mm).

There are five basic types of airgun projectiles: pellets, BBs, lead balls, darts and bolts. Some smoothbores can use several types, but rifled airguns should use only pellets or lead balls. Some rifled airguns have been advertised for use with either pellets or BBs. This use is perfectly safe, but owners have generally found that the steel BBs wear the rifling over time. Subsequent accuracy with pellets suffers.

Pellets are most commonly hourglass shaped, with a wide head, narrow waist and wide skirt. This design is sometimes called a "diabolo" pellet, named after an object of similar shape used in the ancient game of Diabolo. The head, which may be any of several shapes, is positioned toward the muzzle when loaded. The thin flared skirt acts as a seal for the air pressure and rides the rifling in rifled guns. Because of the pellet's deep hollow base, a number of people have noted at least a passing resemblance to a Minie ball. The pellets work well in smoothbore as well as rifled guns, because the weight-forward design stabilizes them in flight. Some pellets are made in cylindrical form, but apparently not for all calibers.

BBs are round balls, generally made of steel, but sometimes of lead. They are of nominal .177-inch diameter, but steel BBs are actually a tiny bit smaller. Steel BBs are the correct projectiles for spring-piston repeating BB guns and also work well in many smoothbore 177 guns of other types. The little balls are coated with copper or zinc to prevent corrosion. Again, it seems a good idea not to use steel BBs in any rifled barrel, even if advertised to be OK for such use.

Lead balls are available in 177, 22 and 25 calibers. They are sometimes used for metallic silhouette shooting with airguns.

Darts and *bolts* are two types of pointed projectiles intended for dartboard targets. It is recommended that they be fired only in smoothbore barrels, although some rifled barrels apparently can use certain types of bolts.

Shooting the Airgun

The safety rules for airgun use are essentially the same as for firearms use. Airguns are not toys; they must be handled in the same safe manner as are firearms. Review the safety rules in Chapter 2.

The fundamentals of shooting air rifles and air pistols are essentially the same as those we've covered for rifle and pistol shooting. Review Chapters 6 and 11, respectively.

Some special aspects of shooting airguns, however, deserve additional consideration. Loading an airgun should be done properly. Because there are so many different designs, the manufacturer's instructions should always be consulted.

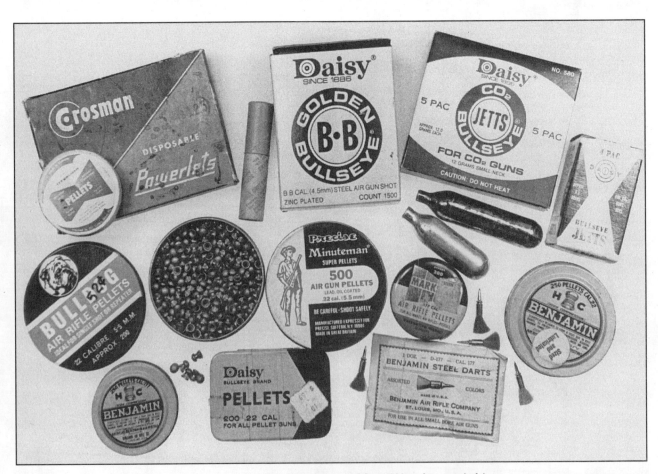

An assortment of pellets, BBs, darts and CO_2 cartridges form a colorful display and indicate the wide variety of airgun ammunition available.

Shooting an airgun is a fun activity that can be done just about any-place. Here, Patrick Malloy tries out a Daisy Model 880, a 177-cal-iber pneumatic.

Dry-firing (shooting an unloaded gun) is of great value in developing shooting skills with firearms. However, many, perhaps most, airguns will be damaged by dry-firing. Reportedly, some precision target airguns are specially designed to allow dry-firing. If you are not absolutely certain that dry-firing is OK for your airgun, *do not* do it!

Unloading an airgun can be different from unloading a firearm. As with loading, the manufacturer's instructions should be consulted and followed. Many airguns cannot be unloaded and must be fired to remove a projectile. I recall a situation in which smallbore rifle shooters and air rifle shooters were both on the same firing line. For some reason, the command "cease fire" was called. The smallbore shooters stopped firing, opened their bolts and removed any unfired cartridges. Air rifle shooters stopped fire and opened their guns, but could not unload pellets already in the guns. No one was quite sure what to do. Obviously, no one could go forward of the firing line under those circumstances, and the air rifles had to be closed again and fired to unload them before the line was safe. Think ahead and plan for situations such as this.

Compression of air causes a rise in temperature. The sudden compression of some spring-piston airguns can cause enough temperature rise to ignite low flash-point lubricants, such as some light petroleum-based oils. This condition is known as dieseling and could possibly injure a shooter or damage a gun. Follow the lubrication guidelines of the manufacturer to avoid this problem.

Some airguns have a provision for mounting an optical sight. Many have been equipped with inexpensive scopes designed for 22-caliber rifles. Be aware that some scopes, while designed to withstand straight-line recoil, may not be resistant to a sudden two-way snap, or to the vibration produced by some airguns. If you are going to scope an airgun, check with the manufacturer of the scope to see if it is suitable.

Air-Powered Shotguns

We have gone on as if the only airguns ever made were rifles and handguns. What about shotguns?

Yes, some air and CO_2 shotguns have been made. They are not common, but a number of different designs were tried. Perhaps the most advanced was the Crosman Trapmaster, a .380-inch-bore CO_2-powered gun introduced in the late 1960s. The gun could be bought separately or as a set with its own miniature trap and targets. It used two CO_2 cartridges and tiny shot-shells that contained about sixty pellets of #8 shot. This design apparently worked well, but its performance was limited and sales were poor. It was discontinued during the 1970s.

Airgun Activities

Airguns can be used safely and legally in many situations in which the use of a firearm might not be legal or appropriate. Let's consider some of them: indoor shooting; plinking and novelty shooting; hunting; qualification and competition; Olympic and international shooting.

Indoor Shooting

Indoor shooting can be done anywhere there is a safe area. Because most indoor shooting, sooner or later, is going to be done on 15-foot or 5-meter (16.5 feet) NRA targets, the range should have at least that much space between the firing line and the face of the target. More space will be needed for firing positions, moving-around space, and so on.

There should be both a primary backstop and a secondary backstop. The primary backstop is to stop and collect the pellets or BBs. It can be a sophisticated pellet trap or it can be a cardboard box filled with newspapers, magazines or telephone books. Targets can be taped to the side of the box. Behind the target, the box should contain loosely wadded newspaper to prevent rebounds. Behind the crumpled news-

Two boys shoot their Red Ryder BB guns on a shooting range. Some people think this is about as much fun as airgun shooting needs to be.

paper, the other filler material should be upright and packed tightly.

What if a shot misses the box? A loosely hung piece of carpet or canvas can serve as a secondary backstop to catch any shots that might miss the primary backstop. For indoor shooting, stick to lower-powered airguns. If you have outdoor space available, then a dirt bank or bales of hay will make an excellent secondary backstop for the more powerful air rifles.

Plinking and Novelty Shooting

Informal shooting at informal targets is a sport made to order for airguns. A safe location, of course, is a must. Know where every BB or pellet will go. Candy mints, aspirin tablets and crackers all make good biodegradable targets. Aluminum drink cans are easily penetrated by airguns and make a satisfying clink when hit. After you finish shooting, be sure to properly dispose of your targets.

Small metallic silhouettes designed for airgun use are available. These targets are used in competition also, but can be shot just for the fun of it. Field Target shooting is a recent development of airgun shooting. The targets are steel silhouettes that have varied shapes resembling crows, squirrels, rabbits and foxes. The targets may be placed along an outdoor course in a natural setting.

Hunting

The taking of small game and pests can be successfully done with airguns. It is important to keep everything in perspective, however. Even the most powerful airguns of today still have less power than that of a 22 Short. This means that if you are unlikely to make a clean one-shot kill on the intended game with a 22 Short, that game should not be hunted with an airgun. Pests such as rats and starlings are within the capabilities of the more powerful of today's airguns. Rabbit and squirrel hunting call for careful head shots.

For a dedicated airgun shooter, hunting presents a challenge. Careful shot placement becomes more important than power. Getting into close range takes great skill, and successful airgun hunters are among the best of hunters.

One of the best airgun hunters I ever knew was a young boy in South Louisiana, back in the 1960s. With five kids in his family, extra meat on the table was always welcome. After school, he would slip into the woods near his home with an open-sighted 177-caliber Benjamin Model 317 air rifle. Taking only head shots at sitting rabbits at close range, he seldom came out of the woods without a cottontail or two. That young fellow was one of the best hunters I ever met.

Several decades later, I made the acquaintance of another patient hunter with a later-model Benjamin Model 347, also a 177. This man viewed squirrels more as pests than as game. He used his Benjamin with careful shots on squirrels to protect his pecan trees. The sound of a firearm might have made them leave temporarily. However, his aim was to eliminate them, not scare them. For quiet, one-by-one control, he felt his air rifle was the best solution. The squirrel stew was just a bonus.

Qualification and Competition

Paper targets are really the best way to see how good you are with an air rifle or air pistol. A lot of people shoot at paper targets just for fun. However, most of us tend to remember our good shots and forget our bad ones. It is worth measuring your skills, by either qualification or competition.

Qualification is simply shooting against a certain set of scores. When you achieve the skill required to reach one level, you can go on to the next level. The National Rifle Association has a number of airgun qualification courses. Shooters may earn certificates, brassards and medals for the stages they complete. Here is listing of the qualification courses available at the time of this writing: 15-foot Air Rifle; 25-foot Air Rifle; 25-foot Air Pistol; 10-meter Position Air Rifle; 25-foot Position Air Rifle; 5-meter BB Gun; 10-meter Running Target Air Rifle; 10-meter Precision Air Rifle; 10-meter Air Pistol.

Competition may be at local, regional or state levels throughout the country. Airgun competitions are coordinated through the NRA and are held in these disciplines: 5-meter BB Gun; Position Air Rifle; International Pistol; International Rifle; International Running Target; Pistol Silhouette; Rifle Silhouette.

For young people, marksmanship training programs are held by the National Guard, U.S. Jaycees and Junior Olympic Shooting Program camps. The Boy Scouts of America permit the use of airguns in earning the Rifle Shooting merit badge. Many Scout councils have airgun shooting for older Cub Scouts and Boy Scouts. The Presidential Sports Award can also be earned in Air Rifle Shooting.

Olympic Shooting

Olympic competition is the highest goal for people involved in many sports. I always like to see someone who is at least approaching my age competing in the Olympics; it seems that only in the shooting events do we see athletes who have passed their twenties. This suggests that not only is shooting a lifetime sport, it is, age-wise, the best equal-opportunity sport in the Olympics.

Air rifle and air pistol events are relative newcomers to the Olympics, but they are very popular events. The reasons for this are the same as for any airgun activity: Every city that hosts the Olympics can find space for airgun shooting, and everyone working toward the Olympics can find space for airgun practice.

Here is air rifle shooting of a more serious sort. These five young men—Andrew Bard, Derek Ritter, Brian Hirte, James Dillahey and Scott Burns—were among the outstanding 10-meter air rifle shooters at the 1994 Florida Junior Olympic Shooting Camp.

International Air Rifle competition is shot entirely from the standing position. This position worked pretty well for Derek Ritter, who won the gold medal for air rifle shooting at the 1994 Florida Junior Olympic Shooting Camp.

Another step up. Bruce Buell, a well-known North Florida Smallbore shooter, gets in some practice for International Air Rifle shooting.

There are three Olympic airgun events:

Air Pistol is fired at 10 meters, with any 177 air- or gas-powered pistol. Men fire sixty shots in 1 hour and 45 minutes. Women, considered more delicate, I suppose, only fire forty shots in 1 hour and 15 minutes.

Air Rifle is fired at 10 meters, standing position, with any 177 air rifle weighing not more than 12.12 pounds. Men fire sixty shots in 1 hour and 45 minutes. Again, women only fire forty shots in 1 hour and 15 minutes.

I think that this separation of men and women dates back to 1976. Through those games, men and women competed on an equal basis. That year, in the 50-meter Smallbore rifle match, Lanny Bassham and Margaret Murdock, both U.S. shooters, took the top two places with identical scores. Apparently, that was just too much male/female equality for all the European men who had been beaten. In later Olympics, women had to shoot different courses.

Running Target is fired at 10 meters with a 177 rifle weighing not more than 12.12 pounds. A 4x riflescope may be used. Men fire thirty slow shots and thirty fast shots. Women fire twenty slow and twenty fast shots.

These same courses are fired in other international competitions, such as the World Games and the Pan American Games.

Airguns have many advantages. They are inexpensive to shoot, require little space and have a low noise level. They can be used in situations and places in which firearms might not be legal or appropriate.

Today's airguns are remarkably accurate. They can provide practice that applies to all firearms, or they can provide sport all their own.

Airguns are free of most of the legal and environmental restrictions placed against firearms. Many school marksmanship programs, set up in years past for smallbore rifle and pistol shooting, no longer can use firearms. The programs still survive because of the use of airguns.

With a few different airguns, a person can enjoy rifle and pistol plinking, qualification and competition. He can dispatch pests and hunt small game. He can shoot in the woods; he can shoot in his living room; he can shoot in the Olympics!

Airgun use in America is growing, and this is a benefit to the entire realm of the shooting sports.

CHAPTER NINETEEN

GUN CARE AND CLEANING

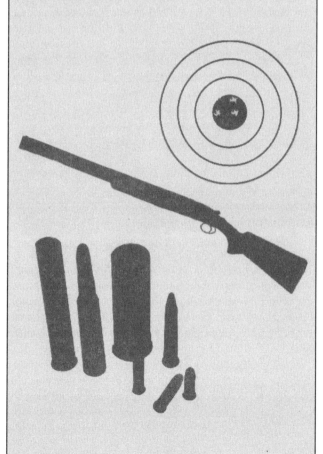

"**NEVER LET THE** sun set on an uncleaned gun."

"A gun can be ruined by too much cleaning as easily as by neglect."

"Clean immediately after each use."

"Leave it alone as much as possible."

These statements were taken from various firearms publications, and all pertain to gun cleaning. Is it any wonder some new shooters are a bit confused about how and when to clean their guns?

Since agreement is not universal as to procedures, let us at least be sure we agree about *concepts.* A gun, even an inexpensive one, is a valuable piece of precision equipment. It can last several lifetimes if properly maintained. If we are in agreement here, then we should agree that cleaning and maintenance are necessary. The purpose of cleaning a gun is to maintain its appearance, performance and value.

Let common sense guide us in how often and how much to clean our guns. We don't want to deliberately ignore our guns and let them deteriorate and malfunction from lack of attention. We also don't want to clean them to death, scrubbing the rifling out of the bore, rubbing off the finish, and saturating everything with solvent and oil.

Also, different types of guns require different types of attention. Obviously, a day of airgun shooting will not call for the same cleaning procedures as a day of muzzleloader shooting.

In general, a gun should be cleaned after a day of use. Also, if a gun has been stored for a long period of time, it's a good idea to at least give it a quick cleaning before using it again.

Cleaning Equipment

For just about any type of gun, we will need to have certain things: a suitable cleaning rod, with attachments; cleaning patches; bore cleaner or solvent; gun oil; soft cloth; and small brush.

Let's look at these items in just a bit of detail.

A *cleaning rod* is a straight rod long enough to go through the bore. Always clean from the breech, if possible. If you are cleaning, say, a bolt-action rifle, the rod should be at least as long as the length of the combined barrel and receiver, not just the barrel.

Steel or brass rods, or rods coated with plastic or nylon, are favored by many, but aluminum rods seem to be the most common. The only thing wrong with aluminum is that it is soft

203

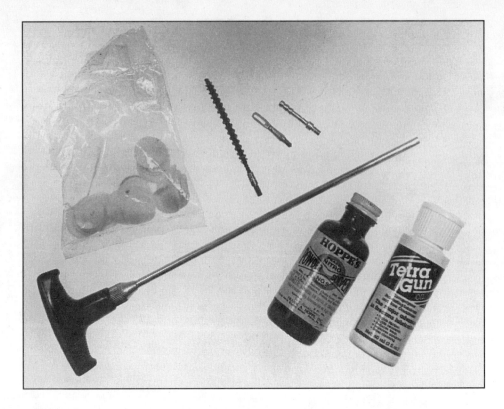

A minimum set of cleaning items to care for a gun are a rod with brush and tips, patches, solvent and oil. A soft cloth and a small brush should also be added.

enough for grit particles to become embedded in the metal. Such grit may then be carried into the bore, so be careful not to let this happen if you use an aluminum rod.

Screw-in cleaning rod attachments needed are a *tip* or two to hold cloth patches and a bore *brush*, generally with brass bristles of the correct size to fit your bore.

Cleaning patches, generally made from white cotton flannel or other absorbent cloth, should be of the correct size for your bore. "Correct size" means they do not stick in the bore, nor do they slip through without cleaning anything. Patches allow you to apply solvent or oil to the bore, and to remove fouling and other foreign material. You can buy patches or you can make them.

Bore cleaning solvent loosens fouling and deposits from powder, lead, copper or plastic, allowing that noxious stuff to be removed from the bore. A number of good commercial solvents are available.

Gun oil is light oil that serves both as a lubricant and preservative to prevent rusting. Any gun shop can supply good gun oil. New synthetic oils are reported to perform better than the older petroleum-based oils.

A soft *cloth* is needed for wiping the exterior surfaces. Cotton flannel is a good choice.

A small *brush* is needed to clean inside actions and receivers and in all the little nooks and crannies every gun seems to have. An old clean toothbrush works well.

Before you begin to clean a gun, make *absolutely sure* that it is unloaded. Check the chamber and magazine. Move all ammunition away from the cleaning area. The action should stay open during the cleaning process.

Our first task is to clean the bore. Bullets or shot or wads or other things have been rushing through it, leaving behind bits of

lead or copper or plastic as they go. Burning powder pushes these projectiles, and it also leaves a residue.

It is true that modern cartridges with smokeless powder and non-corrosive primers do not need cleaning in the sense that guns of yesteryear did. Still, it makes sense not to keep pushing shot after shot through the accumulating foreign material in the bore.

Our next concern is the functioning of the gun. The action came from the factory designed to operate with certain clearances between parts. These clearances fill with grit and powder residue, which can prevent the gun from working, so it doesn't make much sense to let this stuff accumulate.

Another concern is the exterior. I suppose it is possible that a gun covered with rust could shoot as well as one with an unblemished exterior, but if we let rust and corrosion cover the outside, some of it might get into the action or bore. Better not take the chance. Maintain the exterior as part of your routine cleaning, for the sake of performance as well as appearance.

Cleaning for Corrosive Ammunition

Corrosive ammunition is back again! Ah, it was wonderful when all available ammunition was non-corrosive. Non-corrosive primers were introduced to America in 1927 and became essentially universal here before World War II. However, military ammunition used corrosive primers for some time afterward.

For more than two decades following World War II, surplus corrosive ammunition—both U.S. and foreign—was available at low prices. It was wonderful to have this inexpensive ammunition available, and it gave a great boost to the shooting sports. Part of the price, however, had to be paid after the shooting was done.

CLEANING THE RIFLE

Using a copper bristle brush coated with commercial bore solvent, scrub the bore from the breech end to loosen caked-on fouling.

1. Attach a bore brush to the cleaning rod and wet the brush with solvent. Push it back and forth through the bore a few times to loosen residue and fouling. Make sure the brush goes all the way through; do not reverse the bristles inside the bore. When possible, clean from the breech to avoid possible wear of the rifling at the muzzle. Some shooters prefer not to use a brush to clean 22 rifles and use only patches.

2. Put a tip on the rod and push a series of patches through the bore to remove the residue that has been loosened. If, after several patches, they do not come out clean,

go back to step one and use the brush again. When a clean patch comes out, push an oiled patch through the bore to protect it from rust.

3. Clean any foreign material from the rifle's working parts, using a patch, cloth, brush or any combination of these. Use solvent if necessary, then dry and lightly oil the parts.

4. Wipe the exterior with an oiled cloth or rust-preventive wiper. All exposed metal surfaces should be protected from rust. After oiling, handle the rifle by the stock when putting it away.

Be sure to clean all moving parts of powder fouling—otherwise, the action may stick.

After a thorough internal cleaning, always rub down the exterior with light oil to preserve the looks and prevent rust.

Corrosive primers are made with potassium chlorate, which makes an excellent primer. It works well and has a long useful life. However, when fired it deposits potassium chloride in the bore, which is a chemical salt. Potassium chloride is related to sodium chloride, common table salt. It has the same property of absorbing moisture from the air. In a rifle or pistol bore, the moisture is held against the steel and causes rust in a relatively short period of time.

At the time of this writing, surplus military (and some sporting) ammunition with corrosive primers is being imported at attractive prices, from a great many sources. Some of this ammunition is known to be corrosive and is labeled as such; some is called "mildly corrosive." (Whatever can that mean?) Some has been labeled non-corrosive when it really is corrosive. If in doubt about any foreign ammunition, treat it as corrosive. Don't blame the packagers too much. They probably couldn't read English and had no idea what the labels said. At any rate, we are fortunate to have the opportunity to use this ammunition.

However, if you use corrosive ammunition, the only thing you can depend on to keep your bore from rusting is water. Ordinary cleaning methods do not remove potassium chloride from the bore. You must dissolve these salts with water. Sure, ordinary cleaning will physically push some of the salt out with the residue, but there will still be some left, and rusting can start under the oil.

The old military method of cleaning three times came about because of corrosive priming. Before the cause of the rusting came to be understood, military personnel were instructed to clean their firearms completely, three times. Each cleaning pushed out more of the salt. This procedure reduced the effect of the rusting, but did not really stop it.

Once the cause of the problem was recognized, the solution was simple. Flush the bore with water to dissolve the salt into solution, dry it thoroughly, and then clean the gun normally.

A good way to begin this process is to put a few inches of hot, soapy water into a bucket or large tin can. Stick the rifle muzzle into the can. With a tight-fitting patch on a rod, simply

CLEANING THE SHOTGUN

1. Attach a cloth patch to the cleaning rod and wet the patch with solvent. Push it through the bore a few times to loosen residue. If the bore has streaks of lead from shot, or streaks of plastic from wads, first use a bristle brush wet with solvent, followed by a solvent-soaked patch. When possible, clean from the breech to avoid unnecessary wear from the rod in the choke area and at the muzzle.

2. Clean the loosened residue from the bore with a series of clean patches. Continue until the last patch comes out clean. Then run an oiled patch through the bore to protect it from rust.

3. Clean any foreign material from the shotgun's working parts. Use a patch, cloth or small brush as needed, then lightly oil the parts.

4. Wipe the exterior with a lightly oiled cloth or rust-preventive cloth. All exposed metal surfaces should be protected from rust.

Note: For years, some people successfully avoided routine daily cleaning of their shotguns after smokeless powder and non-corrosive primers became common. However, when plastic-cased shotshells arrived, we discovered something new—chamber rusting. Generally, shotguns that were not cleaned regularly had no problem with their bores, but sometimes they developed rust in the chambers. This was a real mystery, because there was nothing in the powder or primer that could cause rust. I'm not sure we understand the mechanism of this yet. It

Don't forget to clean the action after you've scrubbed the fouling from the bore.

occurs only with plastic shotshells, but the plastic itself does not seem to be the cause. Perhaps the waxed exterior of the older paper shells protected the chamber in a way that plastic does not. Whatever the reason, it is easy to prevent. Just clean your gun after you use it.

CLEANING THE HANDGUN

1. Use a solvent-wetted bore brush on the cleaning rod and push it through the bore a few times to loosen fouling and residue. When possible, clean from the breech.

The easiest way to get to the breech of many semi-automatic barrels is to remove the barrel from the gun. Most revolvers and some semi-automatics have to be cleaned from the muzzle. Be careful not to unnecessarily wear the rifling near the muzzle. With a revolver, use the brush in each chamber of the cylinder as well as in the bore.

2. Remove the brush from the rod, put on a tip, and use a series of patches to clean the loosened residue from the bore and chambers. If the last patch is still dirty, repeat the first step. Continue until the last patch comes out acceptably clean. Push an oiled patch through the bore to protect it from rust.

3. Clean foreign material and powder residue from the working parts and from all recesses in the mechanism, using a brush, patch or cloth. Residue forms at the junction between the barrel and cylinder of a revolver, so be sure to clean the barrel, frame, and face of the cylinder here. Some semi-automatic pistols should be partially disassembled for cleaning. Powder fouling often builds up in the mechanism enough to affect functioning. Follow the manufacturer's instructions for disassembly.

4. Wipe all metal surfaces with an oiled cloth or rust-preventive cloth. After the metal has been protected, handle the handgun by the grips.

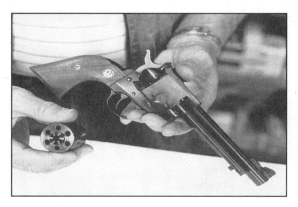

Begin by disassembling the handgun. With many revolvers, the barrel cannot be removed.

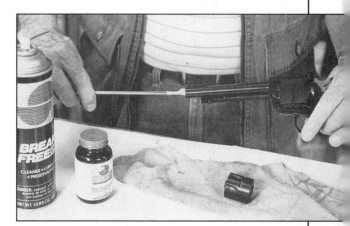

Run a solvent-coated cleaning patch through the bore and each chamber in the cylinder.

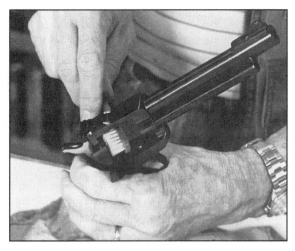

Thoroughly clean the action of residue. An old toothbrush works well.

Remember, gun maintenance is not complete until the exterior has received the same attention as the interior.

pump the water up and down inside the bore. If the water is very hot it will evaporate quickly, and the heat speeds drying of the bore.

The barrel can be removed from some semi-automatic pistols, and water can be pumped through them the same way. Revolver barrels and chambers should be swabbed generously with water-soaked patches.

Different arsenals changed from corrosive to non-corrosive priming at different times. To be on the safe side, consider all U.S. military ammunition made before 1958 as corrosive. Any foreign ammunition from an unknown source should be considered to be corrosive until it can be proven that it is not. A quick water treatment is cheap insurance against a damaged bore.

I hope I am not spending too much time on this, but too many good firearms have been damaged by the use of corrosive ammunition and improper cleaning.

Cleaning The Airgun

Because an airgun uses only air or gas as a propellant, airgun bores require only minimal care.

In spring-piston guns, a tiny bit of lubricant is often blown into the bore from the air compression chamber. This is actually a benefit, as it generally is enough to prevent the bore from rusting. Periodic cleaning of the residue should be done, though.

The situation is different with pneumatics. The air going through the bore may not have any trace of lubricants. Thus, a protective film of oil should be put into the bore to prevent rust.

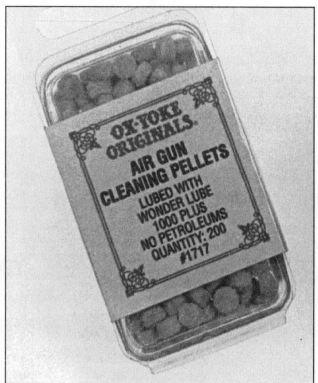

Potassium chloride salts from corrosive primers can be dissolved and flushed out by pumping hot water through the bore with a tight patch on a rod. The writer cleans an 8mm 1938 Turkish Mauser after shooting it with corrosive ammunition.

Airguns can be cleaned with a rod, but another option is simply to shoot a cleaning pellet through the bore. These are for a 177-caliber airgun.

Some pneumatics have barrels made of bronze to prevent bore rusting.

Some pneumatics and some spring-piston rifles drive unlubricated pellets fast enough to leave traces of lead in the bore. Lubricated pellets leave traces of lubrication. All this adds up to the fact that airguns are not totally maintenance-free. Periodic attention to the bore, oiling of moving parts according to the makers specifications, and wiping the exterior metal surfaces are about all the maintenance airguns need.

Cleaning rods and accessories are available for 177 airgun bores. When possible, clean from the rear of the barrel because wear at the muzzle can adversely affect accuracy. If the gun cannot be cleaned from the rear, use special care when cleaning from the muzzle.

Be careful when selecting oil and solvents for cleaning an airgun. Some solvents formulated for firearms fouling may damage the seals of airguns. Follow the manufacturer's recommendations.

One neat little item that airgunners have that other shooters do not is cleaning pellets. These little pellets are generally made of felt or other soft material and are sized to fit the bore of the gun. They are loaded into the airgun in the same way as standard projectiles. When the gun is fired, the pellets scrub the bore as they zip through. An appropriate cleaner or preservative may be on the pellets or may be added before firing. Some manufacturers recommend that two or more pellets be used at a time.

Some shooters use them after a certain number of shots have been fired. When a little oil is applied, cleaning pellets can leave a protective coating in the bore. Used dry, they can remove oil before shooting.

Exterior surfaces should be wiped with an oiled cloth, or a cloth with some other rust-preventing compound. After the gun has been oiled, avoid skin contact with metal parts.

Cleaning the Muzzleloader

The residue from blackpowder is very corrosive, so the gun must be cleaned at the end of each day. Blackpowder residue is also very messy, and some folks manage to cover themselves with it during the cleaning process.

The materials needed for cleaning blackpowder guns are few and simple. You need a rod, patches, a container of soapy water, and some oil. There are some commercial blackpowder solvents that are very effective, but they aren't really necessary. After all, some blackpowder guns over a century old are still shooting, and they were cleaned only with soap and water.

Muzzle-Loading Rifle

It usually makes things easier to remove the barrel. This way, you can place the breech in a container of soapy water and flush the barrel. It also keeps water or solvent from getting into the lock or on the finish of the stock.

For a hook-breech rifle, simply remove the barrel key from the forend and lift the barrel out of the stock. If the barrel is fitted with a breech plug that forms the tang, you can also remove the screw holding the tang and then lift the barrel out of the stock. In many cases, you must first make sure the ramrod has

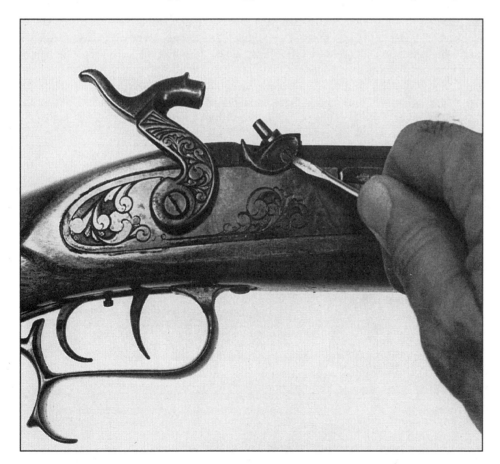

Some muzzle-loading percussion firearms have a cleanout screw that can be removed to aid in cleaning. With the screw out, a straight passage into the bore is opened.

To remove the barrel of a hook-breech muzzleloader for cleaning, tap out the barrel key and pivot the barrel up and forward.

been removed from its recesses before doing this. If it is a percussion rifle, remove the nipple.

Put a patch on a cleaning rod, saturate it with water or cleaning solvent, and swab the bore a number of times to loosen fouling.

Prepare a can or bucket of hot soapy water. Put the breech end of the barrel into the bucket. With a patch on a rod, pump the water up and down the full length of the bore a number of times. You will see the water darken as the fouling is flushed out. Remember that you are cleaning from the muzzle, so do not allow the rod to damage the rifling there.

Follow this same procedure using clean hot water until the barrel is clean. Wipe the bore with fresh patches until they come out clean and dry. The hotter the water used, the quicker the barrel will dry. When the bore is thoroughly dry, oil it lightly with a patch, then oil the outside to protect it from rust.

The lock may get some residue in it and may need cleaning. Remove the screws holding it in the stock, and clean the lock using either solvent or very hot water, then thoroughly dry and oil it.

Clean powder fouling from the stock with water or wood cleaner, *not* blackpowder solvent, which could hurt the finish. When you are done cleaning the rifle, be sure that no water or cleaning fluid is in the space between the stock and the barrel before you reassemble the gun.

There are other ways to clean the bore. On a backwoods hunt of several days, the rifle can be swabbed every evening with a series of wet patches. The patches can be soaked with either hot water or solvent. When the bore is clean, it should be lightly oiled.

Another method, if the gun is difficult to disassemble, is to use a flush-out nipple. This is similar to a regular ignition nipple, but has a much larger internal hole. A piece of plastic tub-

Muzzleloaders that do not have a hook breech can also have their barrels removed for cleaning, but when all bands or keys are removed, the tang screw must also be taken out.

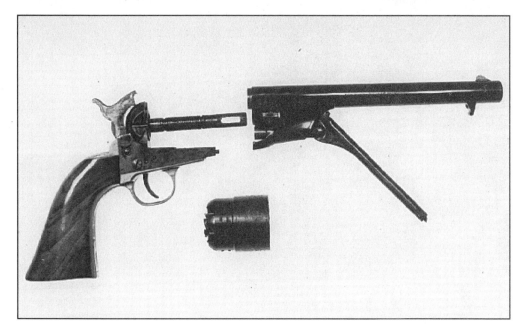

The Colt-style muzzle-loading revolver allows removal of both the cylinder and the barrel assembly for cleaning.

ing can be installed over it, and the other end of the plastic tubing can be placed in a container of soapy water. The water is then pumped slowly back and forth using a ramrod as before. Don't do it too fast or the tubing may pop off the nipple and make a mess.

If you have a flintlock, this latter method will probably not be an option. However, some modern flintlocks have removable flash hole liners. These may be removed and a flush-out nipple installed.

Muzzle-Loading Shotgun

Most of the same techniques apply to the muzzle-loading shotgun as for the muzzle-loading rifle. Because many such shotguns are double barrels, make sure each barrel is cleaned thoroughly. It may be a good idea to change water cans for each barrel (if you use that method) to check the condition of the water.

Muzzle-Loading Handgun

Single shot pistols may be cleaned by following the same general procedure as for rifles.

Muzzle-loading revolvers are more complex mechanically. The cleaning procedure is thus somewhat more complex. Let us consider that muzzle-loading revolvers fall into two general types.

The Colt type has no topstrap. The barrel is attached with a metal wedge to the axis on which the cylinder turns. When this wedge is removed, the barrel and cylinder may both be removed from the frame.

The Remington type has a frame with a topstrap. The barrel is screwed into the frame and is not removable for cleaning. The cylinder, though, may be easily removed from the frame.

For a thorough cleaning, muzzle-loading revolvers need to be taken apart. First, with either type, make sure the revolver is unloaded. Then put the hammer in the half-cock or loading

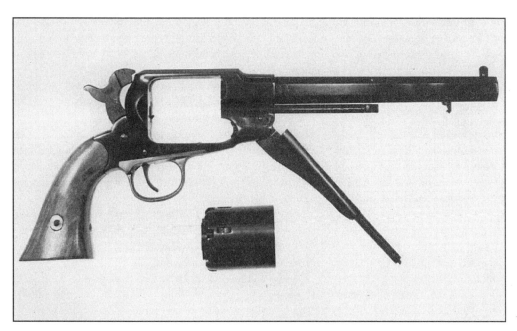

The Remington-style blackpowder revolver can have the cylinder removed for cleaning, but the barrel is fixed to the frame.

Whatever kind of gun you want to maintain, there are a number of excellent solvents, oils and other products from which to choose.

position. At this point, the takedown for the two basic types varies.

For the Colt type, the next step is to remove the barrel wedge that holds the barrel to the frame. It is removed from right to left. Depress the wedge spring and tap out the wedge with a wood or brass tool.

Unlatch the loading lever and rotate it downward. Make sure the rammer is positioned *between* two chambers and push on the lever. The barrel assembly will be forced forward, off the central axis pin. Remove the barrel, then slide the cylinder forward off the axis pin.

For the Remington type, unlatch the loading lever and pull it down. The cylinder pin can now be withdrawn forward from the frame, and the cylinder can be removed from the side. Other revolvers of similar construction can be disassembled in one of these two basic ways.

With the revolver taken apart, wash the barrel and cylinder in hot soapy water. Use your small brush to remove powder residue from the outside surfaces of the cylinder and frame.

It is best to be careful not to get water into the revolver's internal parts. However, I have known shooters who simply submerged Colt-type barrels, complete with their wedges and rammer mechanisms, in hot, soapy water for cleaning. This is OK as long as you flush with clean hot water and make sure you get everything absolutely dry.

However you do it, get everything good and clean. Use several changes of water, if necessary. If you are the sort who wants to take no chances, you may also use a commercial blackpowder cleaner in addition to the water cleaning.

After the gun is clean and thoroughly dry, use an oiled patch to put a film of oil in the bore and in the chambers. With an oily rag, wipe the surfaces of all the parts before assembling. Put a little oil on the working parts. Put a little grease on the cylinder axis or pin, so that it will turn freely without powder fouling binding it. When you have assembled the revolver, wipe it again with the oily cloth; after that, handle it only by its wooden grips.

Proper Storage

Whatever gun we've used today—rifle, shotgun, handgun, airgun or muzzleloader—we have properly cleaned it and it's ready to be put away. It must be stored somewhere. Most shooters are proud of their guns, proud of their participation in the shooting sports, and want to display them. Tempering this desire is a knowledge that guns are often targets of theft, and that untrained persons may not always safely handle accessible guns.

Where you live and your personal situation will determine how you store your guns. Bear in mind always that you do not want unauthorized people to have access to them. Some people successfully combine display with restrictions on who has access to them. Attractive locking glass-fronted gun cabinets accomplish this. Gun racks with a cable or bar lock may also be used. Some gun owners see theft as their greatest concern and store their guns in special safes or vaults.

Guns kept specifically for home defense will be treated differently, of course, but whatever your storage location, it is a good general rule to make sure the gun is unloaded and the ammunition is stored in a separate place.

Be sure to choose a cool, dry spot to store your guns. After all, we didn't go through all these cleaning procedures just to let the guns deteriorate in a damp corner somewhere!

CHAPTER TWENTY

BUYING
NEW OR
USED GUNS

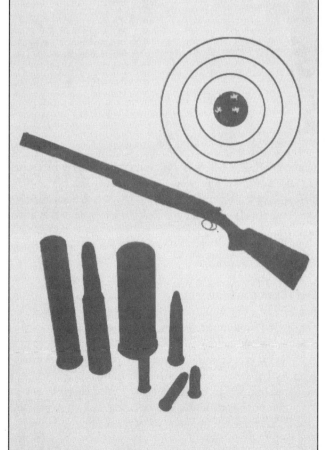

THERE IS A certain type of shooter who will just wander into a gunshop without any thought or intention of buying a new gun. A short while later, he or she will come out with a new gun. It is probably a lot of fun to do it that way.

However, the people who do it that way sometimes wind up with guns they seldom use. There may be nothing at all wrong with the new gun, it just may not really suit any shooting need for that particular shooter.

For most of us, a better way would be to consider what our shooting needs really are, then determine what sorts of guns are appropriate for those needs.

Now, I understand that "need" is not necessarily the best term. It may be said of the man who owns a shotgun that he does not need a second shotgun, because he can only use one at a time. However, if he is thinking about taking up Skeet shooting, and the shotgun he already has is a heavy, long-barreled goose gun, then his shotgun requirements have changed. He needs a new shotgun.

When you decide to buy a new gun, your choice will depend on a number of variables. Some of the main factors will be your intended use, your personal preference, availability, and cost.

Let's add in a few more personal factors such as age, size, strength and personal physical requirements.

Guns for organized shooting sports may have to meet certain requirements; guns for hunting in certain areas may fall under special laws or restrictions. All these are factors to consider, and we haven't even started looking at any guns yet!

How To Buy

Most people, whether or not they actually think about it in formal fashion, go through a certain procedure when buying a gun. Let's try to break this all down into some logical and easy-to-use steps.

Determine Your Requirements

The most basic decision, of course, is whether you need a rifle, shotgun or handgun. Even though some rifles, some shotguns, and some handguns can be used for many types of shooting, in order to narrow the field, a person needs to make this decision first. Often it is made unconsciously, because a certain type of gun is logical for a certain type of shooting, or a certain type of gun is required for a certain type of shooting.

Then, the gun's use comes next. Will it be used for hunting,

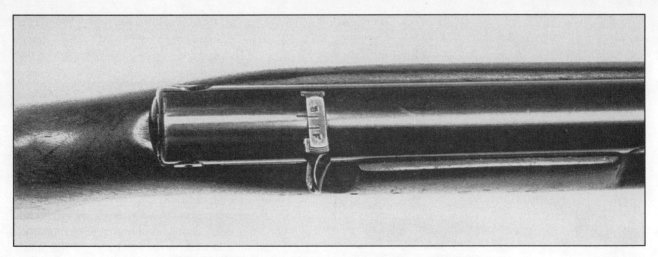

When you buy a gun, be sure you understand how it operates. This Winchester Model 74 22-caliber semi-automatic has its safety in an unusual place—on top of the receiver.

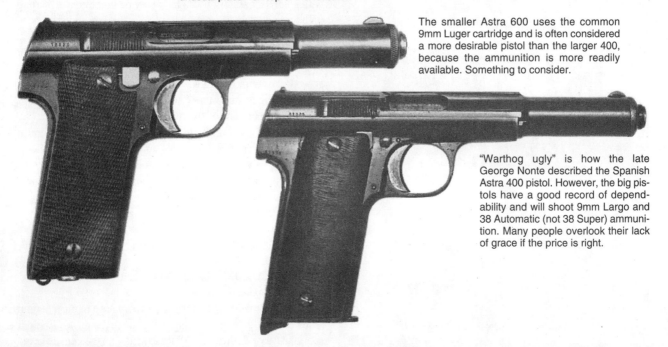

The smaller Astra 600 uses the common 9mm Luger cartridge and is often considered a more desirable pistol than the larger 400, because the ammunition is more readily available. Something to consider.

"Warthog ugly" is how the late George Nonte described the Spanish Astra 400 pistol. However, the big pistols have a good record of dependability and will shoot 9mm Largo and 38 Automatic (not 38 Super) ammunition. Many people overlook their lack of grace if the price is right.

plinking, target shooting, self-defense? Perhaps it will be a multi-purpose gun, serving more than one use.

If it is for hunting, it must be completely legal for the hunting in your area and suitable for the hunting you want to do. In my area, semi-automatic centerfire rifles are perfectly legal for deer hunting—but only if they hold five rounds or less, and only if used outside management areas set aside specifically for shotguns, archery or muzzleloaders.

The popular Savage Model 24 rifle/shotgun combination guns are useful for many types of hunting. Because they have rifle barrels, though, they are often not permitted for shotgun-only hunting.

If the gun is to be used for a specific type of shooting competition, you should understand the rules of that competition. Years ago, someone planned to use a 45-caliber Smith & Wesson Model 1955 revolver for both bullseye and PPC competition.

At that time, however, the big-frame Smith & Wessons were made with $6\frac{1}{2}$-inch barrels; the limit for PPC was 6 inches, and the revolver was not allowed.

If you are left-handed or shoot left-handed, can you operate a standard model, or should you look for a left-handed or ambidextrous version of the gun?

Do Your Homework

While you're looking at guns, be sure to pick up printed data about them, too. Most people do not consider this to be a chore, but a lot of extra fun. Read everything on which you can get your hands. Any firearms-related books or magazines could be a help. Current volumes of annually published books such as *Gun Digest* and *Guns Illustrated* have comprehensive catalog sections. Other publications also have useful catalog listings. If you are not ready to buy a bunch of books, check in at your local library, though copies may be pretty well worn and dog-eared. Other people are doing the same reading and studying you are.

HOW TO CHECK OUT A RIFLE

Look at the bore. It should be clean and shiny, with sharp lands and grooves. Heavy oil can sometimes cover irregularities in the bore, so if it looks suspicious, run a dry patch through it and look again. Don't hesitate to ask to do this; if someone wants to sell a gun, he will try to accommodate you.

Is there a circle or ring visible in the bore? If so, an obstruction has probably been shot out of it. The point where the obstacle was hit is represented by a bulge in the barrel. Run your fingers lightly over the outside of the barrel and see if you feel a slight bump. A tight patch pushed through the bore will jump ahead when it crosses such a spot.

The action should work smoothly. Slowly work it to see if everything works properly. Sometimes worn mechanisms need the inertia of being worked fast for some things to operate as they should. If worked fast, the rifle should stay cocked and nothing should slip out of place or bind. There should not be any obvious abnormal gap or looseness at the breech.

The safety of this early Savage Model 99 is just behind the trigger. Later models had the safety on the tang. Make sure you understand the differences when you look at used guns.

Write the manufacturers of guns in which you might be interested. They want to sell you their products, so they are usually more than willing to supply you with catalogs and other information.

Rule books for specific shooting sports are valuable for making a choice if you intend to compete. They are available from the National Rifle Association or from the governing organization of the sport.

Talk with your friends. What do they use? Visit a local gun club or shooting range. What are those shooters using? If you are going to shoot your new gun in competition, visit matches scheduled for that type of competition. Talk to the shooters. Find out what they like or don't like about the guns they are using. Perhaps they will let you handle their guns or even allow you to fire a few shots.

While you are at a gun shop or sporting goods store to look at the guns, ask the people there about your choices. Ask customers as well as store personnel. Find out all you can before you buy. Getting and exchanging information about guns and shooting is part of the enjoyment of being a gun owner.

Learn What Suits You

When you have narrowed the field a bit, it's time to handle the gun you're interested in buying. Is it simple to operate? Will it be easy to take apart, clean and maintain? Does it really fit you? Gun fit is especially important with shotguns. If the gun doesn't fit, can it be easily modified? When you pick up a handgun, can you easily reach the trigger and all the other controls?

The cost of the gun itself is often a factor. Be realistic about how much you want or can afford to spend.

Buying a Factory-New Gun

There is a problem with terminology for guns. Many is the time a friend has invited me over to see his "new" gun. Sometimes it really was brand-new; sometimes it was a beat-up old military relic of a war long forgotten. In each case, however, the gun was new to the owner. The terminology really is not a big thing. I always enjoyed seeing the guns, whatever they were.

However, we need to distinguish between guns that are really new, and those that are just new to us. Let us say that a gun straight from the factory and never shot by another shooter is a "factory-new" gun. We will consider all other guns as "used" guns, though they are new to us.

If you are going to buy a factory-new gun, you rightfully expect it to be in perfect mechanical condition. There are some things to think about:

What is the reputation of the manufacturer? Are parts and service available now and likely to be in the future? Does the gun itself have a good track record for dependability? If there should be a problem, what is covered in the warranty or guarantee?

If you feel you will be satisfied with a certain gun, where should you buy it? A reputable dealer will stand behind the products he sells. Some gun shops have gunsmithing services available and can handle repairs or modifications for you. If a gun should have to go back to the factory, will the dealer handle it or is it your responsibility?

If you want accessories—scopes, slings, grips—can you get them from the dealer and perhaps have them installed immediately? Or will you have to shop around for them later?

These things make a great deal of difference to many people. It is well worthwhile getting answers to these questions before you buy.

Buying a Used Gun

Used guns may be purchased from a gun shop or sporting goods store in the same manner as factory-new guns. Often, these guns are trade-ins from people moving up to a different gun; they may be excellent buys. In some cases, the dealer will include a limited warranty of his own.

Used guns may also be acquired from individuals. Sometimes these folks may be friends, neighbors or hunting partners. In such cases, you may already know the history of the gun and may be able to shoot it before deciding to purchase.

In other cases, a person unknown to you may advertise a gun, or guns may be sold at gun shows, pawn shops, second-hand stores, estate sales or garage sales. Some excellent values can be had. However, each step you get further from a reputable gun dealer, the greater your knowledge of used firearms must be.

Foremost in that requirement is a knowledge of the applicable laws. The person selling must legally own the gun. You must conform to the law in your purchase of the gun. You have

Whether you're buying a new or used gun, be sure to comply with all local and national laws. Dealers are usually well-versed in the law and will make sure your purchase is entirely legal.

HOW TO CHECK OUT A SHOTGUN

Look at the bore. Again, rings in the bore indicate a slight bulge in the barrel, which can usually be felt by lightly running the fingers along the outside surface.

Pump guns should be worked slowly to make sure all the parts move at the proper time. Parts should operate by mechanical connection and not have to be slammed into place by inertia. They should work smoothly, without binding, when worked either fast or slow.

Check hinge-type shotguns for looseness when they are closed. Many hinge-type guns have automatic safeties that go "on" when the gun is opened. Make sure these and all other safeties operate properly.

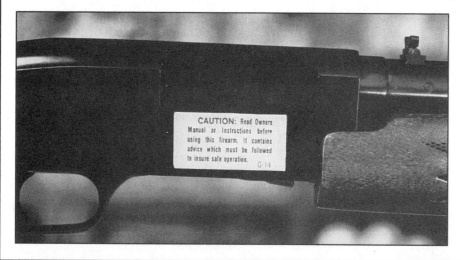

Pump shotguns can be tricky for the used gun buyer to evaluate. Be sure the action works properly fast or slow, and check for tight lockup. Many pump guns have removable barrels that make checking the bore very easy.

a personal responsibility and a legal obligation to know and obey the law.

If this is more than you want to handle at this stage, stick to shopping at a reputable dealer's store. Such dealers know and uphold the law; that aspect will not be a concern to you.

NRA condition standards are used by many sellers, buyers and collectors, but not everyone uses these standards. If you answer an ad for a gun, ask if the condition described is in accordance with the NRA standards. This system is used for condition ranking in *Modern Gun Values* and other books.

Here are the NRA standards for firearm condition:

Factory New—all original parts; 100 percent original finish, in perfect condition in every respect, inside and out.

Excellent—new condition; used but little; no notable marring of wood or metal; bluing perfect except at muzzle or sharp edges.

Fine—all original parts; over 30 percent original finish; sharp lettering, numerals and designs on metal and wood; minor marks in wood; good bore.

Very Good—in perfect working condition; no appreciable wear on working surfaces; no corrosion or pitting; only minor surface dents or scratches.

Good—in safe working condition; minor wear on working surfaces; no broken parts; no corrosion or pitting that will interfere with proper functioning.

Fair—in safe working condition, but well worn, perhaps requiring replacement of minor parts or adjustments; no rust;

Reputable dealers usually describe their guns using NRA standards, and these can be mighty helpful if you understand their meaning and implication.

(Below) Someone put a tremendous amount of work into making this Russian Mosin-Nagant into a nice sporter. There is little demand for such rifles, however, so the price may be moderate. Parts are generally available for military rifles of which large quantities were made.

(Right) Military versions of the traditional 45 Auto, this one made by Remington-Rand during WWII, may be as serviceable as commercial ones, at a lower price. Some are considered collectible, though, and this influences prices.

(Below) Shopping for an inexpensive surplus rifle? Designs such as this Mark III British 303-caliber rifle are reliable, the ammunition is readily available and the guns sell at reasonable prices. Condition is the guiding factor here.

may have corrosion pits which do not render gun unsafe or inoperable.

Poor—major and minor parts replaced; major replacement parts required and extensive restoration needed; metal deeply pitted; principal lettering, numerals and designs obliterated; wood badly scratched, bruised, cracked or broken; mechanically inoperative; generally undesirable as a collector firearm.

Here are some extra things to think about when buying a used gun: A poor appearance may indicate overall abuse or excessive wear; damaged screw slots may indicate disassembly by someone who didn't really know what he was doing, so there may be internal problems; all mechanical controls—trigger, safety, action release, disconnector, etc.—should be checked to make sure they function correctly; if possible, shoot the gun before buying it.

Even if you consider yourself an expert concerning firearms, it is often good to take a knowledgeable friend along when looking at used guns. A second person can spot things you might overlook. I hate to admit it, but I have bought guns with ringed barrels, bent barrels, short firing pins, broken firing pins, worn parts and missing parts. I learned a lot about gunsmithing, but that wasn't why I bought the guns. Be observant.

Buying Military Surplus Guns

There are a great number of military surplus firearms on the market now, and they represent a wonderful opportunity for the shooter and for the shooting sports.

In the years following World War II, nations began to modernize their armament with new military firearms. Something had to be done with the old guns and ammunition. It would cost money to destroy these items, but money could be made by selling them. The best market for the guns and ammunition was in the United States. Large quantities of surplus rifles, handguns and ammunition came into the country in the early 1950s and continued through most of the 1960s. People who never had much interest in shooting bought a rifle and some ammunition just because the price was low. Then they wondered how it would do as a hunting rifle, bought some hunting ammunition and took it into the woods.

Shooting clubs that had never been able to run much of a shooting program suddenly found that everyone could afford what they needed for rifle and pistol matches.

I lived in southern Louisiana during the early 1960s, and I remember our club's first pistol match. There was a smattering of all kinds of handguns for the 22 and centerfire stages, but

HOW TO CHECK OUT A HANDGUN

The act of cocking the hammer on a revolver should turn the cylinder to the next chamber, and it should lock in place. A revolver, when cocked, should have very little side play in the cylinder. Chambers should align with the bore. Push against the spur of the cocked hammer with your thumb; it should stay firmly cocked and not drop.

The crane, which is the part that swings out with the cylinder on some revolvers, should fit snugly against the frame in the front when the cylinder is closed. Many cranes have been loosened because previous owners tried to impress their friends by snapping the cylinder shut the way some guys do on TV.

With a single-action semi-auto, pull back the slide and lock it open. Then press the release and let the slide run forward. The hammer should never follow the slide down.

Check out all the pistol's safeties. If the gun is equipped with a grip safety, it should prevent the trigger from releasing the hammer. A thumb safety, when engaged, should absolutely prevent the hammer or striker from falling. A decocker should allow the hammer to drop without striking the firing pin.

Sometimes you can shoot a gun before you buy it. If you have the opportunity, take it to the range and try it out before you make your decision. The writer here is shooting a military 1911A1 45.

surplus handguns armed 100 percent of the firing line for the 45 match. I recall that I used a 1917 Colt, while a friend shot a converted 455 Webley.

During that time, hunting and target shooting alike boomed. Those who began shooting with surplus guns developed an interest in shooting and bought commercial firearms and ammunition, too. That was a good time for the shooting sports.

Then came a series of tragic assassinations of public figures. The mood in America underwent a metamorphosis, and Congress, upset with the thought of Americans having easy access to guns, enacted the Gun Control Act of 1968 (GCA'68). A major provision of the act was to prohibit the sale of firearms through the mail. Among its other restrictions was a ban on the importation of surplus guns and ammunition. By the late 1980s, though, almost two decades after the GCA'68, importation of foreign surplus firearms and ammunition was again allowed.

This has created another wave of interest in the shooting sports. The entry-level cost for the equipment to get into rifle or pistol shooting has dropped significantly. Once involved, new shooters increase their interest and buy more equipment.

This is not to say that there are no problems. Most of the restrictions of GCA'68 remain. The increasing number of firearms brought into the country has brought further calls for more gun control. Importation of substantial quantities of certain types of firearms and ammunition have already been outlawed. Bans against so-called assault weapons were passed. These guns are mechanically the same as other guns, but look different.

At any rate, we are fortunate again to have surplus firearms

Gun shows can be great places to find good used guns, but you can get stung with a worthless junker if you aren't sure what you're doing. Be sure to do your homework before you buy.

and ammunition available to allow more folks to get into the world of guns and shooting.

When considering a surplus gun to shoot, the price may be attractive, but pay attention to its condition. Most of these guns date back to World War II or earlier, and none comes with a manufacturer's warranty.

On the plus side, no country ever consciously planned to send its troops into battle with inferior weapons. Some are much better than others, but they all were the best some country could provide. Because there are so many of them, getting replacement parts is not usually a problem.

On the minus side, what you see is what you get. Don't like the caliber? Too bad. Stock doesn't fit? Too bad. Sights not adequate? Too bad.

Still, some people like to collect them and tinker with them. Most important, surplus military guns give some folks their first real chance to enter the shooting sports.

Ultimately, we need to do our homework before we buy a "new" gun, acquiring knowledge that will narrow the options. We need to determine if the gun suits us, and if it's the right size, shape and weight. Is it within our price range?

With factory-new guns, we need to consider the manufacturer's reputation and the gun's track record, where we will pur-

chase it, its warranty, and whether we will need different sights or other accessories for it.

With used guns, we need to know if the one we want is a current model or whether it is an out-of-production model that might present a problem if it needs parts or service. We need to be very careful about checking the condition of used guns. However, buying a used gun can get us a level of quality or features we might not be able to afford in a new gun.

Surplus military guns are a special category of used guns, yet they require the same homework you put into studying the commercial guns. Some excellent buys may be made, but only if a military-style rifle or pistol will suit your needs. While they may be satisfactory for a High Power rifle match, deer hunting or home defense, they will not help you at all if you need a Smallbore match rifle or a gun for quail or Sporting Clays.

All this should give you a start toward selecting your "new" gun. It is nice to know, though, that guns hold their value better than a lot of other things. If you find later that something else would suit you better, you can always trade up.

Whatever gun you choose, I hope you enjoy it and do well with it. Good shooting!

CHAPTER TWENTY-ONE

LOADING
YOUR OWN
AMMUNITION

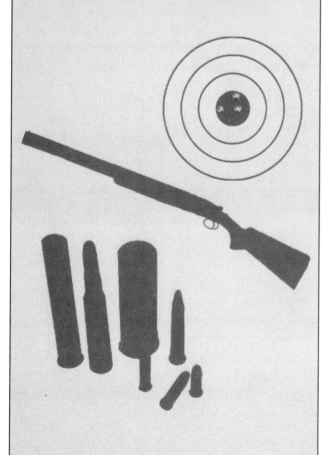

THE LATEST SURVEY I have available from the National Reloading Manufacturers Association indicates that more than six million shooters load their own ammunition. If each shooter loads only about 200 rounds per year (a pretty conservative estimate, I would think) then well over *one billion* rounds of ammunition are loaded by shooters for their own use. The actual number is probably many times that.

There must be something to it.

Before we get too deeply into this, let's consider the proper terminology for this activity. What do we call this process of inserting new components into a cartridge case to produce usable ammunition? Is it reloading or handloading? I'm sure you noticed I have cagily used neither term in the chapter title.

I have heard it presented that if components are assembled into a fired case, the procedure is reloading. If a new unfired case is used, it is handloading.

I mention this because you will probably hear it said many ways during your shooting career. You should be aware that there is no universal acceptance as to when to use what term. I generally use "reloading" and "handloading" interchangeably. With your permission, I shall do so here.

Cartridge Development

We may think of making our own ammunition as something very new, but the origins go back many years.

We don't really know when the first shooter wrapped powder and ball together in twisted paper to speed the reloading of his muzzleloader. The idea of a cartridge, a compact unit to hold everything a shooter needed to reload a gun, went quickly around the world.

After centuries of tentative experimentation with self-contained cartridges, when things began to happen, they happened fast. In 1836, pinfire shotshells were introduced in France. That same year, Dreyse's needle gun was patented in Prussia. It used a paper cartridge with a primer at the base of the bullet; a long needle penetrated the powder to fire the cartridge. The needle was right in the middle of the powder when it went off (not a great place for a thin piece of metal to be), but it worked well enough that it was adopted by Prussia in 1842. It was the world's first military cartridge breechloader, and it terrorized the French.

By 1844, the Sharps breechloader had been patented in America. It had a strong falling block action and used paper or linen cartridges to hold the powder and bullet.

In 1846, a pinfire cartridge with a copper case was introduced in France. On firing, the case expanded against the chamber walls to make a gas-tight seal. It was probably the first self-contained metallic cartridge.

Experimentation went rapidly from there. In 1857, Smith & Wesson introduced the first successful rimfire cartridge, the 22 Short. By 1861, two rimfire rifle cartridges were in production, the 56-56 Spencer and the 44 Henry. They were made in large quantities during the Civil War.

However, the thin metal of a rimfire case could not stand much pressure, and it could not be reloaded. After the Civil War, development centered on the centerfire system. It used a much stronger case and a separate small primer.

In 1866, the United States military adopted its first centerfire cartridge, the 50-70 (50-caliber, 70 grains of blackpowder). It was replaced in 1873 by the 45-70. That was a good year for gun developments. In 1873 Winchester introduced its first centerfire cartridge, the 44-40, and Colt brought out the 45 Colt cartridge in their famous Colt Single Action Army revolver. Interestingly, all three of these old-timers are still in production.

The centerfire cartridge has dominated the firearms scene since that time. Rimfires were still made, but as time went by, centerfire cartridges filled most of the niches, except for that held firmly by the 22 rimfires.

Centerfire cartridges of the 1870s and 1880s were a varied lot. They ranged from low-powered revolver cartridges such as the 32 Smith & Wesson and 32 Short Colt, through medium cartridges that could be used in either revolver or rifle, to the big, powerful cartridges of the buffalo rifles.

These latter cartridges bring us back to the subject at hand. The buffalo hunters of the 1870s and 1880s gave us the first large-scale example of the benefits of reloading. Weight and space could be saved by carrying primers, powder and lead, instead of the huge number of cartridges they would otherwise need. After each day's shooting, they would simply reload their cartridge cases. The tools they used were primitive by our present standards, but the procedures were much the same as those we use to reload ammunition today.

Why Reload?

Unlike the buffalo hunters, today's shooters are not so concerned with the weight and bulk of ammunition. So, why do people reload ammunition, anyway?

For economy, certainly. The brass case of a rifle or handgun cartridge is usually the most expensive part of the loaded round. Even with shotgun shells, where the internal components are costlier, the savings of reloading are substantial.

There are two ways to look at economy of reloading. One is that you can do the same amount of shooting for a lot less money. Another, that has more appeal for most shooters, is

Hand tools such as the Lyman 310 are useful because they can be taken along when you go shooting. Here, the writer is using a 310 while experimenting with different loads for a Marlin 30-30.

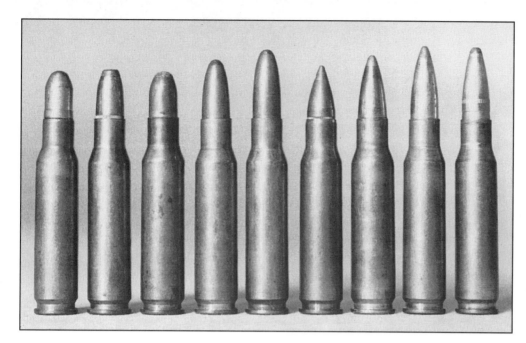

Besides economy, reloading offers versatility. Here are a number of 308 Winchester reloads, many not available as factory ammunition.

that you can do a whole lot more shooting for the same amount of money!

While economy is perhaps the most common reason for reloading your own ammo, it is not necessarily the most important one.

Accuracy is another reason for reloading. This is not to say that there is anything wrong with factory ammunition. But for a specific gun, if you are willing to put out the time and effort, you can often find a load that is more accurate than factory loadings. It is a happy situation when the most accurate load also turns out to be an inexpensive one.

As a matter of fact, because pistol shooting sports use so much ammunition, it is probably safe to say that they are popular *because* of reloading.

Obsolete calibers can be brought back to life through handloading. Cartridge cases no longer available in factory loads may often be formed from the cases of easily obtained ammunition. Then, the newly formed cases may be reloaded using normal procedures. Many old-time rifles and handguns are kept in service this way.

Creating special loads is another good reason for reloading. Light loads can make a full-power big game rifle suitable for small game hunting or for practice. Some factory loads are downloaded because there are still many older, weaker guns in service in some calibers. If you have a strong, modern gun, then you can load ammo for it to its full potential.

The number of different types of cartridges and loads available from the factory, although large, is limited. Ammunition companies cannot afford to tool up for small runs of cartridges that only a few people want. If you are one of those few people, and you are a handloader, you can custom-make ammo to suit your needs.

Shot loads for rifles and pistols, ultra-light loads, blanks, solid ball loads for shotguns—all can be made by careful handloading.

Before you attempt to reload any cartridge, be sure to pur-chase and *read* at least one good reloading manual, the most current one you can acquire. You will need the reloading manual to determine the proper primer, trim length for cases, and charges of the correct powder, as well as for a host of other reference material too numerous to mention here. Two manuals are better than one.

Metallic Cartridge Reloading

Essentially all rifle and pistol cartridges used today have a case of metal, generally brass. We will consider shotshells, with their plastic or paper cases, separately, in a short while.

The components needed for metallic cartridge reloading are cartridge case; primer; powder; bullet.

Cartridge cases for reloading must be in good shape to withstand the pressure when fired. They may be either cases from ammunition you have fired, new cases, or fired cases from other sources.

New brass cases can generally be assumed to be OK, but look them over anyhow. Examine your fired cases a little closer and take a *very* close look at cases of unknown origin. Cracks may be present at the neck, sometimes in the body. Cases may crack from age or because of the number of times they have been fired, loaded and fired again. Once a case develops a crack *anywhere*, it should be discarded.

A more serious problem is a stretch mark near the base of the case. This is a sign of incipient separation of the case. If a cartridge is fired in a chamber with excess headspace, it may be pushed forward by the blow of the firing pin and/or the detonation of the primer. As the burning powder expands the case, it grips the chamber walls. The base, being too far forward, is forced back; the case stretches near the base; and the brass becomes thin with an internal ring around the base. On the outside, this thin spot often appears as a bright ring or a circular crack just above the base. Some reloaders check the inside of suspicious cases with a small hook on the end of a piece of wire. If the hook drops into an area where the thickness of the brass

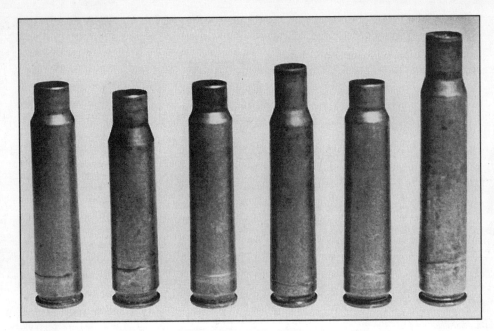

Different forms of incipient head separations. None of these caused a problem, but they could have. Inspect your cases before loading.

has been reduced in this manner, it is easily felt, and the case is discarded.

Primers for reloading have three parts: the cup, priming compound and anvil. When the firing pin hits the cup, it crushes the priming compound against the anvil. The resulting detonation shoots flame through the flashhole of the case, igniting the powder. Because the hole is in the center, the fired primer may be pushed out of the case by a small rod inserted through this hole.

Primers may be purchased at many gun shops and sporting goods stores. They come in four standard sizes: small pistol, small rifle, large pistol and large rifle. These are all Boxer primers.

Another primer type, the Berdan, is commonly used for European cartridges. The anvil is part of the cartridge case instead of being a separate piece. This arrangement does not have a central flashhole. Berdan-primed cases require special decapping tools, and so they are seldom reloaded.

Powder for reloading may be also purchased at many gun shops and sporting goods stores. Powders are classed by their chemical composition. Single-base powders are primarily nitrocellulose; double-base powders are nitrocellulose and nitroglycerine.

Powder may also be classed by granule type. Common types are ball (spheres), flake (discs), and extruded (cylinders). There are useful powders of all types, and the handloader's primary concerns will be the selection of a suitable type and charge, and the accuracy of its measurement.

Bullets fall into two categories, lead and jacketed.

Lead or lead-alloy bullets for pistol reloading are available from many sources, or they may be cast or, less commonly, swaged by the shooter.

Jacketed bullets are almost always bought by the shooter, although some advanced handloaders swage their own. A lead core is covered with a jacket of a harder metal, usually a copper alloy such as gilding metal. Jacketed bullets can be driven to higher velocities than lead bullets.

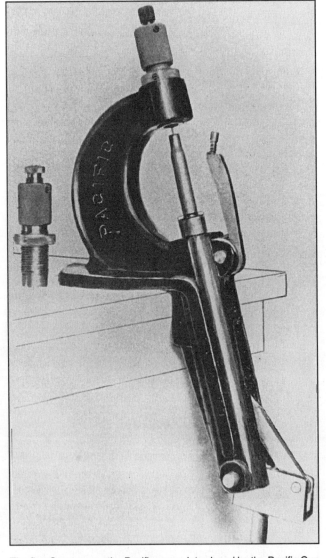

The first C press was the Pacific press, introduced by the Pacific Gun Sight Company in the late 1920s. It set the pattern for bench-mounted reloading tools.

Equipment

In the early days of centerfire ammunition, the supply of cartridges to the frontier areas was unpredictable. Users of the new rifles and revolvers wanted to be sure of an adequate supply of ammunition, so many portable reloading tools made by the gunmaker were sold along with the guns.

As the frontier became settled and shooters relied more and more on factory ammunition, the gun companies stopped making loading tools. However, those who liked the idea of reloading were in luck; in 1884, John Barlow introduced a line of hand-operated loading tools under the name Ideal. Blackpowder had been easy to load. Most cartridges just used a case filled with black to the base of the bullet. When smokeless powder arrived on the scene, the handloader could not simply fill the case with powder, because it had different burning characteristics, so the handloader had little to guide him. John Barlow experimented with smokeless loads, recorded his observations, and worked closely with ammunition companies and firearms makers.

He published this information in the *Ideal Handbook*, the direct ancestor of our modern loading manuals. Presented with a mixture of loading data, pitches for Ideal tools, cartoons and witty sayings, the *Handbook* was very popular and probably was a great force in keeping alive interest in reloading.

Various designs for loading tools, bullet moulds and sizers, and gas checks for lead bullets all came from Barlow. He sold Ideal to Marlin in 1910, and the Lyman Gun Sight Co. acquired it in 1925. Modernized versions of the basic portable hand reloading tool, bullet-sizing equipment and moulds for some of Barlow's original bullet designs are still available from Lyman. The numbering of the *Lyman Reloading Handbook* is a continuation of the numbers of the old *Ideal Handbook*.

After World War I, interest in reloading soared. By the end of the 1920s, the bench-mounted C-type press and the now-standard $7/8 \times 14$ dies had been introduced by the Pacific Gun Sight Co. The first of its type, the C press became the standard type of bench-mounted reloading tool.

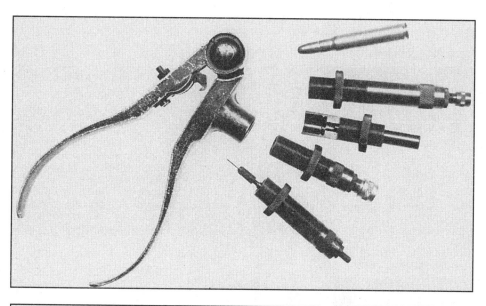

The Lyman 310 tool has dies for decapping and neck sizing, neck expanding, priming, and seating. This set is for 8mm Mauser, and a loaded cartridge is shown with the dies.

(Below) The 310 tool is liked by many reloaders because it gives a good "feel" when seating the primer.

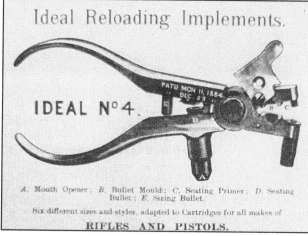

Some Ideal reloading tools combined a cartridge loading tool with a bullet mould. Ten different tools were originally offered, but they were narrowed down to No. 3 for rimmed cases and No. 10 for rimless cases. Eventually they were combined, and the "310" tool is still offered by Lyman.

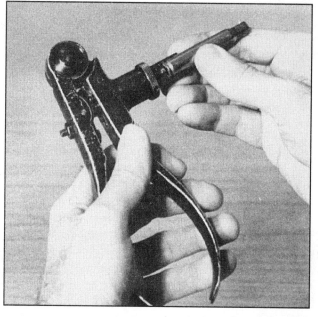

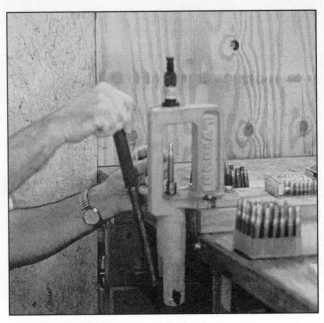

Sizing 30-06 cases in a C press, here a Pacific not much different from the original. A C press allows equal access from either side.

Here the writer is using an O press, this one a Lyman, to seat bullets in 8mm Mauser cases.

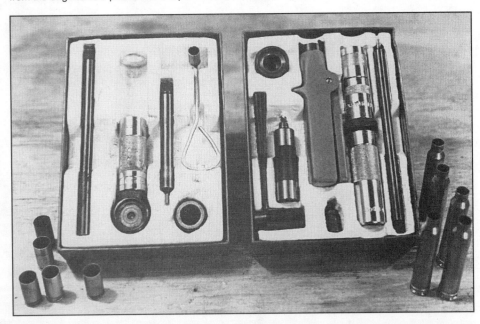

Slow and noisy because every step requires hitting something with a mallet, Lee Loaders make good ammunition. Here are two: a 45 ACP version made back in the 1960s and a more elaborate set for 300 Winchester Magnum made during the 1970s.

During World War II, the American firearms industry was focused on the war effort, and ammunition and cases for civilian shooting were not generally available. Still, civilians were encouraged to keep in practice. A Japanese invasion was always possible, and any man might be called into service. American ingenuity kept many people shooting. New reloading tools and new reloading methods were developed, not by companies, but by individuals.

One such development was the introduction of the O-type press. Fred Huntington, who ran a small reloading equipment business from his garage in the post-war years, introduced the new press. The press sold well, and the company grew to become RCBS.

A number of other companies were formed in these post-war years to provide both components and tools for reloaders.

Handloading grew, and increasingly sophisticated tools were offered. In contrast, very simple tools were offered, too, and they sold well.

Loading Presses: The old Ideal tong tool that the cowboys used is still available as the Lyman 310 tool. It is still favored by some shooters (your writer included) for experimenting with different loads. Everything one needs can be carried in a box to the range.

The least expensive tool is the Lee Loader, introduced in the early 1960s. Power is supplied by tapping with a mallet. This ingenious tool makes good ammunition in small quantities, but requires a firm, solid surface to hit against.

Most reloaders use bench presses. The most popular types are the C and O presses, but others such as turret presses have been and are being made.

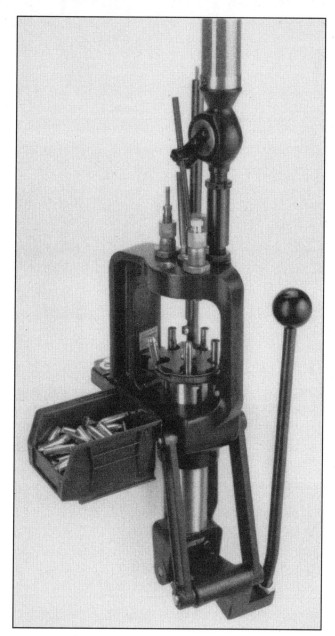

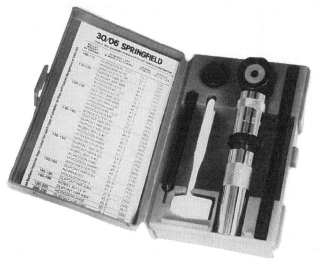

Lee Loaders are available in a variety of calibers. A mallet de-caps/resizes cases and seats the bullet, and a simple powder measure throws a pre-determined charge.

These cutaway dies show the smooth surfaces and internal parts necessary to size and decap a fired case (left) and to seat the bullet to the proper depth (right) after repriming it and charging it with powder. Loading dies are precision tools that, with proper care, will last indefinitely.

Progressive presses can make reloading less of a chore and turn out lots of ammo in a short time, but the initial cost is greater than with a simple press.

C-type presses allow easy access for both right- and left-handers. Presses with an O shape may be less apt to spring during the heaviest sizing or swaging jobs, because the construction is fully supported.

In the C and O presses, the cartridge case moves up to the die on a ram. Some presses have a moving platform that raises the cartridge case on a large single column. H-type presses are similar, but have a member that rises between two smaller columns.

Turret presses hold a number of dies, from four to twelve, each of which is rotated into alignment with the ram as needed.

Progressive presses have become very popular in recent years. The operator inserts a case by hand, and the case progresses from one station to another automatically, without being handled by the reloader. Each pull of the lever produces a complete cartridge. High-volume shooters like the time-saving features of progressive presses, but they are complicated and are generally preferred by advanced reloaders.

Dies: If you use a Lyman Tong Tool or a Lee Loader, the appropriate dies come with those tools. Bench presses, however, use standard reloading dies, all threaded $7/8$x14 on the outside, and they fit almost any press made today.

There are 2-die and 3-die sets, often referred to as rifle dies and pistol dies. Actually, 2-die sets are made for bottleneck cases, and some pistol cartridges are of that design. The 3-die sets are for straight cases, and some rifle cartridges are of that design.

The first die of a 2-die set deprimes the case as it enters the die, by means of a central decapping rod. At the completion of

This O-type press by Lee is the basis of a simple reloading setup.
The remaining tools needed include dies, lube, powder measure,
components, loading data, and good instructions.

the press stroke, the case has been sized. The downstroke of the ram pulls the case neck over the expander button, leaving the neck the correct size for the bullet. The second die seats the new bullet, after the other operations—priming and powder charging—are completed.

The first die of a 3-die set sizes the case. The second die expands the neck. Decapping could take place in either of these dies, depending on the design. The third die seats the bullet, after the case has been primed and powder charged.

Shellholder: The shellholder is the device into which the base of the cartridge case fits, on top of the ram. Obviously, the ram could push a case into a die without benefit of a shellholder, but something must hold the base of the cartridge so that it can be pulled back out.

Primer Seating Tool: Many presses come with a special primer arm for seating primers, or such items can be bought lat-

er to fit the press. Priming devices that sit atop a press are available. Some reloaders use separate hand-held priming tools, claiming such tools give them a better feel for seating the primers to the exact bottom of the primer pocket. They all seem to work well. Your choice.

Chamfering Tool: This simple tool allows beveling of the case mouth, both inside and outside. Beveling eases insertion of the bullet while loading and may help in crimping the case into the bullet (if you crimp). Some shooters claim that crimping helps to feed the loaded round into the chamber.

One useful task for which it was really not designed is cleaning out the primer crimp on large-primer military cases. Many military cartridges have a light crimp to help hold the primer in place during automatic firing. The primer can generally be driven out past this crimp, but the crimp must be removed before the case can be reprimed. There are tools designed specifically

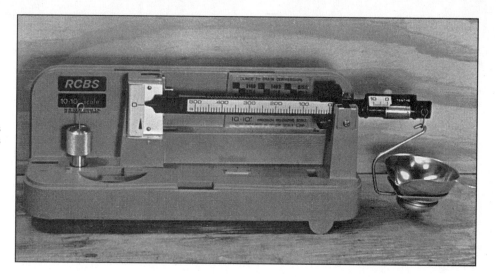

Every reloader should have access to an accurate reloading scale. This one is an RCBS 10-10.

for this, but if you don't have one of them, a pocketknife and a chamfering tool will do the job.

Powder Scale: Accurate measurement of powder is the single most critical step in handloading. You *must* have a good powder scale. With a scale you can weigh each charge, or you can use the weighed charge to make a powder scoop. If you also get a powder measure, you can periodically weigh the thrown charges.

Powder scales are generally of the balance-beam type, although electronic scales are becoming popular. Expensive scales have more features and are faster to use, but inexpensive ones can be as accurate as the average handloader requires.

Powder Funnel: A simple powder funnel can help you put the powder where you really want it to go.

Avoid spilling powder! I have charged almost a whole loading block of cases with powder, then spilled one charge. Did some spilled powder land in some of the already charged cases? Can't tell. Did some powder jostle out of some of the other cases? Can't tell. The only thing to do is pour out *all* the powder from *all* the cases and start over.

Miscellaneous: One of the nice things about handloading is that you start doing it to save money, do more shooting, then buy things so that you can reload more and shoot more and save even more money.

You can never have too many reloading manuals. They make interesting reading, and it is fun to compare them. They really belong in the *necessary* list, although many beginning reloaders share them.

Primer pocket cleaners, reamers and swages are sometimes necessary tools. Bullet pullers, neck reamers, case trimmers, case cleaners, and case tumblers all are nice additions to your loading bench.

Loading blocks to hold the cases are virtually a necessity. You can buy or make them. The trays for miniature ice cubes work well for some handgun calibers. Many other items can be made or improvised.

Case lubricating pads, primer trays, powder tricklers, calipers, adjusting wrenches, special mounting stands, plastic cartridge boxes—well, you get the idea.

Procedures

Once we have the components we need, the procedures for loading ammunition boil down to proper handling and assembly of those components. Some reloaders have tools that will do these procedures in slightly different sequence or combine several steps in one operation, but all of them need to be done.

1. Clean and Inspect the Case. It is a good idea to wipe fired cases with a clean cloth before introducing them into your loading system. Any grit on the cases carried into the loading dies will harm both the case and die. While wiping them off, check for cracks and incipient head separations. We discussed these while we were talking about cartridge cases a short while ago.

If you have a case-length gauge or caliper handy, measure the length of the cases at this time. Brass has a tendency to flow forward with repeated firings. At some point, the cases may become too long and must be trimmed. Consult your loading manual for the correct length.

2. Lubricate the Case. A case must be lubricated before it goes into the resizing die. Lubrication allows the case to enter the die freely and keeps it from getting stuck. It is such an easy step, it is easy to overlook. Cases *can* get stuck. If they do, they are a pain in the neck to get out, so don't forget to lubricate.

There are a number of good commercial case lubricants. It doesn't take much, so a little lasts a long time. A quick roll across a case lubricating pad or a twirl in the fingers with a little lube on them is all that is needed.

3. Decap the Case. The old primer is pushed out with a pin or punch in the loading die. With some simple reloading tools, this is a separate operation. With more sophisticated bench tools, decapping may be combined with either sizing or expanding.

4. Resize the Cases. The case expands on firing. It must be reduced in size in order to fit it back into the gun and to grip the new bullet. There are two possibilities: full-length sizing and neck-sizing. Full-length sizing means squeezing the entire case back to its original specifications. This is necessary so the case will fit any chamber of that caliber.

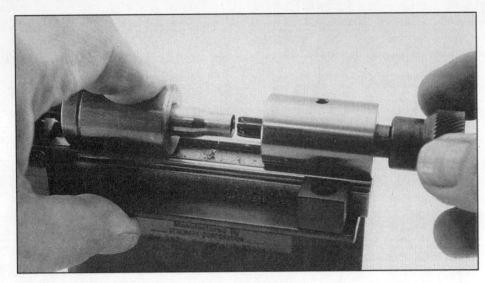

This neck reamer is being used to chamfer a case mouth. This step promotes easier bullet seating and a tighter fit.

Ah, but you only plan to use the cartridges you reload in your own rifle or handgun. Do you really need to full-length size? You may choose to size down only the neck, so it will firmly hold a new bullet. This is called neck-sizing.

The advantage of this is that working the brass cases will unnecessarily shorten their life. They last longer with a minimum of sizing. Also, cases already perfectly formed to a specific chamber are likely to give the best accuracy.

You can get special neck-sizing dies. Many people just use standard full-length dies, but adjust them so the case does not go all the way in, resulting in adequate neck-sizing.

Neck-sizing is not a good choice in all cases, however. If the ammunition might be used in any of several different guns, it should probably be full-length sized, because the chamber dimensions may vary from gun to gun. Hunting ammunition should generally be full-length sized; you don't want to miss the best shot of your life because a cartridge wouldn't chamber properly.

Cartridges for semi-automatics, both rifle and pistol, are generally full-length sized. Most shooters of pump- or lever-action rifles usually full-length size also.

Be advised that some manufacturers do not condone the use of reloaded ammunition in any of their firearms. Consult your owner's manual or the manufacturer for further information.

5. Expand the Case Neck. It would be nice if we could just resize the outside of the case and have the inside dimension be correct. Because cases vary in thickness, however, we must resize every case neck a little smaller than required, then expand the neck to the right size to hold the bullet.

For bottleneck cases, expansion of the neck is generally done in the sizing die. In fact, decapping is also usually done at the same time. A long rod extends through the center of the resizing die. At its end is the decapping pin. Just above the pin is an expander button the exact size the inside of the neck should be. The case neck goes into the die right past this expander button without contact, because the case neck is oversize from firing. The case neck is then sized in the die. On the return stroke, the sized neck, now slightly smaller, is pulled past the expander, which opens it to the proper size.

For straight cases, both rifle and pistol, a separate neck expanding die is used.

No matter which sizing method is chosen, be sure to remove all traces of lube from the resized case.

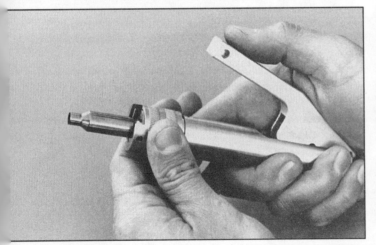

Repriming is most easily done with a hand tool. Those who favor this tool, which operates by thumb pressure, claim it gives a better "feel" than using one's press to reprime.

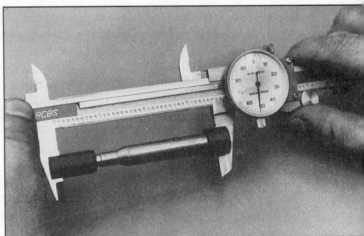

One critical step in the reloading process is making sure your brass is not too long. Check your loading manual, measure each case after sizing, and trim it if necessary.

6. Prime the Case. There are a number of priming devices. Some attach to a bench loading press and can prime a case on the downstroke of the press ram as the case comes out of the die.

Many reloaders prefer to prime as a separate operation, and there are many bench tools and hand tools that will accomplish this. Be sure to wash your hands well before handling primers; even small amounts of oil in the primer may weaken the priming compound and make it undependable.

Be sure to use caution when handling primers. They can detonate with a small blow. Read your loading manual!

7. Charge the Case. Now we are ready to charge our primed cases with powder. The best way to determine the proper charge and powder type is to consult one or more of the excellent reloading manuals put out by a number of companies. Never start with a maximum charge of powder, even if that is your final goal. Begin with a low charge, often called a suggested or starting charge, and see how things go.

If you have several manuals, you will notice that the charges for a specific caliber and bullet may vary from manual to manual. The reason for this discrepancy is that the researchers used different guns to get their figures. Let this sink in. You don't know how your gun compares with the ones the researchers used, so never push the suggested loads. I seldom load maximum charges. To me, this smacks of driving with the accelerator on the floorboard, something I don't do very often either.

Once we've settled on a reasonable charge of a readily available powder, how do we get it into the case? Charges can be weighed on a powder scale. This is the most accurate way, though it is time-consuming. Adjustable powder measures are time savers. The measure is adjusted and a charge thrown into the powder scale's pan. Weigh and readjust as needed. When the adjustment is correct, it can be locked and charges may then be thrown directly into the cases. Check a charge every so often by weighing it, just to make sure the adjustment has not changed. No matter the procedure, make sure you understand what you're doing!

The cheapest way to measure powder is with a scoop. This is the way the buffalo hunter did it, and it still works. You can either buy scoops that are pre-determined for certain charges of

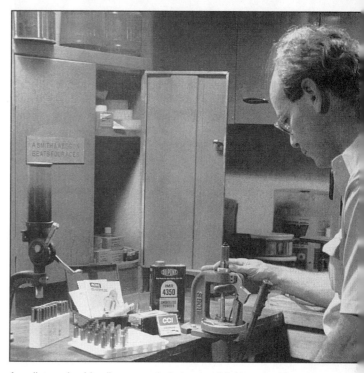

A well-organized loading space includes good light, a stout bench, clean working area, adequate storage, sufficient tools, and no distractions.

certain powders or you can make your own. Old cartridge cases make good scoops. Weigh the charge you want, pour it into a case, mark it and cut it off at that point. Go slowly and keep filing and checking until you get it right. Glue or solder a handle onto your scoop and mark it for that charge.

I recommend using the scoop like this: Pour powder into a small container and plunge the scoop down into it, letting the powder flow inside; raise the scoop straight out, leveling off the powder with a straight piece of thin cardboard. Be consistent each time. A small powder funnel will be an asset in getting the powder into the cases.

This is the most critical time of the entire reloading procedure. Away with all distraction! Turn off the radio! Don't chat with your friends! Pay strict attention to charging the cases with powder.

You must be systematic and uniform in your actions. You must put *one* and *only one* charge in each case. Most reloaders buy or make a loading block in which to stand the charged cases. Develop a system that will let you know which cases are charged and which are not.

When you think all cases are charged correctly, inspect them visually with a strong overhead light. You do not want any cases with no charge or with a double charge.

8. Seat the Bullet. The bullet can now be seated into the neck of the charged case. This simple operation must be done correctly. Follow the instructions that came with your loading tools and press the bullet into the case. Most manuals give you an overall maximum length for the cartridge, and if you have that information, use it. Some bullets have a cannelure, which is a crimping groove. If so, adjust your seating die to position the bullet to that depth. You may want to crimp the case into the groove. If so, follow the directions that come with your dies.

RELOADING STEPS

1. Clean and Inspect the Case
2. Lubricate the Case
3. Decap the Case
4. Resize the Case
5. Expand the Case Neck
6. Prime the Case
7. Charge the Case
8. Seat the Bullet

Shotshell Reloading

The origins of this operation began with simple hand tools. Loading the old brass shotshells was somewhat similar to loading metallic cartridges for rifles and pistols. Then paper shells became common, and techniques changed. Perhaps because shotshells were larger and required more steps than metallic cartridge loading, bench-mounted tools soon appeared.

Economy is the prime reason most people reload shotshells, but it is not as great as that realized by reloading rifle and pistol cartridges. This is because the components that go into the shells are more costly. However, many shotgunners shoot an awful lot of shells, and their savings add up.

The components of a shotshell are shell (or hull); primer; powder; wad; shot.

The *shell* is, in some ways, more important in shotshell reloading than in metallic reloading. Many rifle and pistol shooters recognize the fact that brass cases from different manufacturers may have slightly different capacities. However, for all but the most precise shooting, mixed cases from different manufacturers are often close enough to make no difference.

The situation is different with shotgun shells. Accuracy is not really the problem. Shotshells must be loaded to the brim, so to speak. When all the components are in, the crimp must come down exactly on the top of the shot. With shotshells of differing capacities, things just don't fit right!

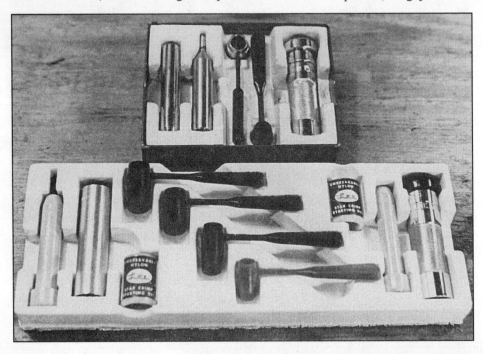

Lee Loaders for shotshells have been around since the early 1960s. At the top, an original set from the '60s. By the late 1970s, the set of tools had grown to that on the bottom.

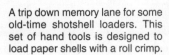

A trip down memory lane for some old-time shotshell loaders. This set of hand tools is designed to load paper shells with a roll crimp.

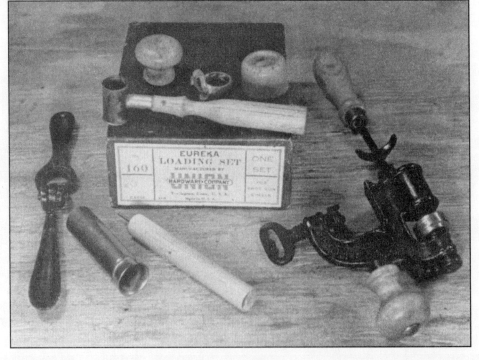

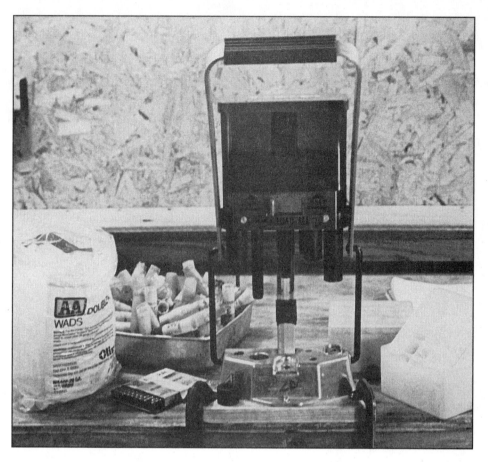

Most shotshell loaders now are of the unitized type, with powder, shot and all dies contained in one tool. This is an inexpensive Lee Load-All.

So, new shotshell reloaders are advised to use only one brand and type of shell. Plastic shells were introduced around the early 1960s, and most shotshells are made of plastic now. Some are all plastic. Some have paper base wads inside plastic cases. A few types of paper shells are still made.

Primers for shotshells consist of four parts, three metal pieces plus the priming compound. They are often called battery cup primers. The head of a shotshell is not rigid as the head of a brass case, so a shotshell primer has the cup and anvil inside a battery cup, which has a small head of its own. This gives it support against the blow of the firing pin and keeps the detonation of the primer from damaging the soft base of the case.

In days gone by, there were different types of battery cup primers for the cases of different manufacturers, and sometimes for different gauges. Things are pretty well standardized now, so this is not a problem.

However, different primers still have different flash characteristics. Reloading tool manufacturers suggest that you use the primer that is recommended by the component manufacturers for the shell, powder, wad and shot charge you are loading. Some slower burning powders in heavy loads require a primer that is hotter, yet still the same size. Follow the recommendations in the loading manual exactly.

Powders for shotgun shells are generally fast burning. The relatively faster powders are used for lighter loads; the relatively slower ones for heavier loads. Charges of different powders fill different volumes. So again, it is important to use the powder type and charge that is recommended for the case, primer,

wad and shot charge of your specific load. Consult a reliable reloading manual.

Wads are mostly moulded plastic now, combining the overpowder wad, spacer, and cup to hold the shot. Thus, the height of the wad column cannot be varied.

In the old days, we could vary the height of the wad column by using more or fewer fiber wads, or even cutting a wad in half. Now, we must match the wad to the other components to get the correct spacing. About the only leeway we have is to add an extra card wad inside the shot cup below the shot. This will fill up space if the shot charge doesn't quite come high enough to give a good crimp.

Shot is what does the job. It breaks the clays and bags the game. Choice of the proper shot size can be a matter of fierce opinion among hunters. In general, use smaller sizes for smaller game, larger sizes for larger game. In some areas, game regulations dictate the shot sizes that are allowable.

For many shotgun sports, the rules tell you what you may or may not use. Some clubs limit the size of shot that may be used on their premises. Load accordingly.

Just one warning: For a long time after steel shot requirements for waterfowl hunting came into being, steel shot was not obtainable for reloading, nor were data available. Now that we are able to handload steel shot, *never* substitute steel shot for lead shot in loading data. The charge of steel shot must be matched to other suitable components.

The way to stay out of trouble and produce good handloads is to follow the recommended loading data *exactly*. Read that manual!

Tools and Procedures

Although older tools are still in use, and simple Lee Loaders have been made in large quantities and are still being used, the modern column-type integrated shotshell loader is most commonly used now.

As we have seen, metallic cartridge loading tools were developed around a basic press to which individual dies and accessories could be added. Scales and powder measures are ordinarily used separately.

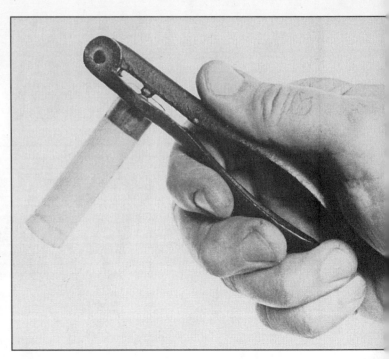

Not much complexity to priming shotgun shells in the old days. Just drop a shell in the hole, put in a primer and squeeze the handles.

Shortly after World War II, the current style of shotshell loader was developed. All holders, dies, and measures for powder and shot were integrated into a single unit. Once the adjustments for crimp, powder and shot charges were made, the unit was ready to turn out reloads without any additional changes. Operating the handle moves the dies and component reservoirs down to the shell. The operator manually moves the shell from stage to stage. Recently, progressive machines that automatically take the shell from operation to operation have become popular.

Regardless of type, the operations for reloading shotshells are basically the same: The case is examined, and the primer removed. The base of the case is resized, and the new primer is seated. The powder charge is inserted, the cup wad is pushed down into place, and the shot charge is dropped in. The crimp at the end of the shell is started, then it is completely formed to finish the shell.

Again, let me emphasize a couple of points about shotshell loading: Stick with the exact components required by the data you are using. Never mix information for steel and lead shot; the pressure curves are very different. Use only steel shot loading data when loading steel shot.

I regularly load shotshells for several gauges and thoroughly enjoy it, so don't misinterpret what I am about to say. Useful as it is, I just don't feel the same romance with shotshell loading as I do with rifle and pistol cartridge loading. There just doesn't seem to be as much opportunity for creativity.

Still, there is something special about making a good score at trap or Skeet, or a great shot on a zig-zagging dove, using your own reloads. It is even more special if someone, impressed, asks where you got the loads you are using, and you can casually answer, "I made them myself."

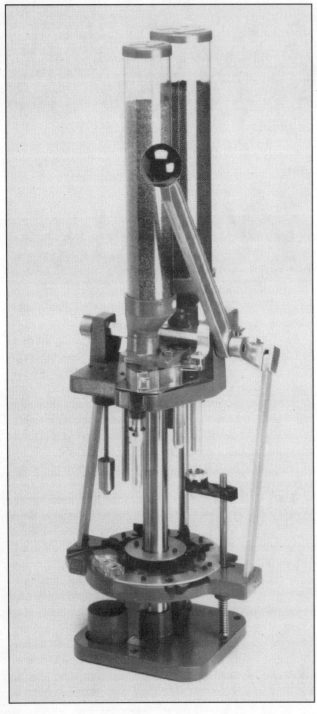

Shotshell reloading tools usually have top-mounted hoppers for shot and powder. The operator feeds in empty shells, and each pull of the handle turns out a fresh reload. Not cheap, these tools can pay for themselves if you shoot lots of shotgun shells.

The tools for bullet casting include a furnace, though it need not be as fancy as this Lyman electric; moulds; a supply of lead alloy, such as wheelweights; and some good flux. These simple tools can cheaply feed handguns or rifles.

Bullet Casting

Bullet casting is a special part of metallic cartridge reloading. It appeals to those who want to have as much control as possible over the performance of the final cartridge.

Cast bullets have a velocity limitation that jacketed bullets can easily exceed. For most pistol loads short of the most powerful, speed limitation is not really a factor. Cast bullets in rifles can be pushed to about 2000 fps, 30-30 velocities, which makes them useful for some hunting purposes as well as for target shooting.

In years past, the selection of store-bought bullets for reloading was not as great as it is today. Now, a handloader can buy just about any bullet he needs. So, why do people bother casting bullets?

Economy is one obvious reason. Cast bullets don't cost much. Other than the brass case, the bullet is the most expensive item in reloading metallic cartridges. Scrap lead (wheelweights are favored) can be used.

Supply is another factor. Some old-timers still remember World War II and the immediate post-war period, when bullets for reloading were simply not available at any price. The bullet caster does not have to depend on outside sources.

The power range of cast bullet loads can suit special requirements. High-power rifles can be used for small game hunting and even for indoor target shooting.

Barrel life is extended. Bore wear with cast bullets is negligible. Some shooters believe cast bullets polish the bore, although there is little research to back this up.

Versatility of diameter is an advantage seldom mentioned. Cast bullets can be made in many diameters not available in jacketed bullets. Guns having worn barrels or odd bore sizes can continue shooting.

Casting Tools and Procedures

Making your own cast bullets is actually pretty simple. The basic requirements are a mould, some lead, a few simple tools, a way to lubricate the bullets, and a way to make them the correct diameter. Be sure to consult a cast bullet handbook before you start.

Here are a few things you will need to get started: Lead alloy such as lead and tin, solder, linotype metal, wheelweights, etc; bullet mould; lead pot and heat source; flux such as wax or grease to help mix the molten metal. You'll also need a dipper or ladle to stir and pour metal, plus a wood stick to open the sprue cutter of the mould. An old hammer handle works well. Be sure to wear gloves and eye protection to guard your hands and eyes from possible spatters.

1. Melting the Metal. Choose a clear, well-ventilated place to work. The traditional iron lead pot works well to melt the metal, as will the sophisticated bottom-pour electric casting furnaces. Small pieces of the lead alloy melt faster than large pieces, so add metal to the pot a little at a time. At the end of a casting session, pour out the unused lead into an ingot mould, discarded muffin tin, or something similar. The small blocks will melt faster next time. Put sprues and rejected bullets back into the pot.

A good alloy of bullet metal should have lead, tin and antimony in it. The metal can come from many sources. A standard alloy for bullets is the Lyman No. 2, which contains the necessary ingredients. H. Guy Loverin, one of the great bullet casters of the past, once said he believed that best accuracy would be obtained with all new metals in the alloy. He admitted, however, that he would not pass up a chance to acquire some scrap lead.

I separate pure lead and save it for casting bullets for muzzleloaders. I use mostly wheelweights for casting my rifle and pistol bullets. I usually add other scrap, such as old bullets, to the wheelweights. Tin makes the bullets cast more easily; if more tin is needed, bar solder is 50 percent lead and 50 percent tin. Blending different lots of metal together keeps different batches of bullets at least fairly uniform in weight. If the weights of bullets cast from different batches are close to each other, everything is fine.

I'm sure I could get better accuracy with pure components, but the hunt for scrap lead has become part of the game for me. I've won matches and killed critters with my cast bullets, so they're plenty good enough for me. For all but the highest velocity loads, I think paying attention to your casting is more important than worrying about your alloy.

2. Preparing the Bullet Mould. While your metal is melting, get your mould ready. If it is a new one, follow the manufacturer's instructions to prepare it for casting. If it is an iron or steel mould that has been oiled for storage, clean it thoroughly, preferably with denatured ethyl alcohol, before using it.

The bullet mould consists of two blocks, each one having half of one or more cavities used to form the bullets. On the top pivots the sprue plate or sprue cutter. There may be other devices used to form hollow points or bases included as part of the mould. Handles allow the user to comfortably hold and use the mould.

3. Fluxing the Metal. When the metal has melted to the point at which it flows almost as freely as water, its surface will look gray and scummy. Part of this scum is made up of impurities, but part of it is tin, and we want the tin mixed back in the alloy. We recombine the tin with the lead by *fluxing* the molten metal.

Drop a small blob of wax or bullet lube into the pot and stir energetically. Light the smoke immediately with a match, so it won't smoke up the place. There are now smokeless fluxes on the market, and they are recommended if the smoke becomes a problem.

Bullets can be lubricated and sized simultaneously in a machine such as this elderly Lyman No. 45, which still does a good job.

The flux causes the tin to mix with the lead. The now-bright surface of the molten metal will still have impurities on the top. Skim these off with the dipper or a spoon and discard them in a tin can or other disposable non-flammable container.

4. Casting the Bullet. The dipper should be left in the pot so that it remains hot. Fill it half full of the molten metal. Take the clean mould in your left hand, turned sideways toward the dipper. Fit the spout of the dipper into the recess of the sprue hole and turn both mould and dipper together to an upright position. Allow a few seconds for the sprue to harden.

Melted alloy can splash, and the fumes need to be properly vented. This bullet caster is well protected with goggles and apron, and a vent fan (not seen) keeps the air fresh.

Put the dipper back into the pot and pick up the wooden stick. Sharply strike the sprue cutter; the sprue will be cut from the base of the bullet.

Open the mould and the new bullet should drop out. Catch it on a soft surface such as an old cotton towel. If the bullet does not drop out on its own, use the stick to tap the *joint* of the handles. Never tap the mould blocks or sprue plate!

5. Lubricating and Sizing. Most bullet casters now use a combination machine that both lubricates and sizes cast bullets. That is, it forces lubricant into the grooves and reduces the diameter of the newly cast bullet to the desired size, in one operation.

Gas checks may also be seated during the lubing/sizing operation. Gas checks are small copper or brass cups that can be added to the base of some pistol bullets and many rifle bullets. They resist gas cutting and allow the bullets to be fired at higher velocities. Bullets designed for gas checks may also be used without them in low-velocity loads.

The use of a lubricating/sizing press is not the only way to lubricate and size, but it is the most common. Some bullets come from the mould the exact size you want them. Lubricant then simply may be smeared on with the fingers, or the bullets can be stood in a pan and melted lubricant poured over them, filling the grease grooves.

Most experts agree that the less sizing done on the cast bullet, the better its accuracy will be. It is also generally accepted that the bullet should be sized as close to the exact groove diameter of the gun as possible.

However, the ability to size a cast bullet is one of its advantages. I have found that by sizing my cast bullets in different dies, I can use the same bullet mould for 30-30, 308, 30-06, 7.62 Russian, 303 British and 7.7mm Japanese.

Safety

Safe bullet casting and reloading is extremely easy if you use common sense.

While casting, always wear eye protection, gloves and long-sleeve shirt. Ventilation should always be good. Use an exhaust hood or fan to assure that fumes are carried away from you. Keep your work area clear. Wash your hands thoroughly after handling lead or lead alloys.

When reloading, keep your work area uncluttered so you can concentrate on what you are doing. Keep distractions to a minimum when handling powder or primers. Wear eye protection. Never, never have more than one can of powder on the bench at one time! Don't get powders mixed up! It is a good practice to have only what you need for one particular operation in your work area at any time.

Recordkeeping

Keeping good records doesn't have to take away any of the fun of reloading. It can make it *more* fun.

Before I started keeping records, I remember finding a box of reloads I'd forgotten about and wondering what they were. I couldn't take a chance on using them for hunting or competition. There was nothing to do but shoot them to find out how they performed. It was a good chance to do some shooting, so it wasn't a real problem.

Two-cavity moulds are perhaps the most common types in use now: (from left) Lyman, Lee, Hensley & Gibbs and RCBS.

I did have a problem preparing ammunition for competition once, by not being able to read the load information on an old cartridge box. The information was not what I thought it was, and my loads did not hit where I thought they should.

Know what you are doing! Keep records. They don't have to be any particular form.

Here is what I do now: I keep a notebook at the loading bench and make notes from each day's loading. These notes are nothing very formal, I just want to be able to duplicate whatever I have done. I put a data label on each box of loaded ammunition. If the box has a separate cover, sometimes I put a label on the cover, too. The label on the box is more important, because covers can get switched. At the range, I record the load data from the box into a small notebook I keep in my shooting kit. After I shoot the load, I record how it did in that particular gun.

This is nothing very fancy, and it doesn't take much time, so I always do it. It is better than trying to remember how many grains of what powder behind what bullet gave me that beautiful group the year before last.

Handloading ammunition is economical, can improve accuracy and allows us to shoot more. It is certainly useful, enabling us to produce ammunition not readily available or perhaps not available at all.

It is recycling at its finest, reusing things over and over instead of discarding them!

Handloading is done throughout the world, but only in America does it really flourish. Millions of Americans handle powder and primers, make bullets and cartridges, billions of them, and all with an excellent safety record.

Handloading is useful, environmentally friendly, and safe!

CHAPTER TWENTY-TWO

THE DOS AND DON'TS OF COLLECTING

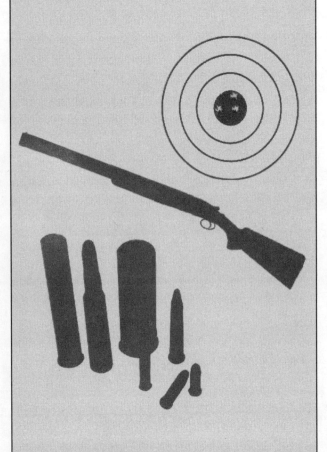

THE URGE TO collect seems to be born in us. Kids collect all kinds of things: comic books, baseball cards, dolls, seashells, rocks, insects. They learn something about them, then move on to other things. Eventually, some of them grow up, discover gun collecting, and have a hobby for life.

Why collect guns? One reason is to preserve our heritage. Firearms figure prominently in a number of historical events. Gun collecting preserves both large chunks and little tidbits of history that might otherwise be lost. Guns as beautiful things, valuable things, as works of art; guns as steps in a mechanical evolution; guns as part of history, romance and adventure—all these are reasons for collecting guns.

Getting Started

What should you collect? There is really no simple answer. Some people plan carefully, know what they are going to collect and then do so. However, most gun collectors probably just stumble into their chosen field.

Many people start out shooting with a 22 rifle, get a shotgun, then a centerfire rifle, perhaps then a handgun. Somewhere along the line, some gun catches their fancy, and they start accumulating similar things. At some point, they realize with shock that the accumulation has become a collection.

In my youth, I bought my first military rifle, an old Russian Mosin-Nagant converted to 30-06. The idea of my rifle actually having been used in some historical event fascinated me, and military rifles held a special place in my eyes. I recall thinking that it would be nice to collect one of every military rifle ever made. I think my real passion for history began at about this time.

I decided to make a list of every military rifle ever made. That was the beginning of my firearms research. It was a bit overwhelming to find out how many there were (even back then) and how much there was to learn about them. I realized I had to give up my idea of getting them all!

Eventually, though, my research paid off in a different way. After I had owned my Russian rifle for more than twenty-five years, I finally put its whole story together. It turned out to be one of sixty personally bought by A.A. Vonsiatsky, a Russian-born naturalized American who had escaped the sweep of the Red Army after the Russian Revolution. He fled to France and then moved to America. He later became the head of a little-known international anti-communist movement, the Russian Fascists. For a short time, the international headquarters of this

This U.S.-made Russian Mosin-Nagant rifle, bought in the 1950s, was one of the things that got the writer interested in history and gun collecting.

(Right) Is my rifle in this picture? A.A. Vonsiatsky, head of the worldwide Russian Fascist movement, was pictured during the 1930s with some of his rifles. The writer bought a rifle formerly owned by him during the 1950s, without any idea of its history, but finally put the whole story together almost thirty years later.

group was in, of all places, Connecticut. Vonsiatsky may have bought the rifles, a familiar rifle chambered for a popular American cartridge, with some thought of using them as training weapons for the overthrow of the communists.

Of course, things didn't happen that way. During World War II the communists became our allies, and in the emotional climate of the war, anti-communist Vonsiatsky was imprisoned on falsified spy charges. The prosecution of Vonsiatsky was the big political career opportunity of Thomas J. Dodd, who later became senator from Connecticut and was instrumental in writing the Gun Control Act of 1968.

There is no telling what the story might be behind any gun you may pick up. Digging that story out is much of the fun of gun collecting.

What to Collect

You may as well know that certain factors influence the demand and, consequently, the price of collectible guns. This is of some interest to all collectors. If you pay a certain price for a gun, you like to believe it is really worth that much and could be sold for about that amount, if necessary.

From another angle, by getting things that are not in demand, you can get them cheaper. The only drawback is that low-demand items are harder to sell if you want to upgrade your collection. At any rate, here are some factors to consider when deciding whether to buy:

Country of origin is always a factor. Most, though not all, people prefer things made in their own country.

Time period of the guns can narrow one's interest. Not specific dates, necessarily, but rather, "flintlock period," "World War II period," and so on. Guns of "big" wars seem to attract more interest than those of "little" wars.

Type of gun (handgun, rifle, shotgun, machinegun) further narrows down the field. Handguns seem disproportionately popular because they take up less space and can be more easily stored, transported and exhibited.

Manufacturer makes a difference. Two breakopen revolvers may have similar mechanical characteristics. However, one by Smith & Wesson will fetch a greater price than an equivalent by Iver Johnson.

Some people collect only by manufacturer. "The Guns of Colt" or "The Guns of Winchester" are the rather ambitious titles of some people's collections. It is hard to get them all.

Your personal interest should be your guide to getting start-

ed. It's probably a mistake to try to duplicate someone else's collection, because it won't satisfy your personal likes.

A friend of mine who was in the Navy began collecting Naval-marked guns and accessories. Another collector friend born in 1938 collects any firearms made during that year. These are both interesting ideas that spark their collecting instincts.

The vast quantities of military firearms that have been imported open the door to collecting variations of particular military guns.

Many of us got started simply accumulating stuff. One gun collector's organization to which I belonged finally added a category for "General Collector" to its application form. It was embarrassing for some people to want to join a collector's club and not know what kind of collector they were.

There are some relatively untouched fields waiting for new collectors. Breakopen revolvers, single shot shotguns, bolt-action shotguns and Spanish revolvers, to name a few, are essentially ignored by collectors. At present, there is not much interest in such things, but lots of them were made, and *somebody* ought to find out something about them.

Most of the early percussion revolvers are already in collec-

Flintlocks, such as this cannon-barrel pistol, are desirable items for many gun collectors.

Walther is famous for its double-action 9mm pistol, the P-38 of WWII. Collectors know the first Walther 9mm was this WWI version, the single-action Walther Model 6.

Unusual mechanical features are often of interest to collectors. This Spanish Jo-Lo-Ar pistol allowed operation of the slide by the shooting hand, using the hinged lever.

tions. However, collecting replicas of these revolvers might be very much worthwhile.

The potential fields of gun collecting are almost limitless: flintlocks, percussion guns, sporting guns, military guns, commemoratives, common guns, variations of common guns, mechanical curiosities, rare guns, historical guns, prototype guns. Well, you get the idea. Whatever you choose, make sure you *like* those items, and count on having fun.

Back in the high inflation days of the late 1970s and early 1980s, a lot of people got into gun collecting. Many of them, unfortunately, looked at guns solely as a way to beat inflation and make a lot of money. They weren't interested in guns as historical items and didn't have any interest in doing any research about them. Many of them got out of collecting very quickly. From a strictly monetary standpoint, they would have been better off doing something else, like buying gold or investing in cattle futures.

Values of guns are based on what the guns are (a constant

sort of thing) and their condition (relatively constant, but which can change for the worse). Another factor is the present demand for those particular guns. This is variable and often completely unpredictable. If you want to make money, try something else. If you like guns a lot, want to have a lot of fun, and maybe make some money, then perhaps gun collecting is worth a try.

Related Items

A collection of guns is always interesting, but related items make it even more so. Flintlock Kentucky rifles displayed with powder horns, knives or other accessories of the period generate greater interest than the rifles alone. Powder flasks, cartridge boxes, swords and bayonets can add to a display of Civil War guns.

Some people get so involved in accessories that the supplemental items sometimes become the main collection. I have seen a large and enormously interesting collection of military holsters. No pistols, just holsters. The collector liked military pistols, got a few holsters just for display, noticed variations, and did some reading to find out more. Eventually the guns were sold and the holsters became the focus of the collection.

Good additions to any collection of cartridge firearms are...cartridges! A youngster may be fascinated by a collection of old Winchester rifles, but many of the early rifles were chambered for cartridges he never heard of. If a 45-60, 38-72 or 40-65 rifle has a cartridge, possibly several, on display with it, the exhibit has a lot more meaning.

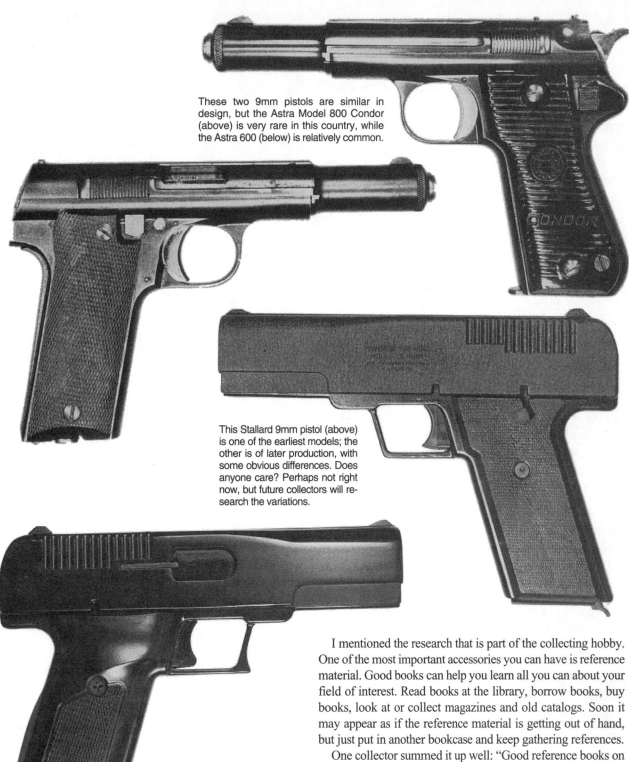

These two 9mm pistols are similar in design, but the Astra Model 800 Condor (above) is very rare in this country, while the Astra 600 (below) is relatively common.

This Stallard 9mm pistol (above) is one of the earliest models; the other is of later production, with some obvious differences. Does anyone care? Perhaps not right now, but future collectors will research the variations.

Cartridge collections are always interesting to me, either as an addition to a gun collection or as a separate collection in its own right. I got my start in collecting by acquiring cartridges—they were much cheaper than guns!

I mentioned the research that is part of the collecting hobby. One of the most important accessories you can have is reference material. Good books can help you learn all you can about your field of interest. Read books at the library, borrow books, buy books, look at or collect magazines and old catalogs. Soon it may appear as if the reference material is getting out of hand, but just put in another bookcase and keep gathering references.

One collector summed it up well: "Good reference books on your shelves will put good guns in your gun cabinet."

Gun collector's associations and museums with good gun collections are also good sources of information.

Care, Repair and Restoration

Care and restoration of a true antique gun is a touchy subject. In the past, some guns have had modifications made or parts replaced that made the gun look like a scarcer, more valuable model. Such practices are considered unethical.

We'll get a little more into the ethics of gun collecting shortly. For now, let us consider caring for a collection piece. The same care given to a "using" gun will generally suffice for a collector's item, but in many cases, the collection gun needs more attention.

Rust is always a problem—perhaps *the* problem—of firearms condition. If a gun is already rusty, go slow. Guns have been ruined by the use of strong commercial rust removers. The rust was removed all right, but so were the markings and the remaining original finish.

Light surface rust can generally be removed by #0000 (the finest grade) steel wool, saturated in lubricating oil. Rub gently. Any repair or restoration of a rare historical firearm should probably be carried out through an expert in that field. Realize that you are holding a little piece of history, and be careful.

For very old guns with missing and unobtainable parts, parts may have to be made. You have a lot more leeway dealing with modern guns, for original parts may be readily available. If a valuable gun has been restored from a much poorer condition, that should be specified when the gun is sold.

Should we shoot old guns we consider collection pieces? Many people who are both shooters and collectors have agonized over this question. This has not been so much of a problem with me. I seem to have a real curiosity as to how guns of all types work and shoot. I am also fortunate to have nothing of any immense value in my collection. Naturally, we do not want to damage either the shooter or the gun. Safety of the shooter is most important, then consider any possible harm to the gun.

Unless a collection piece is likely to be damaged (parts *do* break, you know), or the gun is a rare one-of-a-kind specimen, or it's in factory-new unfired condition, my personal belief is that limited shooting with proper loads is all right for a collection gun. For me, it is much more fun to own if I can shoot it. Note that proper loads may not be the loads for which the gun was designed. Some old guns were not really suitable for their original ammunition in the first place.

If you are going to shoot a collection gun, have it checked over by a knowledgeable expert and shoot reduced loads. For a muzzle-loading gun, this is easily done. If you are a handloader, stick with light handloads. If you decide to shoot a collection piece, please remember that you are the custodian of that little bit of our history. Be careful!

Ethics

There is an unwritten code of ethics to which gun collectors generally subscribe. In addition, some organizations have printed guidelines by which they expect their members to abide.

Obviously, honest gun collectors do not make or sell fake copies of rare or historical firearms. Alteration of markings or serial numbers is also obviously not acceptable. Neither is knowingly misrepresenting a gun by printed or oral word.

Repair, refinishing, replacement of parts and restoration are often done to improve a gun's appearance or return it to original condition, if it has been previously altered. There is nothing wrong with this; such work can bring a gun that was

Gun collectors can be forces in their communities. The late "Pop" Trana, a shooter and collector of Smith & Wesson revolvers, has an annual pistol championship match in Houston, Texas, named after him.

essentially lost to us back into condition for display. However, at the time of sale, it should be noted that this work was done. In some cases, guns have been over-restored. In my eyes, there is nothing wrong with an old gun looking like an old gun.

Condition should always be described as accurately as possible. A good practice would be to use the NRA-derived descriptions given in Chapter 20 on buying a gun.

If you are purchasing a gun of considerable value, check out the seller. If you are not an expert, you may want an appraisal by a qualified expert. Always get a signed, dated bill of sale that gives a very detailed description of the gun. Many collectors also like to have such bills of sale signed by witnesses as well.

Manners and Etiquette

There is another unwritten code of behavior involved with gun collecting. This involves how to behave around other people's guns. Basically, we want to avoid embarrassment, and we want to avoid any harm to people or property.

Assume that a collector *likes* the guns in his collection. Unfavorable comparisons with others you have seen will

Civil War guns are always of interest to collectors. This is a Remington contract rifle of 1862. The modern Zouave replica muzzle-loading rifle is patterned after it.

Mention gun collecting and many people immediately think of old Winchesters. The Winchester Model 1873 was probably the most important model of the company's early years.

Collecting military rifles has always been of interest to many. The tremendous numbers and varieties allow even a beginning collector to assemble an interesting collection. This is a WWII Japanese Arisaka rifle.

An ordinary British SMLE rifle? A well-read collector might tell you that it is a rare Mark IV rifle, the first SMLE with a peep sight. It was never officially adopted.

It looks like a Winchester Model 12, but it is not. The Winchester Model 25, a solid-frame design, was produced for a short time to provide a lower-priced gun for the company's line. It's sure to have collector interest in the future.

probably not make him feel good. Likewise, questions or comments about values are not considered polite. The owner may volunteer what he paid for a gun. He may not. If he does not, he probably considers it his own business, so don't put him on the spot by asking him what he paid for something. If he does tell you, then whatever you do, do not tell him that he paid too much.

When examining a collector firearm, all safety rules apply. Keep any gun pointed in a safe direction, keep your finger off the trigger, and keep the action open. Collection guns may have unusual mechanical features, so make sure you ask for permission to handle a gun, and then make sure you really understand how it works before handling it. Never "snap" (dry-fire) someone else's gun!

Legal Aspects

All laws that pertain to buying and selling firearms must be obeyed. Many collectors have a mix of antique and modern guns, and they should be aware that different laws apply to different guns.

Muzzle-loading guns, both original and replicas, are generally exempt from federal firearms laws, as are airguns. Those firearms made before 1898 are considered "antiques" and are generally exempt from the record-keeping requirements of the federal laws. There is a large category of "curios and relics" which may be obtained by people with a federal collector's license; for those without such a license, they must be acquired as modern guns, through a licensed dealer.

Machinegun collectors are probably the most heavily regulated collectors in existence. Because of this, they are probably the most knowledgeable about the laws. Machineguns can only be transferred through the holder of a Class III federal license, and a transfer tax must be paid.

Besides federal laws, some local laws also apply to buying and selling guns. Local collectors' organizations should keep current on these often-changing local laws.

Looking at things objectively, it's difficult at times to understand firearms laws. There is no way to logically explain why a Winchester '94 30-30 rifle made in December of one year is an antique, exempt from federal law, and an identical rifle made during the first few days of the next year is a modern gun, subject to full restrictions.

These things must be studied and learned. Find out about the laws that pertain to your collecting interest. From a personal

Airgun collecting has become more popular, because the guns are free of most of the restrictions placed on firearms. This is a special Daisy Model 25, a 1913 design reproduced in 1986 to commemorate the company's 100-year history.

Machinegun collectors are probably the most heavily regulated collectors in existence, but they perform a valuable service in preserving part of our history that would otherwise be lost. This is an experimental Thompson 30-06 light machinegun, developed to meet the WWII need for more military arms. It did not work well and was never produced.

standpoint, you don't want to take a chance on violating the law. From the standpoint of firearms ownership in general, we don't want any violations.

Be aware that laws change. Between the time I write this and the time you read it, laws may have already changed. If you own a number of guns, you must be aware of how the law affects you.

Recordkeeping

I've known collectors who were walking encyclopedias of knowledge about their gun collections. However, if they walked across the street just as an oncoming truck lost its brakes, all that knowledge would be lost.

Recordkeeping related to your gun collection is good for you and good for posterity. We get older, new things crowd in with the old things in our minds, and eventually we need permanent records to keep it all straight.

We guard against theft as much as possible, but guns are sometimes stolen. Good records allow us to immediately give a description to the police and may aid in the quick recovery of the stolen items.

Although it isn't likely to happen to anyone reading these pages, people do die. Survivors are often left with no real understanding of what is in a collection. Good records can help. Records can be elaborate and formal, or they can be simple. I prefer to use a simple method; I would be tempted to put it off if it were too involved.

If you haven't already worked out a system of records, here is a possibility to consider. Keep a single sheet of paper for each gun in a notebook or file, or wherever it is convenient. You can make up a simple form and use a copy of it for each gun.

On the top, put the full description, including the model or name, caliber or gauge, serial number, and general description. Then add details on the markings, size, weight, finish, etc., to

further identify that specific gun. The bottom half of the form might consist of two sections. The first section might include historical background and notes. Then, at the very bottom, give details on where, when, and from whom you acquired it, the price paid, and any updates on value you might have done.

If a gun is stolen, destroyed or sold, some of this bottom information may no longer be needed. Then you can fold the bottom of the sheet under, photocopy the rest of it, and present a copy to the police, insurance company or the purchaser.

Photographs of the guns in your collection are always desirable. Try to get a photo of the specific identifying features of each particular gun. High-contrast black-and-white photos will generally photocopy well, so copies of the photos can be provided along with the copies of your record sheets.

Additional material may be filed with the original record sheet, if desired. Such additional items might include the bill of sale, instruction booklets, copies of articles that contain historical background, and so on.

Originals or duplicates may be kept in a safe deposit box. You don't want to take a chance on your guns and your records both being lost!

When the frontiersman of the 1700s primed his Kentucky and headed after game, he probably had no thought that his rifle would someday be a prized collector's item.

The mountain men with their percussion rifles, the Civil War soldiers with their variety of guns, the cowboys with their Colts and Winchesters, the riverboat gamblers with their derringers, the buffalo hunters with their big Sharps rifles—all these people are now part of our history. Their guns, ordinary working guns to them, are now desirable collector's items.

The ordinary guns of today, as well as the exotic and unusual ones, will perhaps be the collector's items of tomorrow. Don't let anyone tell you there is something wrong with some guns, or that we don't need certain types of guns. As far as I'm concerned, *all* guns are part of our heritage!

GLOSSARY OF TERMS

Special terms are often used in a discussion of guns and shooting. A knowledge of such terms helps people understand firearms and the shooting sports, and allows better communication. This listing gives explanations of common terms used in this book and other firearms literature.

Accuracy—a. the ability of a gun to shoot a single projectile close to the aiming point of the target; b. the ability of a gun to shoot a number of successive single projectiles into a small group.

ACP—Automatic Colt Pistol. Used to designate cartridges designed for Colt pistols, for example, 45 ACP.

Action—the combination of moving parts that allow a shooter to load, fire and unload a gun.

Accurize—to improve the accuracy of a rifle or handgun, usually by mechanical improvements or adjustments.

Adjustable choke—a device attached to the muzzle of a single-barrel shotgun to vary the degree of choke, thus varying the size of the shot pattern at different ranges.

Adjustable sights—sights that allow vertical (elevation) and horizontal (windage) adjustments.

Airgun—a gun that propels projectiles through a tubular barrel by the expansion of compressed gas, such as air or carbon dioxide (CO_2.)

Ammunition—a general term covering any material used to shoot any type of gun; depending on context, it may include cartridges, powder, bullets, airgun pellets, etc.

Anvil—the part of a primer or cartridge case against which the priming compound is crushed when the firing pin strikes the primer cup.

Aperture—the hole in a rear peep sight through which the shooter looks at the front sight and target.

Aperture sight—a rear sight that uses an aperture, generally mounted on the receiver or, less commonly, on the tang.

Arm—an abbreviation of firearm.

Arsenal—usually, a place where military guns are made or repaired. The term is often confused with armory, a place where guns are stored.

Assault rifle—a military rifle designed for full-automatic fire with a reduced-power cartridge. The term is incorrectly—but commonly—applied to some semi-automatic rifles.

Autoloading—an action of semi-automatic or self-loading operation.

Automatic—a true automatic firearm (full automatic) is one that continues to fire as long as the trigger is pulled and ammunition holds out.

Automatic safety—a mechanical safety device that usually engages every time an action is opened.

Backstop—material that stops projectiles that have passed through a target; it may be natural, such as a hillside, or constructed for the purpose.

Backstrap—the metal portion of a handgun frame at the rear of the grip.

Balance point—the point of a rifle or shotgun at which the gun will balance.

Ball—a. round lead projectile used in muzzle-loading rifles or pistols; b. military term for rifle or pistol ammunition with jacketed bullets.

Ball powder—propellant powder in which the granules are spherical in shape.

Ballistics—the science or study of projectiles in motion. Interior ballistics deals with the forces acting on the bullet until it leaves the muzzle; exterior ballistics deals with the flight of the bullet.

Barrel—the hollow tube of a gun though which projectiles are expelled; the interior is called the bore.

Base wad—a fiber or plastic component placed inside the base of a shotgun shell to strengthen the base and support the primer. It may be moulded with the shell or attached later.

Battery—the condition of a firearms breechblock in firing position.

BB—a spherical pellet of: a. plated steel of .175-inch diameter for use in airguns; b. lead or steel of .180-inch diameter for use in shotguns.

BB Cap—Bulleted Breech Cap; a small low-power 22-caliber cartridge for short-range shooting. Its ancestry goes back to the 1840s.

Bead—a. a round sight normally used at the muzzle of a shotgun; b. the front sight of some rifles, in which the sight is viewed as a round bead on a narrow post.

Bench or *Benchrest*—a structure used to solidly support a rifle during shooting.

Berdan primer—a primer consisting of a cup and priming compound; the anvil is formed in the cartridge case; cases of this construction are not easily reloaded.

Blade sight—generally, the front sight of a rifle or handgun, seen by the shooter as a post.

Blowback—a type of automatic or semi-automatic firearm in which the breechbolt is not locked in place during firing; the action parts "blow back" by the energy of the fired cartridge.

Boattail—the shape of a bullet with a tapered base; designed to reduce air drag.

Bolt—a. a breechblock, generally circular in cross-section, that moves backward and forward to open or close the action; b. the part of a revolver that locks the cylinder from turning.

Bolt action—an action type that uses a bolt normally operated with an up-and-back, forward-and-down motion.

Bolt face—the forward end of a bolt.

Bolt handle—an operating handle, generally ending in a knob, that extends from the side of a bolt; the shooter grasps this to operate the action.

Bolt release—a. the mechanism that allows the bolt to be removed from a rifle or shotgun action; b. the mechanism that allows the bolt of a semi-automatic firearm to move forward from its open position.

Bore—the hollow interior of a gun barrel.

Bore diameter—the diameter of a gun's bore. For rifles, this may be measured from the bottoms of opposing grooves (groove diameter) or the tops of opposing lands (bore diameter).

Boxer primer—a type of primer, used in most American-made cartridges, that has a cup, priming compound and anvil. The primer pocket in the cartridge case has a central flash hole. This allows the fired primer to be easily punched out, and Boxer-primed cases are easily reloaded.

Box magazine—a removable box-like storage device to hold cartridges and feed them into the action of a firearm at the proper time; often erroneously called a clip.

Brass—term commonly used for empty rifle or handgun cartridge cases.

Breakopen—a gun with a hinged frame that allows opening at the top when unlatched. Also called hinge, top-break or tip-up.

Breech—the rear end of the barrel. The term is sometimes informally used to refer to the breechblock or breechbolt.

Breech plug—the plug that screws into the barrel to close the breech of a muzzle-loading firearm.

Breechblock—a movable block of metal, generally moving in a vertical direction, that closes and blocks the breech of a firearm in preparation to fire.

Breechbolt—a sliding metal part, generally moving in a horizontal direction, that closes and locks the breech of a firearm in preparation to fire.

Breechloader—a firearm that is loaded from the rear or breech end (as distinguished from a muzzleloader).

Buckshot—large (.025- to .036-inch diameter) spherical lead shot pellets used in hunting deer and other large game; also used by military and police organizations.

Bullet—an elongated projectile normally fired through a rifled barrel.

Bullet jacket—the metal covering, generally a copper alloy, of many rifle and handgun bullet designs.

Bullet mould—a device with a cavity or cavities for casting bullets from lead.

Bullet puller—a device for removing bullets from cartridges without firing them.

Bullet trap—a device used to capture and retain fired bullets.

Bullseye—the aiming point of a traditional paper target, generally a black circle.

Butt—the rear portion of the stock of a rifle or shotgun; also, the bottom of a handgun grip.

Buttplate—a metal or composition plate attached to protect the end of a buttstock.

Buttstock—the rear portion of the stock of a rifle or shotgun.

Caliber—a. measurement of the diameter of a rifle or handgun bore, originally in hundredths of an inch; it may now be expressed also in millimeters or thousandths of an inch; b. the cartridge for which a rifle or handgun is chambered.

Cannelure—a groove around the circumference of a bullet or cartridge case.

Cap—percussion cap; primer used for percussion lock firearms.

Cap and Ball—term for percussion blackpowder firearms that shoot round lead balls, with the powder ignited by a percussion cap.

Caplock—a percussion lock.

Carbine—a short rifle; it is a relative term, and the sense of the term has changed with time and geographic location.

Cartridge—a package of components designed to be loaded into a firearm; modern metallic rifle and handgun cartridges consist of primer, powder, bullet and cartridge case. Shotgun shells are correctly, but not customarily, called cartridges.

Cartridge case or *case*—the container that holds the other components of a cartridge.

Case capacity—the volume available inside a cartridge case.

Case head separation—the separation of the cartridge case head, or base, away from the main body of the case.

Case mouth—the open end of a cartridge case.

CB Cap—Conical Bullet Cap; a low-powered 22 rimfire cartridge.

Centerfire—a cartridge, or firearm using a cartridge, with the primer in the center of the base of the cartridge case.

Chamber—the rear portion of the bore, enlarged to permit the loading of an appropriate cartridge; in revolvers, these holes are bored through a revolving cylinder and align with the bore.

Chamber pressure—pressure generated within the chamber by expanding powder gas at the moment of firing. Modern rifles may exceed 50,000 pounds per square inch chamber pressure.

Choke—an internal constriction (or opening and then constriction) at the muzzle of a shotgun barrel. The purpose is to control the spread of the shot pattern, for greater effectiveness at different ranges.

Choke tube—a short hollow cylinder machined to provide a certain degree of choke for a specific type of shotgun. In the past, these tubes were threaded to fit the outside of a single-barrel shotgun; now they are threaded for internal insertion into the muzzle and so may be used with both single- and double-barrel configurations.

Chronograph—an instrument that measures the velocity of projectiles.

Clay bird or *clay pigeon*—a shotgun target, originally made of clay. The shape, an inverted saucer shape, gives it a consistent, soaring flight, and such targets break easily when hit.

Clip—a metal device to hold cartridges for loading into a magazine. A charger clip is loaded into the magazine with the cartridges, while the cartridges are pushed out of a stripper clip.

Cock—a. the act of drawing back, or cocking, the hammer or firing mechanism of a firearm; b. old term for the hammer of a flintlock.

Cocking indicator—a projecting pin or other device that indicates when the action is cocked and ready for firing.

Comb—the upper edge of a buttstock against which the cheek rests.

Combination gun—a hinge-action firearm that has both rifle and shotgun barrels.

Combustion—burning.

Compensator—a device attached to the muzzle of a firearm to reduce the upward movement of the muzzle brought about by recoil; powder gases directed upward pull the muzzle down, compensating for muzzle jump.

Competition—shooting for comparison with the skills of other shooters, often in organized matches or tournaments.

Components—the separate materials that make up a metallic cartridge or a shotshell.

Crane—the pivoting yoke that holds the cylinder of a swing-out revolver.

Crimp—tightening or turning of the case mouth to hold a bullet or shot charge in place.

Crosshairs—aiming device in the form of two thin lines that intersect at right angles in the reticle of an optical sight.

Crown—the rounded edge at the muzzle of most guns, designed to prevent damage to the bore and ensure a uniform surface at the end of the rifling.

Cylinder—a revolver part, cylindrical in shape, with firing chambers that rotate to align with the bore.

Cylinder latch—a latch, ordinarily on the left side of a revolver frame, that allows the cylinder of a swing-out revolver to be opened for loading or unloading.

Damascus barrel—a type of shotgun barrel made in times past by twisting and welding strips of iron and steel together. The patterns formed may be very attractive, but such barrels are not considered safe with smokeless powder.

Dart—a pointed airgun projectile, used primarily for dartboard games.

Derringer—small pocket handguns roughly patterned after pistols made originally by Henry Deringer of Philadelphia.

Dominant eye—the eye that wants to take over when both eyes look at an object.

Double action—a handgun trigger mechanism in which a pull on the trigger can perform the double action of raising the hammer and then dropping it to fire the shot. Most double-action handguns can also be cocked by hand for firing.

Double-action-only—a handgun trigger mechanism in which shots can only be fired by a double-action pull. It cannot be manually cocked.

Dram—a unit of measure for blackpowder charges in shotgun loads; there are 16 drams to an ounce, or 256 to a pound; thus, a dram equals 27.3 grains of weight.

Drilling—a three-barrel combination gun, with both rifle and shotgun options.

Dry-firing—a technique of practicing all the shooting fundamentals, but without actually shooting any ammunition.

Ear protection—devices worn in or over the ears to protect against hearing loss while shooting.

Ejection—removal of a cartridge or cartridge case from a gun, generally done automatically with the opening of the action, by a part called the ejector.

Ejector rod—a rod used for ejecting cartridges or cases from revolvers. In swing-out revolvers, it is in the center of the cylinder and ejects all cases simultaneously. The rod of a solid-frame revolver ejects cases singly.

Electronic sight—a sighting device in which a dot, generally red, appears to be on the target at the point of impact.

Elevation—vertical movement of an adjustable sight that can raise or lower the impact of the bullet on the target.

Extraction—withdrawing a cartridge or cartridge case from a gun's chamber.

Extractor—a part that grips the rim or extractor groove of a cartridge case to withdraw it from the chamber.

Extractor groove—a groove just ahead of the base of a rimless cartridge case to allow the extractor a contact point for extraction.

Eye protection—glasses or goggles worn while shooting to protect the shooter's eyes from possible harm.

Eye relief—the distance between the shooter's eye and the rear lens of an optical sight that allows the eye to see the full field of view available.

Falling block—a single shot action in which the breechblock moves up and down at right angles to the bore.

Feet per second—unit used to measure velocity of a projectile. May be abbreviated fps.

Firearm—a device that propels a projectile or shot charge through a barrel by the pressure of expanding gas produced by burning powder.

Firing line—line from behind which shooters at a target range fire.

Firing pin—the part of a cartridge firearm that strikes the primer of a cartridge in order to ignite it.

Fixed sights—sights that are not ordinarily or easily adjusted.

Follower—a spring-loaded part of a firearm's magazine that controls the cartridges in the magazine and presents them in the proper orientation to be fed into the chamber.

Follow-through—continuing to do, for a brief time after the shot is fired, what the shooter was doing before the shot was fired.

Forearm—the front part of a rifle or shotgun stock, when the stock is of two-piece design. Sometimes used interchangeably with "forend."

Forend—the front part of a rifle or shotgun stock, when the stock is of one-piece design. Sometimes used interchangeably with "forearm."

Forend tip—the extreme forward end of a stock, often made of a different wood or other material that contrasts with the rest of the stock.

Fouling—metal or powder residue left in the bore of a firearm as a result of firing.

Fowling piece—an old term for a shotgun used in hunting birds or fowl.

Frame—for a handgun, the basic structural part to which the other parts are attached or inserted.

Free Pistol—a specialized target pistol, free of most restrictions, used in some forms of international and Olympic competition.

Free Rifle—a specialized target rifle, free of most restrictions, used in some forms of international and Olympic rifle competition.

Front sight—a metallic post, bead or aperture sight mounted near the muzzle of a rifle or handgun, and designed to be aligned with a rear sight.

Gain twist—a form of rifling in which the rate of twist increases toward the muzzle; used in some muzzleloaders, early Colt revolvers, and military rifles and cannon.

Gas check—a shallow metal cup of copper or brass attached to the base of a cast lead bullet to protect the base from powder gases during firing.

Gauge—The size of the bore in a shotgun barrel. Originally, the gauge of a gun was determined by the number of round balls of bore diameter that could be cast from a pound of lead.

Grain—a unit of weight used for measuring powder charges and bullet weights. There are 7000 grains to a pound, thus $437\frac{1}{2}$ grains per ounce.

Grip—*a.* that part of a handgun, or a rifle or shotgun stock, gripped by the shooting hand; *b.* the orientation and pressure of the shooter's hand or hands in holding a handgun.

Grip adapter—a metal or composition filler attached behind the trigger guard of a handgun, generally a revolver, to improve the grip.

Grip cap—a small decorative plate fastened to the base of the pistol grip of a rifle or shotgun.

Grip safety—a mechanical safety device on the backstrap of some semi-automatic pistols and revolvers that prevent the gun from firing until it is gripped in the shooter's hand.

Grooves—the cuts made in the bore of a firearm to produce rifling.

Group—the pattern on a target, made by successive shots from a rifle or handgun.

Gun—a mechanical device designed to propel projectiles through a tubular barrel.

Gun case—a case for carrying or transporting guns.

Gun control—a general term for legislative acts and proposals to restrict private ownership of firearms.

Gunpowder—powder burned in a firearm to propel a bullet or shot charge. Originally applied to blackpowder, the term is now often used for smokeless powders as well.

Half-cock—a notch or detent that holds a gun hammer between its forward position and its cocked position. It serves as a safety for a number of exposed-hammer firearms.

Hammer—a mechanical part that pivots on an axis and can be released by the trigger to go quickly forward to strike the firing pin.

Hammer spur—the grooved or checkered projection of a hammer that allows purchase and leverage so the hammer can be cocked by the shooter's thumb.

Hand—a part of a revolver that turns the cylinder; also called a pawl.

Handgun—a firearm designed to be fired with one hand, although two may be used.

Handloading—processing and assembling ammunition components into cartridges; often called reloading.

Hand trap—a hand-held device used to throw clay targets for shotgun shooting.

Hangfire—a momentary delay between the strike of the firing pin and the firing of the cartridge.

Headspace—the distance from the face of the breech or bolt of a firearm to the part of the chamber that prevents the cartridge's forward movement. If this distance is too great, a condition of excess headspace exists, in which the cartridge case may not be properly positioned and may rupture.

Heel—the upper rear portion of a rifle or shotgun buttstock.

Hinge action—a rifle or shotgun action in which the barrel is hinged to the receiver near the breech and pivoted downward to load.

Hollowpoint—a bullet with a cavity in its nose; designed to expand on impact and often used for hunting.

Hook breech—a design used with some muzzle-loading firearms in which the breech plug ends in a hook; the hook fits into a recess in the tang which remains fastened to the gun; this system allows easy removal of the barrel for cleaning.

Ignition—the process of starting to burn powder.

Inertia firing pin—a firing pin that, when struck by the hammer, flies forward by inertia to hit the primer of a chambered cartridge. With the hammer at rest, the firing pin does not touch the primer.

Iron sights—non-optical metallic rifle or pistol sights.

Isosceles—a two-hand position for shooting a handgun in which the shooter faces the target squarely, with both arms fully extended; the arms and body thus approximate the shape of an isosceles triangle.

Jacket—a thin metal covering over the lead core of a bullet.

Jag—a type of cleaning rod tip to be used with cloth cleaning patches.

Keeper—a loop or clamp used on a rifle shooting sling to hold it in position.

Kentucky rifle—a type of flintlock rifle used by American frontiersmen in the late 1700s. Because most were actually made in Pennsylvania, they are sometimes called Pennsylvania rifles.

Kick—an informal term used to describe the recoil of a firearm felt by the shooter.

Lands—the high surfaces between the grooves in a rifled bore.

Laser sight—a device with a beam generator that projects a beam of intense red light onto the target.

Lever action—a repeating firearm action operated by a lever beneath the grip.

Loading gate—a hinged or spring-loaded cover of the loading port of a rifle or revolver.

Loading press—a bench-mounted tool for reloading metallic cartridges or shotgun shells.

Lock—the action or firing mechanism of a muzzle-loading firearm.

Long gun—a gun designed to be fired from the shoulder, normally a rifle or shotgun.

Machinegun—a firearm capable of full automatic fire.

Magazine—a storage device for cartridges, allowing them to be fed to the chamber at the proper time. A magazine may be part of the firearm, or it may be removable.

Magazine safety—a device that prevents a gun from firing if the magazine has been removed.

Magnum—a somewhat vague name applied to a cartridge—rifle, handgun or shotgun—that is of notably greater power than others of that bore diameter; a firearm chambered for a magnum cartridge.

Master eye—the eye that wants to take over when both eyes look at something; the dominant eye.

Match—an organized competitive shooting event.

Metallic sights—non-optical sights; iron sights.

Minute of angle—an angular measurement equal to $1/60$ of one degree. At 100 yards, one minute of angle is approximately equal to one inch, so has become a common term used in describing firearms accuracy.

Misfire—failure of a cartridge to fire.

Musket—smoothbore military long gun, firing a round ball, in use until about the middle 1800s.

Muzzle—the forward end of a barrel.

Muzzleloader—a gun that is loaded from the muzzle, generally with blackpowder loads.

Muzzle velocity—the speed of a projectile fired from a gun at the instant it leaves the muzzle.

National Matches—annual nationwide rifle and pistol competition held each summer at Camp Perry, Ohio.

Neck—the forward section of a cartridge case.

Neck sizing—squeezing only the neck of a fired cartridge case (rather than the full length of the case) back to its original size, in preparation for reloading.

Nipple—a hollow stem on which a percussion cap is placed, in priming a muzzle-loading percussion firearm.

Open sights—a simple sight system in which the rear sight has a notch open at the top.

Optical sight—a sight that contains glass lenses so that the shooter sees the sighting device and the target in the same optical plane; often called a scope or scope sight; generally (but not necessarily) magnifies the image seen.

Over/under—a double-barrel gun in which one barrel is mounted directly over the other. The British designation for this type of gun is under/over.

Pan—a hollow portion of the flintlock that holds the priming powder.

Patch—*a.* a small piece of cloth used on a cleaning rod to clean the bore of a gun; *b.* a piece of cloth used around a lead ball in loading a muzzleloader.

Patridge sights—a combination of open iron sights that feature a square-topped front sight and a square sighting notch in a flat-top rear sight; named after pistol shooter E.E. Patridge, who introduced this system in the late 1800s.

Pattern—the distribution of a charge of shot. Patterning a shotgun is traditionally done by firing at a large sheet of paper at 40 yards and checking the percentage of pellets inside a 30-inch circle.

Peep sight—informal name for an aperture sight.

Pellet—*a.* individual particle of spherical shot used in a shot charge; *b.* a lead projectile used in airguns.

Percussion cap—a small, cup-shaped thin metal container that holds the priming compound for a percussion muzzleloader; it fits on, or caps, the nipple of the gun.

Percussion lock—a muzzle-loading ignition system using a percussion cap that detonates under the blow of a hammer, thereby shooting flame through a hollow nipple to ignite the main powder charge; this system supplanted the flintlock by the mid-1800s.

Pinfire—*a.* an early self-contained cartridge in which each cartridge had its own small firing pin extending from the side; *b.* a firearm that uses pinfire cartridges.

Pistol—in its restricted sense, a handgun with a fixed chamber, thus a semi-automatic or single shot; in its broader sense, any handgun, including a revolver.

Plinking—informal shooting at informal targets.

Pneumatic—a type of airgun that uses compressed gas held in a reservoir within the gun.

Point of aim—the point on which the sights are aligned.

Point of impact—the point at which a projectile actually strikes.

Powder—chemical compound used as a propellant; it burns on ignition, generating expanding gases that push the projectile through the bore.

Powder charge—a measured amount of powder, ordinarily the amount needed for one shot.

Powder measure—a device used to measure charges of powder by volume.

Press—a bench-mounted reloading tool for handloading ammunition.

Primer—a cup-shaped ammunition component that contains a chemical compound that detonates on impact, thus igniting the powder charge.

Primer pocket—the hole in the base of a cartridge case into which the primer is inserted.

Projectile—as used in shooting terminology, an ammunition component fired from a gun, generally a bullet or shot charge.

Proof load—a cartridge with a load that produces higher than normal pressures, specifically made to test or prove firearms.

Pump action—a rifle or shotgun action in which operation is by backward and forward movement of the gun's forearm; also called slide action.

Qualification shooting—shooting to achieve a certain score or level of proficiency; distinct from competition shooting, which involves shooting against the scores of other shooters.

QD—quick-detachable; refers to firearms accessories that may be quickly removed, such as sling swivels and scope mounts.

Ramrod—a loading rod for a muzzle-loading firearm, used to push (or ram) bullets or wads down the bore.

Range—a. an area designated for shooting; b. the distance between the shooter and the target.

Receiver—the major component of a rifle or shotgun into which the other parts are attached or inserted.

Receiver sight—an aperture sight mounted on the receiver of a gun.

Recoil—energy that pushes a gun to the rear, toward the shooter, when a projectile is fired from the front.

Recoil operation—a semi-automatic firearm design that functions due to the forces of recoil.

Recoil pad—a pad of rubber or other soft material attached to the butt of a rifle or shotgun to decrease the effect of recoil felt by the shooter.

Reloading—a. processing cartridge cases and assembling components to produce loaded ammunition; often interchanged with handloading; b. the act of recharging a gun with fresh cartridges.

Repeater—a gun that is capable of firing a number of shots in succession through mechanical means before reloading becomes necessary.

Reticle—the aiming device in an optical sight, generally an arrangement of crosshairs, sometimes a post or dot, or combinations of these.

Revolver—a handgun with a revolving cylinder; the cylinder has a number of chambers which align with the bore for successive shots.

Rifle—a shoulder-fired firearm with a rifled barrel.

Rifled slug—a lead projectile, approximately bore size, designed to be fired from a shotgun, for use in hunting deer and other large game.

Rifling—the spiral pattern of grooves cut into a gun's bore for the purpose of imparting a spin to the bullet passing through, in order to stabilize the bullet in flight.

Rim—the flange that is at the base of many metallic cartridges and all shotshells; the extractor grips it to withdraw the cartridge or case from the chamber.

Rimfire—a cartridge that contains its priming compound in the hollow rim of its case; crushing of the rim by the firing pin detonates the priming compound and ignites the powder.

Round—a. a single cartridge or shotshell; b. a sequence of twenty-five targets thrown in the sports of trap or Skeet.

Safety—a mechanical device incorporated into the action of a gun and designed to prevent accidental or unintentional firing.

S&W—Smith & Wesson

Scattergun—informal term to describe a shotgun.

Scope—an informal term for a telescopic or optical sight.

Scope bases—scope mounts; blocks or ribs fastened to a firearm to provide an attachment for an optical sight and its rings.

Scope rings—metal rings that fasten around an optical sight to permit attachment to the scope bases or mounts on a firearm.

Sear—part of a firing mechanism that holds the hammer or striker in cocked position, then releases it when the trigger is pulled.

Select-fire—a firearm with a switch mechanism that will allow either semi-automatic or full automatic operation.

Semi-automatic—also known as self-loading or autoloading; a firearm that uses the energy of one shot to work the action to load another cartridge for the next shot.

Shell—informal term for an empty metallic cartridge case, empty shotshell, or loaded shotshell.

Shellholder—an attachment for a reloading press that holds the base of a cartridge case during the various loading operations.

Shoot—a. to fire a gun; b. an organized shooting activity.

Shooting glasses—glasses to be worn during shooting that provide eye protection and may provide better vision.

Shot—a. small spheres of lead or steel used in shotgun shells; b. a round of ammunition fired.

Shotgun—a gun designed to be fired from the shoulder that has a smooth bore for shooting charges of shot.

Shotshell—a loaded cartridge for a shotgun; a shotgun shell, either loaded or unloaded.

Shot string—the elongated arrangement of pellets after they leave the bore of a shotgun.

Side-by-side—a double-barrel gun with the barrels aligned horizontally, one beside the other.

Sight—a device that allows a shooter to aim a gun.

Sighting-in—the procedure of bore sighting, shooting and sight adjustment to bring the point of impact of the bullet to the desired place on the target at a chosen range.

Sight radius—the distance between the front and rear sight of a gun equipped with two sights.

Silencer—a device attached to the muzzle of a firearm that suppresses the sound of the muzzle blast; also called a suppressor.

Single action—a type of revolver or semi-automatic pistol firing mechanism in which the trigger performs the single action of dropping the hammer to fire a shot; the hammer must be cocked either manually or mechanically before the trigger will perform this function.

Single shot—a firearm into which each shot must be manually loaded before it can be fired.

6 o'clock hold—a sight picture in which the top of the gun's front sight is held at the bottom edge of the target's bulls-eye.

Skeet—a shotgun sport that uses a roughly semi-circular field with eight shooting stations; targets are thrown from a high house on the left and a low house on the right.

Slide action—rifle or shotgun action operated by moving a reciprocating forearm backward and forward; a pump gun.

Sling—*a.* a strap of special configuration used as a rifle shooting support; *b.* a strap attached to a rifle or shotgun at the buttstock and forend for carrying the gun from the shoulder.

Sling swivels—elongated steel loops on a gun used for attaching a sling.

Slug—a single projectile designed to be fired from a shotgun.

Slug gun—a shotgun specially designed for shooting slugs, usually equipped with rifle sights.

Small—the grip area of a rifle or shotgun stock.

Softpoint—a jacketed bullet with exposed lead at its tip; the softer lead allows the bullet to expand on impact, and this bullet type is generally used for hunting.

Speedloader—an accessory that allows all chambers of a revolver to be loaded simultaneously.

Spin—rotational movement given to a bullet by the spiral lands and grooves of a rifled-barrel firearm.

Spitzer—a pointed rifle bullet.

Spotting scope—a portable telescope of high magnification, used by target shooters to examine targets from the firing line and by some hunters to spot game at a distance.

Standing breech—informal name for the non-moving vertical part of the receiver of a hinge-action gun.

Steel shot—spherical steel pellets loaded in some shotgun shells; although not as effective as lead shot, steel shot is required by law for waterfowl hunting.

Stock—the wood (or more recently, synthetic) part of a rifle or shotgun that allows the gun to be fired from the shoulder.

Striker—a spring-driven firing pin.

Tang—the extended projections at the rear of a receiver, designed for attachment of the buttstock; a tang sight may be mounted at this location.

Target—a mark to shoot at; may be a paper target or game or any number of informal targets.

Telescopic sight—an optical sight, also sometimes called a scope sight.

Thumb safety—a safety operated by the shooter's thumb.

Toe—the lower rear portion of a rifle or shotgun stock.

Tong tool—a portable hand-held lever-type reloading tool, dating back to at least the 1880s and still available.

Trajectory—the curved path of a bullet in flight.

Transfer bar—a special part of some rifles, shotguns and revolvers which allows a transfer of movement between the hammer and the firing pin only when the trigger is pressed.

Trap—*a.* a shotgun shooting sport that has five positions for shooters behind a single trap house, from which clay targets are thrown; *b.* the device used for throwing clay targets for shotgun sports.

Trigger—a part of a gun's firing mechanism that is pressed by the shooter in order to fire the gun.

Trigger guard—a loop of metal or other material that shields the trigger to help prevent accidental firing.

Tubular magazine—a hollow tube for storage and feeding of cartridges or shotshells, which are inserted one after another into the magazine.

Twist—the spiral formed by the lands and grooves in a rifled bore; the rate of twist is generally given as a ratio, i.e., 1:10 indicating one turn in 10 inches.

Utility gun—*a.* informal term for a gun that offers increased utility because it has both rifle and shotgun barrels that may be installed on the same frame; *b.* any gun kept for utilitarian purposes.

Variable choke—an adjustable choke device that can throw shot patterns of different sizes.

Variable scope—an optical sight that can be adjusted to provide a range of magnification rather than a fixed magnification.

Velocity—the speed of a bullet or shot charge, measured at a certain point in its travel.

Vent pick—a thin wire or special tool used to clean the vent or ignition channel of muzzle-loading firearms.

Wad—a component of a shotgun load that separates the powder and shot; in muzzle-loading shotguns, an over-shot wad may also be used.

Wadcutter—a bullet of essentially cylindrical shape; used primarily in handguns for target shooting because these types of bullets cut clean holes in a paper target and make scoring easy.

Wax bullet—a bullet made of wax, usually used for indoor shooting with handguns.

WCF—Winchester Center Fire; used with many centerfire rifle cartridges introduced by Winchester.

Weaver stance—a two-hand handgun shooting position in which the right arm is straight, pushing the gun forward, and the left arm is bent, pulling the gun rearward; developed by California Sheriff Jack Weaver in the late 1950s.

Windage—the adjustment or adjusting mechanism that moves the sight or reticle in a horizontal direction.

WMR—Winchester Magnum Rimfire; used with a high-velocity 22-caliber rimfire cartridge introduced by Winchester.

Worm—a corkscrew-like attachment used at the end of a ramrod to pull a charge from a muzzle-loading firearm without firing the gun; a wad puller.

WRF—Winchester Rim Fire; used for a 22-caliber rimfire cartridge introduced by Winchester about 1890 that had greater power than other 22s of the time.

X-Ring—a small inner ring inside the 10-ring of a bullseye target, used to break ties in competitive shooting.

Yoke—the crane of a swing-out revolver, which allows the cylinder to be swing outward from the frame.

Zero—*a.* the sight setting that will put the bullet of a particular load on target at a specific range; *b.* the activity of adjusting the sights to put that bullet on target at that range, also called sighting-in.

MANUFACTURERS AND EQUIPMENT DIRECTORY

AMMUNITION, COMMERCIAL

ACTIV Industries, Inc., 1000 Zigor Rd., P.O. Box 339, Kearneysville, WV 25430

Blount, Inc., Sporting Equipment Div., 2299 Snake River Ave., P.O. Box 856, Lewiston, ID 83501

Daisy Mfg. Co., P.O. Box 220, 2111 S. 8th St., Rogers, AR 72756

Dynamit Nobel-RWS, Inc., 81 Ruckman Rd., Closter, NJ 07624

Federal Cartridge Company, 900 Ehlen Drive, Anoka, MN 55303

Fiocchi of America, Inc., 5030 Fremont Rd., Ozark, MO 65721

Hornady Mfg. Co., P.O. Box 1848, Grand Island, NE 68802

MAGTECH Recreational Products, Inc., 4737 College Park, Ste. 101, San Antonio, TX 78249

Omark Industries, Div. of Blount, Inc., 2299 Snake River Ave., P.O. Box 856, Lewiston, ID 83501

PMC/Eldorado Cartridge Corp., P.O. Box 62508, 12801 U.S. Hwy. 95 S., Boulder City, NV 89005

Remington Arms Co., Inc., Consumer Affairs, Delle Donne Corporate Center, 1011 Centre Rd., Wilmington, DE 19805-1270

Speer Products, Div. of Blount, Inc., P.O. Box 856, Lewiston, ID 83501

Winchester Div., Olin Corp., 427 N. Shamrock, E. Alton, IL 62024

AMMUNITION COMPONENTS—BULLETS, POWDER, PRIMERS, CASES

Accurate Arms Co., Inc., Rt. 1, Box 167, McEwen, TN 37101

ACTIV Industries, Inc., 1000 Zigor Rd., P.O. Box 339, Kearneysville, WV 25430

Ballistic Products, Inc., 20015 75th Ave. North, Corcoran, MN 55340-9456

Barnes Bullets, Inc., P.O. Box 215, American Fork, UT 84003

Berger Bullets, Ltd., 5342 W. Camelback Rd., Suite 500, Glendale, AZ 85301

Blount, Inc., Sporting Equipment Div., 2299 Snake River Ave., P.O. Box 856, Lewiston, ID 83501

Buffalo Bullet Co., Inc., 12637 Los Nietos Rd., Unit A, Santa Fe Springs, CA 90670

CCI, Div. of Blount, Inc., 2299 Snake River Ave., P.O. Box 856, Lewiston, ID 83501

Federal Cartridge Co., 900 Ehlen Dr., Anoka, MN 55303

Fiocchi of America, Inc., 5030 Fremont Rd., Ozark, MO 65721

GOEX, Inc., 1002 Springbrook Ave., Moosic, PA 18507

Hercules, Inc., Hercules Plaza, 1313 N Market St., Wilmington, DE 19894

Hodgdon Powder Co., Inc., P.O. Box 2932, 6231 Robinson, Shawnee Mission, KS 66202

Hornady Manufacturing Co., P.O. Box 1848, Grand Island, NE 68802

IMR Powder Co., 1080 Military Turnpike, Suite 2, Plattsburgh, NY 12901

Nosler, Inc., P.O. Box 671, Bend, OR 97709

Omark Industries, Div. of Blount, Inc., 2299 Snake River Ave., P.O. Box 856, Lewiston, ID 83501

Pattern Control, 114 N. Third St., P.O. Box 462105, Garland, TX 75046

Paul Co., The, 27385 Pressonville Rd., Wellsville, KS 66092

Polywad, Inc., P.O. Box 7916, Macon, GA 31209

Remington Arms Co., Inc., Consumer Affairs, Delle Donne Corporate Center, 1011 Centre Rd., Wilmington, DE 19805-1270

Shotgun Bullets Manufacturing, Rt. 3, Box 41, Robinson, IL 62454

Taracorp Industries, Inc., 16th & Cleveland Blvd., Granite City, IL 62040

Vihtavuori Oy/Kaltron-Pettibone, 1241 Ellis St., Bensenville, IL 60106

Winchester Div., Olin Corp., 427 N. Shamrock, E. Alton, IL 62024

BOOKS (Publishers and Dealers)

DBI Books, Inc., 4092 Commercial Ave., Northbrook, IL 60062

GUNS Magazine, 591 Camino de la Reina, Suite 200, San Diego, CA 92108

Krause Publications, Inc., 700 E. State St., Iola, WI 54990

Lyman Products Corp., Rt. 147, Middlefield, CT 06455

Petersen Publishing Co., 6420 Wilshire Blvd., Los Angeles, CA 90048

Ray Riling Arms Books Co., 6844 Gorsten St., P.O. Box 18925, Philadelphia, PA 19119

Rutgers Book Center, 127 Raritan Ave., Highland Park, NJ 08904

Stoeger Industries, 55 Ruta Court, South Hackensack, NJ 07606

Wolfe Publishing Company, 6471 Airpark Dr., Prescott, AZ 86301

GUNS, AIR

Air Rifle Specialists, 311 East Water Street, Elmira, NY 14901

Beeman Precision Airguns, 5454 Argosy Dr., Huntington Beach, CA 92649

Benjamin/Sheridan Co., Crossman, Routes 5 and 20, East Bloomfield, NY 14443

Crosman Airguns, Routes 5 and 20, East Bloomfield, NY 14443

Daisy Mfg. Co., P.O. Box 220, 2111 S. 8th St., Rogers, AR 72756

Dynamit Nobel-RWS, Inc., 81 Ruckman Rd., Closter, NJ 07624

Great Lakes Airguns, 6175 S. Park Ave., Hamburg, NY 14075

Marksman Products, 5482 Argosy Dr., Huntington Beach, CA 92649

Precision Sales International, Inc., P.O. Box 1776, Westfield, MA 01086

Swivel Machine Works, Inc., 167 Cherry St., Suite 286, Milford, CT 06460

GUNS, FOREIGN—IMPORTERS

American Arms, Inc., 715 Armour Rd., N. Kansas City, MO 64116

Armoury, Inc., The, Rt. 202, Box 2340, New Preston, CT 06777

Armsport, Inc., 3950 NW 49th St., Miami, FL 33142

Beeman Precision Airguns, 5454 Argosy Dr., Huntington Beach, CA 92649

Beretta U.S.A. Corp., 17601 Beretta Drive, Accokeek, MD 20607

Browning Arms Co. (Gen. Offices), One Browning Place, Morgan, UT 84050

Cabela's, 812-13th Ave., Sidney, NE 69160

Century International Arms, Inc., P.O. Box 714, St. Albans, VT 05478-0714

Cimarron Arms, P.O. Box 906, Fredericksburg, TX 78624-0906

CVA, 5988 Peachtree Corners East, Norcross, GA 30071

Daisy Mfg. Co., P.O. Box 220, 2111 S. 8th St., Rogers, AR 72756

Dixie Gun Works, Inc., Highway 51 South, Union City, TN 38261

Dynamit Nobel-RWS, Inc., 81 Ruckman Rd., Closter, NJ 07624

E.A.A. Corp., P.O. Box 1299, Sharpes, FL 32959

EMF Co., Inc., 1900 E. Warner Ave. Suite 1-D, Santa Ana, CA 92705

Glock, Incorporated, 6000 Highlands Parkway, Smyrna, GA 30082

Great Lakes Airguns, 6175 S. Park Ave., Hamburg, NY 14075

Griffin & Howe, Inc., 33 Claremont Rd., Bernardsville, NJ 07924

Hammerli USA, 19296 Oak Grove Circle, Groveland, CA 95321

Heckler & Koch, Inc., 21480 Pacific Blvd., Sterling, VA 20166-8903

Interarms, 10 Prince St., Alexandria, VA 22314

Magnum Research, Inc., 7110 University Ave. NE, Minneapolis, MN 55432

MAGTECH Recreational Products, Inc., 4737 College Park, Ste. 101, San Antonio, TX 78249

Mandall Shooting Supplies, Inc., 3616 N. Scottsdale Rd., Scottsdale, AZ 85252

Marksman Products, 5482 Argosy Dr., Huntington Beach, CA 92649

Mitchell Arms, Inc., 3400-I W. MacArthur Blvd., Santa Ana, CA 92704

Nationwide Sports Distributors, Inc., 70 James Way, Southampton, PA 18966

Navy Arms Company, 689 Bergen Blvd., Ridgefield, NJ 07657

Para-Ordnance, Inc., 1919 NE 45th St., Ft. Lauderdale, FL 33308

Precision Sales International, Inc., P.O. Box 1776, Westfield, MA 01086

Sigarms, Inc., Corporate Park, Exeter, NH 03833

Sile Distributors, Inc., 7 Centre Market Pl., New York, NY 10013

Springfield, Inc., 420 West Main Street, Geneseo, IL 61254

Stoeger Industries, 55 Ruta Court, South Hackensack, NJ 07606

Taurus Firearms, Inc., 16175 NW 49th Ave., Miami, FL 33014

Uberti USA, Inc., 362 Limerock Rd., P.O. Box 469, Lakeville, CT 06039

Weatherby, Inc., 3100 El Camino Real, Atascadero, CA 93422

GUNS, U.S.-MADE

Accu-Tek, 4525 Carter Ct., Chino, CA 91710

American Arms, Inc., 715 Armour Rd., N. Kansas City, MO 64116

American Derringer Corp., 127 North Lacy Drive, Waco, TX 76705

AMT, 6226 Santos Diaz St., Irwindale, CA 91702

A-Square Co., Inc., One Industrial Park, Bedford, KY 40006-9667

Beretta U.S.A. Corp., 17601 Beretta Drive, Accokeek, MD 20607

Browning Arms Co. (Parts & Service), 3005 Arnold Tenbrook Rd., Arnold, MO 63010-9406

Century International Arms, Inc., P.O. Box 714, St. Albans, VT 05478-0714

CHARCO, 26 Beaver St., Ansonia, CT 06401

Colt's Mfg. Co., Inc., P.O. Box 1868, Hartford, CT 06144-1868

CVA, 5988 Peachtree Corners East, Norcross, GA 30071

Davis Industries, 15150 Sierra Bonita Ln., Chino, CA 91710

Dayton Traister, 4778 N. Monkey Hill Rd., P.O. Box 593, Oak Harbor, WA 98277

Gonic Arms, Inc., 134 Flagg Rd., Gonic, NH 03839

H&R 1871, Inc., 60 Industrial Rowe, Gardner, MA 01440

Hatfield Gun Co., Inc., 224 North 4th St., St. Joseph, MO 64501

Intratec, 12405 SW 130th St., Miami, FL 33186

Ithaca Aquisition Corp., Ithaca Gun, 891 Route 34B, King Ferry, NY 13081

Jennings Firearms, Inc., 17692 Cowan, Irvine, CA 92714

Kimber of America, Inc., 9039 SE Jannsen Rd., Clackamas, OR 97015

Knight's Mfg. Co., 7750 9th St. SW, Vero Beach, FL 32968

Magnum Research, Inc., 7110 University Ave. NE, Minneapolis, MN 55432

Marlin Firearms Co., 100 Kenna Dr., New Haven, CT 06473

Maverick Arms, Inc., 7 Grasso Ave., P.O. Box 497, North Haven, CT 06473

Mitchell Arms, Inc., 3400-I W. MacArthur Blvd., Santa Ana, CA 92704

O.F. Mossberg & Sons, Inc., 7 Grasso Ave., North Haven, CT 06473

New England Firearms, 60 Industrial Rowe, Gardner, MA 01440

Phoenix Arms, 1420 S. Archibald Ave., Ontario, CA 91761

Ram-Line, Inc., 545 Thirty-One Rd., Grand Junction, CO 81504

Remington Arms Co., Inc., Consumer Affairs, Delle Donne Corporate Center, 1011 Centre Rd., Wilmington, DE 19805-1270

Savage Arms, Inc., 100 Springdale Rd., Westfield, MA 01085

Smith & Wesson, 2100 Roosevelt Ave., Springfield, MA 01102

Springfield, Inc., 420 W. Main St., Geneseo, IL 61254

Sturm, Ruger & Co., Inc., Lacey Place, Southport, CT 06490

Taurus Firearms, Inc., 16175 NW 49th Ave., Miami, FL 33014

Thompson/Center Arms, P.O. Box 5002, Rochester, NH 03867

U.S. Repeating Arms Co., Inc., 275 Winchester Ave., Morgan, UT 84050

Wesson Firearms Co., Inc., Maple Tree Industrial Center, Rt. 20, Wilbraham Rd., Palmer, MA 01069

HEARING PROTECTORS

Blount, Inc., Sporting Equipment Div., 2299 Snake River Ave., P.O. Box 856, Lewiston, ID 83501

Browning Arms Co. (Gen. Offices), One Browning Place, Morgan, UT 84050

David Clark Co., Inc., P.O. Box 15054, Worcester, MA 01615-0054

CRL, Inc., 420 Industrial Park, P.O. Box 111, Gladstone, MI 49837

Hoppe's Div., Penguin Industries, Inc., Airport Industrial Mall, Coatesville, PA 19320

Peltor, Inc., 41 Commercial Way, East Providence, RI 029141

Penguin Industries, Inc., Airport Industrial Mall, Coatesville, PA 19320

Silencio/Safety Direct, 56 Coney Island Dr., Sparks, NV 89431

Willson Safety Prods. Div., P.O. Box 622, Reading, PA 19603-0622

MUZZLE-LOADING GUNS, BARRELS AND EQUIPMENT

Armoury, Inc., The, Rt. 202, Box 2340, New Preston, CT 06777

Armsport, Inc., 3950 NW 49th St., Miami, FL 33142

Colt Blackpowder Arms Co., 5 Centre Market Place, New York, NY 10013

CVA, 5988 Peachtree Corners East, Norcross, GA 30071

Dixie Gun Works, Inc., Highway 51 South, Union City, TN 38261

Euroarms of America, Inc., 208 E. Piccadilly St., Winchester, VA 22601

Gonic Arms, Inc., 134 Flagg Rd., Gonic, NH 03839

Hornady Manufacturing Co., P.O. Box 1848, Grand Island, NE 68802

Lyman Products Corporation, Route 147, Middlefield, CT 06455

Modern MuzzleLoading, Inc., 234 Airport Rd., P.O. Box 130, Centerville, IA 52544

Traditions, Inc., P.O. Box 235, Deep River, CT 06417

Uberti USA, Inc., 362 Limerock Rd., P.O. Box 469, Lakeville, CT 06039

White Shooting Systems, Inc., P.O. Box 277, Roosevelt, UT 84066

RELOADING TOOLS AND ACCESSORIES

Ballistic Products, Inc., 20015 75th Ave. North, Corcoran, MN 55340-9456

Blount, Inc., Sporting Equipment Div., 2299 Snake River Ave., P.O. Box 856, Lewiston, ID 83501

Corbin, Inc., 600 Industrial Circle, P.O. Box 2659, White City, OR 97503

Dillon Precision Products, Inc., 8009 East Dillon's Way, Scottsdale, AZ 85260

Forster Products, 82 E. Lanark Ave., Lanark, IL 61046

4-D Custom Die Co., 711 N. Sandusky St., P.O. Box 889, Mt. Vernon, OH 43050-0889

Hensley & Gibbs, Box 10, Murphy, OR 97533

Hollywood Engineering, 10642 Arminta St., Sun Valley, CA 91352

Hornady Mfg. Co., P.O. Box 1848, Grand Island, NE 68802

Huntington Die Specialties, 601 Oro Dam Blvd., Oroville, CA 95965

Lee Precision, Inc., 4275 Hwy. U, Hartford, WI 53027

Lyman Products Corporation, Route 147, Middlefield, CT 06455

MEC, Inc., 715 South St., Mayville, WI 53050

Midway Arms, Inc., 5875 W. Van Horn Tavern Rd., Columbia, MO 65203

Omark Industries, Div. of Blount, Inc., 2299 Snake River Ave., P.O. Box 856, Lewiston, ID 83501

Ponsness/Warren, P.O. Box 8, Rathdrum, ID 83858

RCBS, Div. of Blount, Inc., 605 Oro Dam Blvd., Oroville, CA 95965

Redding Reloading Equipment, 1089 Starr Rd., Cortland, NY 13045

Speer Products, Div. of Blount, Inc., P.O. Box 856, Lewiston, ID 83501

Star Machine Works, 418 10th Avenue, San Diego, CA 92101

RESTS (Bench, Portable) AND ACCESSORIES

Blount, Inc., Sporting Equipment Div., 2299 Snake River Ave., P.O. Box 856, Lewiston, ID 83501

Decker Shooting Products, 1729 Laguna Ave., Schofield, WI 54476

Harris Engineering, Inc., Rt. 1, Barlow, KY 42024

Hoppe's Div., Penguin Industries, Inc., Airport Industrial Mall, Coatesville, PA 19320

Midway Arms, Inc., 5875 W. Van Horn Tavern Rd., Columbia, MO 65203

Millett Sights, 16131 Gothard St., Huntington Beach, CA 92647

Penguin Industries, Inc., Airport Industrial Mall, Coatesville, PA 19320

Wichita Arms, Inc., 923 E. Gilbert, P.O. Box 11371, Wichita, KS 67211

SCOPES, MOUNTS, ACCESSORIES, OPTICAL EQUIPMENT

Aimpoint, Inc., 580 Herndon Parkway, Suite 500, Herndon, VA 22070

Bausch & Lomb, Inc., 42 East Ave., Rochester, NY 14603

Blount, Inc., Sporting Equipment Div., 2299 Snake River Ave., P.O. Box 856, Lewiston, ID 83501

Burris, P.O. Box 1747, 331 E. 8th St., Greeley, CO 80631

Conetrol Scope Mounts, 10225 Hwy. 123 South, Seguin, TX 78155

Ironsighter Co., 5555 Treadwell St., Wayne, MI 48184

Kris Mounts, 108 Lehigh St., Johnstown, PA 15905

Kwik Mount Corp., P.O. Box 19422, Louisville, KY 40259

Kwik-Site Co., 5555 Treadwell, Wayne, MI 48184

Leupold & Stevens, Inc., P.O. Box 688, Beaverton, OR 97075

Millett Sights, 16131 Gothard St., Huntington Beach, CA 92647

Nikon, Inc., 1300 Walt Whitman Rd., Melville, NY 11747

Pentax Corp., 35 Inverness Dr. E., Englewood, CO 80112

Redfield, Inc., 5800 E. Jewell Ave., Denver, CO 80227

S&K Mfg. Co., P.O. Box 247, Pittsfield, PA 16340

Schmidt & Bender, Inc., Brook Rd., P.O. Box 134, Meriden, NH 03770

Shepherd Scope Ltd., Box 189, Waterloo, NE 68069

Simmons Outdoor Corp., 2120 Killearney Way, Tallahassee, FL 32308-3402

Swift Instruments, Inc., 952 Dorchester Ave., Boston, MA 02125

Tasco Sales, Inc., 7600 NW 26th St., Miami, FL 33122

Weaver Products, Div. of Blount, Inc., P.O. Box 39, Onalaska, WI 54650

Wideview Scope Mount Corp., 13535 S. Hwy. 16, Rapid City, SD 57701

Williams Gun Sight Co., 7389 Lapeer Rd., Box 329, Davison, MI 48423

Carl Zeiss Optical, 1015 Commerce St., Petersburg, VA 23803

SIGHTS, METALLIC

Bo-Mar Tool & Mfg. Co., Rt. 12, Box 405, Longview, TX 75605

CRL, Inc., 420 Industrial Park, P.O. Box 111, Gladstone, MI 49837

Hesco-Meprolight, 2821 Greenville Rd., LaGrange, GA 30240

Lee's Red Ramps, Box 291240, Phelan, CA 92329-1240

Lyman Prod. Corp., Route 147, Middlefield, CT 06455

Millett Sights, 16131 Gothard St., Huntington Beach, CA 92647

Williams Gun Sight Co., 7389 Lapeer Rd., Box 329, Davison, MI 48423

ASSOCIATIONS

Amateur Trapshooting Association
601 West National Road
Vandalia, OH 45377
National trapshooting organization

American Legion
P.O. Box 1055
Indianapolis, IN 46206
Junior shooting sports programs

Brigade of American Revolution
32 Douglas Road
Delmar, NY 12052
Revolutionary War period muzzleloader competition

Civil War Skirmish Association
7511 Winding Way
Fair Oaks, CA 95628
Civil War reenactments, west of Mississippi River

International Handgun Metallic Silhouette
Association
P.O. Box 368
Burlington, IA 52601-0368
Metallic silhouette competition

National Bench Rest Shooters Association, Inc.
2020 Buffalo
Levelland, TX 79336
Benchrest rifle shooting competition

National Guard Marksmanship Training Unit
Camp Robinson
North Little Rock, AR 72118-2200
Junior marksmanship program

National Muzzle Loading Rifle Association
P.O. Box 67
Friendship, IN 47021
National muzzle-loading competition

National Reloading Manufacturers Association
1 Centerpointe Drive, Suite 300
Lake Oswego, OR 97035
Ammunition reloading

National Rifle Association of America
11250 Waples Mill Road
Fairfax, VA 22030
General information on shooting for competition, qualification and recreation.

National Shooting Sports Foundation
Flintlock Ridge Office Center
11 Mile Hill Road
Newton, CT 06470-2359
General information on recreational shooting

National Skeet Shooting Association
P.O. Box 68007
San Antonio, TX 78268-0007
Skeet shooting competition

National Sporting Clays Association
P.O. Box 68007
San Antonio, TX 78268-0007
Sporting Clays competition

North-South Skirmish Association
4815 Oglethorpe Street
Riverdale, MD 20737
Civil War reenactments, east of Mississippi River

U.S. Olympic Training Center
1750 East Boulder Street
Colorado Springs, CO 80909
International competition

U.S. Practical Shooting Association
P.O. Box 811
Sedro Woolley, WA 98284
Practical shooting competition

United States International Muzzleloading Committee
Weldon Road #4
Lake Hopatcong, NJ 07848
Muzzle-loading competition

United States Junior Chamber of Commerce
P.O. Box 7
Tulsa, OK 74121-0007
Daisy/Jaycees airgun shooting programs

United States Revolver Association
40 Larchmont Avenue
Taunton, MA 02780
Pistol competition via postal matches

PUBLICATIONS

American Handgunner
591 Camino de la Reina, Ste. 200
San Diego, CA 92108

American Hunter
National Rifle Assn.
11250 Waples Mill Rd.
Fairfax, VA 22030

American Rifleman
National Rifle Assn.
11250 Waples Mill Rd.
Fairfax, VA 22030

Arms Collecting
Museum Restoration Service
P.O. Box 70
Alexandria Bay, NY 13607-0070

Black Powder Times
P.O. Box 1131
Stanwood, WA 98292

Field & Stream
Times Mirror Magazines
Two Park Ave.
New York, NY 10016

Gun List
700 E. State St.
Iola, WI 54990

The Gun Report
World Wide Gun Report, Inc.
Box 38
Aledo, IL 61231-0038

Gun Show Calendar
700 E. State St.
Iola, WI 54990

Gun Week
Second Amendment Foundation
P.O. Box 488, Sta. C
Buffalo, NY 14209

Gun World
Gallant/Charger Publications
34249 Camino Capistrano
Capistrano Beach, CA 92624

Guns
Guns Magazine
P.O. Box 85201
San Diego, CA 92138

Guns & Ammo
Petersen Publishing Co.
6420 Wilshire Blvd.
Los Angeles, CA 90048

Handloader
Wolfe Publishing Co.
6471 Airpark Dr.
Prescott, AZ 86301

Muzzle Blasts
National Muzzle Loading Rifle Assn.
P.O. Box 67
Friendship, IN 47021

Muzzleloader Magazine
Rebel Publishing Co., Inc.
Dept. Gun, Route 5, Box 347-M
Texarkana, TX 75501

Outdoor Life
Times Mirror Magazines
Two Park Ave.
New York, NY 10016

Petersen's HUNTING Magazine
Petersen Publishing Co.
6420 Wilshire Blvd.
Los Angeles, CA 90048

Rifle
Wolfe Publishing Co.
6471 Airpark Dr.
Prescott, AZ 86301

Shooting Times
PJS Publications
News Plaza, P.O. Box 1790
Peoria, IL 61656

Shotgun Sports
P.O. Box 6810
Auburn, CA 95604

U.S. Airgun Magazine
2603 Rollingbrook
Benton, AR 72015

Women & Guns
P.O. Box 488, Sta. C
Buffalo, NY 14209